Fr. Gribble's monograph on the ⟨ ⟩
ley, C.S.C., brings to life a man o
he was called by his superiors. Fɪ᎐᎐᎐ ᴛʜᴇ ᴜ.᎐. ᴛᴏ ᴀᴀᴀ ᴀɴᴅ ᴀᴀɴɪ
to Africa, Vincent McCauley inspires one with his exemplary
religious life as it is lived in the Congregation of Holy Cross,
his sense of humor, and his devotion to spreading the Gospel. I
heartily recommend this timely piece.

John I. Jenkins, C.S.C.
President, University of Notre Dame

In this engaging work, Fr. Gribble provides us with insight into
both the life of a revered Holy Cross missionary and the places
where he served. For anyone interested in the life of Bishop
McCauley and the history of Holy Cross in Asia and East Africa,
this book is essential reading.

Amy Cavender, C.S.C.
Professor of Political Science, Saint Mary's College

Father Gribble, the hardest working man in the field of U.S.
Catholic history, has written a splendid biography of that "valiant
man of God," missionary priest and bishop, Vincent McCauley,
C.S.C. This book works as both a spiritual and historical biog-
raphy and makes a significant contribution to mission and East
African studies. I highly recommend it.

Jeffrey Burns
Archivist, Archdiocese of San Francisco

Vividly portrays the missionary journeys of Vincent McCauley
and is very timely as his cause for canonization moves ahead.

Joseph Healey, M.M.
Superior, Maryknoll Society House
Masaki, Msasani

VINCENT
MCCAULEY, C.S.C.
BISHOP OF THE POOR, APOSTLE OF EAST AFRICA

Richard Gribble, C.S.C.

ave maria press AmP notre dame, indiana

Founded in 1865, Ave Maria Press is a ministry of the Indiana Province of Holy Cross.

www.avemariapress.com

ISBN-10 1-59471-110-0   ISBN-13 978-1-59471-110-7

Cover and text design by John R. Carson.

Printed and bound in the United States of America.

Library of Congress Cataloging-in-Publication Data

Gribble, Richard.
  Vincent McCauley, C.S.C. : bishop of the poor, apos-
tle of East Africa / by Richard E. Gribble, Jr.
      p. cm.
  "A Holy Cross book."
  Includes bibliographical references and index.
  ISBN-13: 978-1-59471-110-7 (pbk.)
  ISBN-10: 1-59471-110-0 (pbk.)
  1. McCauley, Vincent, 1906-1982. 2. Missionaries--Africa, East--Bi-
ography. 3. Missionaries--United States--Biography. 4. Congregation of
Holy Cross--Missions--Africa, East. 5. Amecea--History. I. Title.

BV3705.M37G75 2008
266'.2092--dc22
[B]
                                            2008014388

Service to God's people in foreign lands is, I believe, a special vocation for priests and religious. Taking the message of Jesus Christ abroad, as did the first apostles, has never been easy, but rather fraught with obstacles, suffering, and many frustrations. Yet, since the very foundation of the Congregation of Holy Cross, priests, brothers, and sisters have made the sacrifice and risked their lives in service to God's people across the globe. Since this book tells the story of a missionary, it is appropriate that it be dedicated to the men and women of Holy Cross who, like Vincent McCauley, heard the call of the Lord and answered through service in foreign lands. It is with the highest admiration for their ministry and lives of faith that this biography of one of their own is dedicated.

Contents

Preface

On February 3, 2003, I received a letter from Father Tom Smith, C.S.C., director of the Holy Cross Mission Center, located in Moreau Seminary at the University of Notre Dame. He informed me of the forthcoming golden jubilee of the Congregation of Holy Cross's mission in East Africa, which began in November 1958. As a part of the celebration of this accomplishment, the Mission Center invited me to research and write the life of Bishop Vincent J. McCauley, C.S.C., who, along with three newly ordained priests, inaugurated the East Africa mission. My acceptance of this task gave me the privilege to meet and know closely, although not firsthand, the life of a dedicated religious and priest, who now has been granted the title "Servant of God," as the formal introduction of his cause for canonization has been introduced in Rome and accepted by the Diocese of Fort Portal, Uganda.

The privilege granted me to carefully and completely investigate Bishop McCauley's life has proved to be a great blessing indeed. This project has allowed me to travel extensively and interact with many people and different cultures. While initially a bit apprehensive about my trip to East Africa, due in large measure to fears about illness, the experience was in many ways transformative for me. I was given the opportunity to experience a completely different culture in lands totally foreign to me. While I had traveled extensively in the past, I had never been to sub-Saharan Africa. Not a man who normally keeps a journal, I religiously kept notes on my daily activities as well as my thoughts and feelings during my sojourn. I did not want to lose close contact with my emotions at that time. The experiences of new people, foods, and customs, the awareness of being a minority, plus the daily reality of not having the basic infrastructure assumptions common in the United States, things like functioning electrical, water, and road systems, provided much food for thought and significant opportunities for serious prayer and reflection. As I discovered much about myself, I also learned about the life of Bishop McCauley, widely regarded in Eastern Africa as a saint, and the significant influence he had upon the people and Church of that region. McCauley was a special man and certainly worthy of this study. I only hope my work has done justice to his life, mission, and ministry.

There are numerous people who contributed greatly to the completion of this project. First and foremost, the initial invitation, plus financial and moral support, given me by Father Tom Smith, C.S.C., and the Holy Cross Mission Center made this project possible. In my travels I was always treated with the utmost respect and consideration. In East Africa I was welcomed by the Holy Cross community, especially the district superior, Father James Burasa, C.S.C., Brother Joseph Kaganda, C.S.C., my host in Fort Portal, and Brother Cleophas Kyomuhendo, C.S.C., and Father Willy Lukati, C.S.C., my hosts at the McCauley Formation House in Nairobi. The East Africa community collectively gave me every support and cooperation possible, especially their time, guidance, and knowledge, to assist my efforts. Brother Jim Nichols, C.S.C., was particularly helpful in the congregation's archives in Kampala, as was Father Thomas McDermott, C.S.C., who provided emotional and logistical support to me when my mother's sudden death necessitated my return to the United States to preside at her funeral. In Fort Portal, I wish to thank Father Chris Mukidi, archivist for the diocese, and his assistant, Ms. Olive Komuhendo, who provided me with total access to any and all materials needed for this project. In Nairobi, I am grateful to Father Pius Rutechura, the secretary-general of AMECEA, and his staff for their warm welcome and assistance.

Numerous people in the United States were also instrumental in the completion of this project. Father William Simmons, C.S.C., and Mrs. Jackie Dougherty were invaluable in aiding me to find materials about McCauley in the archives of the Indiana Province of Holy Cross. At the University of Notre Dame Archives, which houses the records of the general administration of Holy Cross, the assistance of the director, Dr. Wendy Schlereth, and Dr. Kevin Cawley was greatly appreciated. Brother Robert Gilroy, C.S.C., archivist for the Eastern Brothers of Holy Cross in Valatie, New York, was also of great help. My thanks is also extended to numerous Holy Cross religious who sat for interviews, provided insights on McCauley, and took the time to read and critique this manuscript, correct names, add additional facts, and provide clarity in many areas. Lastly, I wish to thank my friend, Sister Tania Santander Atauchi, C.D.P. Her constant care, interest in my work, and support while I was in Africa will always be fondly remembered.

Richard Gribble, C.S.C.

Introduction

On November 1, 1982, "a valiant man of God died, but a saint was born."[1] This statement by Father John Croston, C.S.C., about the death of Bishop Vincent McCauley, C.S.C., at the Mayo Clinic in Rochester, Minnesota, heralded the end of a gallant life. Many men and women in history could rightly be given the appellation "valiant," yet it is a term, not widely applied, that is given to those few people whose lives positively impact the world through dedication, hard work, and perseverance. Such was the life of Vincent Joseph McCauley, a man from simple roots who, while maintaining his simplicity of life and action, achieved greatness through concern for and service to people on three continents.

Vincent McCauley's early life was a foreshadowing of his simple but efficacious work as a priest and bishop. Born and raised in the Midwest community of Council Bluffs, Iowa, McCauley came from a strong Catholic family with traditional religious practices of the era. He, along with his five younger siblings, attended the local parish school, St. Francis Xavier. It may have been providential that his education came under the patronage of one of Catholicism's most famous missionaries. After

1

graduation from Creighton Prep in nearby Omaha, Nebraska, McCauley heard the call of the priesthood and joined the formation program for the Congregation of Holy Cross at the University of Notre Dame. After completing his theological training at the Foreign Mission Seminary in Washington, D.C., he was ordained to the priesthood in 1934. The world would become his stage in the accomplishment of his work for God's people.

The Great Depression and its economic ramifications directly impacted the life of the new priest. His desire to join the congregation's mission in East Bengal was placed on hold for two years until sufficient funds became available to sustain him in that distant land. Thus, for two years McCauley lived and worked in southeast Massachusetts, assisting in the formation of seminarians, while attending classes at Boston College. In October 1936, when economic conditions were more satisfactory, McCauley and three other Holy Cross religious sailed to Bengal, arriving in mid-November. Vincent McCauley's missionary experience had begun.

The Holy Cross mission in Bengal was initiated in 1853 and had been continuous since 1888. Still, despite a considerable amount of time in the area, the community's mission was rather primitive, although the zeal for ministry among the people, of whom very few were Christians, was always high. In Bengal, Vincent McCauley learned firsthand about suffering and hardship, from his personal experience and the people he served. His principle work was in religious formation as assistant and later rector of Little Flower, the minor seminary in Bandhura. He also spent close to two years in the northern mission district of Agartala working with the Kukis, a tribal people from the Lushai Hills, who had migrated northwest, and had been served by Canadian Holy Cross religious. Severe illness, however, forced him to return to Bandhura. In late 1943, McCauley was struck by a serious case of phlebitis that did not respond to treatment. Fearful that some blood clot caused by this condition might lodge in the heart and cause death, McCauley was sent home in May 1944. The trip was made possible through U.S. Army Air Corps personnel whom McCauley had known since his childhood in Iowa. His rather miraculous rescue from harm's way in Bengal indicated God had important plans for his future.

McCauley spent almost a full year in recovery at home and at Notre Dame before being assigned to his alma mater, the Foreign Mission Seminary (the Bengalese) in Washington, D.C. Initially he served as assistant superior and rector, but in the summer of 1946 he was assigned as superior. For six years McCauley continued his work with seminarians, now in a United States context. He was well liked and appreciated by all, including the seminarians at Holy Cross College, the principal theologate for the congregation in the United States, physically located only a five-minute walk from the Bengalese.[2] After his tenure as rector ended in 1952, McCauley continued on in Washington, serving as procurator of the missions. He spent the vast majority of his time on the road in mission appeals. Yet, he never lost his touch with the seminarians. As one related, "He was always pleasant, even in the early morning after [returning from] a long trip."[3]

While McCauley was effective as a religious formator and possessed a "Midas touch" in his ability to raise money, his desire and life had always been oriented toward the missions. In April 1958, McCauley and fellow Holy Cross priest, Arnold (Gus) Fell, journeyed to Uganda, East Africa, to evaluate an offer from Bishop Jean Ogez, W.F., and the White Fathers community (today known as the Missionaries of Africa), to assist in the Diocese of Mbarara in the western section of the country.[4] McCauley and Fell gave a glowing report of their trip, leading directly to the inauguration of a Holy Cross mission in that land. McCauley, together with three newly

ordained priests, Burton Smith, Francis Zagorc, and Robert
Hesse, arrived in Entebbe, Uganda, on November 4.
With McCauley's appointment as superior of the mission,
the Holy Cross presence expanded in the region over the
ensuing years. As more religious came and Holy Cross took
responsibility for parishes and schools, Ogez's desire to split
the diocese north and south, an idea that had circulated from
the outset of the congregation's presence, became stronger.
Eventually on April 19, 1961, the Diocese of Fort Portal was
canonically erected with Vincent McCauley appointed bishop.
While McCauley continually argued his unworthiness and
lack of qualifications, he was the natural choice for ordinary,
as the region was now largely under the watchful care of Holy
Cross religious. After his episcopal ordination at Notre Dame
on May 17, McCauley returned to take stock of his new realm.
After an initial tour of the diocese he reported to his provincial, Father Theodore Mehling, C.S.C., "Every day the job
looks bigger and more complicated."[5]

McCauley served the Church in Uganda as bishop of Fort
Portal from 1961 to December 1972. Starting with virtually
nothing, McCauley built the institutions, administrative structure, and *esprit de corps* required for this new mission effort.
He was responsible for the foundation of numerous parishes,
a diocesan structure of operation, including a senate of priests
and board of consultors, and the construction of a new cathedral after a massive earthquake in March 1966 destroyed
the existing church. Always a strong proponent of the local
church, McCauley transformed a local secondary school into
St. Mary's Minor Seminary and became a second founder
to the Banyatereza Sisters, an indigenous group of religious
women from western Uganda. Ever compassionate, he made
significant efforts to assist refugees, materially and spiritually,
from Rwanda, the Congo, and the Sudan who migrated to
western Uganda during various periods of the 1960s. Almost

immediately he became a leader in the Uganda Episcopal
Commission (UEC), serving at different times as the chair
of the Medical Bureau and Social Communications Department. When Uganda needed a national seminary, the bishops
turned to McCauley to lead the development campaign and
to oversee construction of Gaba National Seminary, which
was dedicated on October 20, 1970. As a visionary bishop in
the spirit of Vatican II, McCauley championed the Church's
efforts in ecumenism through his organization and leadership
in the Uganda Joint Christian Council (UJCC).

Vincent McCauley's talent, boundless energy, and foresight
took him beyond the borders of Uganda in a mission to the
broader Church of Eastern Africa. In 1964, at the third session of Vatican II, McCauley was elected chairman of the
Association of Member Episcopal Conferences of Eastern
Africa (AMECEA).[6] McCauley served this role with great
distinction. Working with Father Killian Flynn, O.F.M. Cap.,
secretary-general of AMECEA, McCauley was responsible for
organizing the body's triennial plenary meetings, as well as
significant regional conferences on ecumenism. His organizational and financial wizardry was tapped to rescue AMECEA
from a severe economic crisis in the late 1960s and early
1970s, and to inaugurate the Gaba Pastoral Institute, a year-
long academic program designed to instruct religious leaders
in the theology and pedagogy of the post–Vatican II era.

When Killian Flynn died in December 1972, a time that
coincided with McCauley's resignation as bishop of Fort Portal,
it was natural for him to move to AMECEA headquarters in
Nairobi and assume the position of secretary-general. Between
1973 and 1979 McCauley led the AMECEA to new heights
through his vision, continued high energy, and ever-faithful
commitment to the Church in Eastern Africa. He was responsible for the initiation of a one-year accountancy program at
the Nyegezi Social Training Center in Tanzania and numerous

ecumenical efforts, such as a 1974 urban seminar, outreach to
the World Council of Churches and the All Africa Conference
of Churches (AACC), and in welcoming the Christian Organizations Research and Advisory Trust (CORAT) to Eastern
Africa. Additionally, as in Fort Portal, McCauley was at the
forefront of education, leading the charge for the creation of
a secondary-school religious education syllabus for use in all
schools in Eastern Africa. The project bore great fruit in its two
phases, with its implementation in twenty African countries
by 1979. On a more personal level, McCauley never forgot the
disenfranchised of society, especially refugees, who flocked to
him at the height and during the aftermath of Idi Amin's reign
of terror in Uganda.

After fifteen years in a position of leadership with
AMECEA, Vincent McCauley stepped down in August 1979
and was replaced by his protégé, Father Joseph Mukwaya.
McCauley's life of retirement was anything but quiet, however, as he continued to make significant contributions while
in residence at AMECEA headquarters. He served as acting
chairman or secretary-general when the sitting officials were
not available. Undoubtedly the greatest contribution in this
final stage of his life, and one of the most significant in his
episcopal career, was his association with the foundation of the
Catholic Higher Institute of Eastern Africa, today known as
the Catholic University of Eastern Africa. Serving on academic
and financial committees, McCauley continued to apply his
skill and zeal for the apostolate to assist the local church
through education.

The accomplishments of Vincent McCauley, especially in
Eastern Africa, were many and significant, but his story cannot
be adequately told without some reference to his association
with people and his personal suffering. A victim of facial skin
cancer for close to forty years, he never complained about
many painful and at times disfiguring surgeries. On the

contrary, he often joked about it. In a salutation to one of his fellow African bishops he wrote: "Do keep well and say a prayer once in a while for the scar-faced Bishop of the Mountains of the Moon."[7] McCauley was generous, often to a fault, and always had time for others. He was warm, welcoming, and compassionate. He expressed his care in many ways, by action and word; his sincerity was never questioned by anyone. One Fort Portal priest succinctly stated what many believed: "We felt the Bishop had great love for Jesus and for the people."[8]

The story of Bishop Vincent McCauley is an important one for several reasons. First, with the Congregation of Holy Cross celebrating fifty years of ministry in East Africa in 2008, it is appropriate to celebrate its best-known and most significant missionary to that region of the world. Secondly, no scholarly research has been done on McCauley or Holy Cross in the region, save a booklet published in 1980 and references in a few books and articles.[9] While the amount of scholarly research on American mission efforts is increasing, much more needs to be done.

This biography conveniently divides McCauley's life into its three principal parts. Chapters 1 through 3 describe his time before his 1958 mission to Africa, including his childhood, early years as a priest, missionary experience in Bengal, and twelve years in Washington, D.C., at the Foreign Mission Seminary. Chapters 4 through 9 provide detailed information on McCauley's life as bishop of Fort Portal. The early days of the congregation's mission in Uganda are followed by the formation of the diocese and his involvement with many groups, initiatives, and programs. His efforts served both the local church and the Church in Uganda collectively, through his significant participation in the Uganda Episcopal Conference. This section ends with his resignation and move to Nairobi. The last third of this monograph tells McCauley's story with AMECEA, both as chairman and secretary-general. Bringing

his broad vision to the regional bishops' conference allowed
McCauley's talent and goodness to be experienced by more
people with many significant positive results, especially the
foundation of the Catholic University of Eastern Africa. A
short epilogue is provided to synthesize McCauley's spirituality and his legacy for the Church and to history.

This biography comes at a very appropriate time for Holy
Cross, the Church in Eastern Africa, and Vincent McCauley.
In August 2006, the cause for canonization of Bishop Vincent McCauley, C.S.C., was introduced in the Congregation
of Saints and has been accepted for review by the Diocese of
Fort Portal, Uganda. Thus, McCauley rightly bears the title,
"Servant of God." It is neither the purview nor the task of
historians to determine the sanctity of individuals. Rather,
biographers report and interpret the facts of individual lives
to provide a full and clear picture of the time period and the
life of the person in question. This historian makes no claims
to Bishop McCauley's merit as a saint, but unquestionably
he was a valiant man of God who brought his faith, talent,
energy, and joyful personality to people on three continents.
This fact alone makes his life meritorious and a model for others to follow.

CHAPTER 1

The Early Years: 1906–1936

Since the time of Jesus Christ, the missionary spirit has been active among the Christian faithful. Jesus' exhortation to his disciples was crystal clear: "All authority in heaven and on earth has been given to me. Go therefore and make disciples of all nations, baptizing them in the name of the Father and of the Son and of the Holy Spirit and teaching them to obey everything that I have commanded you" (Mt 28: 18b–20a). Church historian Stephen Neill gives three prominent reasons for the initial Christian evangelization process. First, since Jesus did not return as soon as anticipated there was a need to spread his teaching to the then-known world. Secondly, unlike Judaism, which saw the movement of faith from the periphery to Jerusalem, Christians saw the need to move from the center to the periphery. Lastly, the destruction of Jerusalem and subsequent Diaspora of 70 CE sent disciples of the "New Way" to all regions to preach (Acts 8:4).[1]

This missionary spirit was first and foremost exemplified in
the life of Saul of Tarsus. Converted on the road to Damascus,
Saul, who took the Christian name Paul, became the great
evangelist to the Gentiles. On three long and arduous journeys, Paul, buoyed by the decision at the Council of Jerusalem
in 49 CE,[2] brought the message and mission of Jesus to the
then-known European world. Not only did Paul start several
Christian communities of faith, but additionally he left to
posterity his corpus of writings which even today serves to
articulate the basic teachings of Christian theology.

Paul's initial efforts to bring the message of Christ to the
world have been repeated and advanced throughout the two
thousand years of Christian history. While the faith spread
rapidly within the Roman world, it took several centuries
before Christianity reached beyond the Mediterranean region.
It was the dawn of the era of exploration that re-energized
Jesus' initial challenge to "make disciples of all nations." The
desire to bring products and goods from the regions of Asia
to Europe, and the spirit of adventure associated with new
discoveries, prompted explorers to venture both east and west.
Traveling east, the Portuguese brought their Catholic faith
with them when they reached the Indian subcontinent. The
efforts of the famous Jesuits Francis Xavier, Mateo Ricci, and
Robert de Nobili to evangelize peoples in India, China, Japan,
and neighboring lands are both legendary and heroic. Using
an inculturation method that was certainly forward thinking
for the time, these courageous followers of Christ established
the roots of Christianity in lands that for many centuries had
been the stronghold of Eastern religions, such as Hinduism,
Buddhism, and Confucianism. Seen in the context of their
day and the adverse and hostile conditions they found, their
endeavors can only be described as highly successful. In the
West, led by the Spanish, the New World was evangelized
principally through the efforts of religious orders, especially

the Franciscans and Jesuits. Using a more forceful approach of acculturation, the Spanish missionaries rapidly converted the whole of Central and South America. In North America, the French, utilizing inculturation, came to the regions of what is today New England, eastern Canada, and the upper Midwest to work with various Native American tribes. Numerically their success was small, but their spirit, as exemplified by the heroic martyrdom of Saints Isaac Jogues and John de Brebeuf, continued the centuries-old tradition of making disciples of all nations.[3]

The missionary spirit that was so endemic to the Christian culture of Europe continued in the United States after the Church's establishment with the erection of the See of Baltimore in 1789 and the appointment of its first bishop, John Carroll. In 1830, John England, the first bishop of Charleston, South Carolina, spoke with Pope Gregory XVI about fostering the sacramental life among African Catholics who had settled in Liberia, a nation founded by freed American slaves. England brought the concept of pastoral care of these people to the First and Second Provincial Councils of Baltimore in 1829 and 1833, respectively. The Jesuits were asked to take the Liberian mission, but they refused, citing too many ongoing responsibilities in western North America. In 1841, however, Propaganda Fide (today the Congregation for the Evangelization of Peoples) issued an appeal to the United States bishops for assistance to areas outside of the United States. Thus, a three-man team, Edward Barron, vicar general of the Diocese of Philadelphia, John Kelly from Albany, New York, and Denis Pindor, a lay catechist from Baltimore, journeyed to Liberia. The mission continued until 1884 under the leadership of the Society of the Immaculate Heart of Mary, which soon amalgamated with the Holy Ghost Fathers.[4]

In the mid-nineteenth century, United States missionary efforts expanded further. In 1860, Propaganda Fide requested that the Diocese of Charleston, South Carolina, oversee the spiritual needs of the few Catholics in the Bahamas. Unable to mount any sustained effort, Charleston passed the project to the Archdiocese of New York. St. Francis Xavier Church in Nassau was constructed in 1885. A few years later, the Sisters of Charity and Benedictines from Newark, New Jersey, got involved in the mission. By 1896, the former had started two schools in Nassau. The Benedictine mission also continued, slowly but gradually, growing with support from its parent community in Minnesota. Through the Benedictines and the Sisters of Charity, the New York archdiocese maintained its missionary activity in the Bahamas until 1931.

Religious congregations were also independently active in mission work. Pope Pius IX asked the Redemptorists to assist in the Caribbean mission on St. Thomas and St. Croix. Religious arrived there in 1858. The Passionists established a foundation in Mexico City in 1865. Later they moved south into Argentina and Chile. Franciscan sisters from Albany, New York, went to Jamaica in 1879. Additional Franciscan sisters from Syracuse, New York, under the direction of Blessed Marianne Cope (1838–1918), went to Hawaii. In November 1883, Cope, along with six other sisters, arrived in Honolulu to work in hospitals specializing in leprosy. By April 1884, the sisters were in charge of Kakaako Hospital on Molakai, as they had requested before coming to the region. In 1893, the superior general of the Jesuits asked the Missouri Province to take a mission in British Honduras (today Belize). In 1898, the Jesuits invited Sisters of the Holy Family (founded in New Orleans in 1842) to assist them in mission schools. In addition to institutional commitments, several individual religious went to the missions abroad, including to China and New Zealand.[5]

The Congregation of Holy Cross, a religious order of priests and brothers established in 1837 in LeMans, France, took up the missionary challenge of Jesus almost from its foundation. The congregation's founder, Blessed Basil Anthony Mary Moreau, a secular priest of LeMans, envisioned a congregation of clerics and lay brothers who would assist the local bishop as necessary to rebuild the Church in the wake of the destruction wrought by the French Revolution and its aftermath.[6] On March 1, 1837, the congregation was formed when a fundamental pact was signed uniting the Brothers of St. Joseph, founded in France by Father Jacques Dujarie in 1820, and the Auxiliary Priests (band of diocesan clergy) from the Sainte-Croix district of the city of LeMans, headed by Father Moreau. By 1839, the new religious community had 34 houses in France and 127 members—12 priests, 115 brothers (24 professed, 78 novices, and 13 postulants).[7]

Moreau, the leader of the congregation, placed the community under the guidance of the local bishop for service to the Church. In 1840, Moreau accepted the invitation of the bishop of Algiers to initiate a mission in northern Africa, then a "department" of France. While the project was short-lived and unsuccessful, Moreau's effort led later to other more successful initiatives. In 1841, Father Edward Sorin, C.S.C., one of Moreau's most promising men, traveled with six brothers to the wilderness of northern Indiana and the Diocese of Vincennes. In November 1842, Sorin founded the University of Notre Dame, which today stands as the principal institution of the congregation in the United States. In 1853, Holy Cross went to East Bengal, as part of an agreement made with the Holy See to secure the Congregation's canonical erection.[8]

The dawn of the twentieth century, most especially the destruction wrought by World War I, caused great upheaval for world missions. The retrenchment of European Catholics, due to the destruction of so many institutions and loss of personnel, gave Americans a golden opportunity to serve. It was the hour for the United States' mission to shine through four significant manifestations: (1) creation of student organizations for mission education and promotion, (2) nationalization and coordination of mission agencies through the hierarchy, (3) outreach to Catholics in Latin America, and (4) convergence on China of United States Catholic missionaries. In July 1918, the Catholic Students Mission Crusade (CSMC) was launched, headquartered in Cincinnati with Thomas Shahan, rector of the Catholic University of America, as leader. The CSMC was highly influential in energizing people for mission work and providing an alternative to the capitalist and bureaucratic aspects of America. The mission division of the National Catholic Welfare Conference (NCWC), established at Notre Dame in July 1919, was responsible for the formation of the American Board of Catholic Missions (ABCM). The ABCM was approved in 1922 but did not have a constitution or begin its official work until January 1, 1926. From its foundation until the mid-1930s, the NCWC was involved with church and state affairs in Mexico. As described by historian Douglas Slawson, the NCWC and its Latin American Bureau branch of the Social Action Department were able to assist in returning stability and peace to the Mexican people.[9]

In June 1925, the Catholic Hospital Association and the Catholic Medical Mission Board (CMMB) was formed. Its purpose was to ascertain the needs of missionaries and to collect and distribute medical supplies and medicine to them. By 1934, the organization had distributed 23,000 surgical instruments to almost 900 mission stations and 295 religious congregations worldwide.[10]

At this same time the Society for the Propagation of the Faith began to promote the idea that women missionaries needed to work with women, especially concerning healthcare issues. The most significant spokesperson for medical missions was Dr. Anna Dengel (1892–1980). Observing this need, and believing that white people owed a debt "to peoples subjugated and exploited by their forefathers," she formed a religious congregation devoted to medical missions. In September 1925, with the help of Father Michael Mathis, C.S.C., who helped her write the congregation's constitution, Dengel started the "Pious Society" of Catholic Medical Missionaries, "whose purpose was to provide professional medical help where it was most needed." In 1936 the society became a religious congregation.[11]

This same spirit of adventure and desire to bring the gospel message to all peoples was present in the mind of Vincent McCauley, who understood well and lived fully his Christian call to evangelize the world to Christ. In a career that would span almost five decades, McCauley, as priest and bishop, brought Jesus' message to peoples in Bengal and Eastern Africa. A man of great vision and unbounded energy, despite a lifetime bout with cancer, Vincent McCauley represented the mid-twentieth century missionary in his finest hour. Never cowed by difficult conditions, discouraging results, or lack of support, McCauley courageously and successfully planted and nurtured the faith in far-off lands for over thirty years.

Early Life and Religious Formation

Vincent Joseph McCauley, the eldest of six children of Charles McCauley and Mary Wickham, was born in Council Bluffs, Iowa, on March 8, 1906. He was baptized ten days later, on March 18, at the family parish, St. Francis Xavier, certainly an appropriate church for the future missionary priest and bishop. Vincent received the sacrament of confirmation at this same parish on May 6, 1917.[12]

McCauley's home life in Council Bluffs centered itself about family and activities associated with the Church. His father, Charles, described as a "perfectly integrated man with whom you felt comfortable,"[13] was a wire chief for American Telephone and Telegraph (ATT) in Omaha. His mother tended the home front, meeting the needs of Vincent's five younger siblings, Mary Margaret, Robert, Paul, Eleanor, and Eileen. As was common for many Catholic families of the era, especially those of Irish heritage, the McCauley clan recited the daily family rosary, a practice that undoubtedly was highly influential to Vincent for his future spirituality, which emphasized strong Marian devotion and recitation of the rosary. Charles McCauley was an active member of the Knights of Columbus at St. Francis Xavier parish while his wife, Mary, was an active participant in the altar guild and various parish prayer circles. Years later, these prayer groups would become the locus for financial assistance for Vincent during his missionary efforts, especially during the troubled period of the Great Depression and World War II.[14] The family regularly attended missions and many other parish-sponsored events. As with many Catholic families of the period, the parish was central to the McCauley family's religious and social life.

As the eldest child of six, Vincent took very seriously his responsibilities toward his younger siblings. He was the surrogate parent on the rare occasions when their parents were both out of the house. He commanded his siblings' respect, for he was never domineering, but rather demonstrated a gentle, yet at the same time forceful, way with his brothers and sisters. He had a special touch, another characteristic that would be invaluable and widely demonstrated later in his priestly life, that drew others to him. McCauley was especially helpful to his siblings, as well as his parents, when tragedy struck the family. In 1930, his brother Paul, who had finished high school and was ready to enter the Jesuits, was killed in a car accident. Years later, he was the source of strength for his sister Eileen, when her husband of only six months died tragically of measles at a U.S. Army camp.[15] McCauley was always extremely grateful for his family, especially the support they gave him in his life. In 1948 he wrote,

I would be less than grateful if I did not remember all you have done, all you have been, and if I did not try in some way to make a return. You realize, I am sure, that as a Religious I have nothing that I can call my own and am not, therefore, free to express gratitude in a material way. But things spiritual are to me very real. . . . My Mass is to me my greatest treasure and I daily ask God to share its fruits with all of you.[16]

In typical fashion for the day, McCauley was a product of the Catholic education system. He and all his siblings attended the parish school, St. Francis Xavier. He then matriculated to Creighton Prep in Omaha where he excelled in sports, especially baseball, which was his true love.[17] He played first base and was known as a good "long ball hitter." He was adept enough to play a summer of semi-pro baseball in Omaha in order to make a little extra money.[18] After finishing the program at Creighton Prep, it was a natural move to Creighton University's College of Arts and Letters where he matriculated as a member of the class of 1928.[19]

His time at Creighton was cut short rather unexpectedly, however, when members of the Congregation of Holy Cross gave a mission at St. Francis Xavier parish in the early fall of 1924. Like many American Catholic young men McCauley, during his youth, was enamored by the mystique of Notre Dame. As a sports fan, he and his brothers listened almost religiously to Notre Dame football games on the radio. McCauley was very impressed by the mission and more especially the messengers. He spoke with one of the priests, Father Joseph Boyle, C.S.C., about Notre Dame and the Holy Cross community. The encounter sparked in him the desire for the priesthood, a latent feeling that was, according to family members, rarely expressed.[20] In a letter to Holy Cross officials at Notre Dame, however, McCauley claimed "that this calling [priesthood] has been the aim of my life for many years." In

a letter to the vocation director, he spoke of his desire to join
Holy Cross: "Trusting that God wills it, my only desire now is
for a favorable reply from you."[21]

McCauley left Council Bluffs in November 1924 to join
the Congregation of Holy Cross. McCauley spent the next five
years of his initial formation at Notre Dame. Because his entry
was mid-year, he was sent initially to the minor seminary at
Holy Cross Hall at the University. On July 1, 1925, he entered
the novitiate on campus and professed his first vows on July 2,
1926. He spent three years in temporary vows as he completed
his undergraduate education. He professed perpetual vows on
July 2, 1929, and graduated from Notre Dame in June of the
next year.[22]

As a finally professed religious, McCauley continued his
training at the Foreign Mission Seminary (FMS, commonly
called the Bengalese) at Washington, D.C. The FMS was the
brainchild of Father Michael Mathis, C.S.C., who, although
not a veteran of the Congregation's mission in Bengal, held
an untiring interest and love for this apostolate. In 1917 he
founded the Holy Cross Foreign Mission Society and in 1919
started *The Bengalese*, a monthly magazine that chronicled
the stories of missionaries and their work as a means to raise
money for the mission. On September 23, 1924, the Foreign
Mission Seminary was opened as a residence for seminarian
mission candidates with Mathis appointed as the first rector and procurator of the missions. This establishment was
a significant achievement for Holy Cross and especially the
Bengal mission. As Edmund Goedert, C.S.C., has commented
about the foundation, "From this point on, a steady flow of
men began coming to Dacca and the greatest problem of the
missions [adequate personnel] was solved." When McCauley
arrived in Washington in September 1930 to begin theological study, Mathis was still superior, although George Marr,
C.S.C., took over in the fall of 1931.[23]

McCauley and everyone at the FMS attended classes at Holy Cross College, the principal theologate for the congregation in Washington, and a mere five-minute walk down Taylor Street to Harewood Road. Holy Cross College, founded in 1895, was one of the first religious establishments in response to the call by the American bishops to centralize religious houses of formation around the new Catholic University of America, which opened in 1889.[24] During these years he received all the minor orders, including the order of deacon on October 1, 1933. He was ordained with his classmates, John Lane and Joseph Corcoran, on June 24, 1934, by Bishop John Noll of Fort Wayne at Sacred Heart Church at Notre Dame. He immediately returned to Council Bluffs for a brief vacation. There he conducted mission appeals in local parishes before moving to his new assignment. At the conclusion of this work, stating he was ready for any assignment given to him, McCauley demonstrated his lighthearted side, comically writing to the provincial, James Burns: "I have not been excommunicated, jailed or ostracized in this land of burnt-up cornfields."[25]

McCauley's desire to train for the missions at the Bengalese requires some analysis. Interviews with members of his family reveal little as to his motivation for this specialized ministry. However, years later in a lecture at Creighton University, McCauley revealed at least partially his motivation for this narrow and more difficult road (Mt 7:13–14):

> For more than thirty-five years I have had the conviction that it was the Faith and zeal and generosity of the Christian Community in Council Bluffs and Omaha that produced the situation, conditions, [and] atmosphere that enabled me and many others to receive the privilege of serving in the missions.[26]

Thus, it appears that McCauley chose to be a missionary from the example of sharing and self-sacrifice he experienced from family and friends at home. As the story of Vincent McCauley's life unfolds, it will be clear that this same spirit of personal sacrifice and self-giving was part and parcel of his ministry as priest and bishop for almost fifty years.

Besides his desire for mission work, the basic spirituality that McCauley possessed and practiced needs explanation to assess its origins. Vincent McCauley was a simple man, who found this virtue from his Midwest roots. Fellow Holy Cross religious speak of how "he never really cared for material things." He was a man of hope who refused to give up on any endeavor or individual.[27] While McCauley, unlike his contemporary and fellow Holy Cross religious Father Patrick Peyton, never wore his spirituality on his sleeve, all knew he was a man of great prayer and personal holiness.[28] The one area that was more obvious was his devotion to the Blessed Virgin Mary. Many contemporaries speak of rosary recitation as essential at the outset of any trip McCauley took by car. He made regular visits to the shrine at Lourdes, seeking strength for his work in the missions. He was convinced that if he was willing to serve, Mary's intercession with Christ would provide the strength necessary. McCauley's devotion to the Blessed Mother was demonstrated in a homily delivered on the Feast of the Immaculate Conception:

> When God so honours His mother, can we do less? When God makes His mother sinless can we fail to rejoice? When God shows His life and His Divine work with His Mother, can we His redeemed children neglect her? . . . . We fulfill God's plan when we honour Mary and we make our own lives pleasing to God when we let Mary be in all things Our Mother.[29]

McCauley's time at the Bengalese had prepared him for assignment to the Bengal missions, but the economic shortfall resulting from the Great Depression forced Holy Cross to restrict the number of men assigned to the mission, due to costs for travel as well as maintenance in the mission field. Bishop Timothy Crowley, C.S.C., of Dacca (Bengal) had informed the provincial, James Burns, of the situation in mid-1934. Thus, Burns, with the approval of the superior general, assigned McCauley "as a member of the faculty at our seminary at North Dartmouth, Mass[achusetts]."[30]

While Holy Cross had established educational and parochial foundations in the Midwest, South, and West, the East did not attract the congregation until the period of the Great Depression.[31] James Wesley Donahue, superior general of the congregation from 1926 to 1938, had been favorably impressed with the area from his initial visit there in 1912 as a member of the community's mission band.[32] In November 1931, James Cassidy, apostolic administrator and auxiliary bishop of Fall River, Massachusetts, wrote to Donahue inviting him to start a seminary in the diocese. Favorably disposed to Cassidy's offer, Donahue proposed to the 1932 General Chapter of Holy Cross that the community purchase property in southeast Massachusetts in order to open a minor seminary. The proposal was approved and, after some negotiations with the diocese and local officials, the former Crary Hospital and its sixty-eight acres of property were purchased at North Dartmouth. On December 8, 1933, the superior general celebrated the first Mass at Our Lady of Holy Cross.[33]

McCauley taught at North Dartmouth while simultaneously taking classes in English and speech at Boston College. One of his collateral duties at the seminary was director of maintenance. This kept him busy, as the repairs to the old building were numerous and thus very time consuming. Although not enrolled in a degree program, McCauley honed his academic skills while commuting to Jesuit-sponsored Boston College.

Meanwhile, Holy Cross's presence in the East continued to expand. On March 2, 1935, Thomas Duffy, C.S.C., arrived at Our Lady of Holy Cross to assume duties as superior of the eastern mission band. During the visit he and seminary superior William Doheny traveled to North Easton, about forty miles north, to tour the Frederick Ames estate, which was being offered for sale.[34] The facility was perceived by Duffy as the ideal location and environment for the realization of his dream of a college foundation.[35] In August 1935, after negotiations on price were completed, Holy Cross purchased the Ames estate, consisting of approximately 350 acres of land and several buildings. The community chronicle reported that the sale "assures the Congregation of an enviable and an ideal location for the expansion of its Eastern apostolate."[36]

Transfer of the seminary from North Dartmouth to North Easton was accomplished after the sale was finalized. As director of maintenance, McCauley directed the physical move of five carloads of furniture and other household and personal items to North Easton.[37] He was very impressed with the North Easton property, calling it "one of the niftiest layouts in all New England, barring none." He did realize, however, that the expansive area and assorted buildings would necessitate much maintenance. As he put it to his family, "Our biggest problem now is taking care of this place."[38] While there, McCauley continued both his duties as teacher and student.

After two years in the East, Vincent McCauley was ready and eager to begin new adventures in his life and priestly ministry. He spent the summer in New York City at Blessed Sacrament Parish on West 71st Street awaiting his new assignment. He spoke of his time as "a pleasant and profitable change from North Easton, much as I enjoyed the past year there."[39]

Summary

The vast Midwestern plains of western Iowa played host to the early years of Vincent McCauley. Raised in a typical blue-collar family, McCauley found his initial call to follow Jesus' exhortation to evangelize all peoples through his Catholic education and the missionary efforts of the Congregation of Holy Cross. After his initial training at Notre Dame, McCauley was sent for formal preparation for his mission dream at the "Bengalese" in Washington, D.C. Under the influence of one of Holy Cross's twentieth century mission heroes, Michael Mathis, C.S.C., McCauley readied himself for the mission field. After ordination, however, due to insufficient funds to maintain him in Bengal, he was asked to wait two years and was, thus, assigned to Holy Cross foundations in Massachusetts. After two years, however, with the economic hardships of the Great Depression lessening on the American people, Vincent McCauley was ready to begin his first great adventure as a missionary in Bengal. It was only the beginning of a life dedicated to bringing Christ's gospel message to the world.

CHAPTER 2

Missionary to Bengal: 1936–1944

The missionary spirit that had inspired countless Christians over the centuries to venture to foreign lands and cultures was present with Vincent McCauley since his days at the Foreign Mission Seminary. With the economic effects of the Great Depression abating, it was now possible for him to fulfill his earlier dream to bring the gospel to those who did not know Christ. McCauley's two years in Massachusetts provided him with some seasoning, allowing him to be better grounded in his priesthood and, thus, better prepared for the difficult path that lay ahead. Equipped in every possible way for this mission, Vincent McCauley now entered into the missionary life that would mark his ministry and direct his future in Holy Cross.

Christianity in Bengal

Christianity in the Indian subcontinent traces its origins to Portuguese efforts during the era of exploration. In 1497, Vasco de Gama first reached India. While the ruling Moghul government of the region did not cater to foreigners or Christianity, the Portuguese were tolerated because they brought profitable trade. Each year Portuguese traders arrived in June on the monsoon winds and they left in October. To make certain, however, that no permanent settlements were made, the quarters occupied by the Europeans were annually burned. In 1577, however, Akbar, the Moghul emperor, gave permission for permanent settlements and, thereby, paved the way for the future growth of Christian institutions.[1]

Akbar's decision allowed Christianity to gain its first foothold in Asia. These first Christians were Portuguese settlers, many of whom were rogues or "less-desirables" who came to India to escape punishment in their homeland. The initial reaction of the local people to Christianity was, quite naturally, not positive. Goa was established as an episcopal see in 1534 and an independent archbishopric in 1557.[2] Three prominent religious orders, Jesuits in 1598, Augustinians in 1599, and Dominicans in 1600, arrived to evangelize the region. The latter stayed only until 1603, suggesting that the moral depravity they found among the permanent Portuguese settlers was an impossible barrier to evangelization. The Jesuits only lasted one more year initially, but returned a few years later. By 1653, there were no fewer than 240 Jesuits in the Indian province, including thirty local novices. The Augustinians remained in Bengal for 250 years, establishing several parishes in Tejgoan, Nagori (their principal foundation), and Hashnabad.[3]

In a system similar to that used by the Spanish in Latin America, the Portuguese government was given *Padroado,* or patronage, in Bengal.[4] At the outset, this system worked well, but later when the Portuguese could not meet the demands for personnel and money, the Church began to suffer, as it had no authority to act independently. The Vatican wanted to send missionaries, but it was prevented under the *Padroado*. Finally in the early nineteenth century, after numerous Church protests to the Portuguese crown fell on deaf ears, the Vatican acted. In 1834, the Vicariate Apostolic of Bengal was established and placed under the jurisdiction of the Sacred Congregation for the Propagation of the Faith (Propaganda Fide). This in practice ended the Portuguese monopoly.[5]

Rome, however, was far from being in charge. The establishment of the vicariate did not sit well with Portuguese clergy who declared the Vatican had no right to act as it had, without permission from the Portuguese government, under the stipulations of the *Padroado*. Thus, a scandalous period where clergy loyal to Portugal or Propaganda Fide began a struggle for power, with the laity caught in the middle. Some resolution was seen in 1845 when East Bengal (today Bangladesh) was cut off from Calcutta and placed under the care of Bishop Thomas Olliffe, an Irish missionary. The region was called the Vicariate of Chittagong, although the bishop resided in Dacca. Olliffe was rarely in his vicariate, however, as he traveled to Europe begging religious communities to assist his three priests, who covered a vast area of over 100,000 square miles. Disease and a harsh climate made the region very uninviting.[6] The bright spot for the Church in Bengal in the early 1850s happened when the battle between Rome and the Portuguese crown over jurisdiction in the region ended with the Vatican's capitulation.

The Congregation of Holy Cross became a player in the Bengal mission even before its final approbation from the Vatican. At the same time that Bishop Olliffe was in Rome seeking a religious community to assist his mission, Father Basil Moreau, the founder of Holy Cross, was in the Eternal City seeking approbation for his nascent congregation. The Prefect of Propaganda Fide, speaking on behalf of Pope Pius IX, told Moreau, "The prompt expedition of these missionaries [to Bengal] will tend greatly to the obtaining for your society the approbation of the Holy See which you ardently solicit."[7] Moreau clearly heard the message and accepted the mission that nobody else wanted. By the end of 1853, twelve Holy Cross religious (four priests, three brothers, and five sisters) were in Bengal, led by Father Michael Voisin.

Tragedy and much suffering marked the first few years of the congregation's time in Bengal. Several of the original twelve religious died, including Voisin. Many of their replacement recruits experienced the same fate, some not even reaching their destination. In 1856, Bishop Olliffe was transferred to Calcutta, prompting the pope to request Holy Cross to take full responsibility for the Vicariate of Chittagong. Moreau acceded to the request. Father Louis Verite, C.S.C., was thus named pro-vicar apostolic. In 1858, however, Verite died while in route to France. Father Pierre Dufal, C.S.C., took Verite's position and in 1860 was named the first bishop in charge of the Vicariate of Eastern Bengal. Moreau's decision to take responsibility for Bengal raised a firestorm of protest among his religious. Many felt the mission was ill-conceived. Edmund Goedert, C.S.C., has commented, "The sad truth was that the community did not feel committed to Bengal and many considered the whole venture a mistake."[8]

Significant opposition to the Holy Cross mission in Bengal continued for several years. Edward Sorin, C.S.C., founder of the University of Notre Dame in 1842, was asked to head the mission to Bengal, but openly refused, stating that if ordered under obedience to go, he would secede from the congregation, taking with him his American compatriots.[9] The human toll on the congregation was great. In a short period of time six religious died and seven others returned to France sick.

In 1872, the General Chapter of the Congregation voted to relinquish the Bengal mission. In 1876, the Holy See formally transferred the Vicariate to the Benedictines and Holy Cross withdrew.[10]

The Benedictine tour in Bengal was short-lived, however. In 1888, Holy Cross returned with five religious, three from the United States and two from Canada. Father Michael Fallize, C.S.C., served as the administrator.[11] In 1890, Father Augustin Louage, C.S.C., was appointed Bishop of Dacca. Although he only lived until June 4, 1894, he was able to open several new parishes with an expanding work force of fifteen priests, one brother, and seven sisters. On December 18, 1894, Peter J. Hurth, C.S.C., took possession of his See as the second bishop of Dacca. Like his predecessors, however, Hurth was hampered by the niggardly attitude of Holy Cross toward the mission, both in the assignment of personnel and in financial support.[12] The situation became even more critical on June 12, 1897, when a severe earthquake struck Bengal, damaging or destroying virtually all church buildings, including the cathedral.

It took some time, but the community's less-than-generous attitude toward Bengal began to change. Following the earthquake, Hurth made an appeal to the 1898 General Chapter for more assistance in personnel and finances. Only in 1906, however, did the General Chapter decree that annual subsidies of $1,250 from the United States Province of Holy Cross and $500 from the Canadian Province be given to the Bishop of Dacca. Additionally, one of the assistants in the general administration was charged with mission interests. Having made some progress, Hurth resigned as bishop in February 1908. However, Rome was slow to act and his replacement, Frederick Linneborn, procurator general of the congregation, did not arrive in Bengal until December 24, 1909. Linneborn died suddenly on July 21, 1915, without gaining significant new

personnel. Again, Rome was slow to act as Joseph Legrand, the
fourth bishop of Dacca, only arrived on June 1, 1917.[13]

During the administration of Legrand, the attitude of Holy
Cross toward the Bengal mission became dramatically more
favorable. However, things did not start out well. On September 24, 1919, a devastating cyclone struck the area, creating
more damage than the 1897 earthquake. Despite the damage,
there was good news. Unlike previous periods, the spirits of
Legrand and his Holy Cross religious were not dampened by
the loss; a greater sense of commitment resulted. Education,
the primary *raison d'etre* of Holy Cross from the outset, played
a significant role in this renaissance. Historian Father Raymond Clancy, C.S.C., comments, "Next to the exercise of the
Sacred Ministry itself, the missionaries s[aw] in education the
proper method of safeguarding the Catholic people."[14] Bishop
Hurth's earlier efforts toward the establishment of primary
schools was crowned in 1918 when St. Gregory's, the most
prominent preparatory school run by the Sisters of Our Lady
of the Missions, came under the control of Holy Cross Brothers.[15] Interest in the mission was greatly enhanced by two new
publications, *The Bengal Witness*, under the direction of Father
James French, C.S.C., and most prominently, *The Bengalese*,
the organ of the Holy Cross Foreign Mission Society which
was championed by Michael Mathis, C.S.C.[16]

Legrand's time was highlighted by the period 1923 to
1927, known as "the Golden Years" of the mission. Several significant events rightly label this period as the mission's heyday.
In 1923, Holy Cross proposed a canonical separation of Bengal into two regions, Dacca under the jurisdiction of American
religious and Chittagong under the control of Canadians. In
1926, the General Chapter gave formal approval to the two-district proposal. On May 25, 1927, the Diocese of Chittagong
was erected with Alfred LePailleur, C.S.C., consecrated bishop
on October 30. More religious joined the mission so that by

1935 the Holy Cross presence had doubled in size from the time of division of the region. As mentioned previously, the Foreign Mission Seminary was opened under the guidance of Michael Mathis in September 1924. Beginning in 1922, John B. Delaunay, C.S.C., first published a pamphlet, "The Bandhura Tin Horn," using it to solicit funds for a proposed minor seminary. Eventually in 1926, Little Flower Minor Seminary opened.[17]

The mission in Bengal entered a new era on May 1, 1927, when Irishman Timothy Crowley, C.S.C., who had served the diocese as vicar general since 1915, was ordained as coadjutor bishop to Legrand in Dacca. On November 11, 1929, realizing that Crowley was doing all the work, Legrand resigned and the former automatically succeeded him. Crowley "assumed office at a time when prospects for the conquest of souls were unprecedented."[18]

Bengal's "Golden Years" and the energy and talent of its new bishop could not, however, stem the tide wrought by the Great Depression and its financial impact on the mission. Europe's post–World War I financial disaster struck the United States in October 1929 suddenly with a ferocity never before experienced. The stock market crash forced all to tighten their financial belts, leading to significant loss of resources for the Bengal mission. Crowley was forced to cut his catechist corps by one-half and canceled all expansion plans for 1931. He reported that he was able to keep the mission going, but barely.[19] He pleaded with the United States provincial, Father James Burns, C.S.C., suggesting America had a responsibility to Dacca:

> The point I want to make is that we may not ask for alms in Europe, which has its own mission fields to support. Our homefolk must bear with our importunity when we appeal on behalf of Dacca. To whom except to you shall

we appeal? Dacca is America's *Front* [Crowley empha-
sis] in the great campaign of the Church in India.[20]

In the first years of the 1930s, as the Depression deepened
in the United States, so too the misery in Bengal grew more
profound. With a slight note of optimism, Burns reported to
Crowley:

> I need not tell you that times are even worse than when
> you were in the States. Money is tighter and although
> there is a renewal of confidence since the new administra-
> tion took the reins the effects are not yet perceptible in a
> financial way. But all indications point to the conclusion
> that the tide has turned. Let us hope so.[21]

Crowley, however, could not be so positive:

> We hear all kinds of rumors that [the] depression is lifting
> off America and that prosperity is definitely coming back.
> So far as myself and the missionaries are concerned, we do
> not experience the happy reaction up to the present. . . . The help
> that normally [we] would receive from special benefactors
> has dwindled to almost nothing. We have to cut down our
> expenses to close to 40% of what they were a year ago.

He further told Burns that he was struggling to "keep what
we have," describing the current situation as "a hand to mouth
existence."[22] He concluded, "I never imagined three years ago
or even last year that the mission would come upon such anxious days."[23]

The situation in Bengal forced Holy Cross to cease sending men to the mission, as they could not be maintained
financially. The superior of the mission, Father Michael Mangan, C.S.C., informed the superior general: "We are obliged
to reduce the allowances of all men in accordance with our
income."[24] In August 1933 Crowley was much more explicit:

> I feel obliged after consultation with Father Mangan to
> suggest to you that you keep the missionaries home this

year and send only Brother John [Heim] whose support can be met without great difficulty either here or in
Bandhura. . . . Unless you see that conditions from the
financial point of view have very definitely improved it
would be imprudent to send the three young priests to us
this year.[25]

Crowley's recommendation to keep the missionaries home
extended into 1934. The next year, however, prompted by
pressing needs at Holy Cross High School at Bandhura, and
with some ease in the financial picture, Crowley again began
to look for recruits, effectively opening the door for Vincent
McCauley to fulfill his ambition as a missionary.[26]

Journey to Bengal

In 1936, buoyed by Crowley's new confidence, Superior
General (1926–1938) James Donahue, C.S.C., made ready to
send new men to Bengal. Crowley cabled the superior general,
saying that four new men could be accommodated, although,
"receipts are still very poor."[27] His provincial, James Burns,
C.S.C., informed McCauley that Donahue had assigned him
to Bengal. Donahue explained his assignment:

I chose Father McCauley in preference to Father [name
withheld]. Let me tell you why. Father McCauley's record
as religious and student is one of the finest. Much better than that of Father [name withheld]. His judgment
is excellent and his zeal is all-consuming. He has never
caused his superiors the least worry. The doctor's report
shows him to be in the best of health. There is, I understand, some deafness in one ear, but if I were a parish
priest in the United States today I would gladly take him
as an assistant knowing that no curate would hear more
confessions than Father McCauley. He is beloved by all
who know him.[28]

Burns agreed with the summary and welcomed the young priest's open attitude toward the mission: "I know you have placed yourself unreservedly in the hands of the Superior General, and have been willing to go to India any time he should say so." McCauley was asked to receive a thorough medical examination before he left.[29]

Before leaving for Bengal, McCauley was asked to make mission appeals in the Washington, D.C., area. He had conducted a similar task immediately after ordination and would later spend six years (1952 to 1958) on the formal "begging circuit." These were all future contacts for his numerous forays seeking funds during his time as bishop of Fort Portal (1961 to 1973). Burns instructed Father Francis Goodall, C.S.C., procurator of the missions, to keep McCauley on the tour as long as he was productive. Goodall reported to the provincial, "Father McCauley . . . seems to be meeting with small success in his efforts to secure the approval of Bishops for his preaching."[30]

Possibly because no new missionaries had been sent to Bengal in three years, confusion arose in Washington, D.C., concerning which four religious would be assigned. Records show that in July 1936 McCauley was scheduled to travel with Lawrence Graner, C.S.C., who was returning to Bengal and two brothers. By September, however, it was decided that Raymond Switalski, C.S.C., another veteran missionary, would go with the party in place of Graner. Switalski had requested to travel west to Bengal, but Burns decided that "Father Switalski's experience in oriental travel would be of great benefit to the others who are going for the first time."[31]

Before his departure McCauley was feted by his family and friends back home. A benefit was staged in his honor in Council Bluffs at the St. Patrick Hotel. In Omaha, Mrs. John Jesse, head of the Bengal Letter Club, sponsored a second party at the Miller Park Country Club.[32]

McCauley and his companions, Raymond Switalski, C.S.C., and Brothers Matthew Gara, C.S.C., and Felix Schoen, C.S.C., left New York on the *S.S. Franconia* on October 12, 1936, after a "decided[ly] success[ful]" departure ceremony the previous day in Washington at the Foreign Mission Seminary.[33] The original travel plan called for the missionaries to travel to London and then board a second vessel, the *Strathmore*, for the journey to Bombay. Demonstrating an adventuresome and independent spirit, however, McCauley and Brother Matthew, after two days in London, made other plans. Discovering it was of equal cost to travel via train or ship to Marseilles, the two decided to travel to Marseilles by rail, visiting Paris, Lisieux, and Lourdes in route. They boarded the ship in Marseilles after taking a short tour of the city. McCauley wrote: "At Marseilles we bargained with a cab driver for a quick 'look see' of the city: visited Notre Dame de la Gorde, the cathedral, the water front and zig-zagged around the business district."[34] Donahue noted the deviation and asked McCauley for an explanation. The general accepted the young priest's rationale, but concluded: "I think it would have been more religious for you to have gone to India as your superiors arranged."[35]

McCauley and his compatriots arrived in Dacca on November 16, 1936. He explained, "Well, we arrived safe, sound and in the best spirits one month and four days after we threw a parting kiss to the Statue of Liberty. The trip was quite pleasant on the whole." The local Holy Cross community, headed by Michael Mangan, C.S.C., and Bishop Crowley "gave [them] a royal reception when [they] arrived."[36] McCauley promptly traveled via boat the rather short (twenty miles) but very long (fifteen hours) trip from Dacca to Bandhura and Little Flower Seminary to which he had been assigned. He was welcomed by Father John Harrington, C.S.C., the local superior.[37]

McCauley's initial reaction to the mission focused on the frustration caused by poverty in the region. He wrote to Goodall:

> The missionaries are certainly living close to the budget these days, and how scanty the budget is you know better than I. Everyone has a long list of absolute necessities that simply can't be procured. The Bishop received a report from one of the principal catechists the other day regarding a section [of the country] where ten thousand depressed class [people] have become disgruntled with Hinduism and want to learn more about Christianity. Kane also sent in a letter saying that he can get two hundred near his place with absolute certainty. What he needs is money and catechists at once. Voorde says the Garo men are swamped with demands that they cannot possibly satisfy on their meager allowance. The impression that I get is that all the men are doing what they can with the means at hand[,] but slice and pinch as they will, there isn't enough coming in to satisfy half the need.[38]

After a few months he became more acclimated to the reality of his new environment, but realized it would be a long process. In his usual comical style he described his adjustment to the mission:

> The contest between myself and the rest of Bengal is settling down to a steady pace now that the surface green of the stranger has become worn off a bit. I do not claim to be fully initiated as yet, nor do I bite off large chunks of the Bengali language when I talk, but at least I no longer walk around in a daze and manage to show some signs of intelligence when I am spoken to. The first month or two was one living nightmare. At present, however, there are slight traces of dawn breaking through the attic windows of my mind. Unless the pace increases I can't expect the

full daylight of comprehension for a couple years yet. But it is encouraging to see traces of light, however dim.[39]

As a new missionary, McCauley's ideas and reflections were highly prized by Goodall, who wished to use them for *The Bengalese*. Goodall wrote to the new missionary:

> I do hope that your spirit of cooperation will remain as keen as it has always been and you will give us helpful excerpts of mission life and interesting articles from time to time. No, I do not expect something every month but if you will give us an article once a year or three or four interesting episodes that we could use in connection with mission snapshots that would quite fit the bill.[40]

McCauley made several contributions during his time in Bengal, including eleven articles and several "snapshots" from letters that were published.

Mission to Bandhura: 1936–1939

Immediately after his arrival in Bengal, McCauley was assigned to Bandhura and its educational apostolate. In 1922, Father Omer Desrochers, C.S.C., opened St. John's Apostolic School on the grounds of Holy Cross High School. Its purpose was to train native boys as catechists. The first year there were only four boys enrolled, but by 1926 there were sixty, all of whom took classes at the high school. In late 1922, Father John Delaunay, C.S.C., came to East Bengal. In 1926, through Delaunay's efforts, Little Flower minor seminary "for Bengali and Garo boys" was established alongside St. John's. More accomplished students from St. John's often matriculated to Little Flower for four years of pre-theology training. From Little Flower, students who were successful in the Calcutta University matriculation examinations were sent to St. Albert's major seminary in Calcutta, operated by the Jesuits. McCauley was assigned to assist John Harrington, C.S.C., at

the Bandhura site, a ministry that placed him in both educational camps.[41]

McCauley was kept very busy in his new ministry as he
continued to acclimate to the area. Generally he taught six
classes per day at St. John's plus Latin at Little Flower. He
spoke of "being up to my chin" with respect to his workload.[42]
The day-to-day ministry was made more complicated by the
local conditions, especially the rampant illnesses that plagued
the students, and the oppressive climate. McCauley described
the situation:

> Bandhura is just beginning to sizzle now that the Old Sol
> [sun] is hitting his stride. In another couple of weeks we
> will be fritters. And they tell me that this is the coolest
> March in years. So far though, all we have done is shed
> the extra poundage accumulated over the winter months.
> Some of the boys are not so fortunate. We have had a
> couple cases of intermittent fever that turned plump
> youngsters into chocolate colored skeletons. Our [rose–]
> colored glasses gave out during a siege of "pink eye," and
> the ranks of the "beri-beri" victims are still growing.[43]

Floods were almost an annual event during the monsoon. An
especially bad situation arose in 1938. McCauley graphically
described the state of affairs:

> If we had a theme song it would be "River Stay Away
> from My Door," and believe me we would do some lusty
> bellowing these days. It will be three weeks or more before
> the water reaches its peak and already we are a foot above
> last year's "high." The rise was so rapid this year that
> many washouts occurred along the river. The [rice] pad-
> dies couldn't keep up with the water and a great deal of
> it has been ruined. The jute was skimpy at best and there
> was little of it, so a "blues" song might do for [a] second
> choice if we had any choice. Tonight is "new moon" which
> means the water will rise considerably, and that when only

five inches are needed to bring the fish wiggling through my room. . . . The bazaar shops are knee-deep in water already. Our rice man is having a hard time keeping his supply dry, and today the bread man told us that his oven is only three inches out of the river.[44]

The aftermath of the July-to-September 1938 monsoon was equally traumatic if not more problematic. McCauley's description illustrates the gravity of the situation:

Among our boarders we had typhoid, appendicitis, three kinds of malaria, and beri-beri; fifteen boys in all. I was alone on the job at the time and believe me it was no picnic. The other thirty-five boys kept their health but the water was always a menace. Nearly all had cracked skin due to some chemical in the water, and they *would* [McCauley's emphasis] splash around. Dyssantary [*sic*] threatened us but we fought it off; cholera hit a few times in the nearby village but didn't cross the river. Naturally everything was soaking wet all the time: clothes became mouldy [*sic*], food sp[o]iled in a short time; books began to fall apart. What mildew didn't damage the hordes of ants and termites did.[45]

Besides the elements of nature St. John's and Little Flower fell victim to financial difficulty as well. While the effects of the Depression had eased somewhat, the missions perpetually lived a day-to-day financial existence. The main problem for the seminary was maintenance of the seminarians; reduced funds meant fewer boys could be accommodated. McCauley reported, "Bandhura's allowance is still about one-third of what it takes to run the place." In a humorous way he thanked Goodall for an unexpected contribution:

The fifty-dollar check looked like the fulfillment of the dream I had the other night. Many thanks. Don't send more than a dozen like that a month or we will have to go back to suspenders. The belts won't be able to reach.[46]

The financial need, coupled with the misery wrought by nature, caused McCauley to vent his frustration, but he always kept perspective. Returning from a month vacation in the mountains of Shillong, India, he wrote:

> In any case that month was certainly a lifesaver. I went out of here fed up with the scummy, jungle-dominant life here, but it wasn't long before the perspective cleared a bit, and I could look at things with less pessimism and gradually with enthusiasm.[47]

The educational mission at Bandhura initiated in Vincent McCauley a lifelong commitment to the promotion of indigenous clergy and the local church. Beginning in Bengal, it was a recurrent and well-respected theme in his ecclesiastical career. *The Bengalese* stated succinctly, "It was the work of building an indigenous clergy . . . [with which] Father McCauley was most closely associated."[48] Certainly McCauley's belief in establishing the local church and clergy was shared by his local ordinary, Timothy Crowley, C.S.C.:

> The forming of a native clergy and a competent corps of catechists must continue to be the large claim on our program. The Congregation of Holy Cross could never hope to supply the necessary personnel, even if it were desirable that it should do so. The Holy Father has made it clear that he wants the sons of the soil to minister to their own people. . . . The Little Flower Seminary and its feeder, the Bandhura Apostolic School, must be kept packed full with the best boys of the mission.[49]

McCauley often expressed his conviction for the need of an indigenous clergy. He often stated that establishment of a native clergy had been in the mindset of the Church from the apostolic age. He suggested, "The wisdom of that policy is undeniable. Missionaries are sent out to plant the seeds of the Faith and to nourish the tender plants in foreign gardens.

Plantare Ecclesiam. It is the part of the native clergy to consoli-
date the gains and to extend the fields."[50] The role of nation-
alism was an important factor in the movement toward local
clergy. He wrote to his parents, "The time is coming when the
Indian clergy will have to assume more and more direction of
Catholic interests in this country."[51] Later, when the onset of
World War II all but ended the expatriate supply of clergy to
Bengal, McCauley described the situation:

> Our work of building up a native Indian clergy has taken
> on added significance since the war began. A native priest-
> hood is, indeed, the ideal toward which the Church aims
> at all times, but often the stimulus that pushes that ideal
> into realization is of a very earthy nature.

Knowing that the prospect of receiving European men and
resources would not be promising for years, he concluded,
"Hence the urgent necessity of raising up a native clergy to
look after the needs of the Church."[52]

Nationalism, as best expressed through the independence
movement led by Mahatma Gandhi, was another catalyst
that drove the indigenous clergy train. Perceptive to this reality, McCauley wisely used it to promote his drive for native
priests. He wrote to his family:

> We need native priests badly and may soon have to depend
> on them more than ever. . . . We have no time to lose to
> build up a stronger and more numerous Indian clergy, for
> as in Japan and parts of China, the time may come when
> we will be told to get out. Even if we are not chased our
> position will not be nearly so favorable as it is now, for the
> strong arm of the English is unmistakeable [*sic*]. We must
> prepare for a possible less favorable eventuality.[53]

Two years later he echoed the same theme: "The day is coming—
how fast is a matter of conjecture—when the white man will
be scarcely tolerated in this country."[54]

One of the great obstacles, although periodic, that Catholic missionaries faced in Bengal in their drive to promote indigenous clergy was severe local prejudice against Catholics and priests. McCauley once commented, "Prejudice, ignorance, fear, and a long list of superstitions work against the champions of a native priesthood." He elaborated on the "entangled jungle of ancient superstitions" that needed to be negotiated:

> The concept of priesthood, so clearly understood and so generally admired among our Catholic people at home, had to be planted and carefully cultivated in the minds of our people in the villages. And the task was not easy for the idea of giving up their sons to the service of God was unthinkable as beaf [sic] eating to the Hindu. The culture and customs of the country dictate the very opposite.[55]

A thread of superiority often ran through the attitudinal fabric of many Western missionaries, leading them to believe that native clergy were inadequate for the task. Countering this attitude, McCauley wrote:

> We have still a long way to go, to be sure, but when you consider that the missionaries themselves are now more generally "sold" on the idea of building up a native clergy, and that the sentiments of the Catholics "for" their own priests has and is strengthening, that many more young men want to "join the seminary," then it does seem that things are beginning to "look up a bit."[56]

McCauley understood that the establishment of a native clergy would require much sacrifice and outside support. Encouraged that more boys were showing interest in Little Flower, but cognizant of the situation, he wrote, "We are not sure we shall be able to keep all the young men here, but such is the importance attached to recruiting a native clergy that the authorities are willing to make all possible sacrifices to keep the seminary going."[57] Conscious of the prevailing conditions and the obvious need to bring security to the local church, and grateful for the "sound mission backing and the prayers which are daily enriching the roads of priests and priests-to-be,"[58] McCauley could report some success to his provincial: "In Dacca the efforts to build up an indigenous clergy have been on the whole quite successful and prospects for the future are encouraging."[59]

Mission to the Kukis: 1939–1940

From the mission's foundation in 1853, the evangelization efforts of Holy Cross religious in Bengal were concentrated on peoples located in the immediate areas of the community's schools and parishes. However, in 1909, representatives of the Garos, an aboriginal matriarchal people with Mongolian origins, came to Bishop Hurth asking for a priest. In 1910, after the Garos had made two additional overtures to Hurth, Father Adolphe Francais, C.S.C., was sent to Ranikhong to initiate a mission to these people. Within thirty years, some fifty thousand Garos had been baptized and two important parishes, at Mymensingh and Biroidakuni, had been founded.[60]

During his time at Bandhura, McCauley visited the community's foundation with the Garos on a few occasions. Shortly after his arrival, he traveled to the region with Father Richard Patrick, C.S.C., to attend a priest conference and experienced firsthand the harsh living conditions and difficulty of the mission. In June 1937, he filled in temporarily for three weeks in the region. He wrote, "What I wanted was a taste of village life and more opportunity to speak Bengali. I got both in large doses and enjoyed every moment of my stay."[61]

The Kukis, a hill tribe akin to the Garos, lived in the Lushai Hills in the jurisdiction of the Diocese of Chittagong. Due to government restrictions, however, missionaries were not allowed to evangelize the Lushai region. However, in 1936,

many Kukis migrated into the Longtorai Hills of Tripura
State, a region outside the restricted area. These people, like
the Garos some twenty-five years earlier, sought the ministra-
tions of a priest. A meeting was held between representatives
of the Kukis and Holy Cross to discuss the establishment of
a mission.[62] While it was clear "that no little sacrifice will be
expected," and language difficulties would abound, eventually
in December 1937 two Holy Cross priests, Joseph Voorde
and Raymond Massart, founded the mission at Mariamnagar
(Mary's Town) in the District of Mymensingh.[63] The local
superior, John Kane, C.S.C., was enthusiastic about the
possibilities:

> We have some wonderful prospects here. To the North
> there is a community of some 40,000 Low Caste Hindus
> who are seeking social uplift and as they cannot get it in
> the Hindu society they are prepared to join where they
> can better their condition. This is a golden opportunity
> for us if we can once make a start.[64]

The opportunity that Kane saw was described more completely by Joseph Voorde:

> The Kuki section of our mission is booming and begin-
> ning to show signs of becoming a mass movement. It
> took two years to get it started and now it is becoming
> pretty big, and coming so fast that it will break their back
> if something does not happen soon. We have 300 under
> instruction now with more getting ready to come in. They
> are simply hot after the faith, almost fighting for it.[65]

In January 1939, McCauley was transferred from Bandhura to Mymensingh to prepare for ministry to the Kukis.
The move was necessitated by Raymond Massart's return to
the United States.[66] McCauley spent a "six month novitiate"
at Mymensingh before moving to Agartala and the village of
Mariamnagar.[67] His residence changed "from a brick house

in town to a bamboo one-room set-up out in the middle of a swamp."[68] McCauley described the poverty of the region and harsh living conditions of his residence:

> The floor is mud, damp of course at this season and crawling with a dozen kinds of ants at any time, hence no piling stuff on the floor or in the convenient corners. The bamboo walls offer no storage space either. Bugs by the thousands haunt every fold and crevice and use the criss-cross stripes as up-and-down highways. Two clothes presses hold our articles of daily need; the rest are kept in tin boxes piled head high on a platform of ant-proof wood.[69]

The lack of drinking water and the real danger of cholera and typhoid was significant motivation for Crowley to petition the superior general, Albert Cousineau, C.S.C., to provide sufficient funds to build a habitable place for the missionaries.[70]

Despite the day-to-day harsh conditions, McCauley was not daunted in his desire to serve. He wrote,

> Still, I am encouraged, for poverty has never been the chief obstacle to the spread of the Church, nor has money been the measure of internal strength. If the faith is there and if it is alive and strong, then the means of making it produce good works will be found in one way or another.[71]

He was very pleased to be in Agartala and to have the opportunity to serve in the more traditional mission field. He voiced his pleasure, yet prophetically forecasted the future:

> I am more than pleased by the shift because it [is] the real front line, and everyone wants a try at it some time or other. I may not last long, but I'll make the best use of my stay while it lasts. The reason why I have doubts about its being permanent is that I seem to be pretty well loaded up with malaria, and this place is about as bad as they go in that respect.[72]

McCauley's ministry to the Kukis centered on evangelization and the sacramental life. He and Voorde received reports that people in remote villages sought instruction, but as valiant as they were, sometimes the isolated conditions, difficulty of travel, and lack of financial resources proved insurmountable barriers to progress. Still, McCauley reported, "We are still baptizing, marrying and burying them as usual and try to keep a fresh look-out for new people to instruct."[73] He was very pleased, yet surprised, with the fervent hunger for the faith demonstrated by the people. Catechists were kept busy from dawn to dusk instructing new converts.

The remote nature of the ministry raised some challenges, but McCauley felt more angst at the need to teach even in this remote area. He felt his move from Bandhura would give him a new ministry, but this was not the case. He vented in a letter to his family:

> When I walked out of Bandhura class-rooms I thought I would be finished with that sort of work, but here in this mission I have to look after the readin' – writin' -n- 'rithmetic in a dozen grass hut village schools. . . . You ought to thank your lucky stars that you have sisters to teach your kids. The school regime here is a topsy-turvy mess that needs at least a couple generations of tooth-drilling tactics to get rid of the noxious corrosion.[74]

The main problem that the Kuki mission experienced was insufficient financial resources. He reported in January 1940 that eight catechists were assisting in the mission, but this was more than could be supported.[75] Thus evangelization efforts were being curtailed due to the lack of funds. McCauley lamented the situation: "The spreading process [evangelization] has received a few setbacks of late for it costs money to branch out even in the jungles, and money is what we have been getting less and less of as time goes on."[76] He claimed that monies provided could not even sustain the mission as it was, let alone allow for expansion. Catechists, who were vital to the effort, could not be paid and, thus, were not retained. Still, in a more positive tone McCauley could state, "But, Oh well, we are still here, and though we are on precarious footing the house hasn't tumbled down yet."[77]

McCauley's early prediction that his stay "on the front lines" would be brief came to fruition. In June 1940, he wrote to his family from Shillong, where he went for recuperation and holiday:

> The mosquitoes have been getting after me for some time and my superiors made me get out of the swamp. Up here I have been taking it easy and getting my injections regularly. I hope that by the time I leave my 25 grains of quinine a day will have cleaned out the malaria bugs.[78]

While there McCauley received word that he was to be transferred back to Bandhura. He relayed the message to his family:

> The brass hats evidently think that the jungle jaunts are a little too much for my bag of bones. It would have been all right if I hadn't got so much fever during the last six months, but now they are afraid to take a chance on me.[79]

World War II and the Bengal Missions

The sense of renewed confidence manifested by Bishop Crowley when McCauley arrived in 1936 was also seen in Father Albert Cousineau, C.S.C., who became the superior general of the congregation in 1938. In his first circular letter to the community, Cousineau spoke of the importance of the mission and his support:

> Dacca and Chittagong are fields of untiring devotedness,
> of consoling apostolates and of unbounded love for souls.
> . . . The Congregation is bound always to give of its best
> to Bengal, and I beg their excellencies, Bishops Crowley
> and LePailleur, to believe in my utmost devotedness and
> co-operation.[80]

He continued, "Let me say . . . that Bengal has in its new
superior general a father who belongs to it by his fourth
vow. . . . I pray that we will all stand by the sacrifices, apostolic
spirit and love for souls of the men in Bengal."[81]

The onset of World War II on September 1, 1939, however,
brought significant problems to the Bengal mission. Initially
the ramifications of the war were manifest in the loss of European support, both monetarily and in personnel. However,
after the Japanese attack on Pearl Harbor on December 7,
1941, and the rapid expansion of the war into Indochina and
the subcontinent, the situation became quite severe. The physical proximity of the war to Bengal was certainly on the mind
of the Holy Cross regional superior, Father John Kane.[82] Kane
regularly corresponded with Albert Cousineau, providing
updates on the situation. In December 1941, he was confident
that the British would stop the Japanese onslaught. By March
1942, however, he was much more concerned. He acknowledged that the capture of Singapore was a "serious situation,"
and concluded: "The Japanese are advancing in Burma and if
Rangoon goes, which seems quite likely . . . we are sure to have
the Japanese here in Bengal." In May 1942, Kane was contemplating his options should the Japanese invade the mission.[83]

Bishop Crowley was also concerned about the increasingly
dangerous situation the war created. Before the war expanded
to the subcontinent its effects were felt. The lack of normal
monetary contributions forced many missions in India to
close their schools and dismiss seminarians, teachers, and
catechists. Even the normal allocation from Propaganda Fide

did not come in 1940, but Crowley realized this was only the beginning of an extended economic dry period. Receipts from individual contributors to the mission and specific missionaries dipped a full 90 percent.[84]

Vincent McCauley was equally fearful of what the war might do to the mission. Initially he worried that fighting would envelop the region as "the war is all about us." While soldiers did not arrive as he expected, nonetheless he warned, "We are by no means secure. Everyone says we are enjoying only a temporary respite in the area. The real thing may flare up any day." In a pragmatic way he realized that he might be chased out at any time, but proclaimed, "We intend to keep plugging away for all we are worth."[85] Still, the reality of the war's effect wore on McCauley's general optimism. He described the situation to his family:

> Our Tripura State skies are clouding fast. Seeing our rosy opportunities—right within our grasp—on those jungle hill-tops (hills that we can't climb because there is no fuel in our mission machine) makes me more sick than any amount of malaria. We are not beaten yet. We are still determined to baptize two hundred or more Kukis after the rains. . . . These first converts were to be merely an opening wedge. Now it looks as though we will be hard put to keep the wedge in place, much less force it further into the breach.[86]

McCauley, like Crowley, worried about the loss of money, but he understood the mission was truly the work of God through the hands of people. He wrote, "We realize that for the success—even moderate of this work, most of the burden falls on Him, but we also feel He wants us to share in His labors."[87] In an unusually frank manifestation of his spiritual feelings he wrote:

Maybe we are too pessimistic. Maybe it is God's plan
that things continue to move the hard way. After all, it is
the cross we preach and the Man of Sorrows we call our
leader. In truth we can't hold a candle to the followers of
Christ in mad Europe when it comes to suffering. We are
just too soft, I guess.[88]

Little Flower Seminary

The war caused many difficulties for the Bengal mission
and its people, but this reality did not dampen the spirit of
Vincent McCauley as he returned to his former home at Bandhura. He explained his transfer to his friends,

I was moved from there [Tripura State] when it became
evident that I could not shake off the malaria while living in the midst of it. The superiors sent me back to the
Seminary and Apostolic School to get back on my feet
and to help Fr. Harrington who had been hard pressed
for lack of help.[89]

McCauley was soon appointed superior and rector at Little
Flower on October 1, 1940, when John Harrington, C.S.C.,
was accepted for service as a military chaplain.[90] He was assisted by Jacob Desai, a diocesan priest. The two shared weekend
parish ministry at Golla, a nearby village.[91] McCauley admitted the difficulty of his new assignment, but welcomed his
ministry with open arms since it again allowed him to promote indigenous clergy and the local church. He wrote,

The change was like jumping out of the frying pan into
the fire. Fortunately there is little travel connected with
the work here; it's practically all class work. Still, the
responsibility for training . . . a native clergy and the task
of supporting the institution is even greater than we know
in the jungle front-line. To be teaching again, to be with
the boys, especially seminarians, is very much to my

liking, but I will trade the position of "Seminary Rector,"
for that of "professor" to the first one who may apply.[92]

While McCauley had escaped from the malaria fields of
Tripura State, his health continued to remain fragile at Bandhura. Relapses with malaria and other tropical maladies struck
with regular frequency. He at times described himself as a
"semi-invalid." He began to experience problems with his legs
to the point that his superiors considered moving him to the
cathedral in Dacca, "but [he] talked them out it." He asked for
prayers to get his strength back:

> I do hope you will continue your prayers for me, though as
> it is getting tiresome to go along in low-gear all the time.
> It is a year this month since the trip to the Kuki hills—the
> one that finished me on the front line. Please don't get the
> idea that I have been discouraged. I am not that far yet
> and the Lord has been good enough to let me be willing
> to go at half-speed just so long as it pleases him.[93]

McCauley's precarious health did not seem to impede his
work as rector and superior at Bandhura. The two schools,
Little Flower and St. John's, worked in tandem. New students
stayed for two to three years at St. John's until they were found
qualified to enter Little Flower. McCauley was kept very busy,
not only with the administrative element of his ministry, but
with his teaching duties as well. He often taught six classes
a day of religion and, to older seminarians, Latin, at Holy
Cross High School, where the seminarians took their classes.
McCauley was very appreciative of the significant role played
by the Holy Cross brothers in the formation program: "Without the facilities of a school conducted by our own Brothers
it would be impossible to provide adequate education for our
seminarians."[94] In complementary fashion, Andrew Steffes,
C.S.C., headmaster of the high school "had great respect for
Father McCauley" for "he could get things done."[95]

McCauley was pleased with the students sent to him. He stated, "They are really a fine group and I hope with the help of God's grace that we get some fine priests from them."[96] The numbers at St. John's and Little Flower varied year to year, but in 1944 he reported ten in the regional major seminary, seventeen in Little Flower, and twenty-one in St. John's Apostolic School.[97] He noted a more positive attitude toward the priesthood:

> Our numbers and our prospects [for the seminary] are on the increase. Bengali Catholics are growing in appreciation of the priestly vocation. Where ten years ago every boy who signified his intentions of becoming a priest had to overcome stiff opposition, particularly from parents and relatives, now the majority will find a much greater degree of encouragement, though not a few still meet formidable obstacles.[98]

McCauley's love for the students was totally reciprocal. Michael D'Rozario, C.S.C., retired bishop of Khulna, commented about McCauley's presence at Little Flower:

> We seminarians were very happy to have Fr. McCauley as our Rector. He was a very kind-hearted person and a very holy and enlightened priest. He was a very jovial and cheerful person in spite of the physical sufferings he underwent from time to time. He was always very enthusiastic and inspired us.[99]

The respect clearly noted by D'Rozario was one of McCauley's trademarks. It was the way he treated all who graced the Bandhura compound, setting the proper example for the seminarians.

McCauley's return to Bandhura during the war created several additional challenges for his ministry. In general the war brought great instability and, for expatriate missionaries like McCauley and his Holy Cross confreres, great uncertainty concerning their status. The persistent problem was, as earlier with the effects from the Great Depression, lack of monetary resources. Not only was the money supply cut, but equally damaging was the great rise in inflation. McCauley explained, "All last year the food supply problem was a daily struggle involving a lot of running about, string-pulling and haggling. It isn't over yet."[100] He elaborated further:

> I am having an awful time feeding my gang of forty. Prices are terrible and many things are very scarce. Kerosine[sic] oil is not available much of the time. I am now getting the boys up at four A. M. After morning prayers and Mass they begin study at five-thirty. We hold off breakfast till seven in order to save coal in the kitchen. Then the boys go to bed at eight-thirty because we can't get kerosine for the lamps.[101]

Despite the problems, with optimistic faith he could still write, "Still, we continue to eat, and somehow or another we hope to struggle along but we are certainly in the hands of Providence now more than ever."[102]

Optimism aside, McCauley was forced to face reality. Because he wanted the seminary to "continue so long as it is at all possible," he initiated an earnest campaign with family and friends to solicit contributions. He wrote to his family, "The importance of our little Seminary and Apostolic School is magnified by the spectrum of the times. Anything you can do to bring it to the notice of kind, mission-minded friends, will be of inestimable value."[103] Despite his efforts, it was necessary to close the apostolic school and seminary in March 1943 for one month.[104]

The effects of World War II were not the only problems McCauley faced at Bandhura. He was in a constant battle against non-Catholic and anti-Catholic forces, yet he did note some improvement with time: "There has been a substantial

improvement in the general attitude of the people toward the
seminary and toward the native clergy."[105] The seminary routine and work was interrupted several times during the war
years by Mahatma Gandhi's Indian freedom movement. He
suggested that while Gandhi's efforts were important for the
"untouchables" of the Hindu caste system, their timing "in
the midst of war . . . was certainly untimely."[106] Additionally,
the constant battle against disease and the harsh climate took
its toll. The monsoon rains often dictated the schedule and
seminarians were constantly plagued with malaria and typhoid,
a situation that caused additional periodic closures.[107]

Despite effects of the war, interference from Gandhi's
freedom movement, and the hardship of disease and harsh
weather, McCauley's enthusiasm and dedication for his ministry could not be dampened. Speaking of the seminary as "a
source of great comfort," he was very pleased with the new
seminarian candidates, seeing a marked improvement over
time in their qualifications.[108] He explained more fully,

> I may find myself with more mouths to feed next year [at
> Little Flower] and perhaps less to provide them with—if
> this war keeps getting worse. But there is no doubt about
> the necessity for this move. We will have to trust in Divine
> providence to supply the means—and the means will be
> provided if the project has the approval of heaven.[109]

McCauley credited Bishop Crowley's support for the progress
of the seminary:

> Bishop Crowley is without doubt the single greatest reason
> for the growth and success of the Diocesan Seminary. It
> is the "Bishop's Seminary" in more than a technical sense.
> He followed and supported every step in its evolution and
> how much of the progress was due to his instigation none
> but himself knows.[110]

The local superior, John Kane, noted McCauley's efforts: "At the seminary there is a fine spirit. Fathers McCauley and [Frederick] Bergmann with the help of Father Jacob Desai are giving the boys a good training."[111]

Neither the hardships of war and environment nor physical distance from home ever compromised McCauley's constant dedication to his blood family. He regularly corresponded with many members of his family and was ever grateful for their prayerful and financial assistance. Even at such a distance he remained the faithful older brother, especially to his sisters. He was willing to assist in any way possible. He wrote to his sister Eleanor,

> You can be sure that if the rice field padre can do anything for you at any time at all, well it's as good as done. You probably overestimate the value of his prayers, but such as they are, they are yours to draw on.[112]

He was happy to provide advice when he felt it was needed. Again, writing to Eleanor about her forthcoming marriage, he offered his opinion:

> For a practical demonstration of what the ideal wife should be study your Mother. If you do one fractional bit as well as she, the ups and downs that come to you will only serve to mellow you, not break you; your life will expand, not narrow down; you will then be all that God wants you to be; your marriage, your life will be a success—your salvation assured.[113]

Vincent McCauley never forgot his roots nor the sources of his strength for ministry to God's people abroad.

Illness and Return to the United States

McCauley's enthusiasm for family, mission, and, more specifically, the seminary, could not triumph, however, over his

persistent health problems that flared anew in late December
1943. While on a trip to Dacca to acquire various supplies for
the seminary, McCauley became very sick and was admitted
to a hospital where he stayed for two months. In early January 1944, John Kane reported to the superior general: "Father
McCauley is now in [the] hospital with phlebitis. We hope
nothing serious will develop, but he must remain absolutely
quiet for a month or six weeks at least."[114] In an optimistic
tone, Bishop Crowley elaborated further one month later in a
letter to the American provincial, Thomas Steiner, C.S.C.:

> Father McCauley has been in [the] hospital for a month
> caring for a development called phlebitis of varicose veins.
> The blood clot could be serious if it attached to the heart
> or the brain. Happily in Father's case, rest and very expert
> treatment appear to keep the trouble from becoming
> serious.[115]

Steiner responded, "We trust that Fr. McCauley's case may not
become serious."[116]

Over the next couple months, however, McCauley's condition only grew more severe. Kane reported to the superior
general, "Father McCauley's case turned out more serious than
we first thought. . . . He has a case of serious chronic varicose
veins in both legs . . . an ideal condition for phlebitis and
thrombosis."[117] He was examined by a team of six American
physicians, who stated that he needed six to twelve months
of rest. However, they said a return to the States was not
needed nor warranted at the time. McCauley left the hospital
and resided with Bishop Crowley in Dacca. Examinations,
however, continued to show deterioration, with the blood
clots moving closer to the heart. Additionally, McCauley was
experiencing some very severe and acute attacks of pain. Kane
reported, "I am truly worried. . . . [I] do not know what more
I can do for him."[118]

Fearful of McCauley's deteriorating condition and possible death, Kane acted swiftly to send his sick priest home. During the war years, McCauley, while on vacation, had been in contact with British and American soldiers, but not in any formal capacity. Still, by coincidence, one of his friends from Council Bluffs and Creighton Prep, Hugh Higgins, then a U.S. Army officer serving in the area, heard about McCauley's condition and went to Dacca to visit him. Kane prevailed upon him to use his influence to transport McCauley home. However, the war had basically grounded all civilian air transport and, thus, McCauley was given military orders by General C. R. Smith to be returned as a "wounded soldier." McCauley was given a chaplain's military uniform and proper identification for the trip. In late August, Kane informed the superior general, "Expect Father McCauley next week."[119] McCauley described the experience:

> The six-day trip from Calcutta to Washington was a grand experience. It is certainly the way to travel. Two of the hops were rather rough on the carcass, but there were no plans to hole up. So we just kept on going.[120]

McCauley's return, while necessary, was a hard blow for the mission. His immediate successor at Little Flower, Al Neff, C.S.C., wrote, "Everybody misses Father McCauley and they will for some time."[121] He arrived back in Washington in early September to begin a long period of recuperation.

Summary

Although delayed two years due to the mission's inability to financially support him, Vincent McCauley finally fulfilled his dream to bring the gospel message to the people of Bengal. While desirous of spending more time on the front lines of the mission in the work of evangelization, McCauley, due to the need of the apostolate and his own health, spent almost 75 percent of his time in education at St. John's Apostolic School and Little Flower Minor Seminary. These latter experiences, however, provided him with great insight into the need for indigenous clergy and support for the promotion of the local church, ideas that would be very important in his future ministry in Eastern Africa. Living often in extremely harsh and adverse conditions, he sometimes fell victim to a sense of defeatism and frustration, but he always returned to an optimistic perspective that characterized his approach to ministry and life. It was this same optimism, and his experience as a seminary rector, that he now brought to his new apostolate in Washington, D.C., as he returned home to take the reins of his alma mater, the Foreign Mission Seminary.

CHAPTER 3

The Foreign Mission Society:
1944–1958

Vincent McCauley returned to the United States a broken man in body, but ever richer in soul, character, and experience. His days in Bengal had tested him physically and spiritually, and provided the base upon which his future life as an African missionary would blossom. Although the environment of the Indian subcontinent proved too great an obstacle, McCauley never lost his thirst for adventure, nor his missionary spirit. It seemed natural, therefore, upon his return that he engage in a ministry, which while not a front line missionary soldier position, would nonetheless contribute greatly to the congregation's and the Church's efforts to promote the gospel in distant lands. McCauley spent the next fourteen years associated with the Foreign Mission Society, first as rector of the Foreign Mission Seminary (the Bengalese), from which he had graduated some ten years earlier, and later on the road as an advocate and fundraiser for the missions. In these roles he was able to form men for evangelization and to provide the economic support so necessary for the maintenance of missionaries, something he knew so well from his days of need and want in Bengal. A transition period between his two missionary experiences, McCauley's days in Washington demonstrated his forward thinking and ability to be ahead of the game in all his endeavors.

Return and Recovery: 1944–1946

Upon arrival in the United States it was clear that McCauley's physical condition was serious and needed immediate medical attention. Speaking of McCauley, *The Bengalese* reported in November 1944, "Though his condition was very critical when he arrived here, his doctors assure him that rest and medical treatment will renew his health."[1] John Kane, C.S.C., was glad to hear of McCauley's safe arrival home, but lamented his loss to the mission:

> I do hope he is now improving and will soon be able to work for the mission back home. We are certainly hard pressed and we hated to see him go, such an exemplary religious and zealous priest. It's a great loss to us.[2]

McCauley "hated to fade out" on the mission but realized that he had "no choice" as he was not reliable with such precarious health.[3] Steiner, grateful for his safe return, told him, "Take several weeks of good rest now, which I am certain will do wonders for you." He continued, "We want to take care of you, so we will spare no efforts to put you back on your feet." He encouraged McCauley to go to the Mayo Clinic to obtain "a thorough check-up" and, after significant rest, come to Notre Dame.[4]

Almost immediately after his return McCauley started his program of recovery and rehabilitation. He was initially sent to the French Hospital in New York City, where he was treated for malaria and infections from numerous insect bites on his face. After a short stay, McCauley, after visiting with the superior general, Albert Cousineau, C.S.C., traveled to the Mayo Clinic in Minnesota, a place he would come to know well through numerous visits in the ensuing years.[5] His provincial, Thomas Steiner, C.S.C., hoped "he may get some relief." At Mayo, McCauley had surgery to correct varicose veins, but his recovery was rather slow. His former colleague, Joseph Voorde, C.S.C., in the United States on home leave, reported after visiting McCauley, "He is having trouble every few days."[6]

Despite the apparent problem in his recovery, McCauley was released from Mayo and, with Steiner's permission, went home to Council Bluffs for a period of recuperation. McCauley described the situation: "Last Saturday I was released from the hospital but for all practical purposes I might as well have stayed a little longer. Still, I was anxious to get home, even though I am not very active."[7] Progress was slow, as he reported to Steiner in November:

> When I was in the hospital there were a couple bad days when a clot lodged in my chest. Then a few days ago one came in my leg. There have been other times when small clots cause brief disturbances in non-vital parts. They do indicate, however, that the phlebitis has not cleared up.

Disheartened by his situation, he continued, "Personally, I have no desire to prolong my stay in Iowa. Twice I had set a date to leave but had to call it off both times. Now it looks as though I am stuck again." McCauley was very anxious to get back to work, having received a letter from the Foreign Mission Society requesting his assistance. He lamented, "I am entirely willing to do what I can, but I am afraid I won't be able to travel very soon."[8] In a cautionary response, the assistant provincial, Christopher O'Toole, C.S.C., wrote:

You will be making a serious mistake to leave Council
Bluffs until you are well. I am sure that it is Father Steiner's wish that you remain until your health is quite secure.
Do not worry about getting to work. There is plenty of
time for that. The procedure may take some time, but be
patient and all will be well.[9]

As the end of 1944 drew near, McCauley still had not recov-
ered sufficiently to resume ministry. In mid-December, Joseph
Voorde, C.S.C., reported: "I got a letter from McCauley. He
is in bed again. Boy, is he having a tough time. I hope he gets
fixed up pretty soon. If not, it may be a long time before he
is well enough to do much."[10] However, in mid-January 1945
significant improvement had been noted by a local Council
Bluffs physician who reported to Steiner that McCauley still
had "considerable trouble" with his legs, but he expected a full
recovery. He recommended that McCauley "not be put to too
strenuous duties at the time, but rather that he be permitted
to coast along and do the lighter type of duty which he could
easily handle." O'Toole, extolling McCauley as "one of our finest younger priests," responded that he would not be sent back
to Bengal anytime soon.[11]

McCauley's improved condition allowed him to travel to
Notre Dame to continue his needed rest and rehabilitation.
There, "after his long divorce from his community and his
school," he continued to recuperate while visiting friends. By
March he was sufficiently well to rejoin the mission preaching
circuit, traveling throughout the east. *The Bengalese* reported,

All of Father Vincent McCauley's friends will be happy
to learn that he has made a strong comeback to health.
Although he is not yet his robust old self, he insists upon
getting around and working for the missions. What he has
seen at first hand in Bengal, the crying needs of the poor
and the tremendous opportunities to win souls for Christ,
seems to be a burning goal which pushes him constantly.

> We need hardly mention that he is a valuable asset to the
> Bengalese organization.[12]

By the summer of 1945, McCauley was back to full-time
ministry, assisting mission operations in Washington. In June
he was assigned as assistant superior of the Foreign Mission
Seminary. His ministry included some administrative assistance to the superior, Joseph Fiedler, C.S.C., but his primary
work was teaching three classes of Bengali and making mission
appeals on weekends, during short local trips, and occasionally
on more extensive journeys during school breaks.[13]

Superior and Rector of the Foreign Mission Seminary

In the summer of 1946, Vincent McCauley was appointed
superior and rector of the Foreign Mission Seminary. *The
Bengalese* reported, "The new superior is eminently fitted for
the task of training Bengal's future missionaries, having spent
eight years in the Bengal mission field."[14] He was seen by the
seminarians he trained as a man who possessed "a broad vision
of [the] Church in pastoral dimensions." He was always seen
as enthusiastic and was well respected. He never lost his zeal
for the mission or for Bengal, even though he seldom spoke to
staff or students about his past experiences.[15]

McCauley's style as a seminary rector can only be described
as progressive for his day. Many of his seminarians described
him as "ahead of his time" with respect to his religious formation methods. His progressive methodology was centered
about a lack of regimen and formality, concepts that were
normative, even endemic to seminary training in the post–
World War II American Church. McCauley was not one to
dominate others or use his position to affect his own ideas.
On the contrary, he encouraged seminarians to make their
own decisions as part of their maturation process. He made
personnel decisions through dialogue with individuals, not

edict as was common at that time. Seminarians were all treated with the respect of peers; he allowed no favoritism to invade his thinking. One comment illustrates this point: "I never got the impression he was a ruler, but always a companion, one who shared everything."[16]

McCauley's leadership style stressed cooperation, made accommodation for differences, and was always enthusiastic. Unlike many of his peers, McCauley was never overbearing. He never "ordered people around"; on the contrary he respected various views and made allowance for different opinions. He never built barriers between himself and seminarians, thus isolating himself from his young charges, but rather associated with them freely. One seminarian described his experience: "It was a pleasure to be with a man who was so open, so friendly and so welcoming. He would chat with you, share a cup of coffee or cake with individuals or the group." Seminarians felt very close to him.[17]

One way to understand the gravity of change that McCauley brought to the FMS is to compare his ideas with those of his peer Holy Cross priests at Holy Cross College, a five-minute walk from the Bengalese. Many seminarians from the college made the short uphill trek to visit with McCauley, who was viewed as "a breath of fresh air," especially when he was compared with others who ruled more with an iron fist. One seminarian put it this way: "He was quite different from my past superiors. . . . They were more stern. I was aware they were superiors. With McCauley there was never a domineering, superior attitude."[18]

McCauley maintained a strong pastoral presence as rector. He understood human relationships better than most, especially the fact that seminarians were often placed in awkward positions with little or no voice. Thus, McCauley often became their voice, their advocate, especially in situations that involved leadership in the community. When unusual circumstances arose and seminarians needed special permission, McCauley often went to bat for them with the provincial or general administrations.[19] Seminarians always felt free to speak with McCauley. One seminarian explained:

> McCauley had an interest in the person. He was not interested in externals. He wanted to know what made a person tick. What were your problems? You could be yourself; you could be open. There was a certain spontaneity in relating to him.[20]

The staff at Holy Cross College noted McCauley's pastoral gifts as he served as a confessor and spiritual director for the seminarians at the college. Many took advantage of this privilege and chose McCauley to serve them in these vital roles. As a confessor he was extraordinary. One seminarian wrote, "I found him as a confessor as much more than one who could grant absolution. He combined spiritual direction, in an appropriate way, with the sacrament itself." Another contemporary stated, "I put more trust in him than even my spiritual director. He was a great facilitator and a good confessor."[21] McCauley took his role as confessor so seriously that he even questioned himself when three seminarians who regularly confessed to him left the seminary:

> The withdrawal of three men from so small a house in the course of a year makes me wonder a great deal. Perhaps you know of some reason for it that escapes me. I have asked the other priests in the house if they had any idea of the causes of this unusual trend, but they have not bee[n] able to point it out. I would like to know if there is a remedial fault on my part or if you think it is because of my influence on the men please do not hesitate to replace me. I certainly do not want to be responsible for the disintegration on the mission effort of the Community. I think too much of this Community and the missions to even think of hindering the development of either, and would

urge a change that might halt this deterioration. Believe
me, I'm serious about this and want only what you think
is best for the Community.[22]

The provincial administration responded with full confidence
in McCauley: "Everyone says you are doing a very fine job at
the Foreign Mission Seminary, so you can put your mind at
rest on that score."[23]

What was the source of McCauley's progressive religious
formation leadership style? One could possibly point to his
recent experience in Bengal, viewing his more open style as
completely consistent with the needs and day-to-day ministry in that mission field. McCauley was forced in Bengal to
accommodate and adjust; rigidity would not have been helpful in such an environment. People who lived with McCauley
and experienced his pastoral approach, while not discounting
his experience, suggest, however, that his personality drove his
leadership style. His natural mode of operation was coopera-
tive, nonconfrontational, and open to the ideas and possibilities that others brought. While McCauley certainly believed
in structures and planning, he was not rigid, believing and
practicing that others had something positive to contribute.[24]

McCauley's pastoral style at the FMS was complemented
by strong gifts as an administrator. On a day-to-day basis, the
FMS operated on a fixed schedule of common prayer exercises,
classes (save Bengali) at Holy Cross College, meals, study, and
recreation. Each week McCauley gave the seminarians a spiritual talk. Students experienced them as "not deep, but very
personal and to the point."[25] An annual "departure ceremony"
was held for those missionaries traveling to Bengal. In 1950,
McCauley secured Bishop Fulton Sheen, newly appointed
head of the Propagation of the Faith in the United States, as
the guest speaker.[26]

McCauley used the Foreign Mission Seminary as a house of
hospitality where missionaries, especially those who served in

Asia, were always welcome. Seminarians spoke of McCauley's "open door policy" and his ever-welcoming attitude toward all.[27] McCauley himself described to the provincial the high level of visitor traffic:

> Our house has recently become a hotel for missionaries, particularly bishops. We have had three archbishops—Archbishop Yu Pin of China, Archbishop Kerkels, Apostolic Delegate to India, and Archbishop Mathias of Madras. The rank and file missionaries without titles come and go frequently.[28]

Besides his duties as rector, McCauley was invited to promote the missions on the radio. In September 1947, he was invited by William C. Smith, radio director of the National Conference of Catholic Men (NCCM), to speak on the nationwide radio program "The Faith in Our Time."[29] Two years later, in October 1949, McCauley gave a series of five talks for the NCCM's "Hour of Faith" program. In each case he ended his talk with an invitation for listeners to participate in a new program, the "Unseen Army," a spiritual way to support missionaries around the world. Using St. Therese of Lisieux's "little way" of prayer as a model, McCauley challenged his listeners to spiritually support missionaries. Typically, he stated,[30]

> Missionaries everywhere want and need the spiritual power of your prayers and sacrifices. So send me your name and address and I'll mail you a membership certificate to fill in with the name of your missionary, and the day of the week on which you will make your spiritual offering. In this way . . . you, too, will be a missionary—one of the essential members of Christ's UNSEEN ARMY working on the home front for those who are fighting for His Kingdom in a thousand missions all over the world.[31]

The Unseen Army became the primary vehicle for McCauley to promote the missions during his time in Washington, D.C. The program was actually initiated in 1946, but launched early in 1947 as a way "to stimulate interest in the missions."[32] Members prayed for their missionary, but also did what they could to raise money for his assistance. McCauley described his hopes for the program: "We'll never get rich. We don't want to, in a monetary way, but we do hope that the spiritual riches of the Unseen Army members will pile up spiritual riches that will purchase the graces our missionaries need to make Christ known and loved in all the missions of the world."[33] Highly prized members of the Army included shut-ins, the handicapped, and others who suffered pain or discomfort. McCauley scrupulously avoided any mention of money in his promotion of the Army. Donations were gratefully accepted, but this was not the emphasis.[34]

Integral to his role as rector and superior was McCauley's responsibility for the academic preparation of his seminarians. From his position as rector of the Foreign Mission Seminary and the Bengali classes he taught, McCauley enjoyed faculty status at Holy Cross College, providing him a platform for more influence in the seminary's academic program.[35] McCauley's role as a teacher was both formal and informal. Academic study of Bengali was coupled with its practical application. During recreation periods and often at meals McCauley taught the FMS seminarians important and useful Bengali expressions. Sometimes, as a special privilege McCauley allowed Bengali conversations at dinner in lieu of spiritual reading.[36] Seminarians in general were very impressed with McCauley's teaching method. He was an outstanding speaker and kept your attention. He could relate well to students and was never judgmental. He had the ability to correct errors in Bengali without ever stating the student was "wrong." Some students were a bit frustrated when McCauley missed class due to some mission appeal, but generally they were grateful for his pastoral presence. One seminarian commented: "He had a remarkable gift of making us feel special for our achievements and honestly correcting us when needed without hurt."[37] McCauley liked teaching and considered his students, "on the whole, a group of good average students."[38]

McCauley's days as rector at the FMS were filled with additional responsibilities. One major difficulty that eluded final resolution was to better define the relationship between the FMS, the Foreign Mission Society, and *The Bengalese*. In order to keep the tasks separate and allow each entity to perform its function completely and independently, the rector was not an officer of the society nor a member of *The Bengalese* staff. Despite the separation of duties, McCauley, as mentioned earlier, was often away from the seminary on mission appeals. At times he grew weary with "more than a taste of road work." In a typical letter, McCauley explained his preaching schedule: "I expect to take a two-week jaunt through the Midwest at the end of January. 1 have three dioceses to contact and several pastors and a couple mission clubs."[39] McCauley also gave numerous mission conferences in the capital area. Lastly, for his own academic challenge, McCauley took classes at Georgetown University in the origins of languages.[40]

In the summer of 1952, after having served two three-year terms as rector and superior of the Foreign Mission Seminary, Vincent McCauley was assigned as procurator of the missions. Father Alfred Neff, C.S.C., succeeded him at the seminary. During this period McCauley began in more significant ways a lifelong battle with facial skin cancer. One seminarian recalls, "I remember the day he showed up for a weekly conference with a tiny piece of tape on his cheek. He passed it off as some minor work of the doctor." In September 1952, he again went to the Mayo Clinic, trips which became frequent over the ensuing years. In only five years he reached his seventeenth visit.[41] As would always be the case, McCauley resolutely accepted the situation in a positive tone:

> I think the Good Lord decided I needed a slap—it *was* [emphasis McCauley] overdue. But Our Lady prevailed on Him to take the sting out of it. In another week or two my new face will be merely a reminder of Her kindness and solicitude.[42]

His new assignment provided the opportunity to have more contact with his family. He corresponded regularly, both in letter and phone conversation, with relatives in Iowa and the surrounding environs.[43]

As the chief fundraiser for the Foreign Mission Society, McCauley used his recent experience and his earlier work in 1936 to canvass the countryside on "begging" tours. He claimed to drive[44] 80,000 miles annually in his efforts to give missions and raise money.[45] A typical trip would involve preaching in a given region for four consecutive weekends at different parishes. McCauley often went on his trips accompanied by Robert Hoffman, C.S.C., one of his former students at the FMS and a veteran of the Bengal mission. Hoffman says the two called themselves "nomads," living out of suitcases and never spending much time in any location.[46] While parishes were the main emphasis of the mission drive, area schools were also canvassed to give presentations in an attempt to generate more interest. McCauley literally crisscrossed the country on numerous trips in support of the Bengal mission. Besides giving missions, it was especially important for these "road warriors" to assure that they would be invited back in following years. Thus, McCauley always set up his next visit while conducting his mission. Additionally, it was the custom of all on the begging circuit to visit the families of missionaries if any were in the area of a mission appeal.

While the monetary and pastoral portions of his work for the Foreign Mission Society were important and valued, for McCauley, the most significant benefit was the spiritual aspect. He once commented,

> The abundance of spiritual benefits that flows from our zeal for the missions is too rarely appreciated; never fully understood for its source is hidden in the Divine prodigality of the First missionary. He made mission work fundamentally spiritual. He insisted that it operate primarily on spiritual resources. The returns He grants are basically spiritual for the missionaries and for their mission friends.[47]

Like his earlier promotion of the Unseen Army, McCauley instituted additional specialized groups for mission promotion while serving as procurator. He created quite a following and was able to establish several local "cells" of lay men and women to promote the mission, financially and spiritually. New York and especially Council Bluffs (The Father Vince Mission Club) were the locations of the two main groups.[48] McCauley's love for people and his social ease made him a natural to seek money from donors. This ability would aid him significantly in later years as bishop of Fort Portal, Uganda.

In addition to local clubs, McCauley started two additional groups for mission promotion. In the mid-1950s, he started the "Bricklayers," a group similar to the Unseen Army in its spiritual support of the mission. The group's organ stated as its motto: "Wanted: To build a better world: Few architects . . . more bricklayers." McCauley invited people to join: "Since building the Church in the missions is the privilege of all Catholics, we invite all—barbers, lawyers, miners, doctors, housewives, office and factory workers—to join us as Bricklayers." He also explained the mission of the group:

> Their prayers, sacrifices, and multifashioned bricks are
> vital to the project. They keep your Holy Cross missionar-
> ies at work on the scaffold building for Christ. In all they
> do for Our Lord they credit your spiritual account, asking
> that He reward you as only He can.[49]

In addition to the Bricklayers, McCauley also started, in 1956,
"The Men of Holy Cross," a group of prominent Washington
area laymen. Initially, each member agreed to financially support one seminarian at the FMS.[50]

While McCauley's responsibilities took him away from the
Bengalese on regular and often extended trips, he always tried
to remain connected to the house and its life. In 1956, in addition to his responsibilities as procurator of the missions, he
gained an additional hat as assistant to Father Thomas Fitzpatrick, C.S.C., director of the Foreign Mission Society. He also
served as councilor at the FMS from 1955 through 1957.[51]
Possibly his most important support came through his presence at the annual Departure Ceremonies. The October 16,
1953, ceremony was especially relevant, for it commemorated
the centennial of the departure of the first Holy Cross religious
to Bengal. McCauley spoke on that occasion, describing the
challenge faced by the new missionaries and those who supported them back home:

> In the missions they will find much that is different, much
> that is difficult. Every day will be a new challenge. Confi-
> dent that they are setting out to do God's Will, they will
> rely on His help. They will depend too on the prayers and
> sacrifices of us here at home whom they represent.[52]

While Vincent McCauley had physically left the mission
fields some years earlier, he never lost his desire as a missionary.
Wil Menard, C.S.C., who was a seminarian during McCauley's tenure at the FMS, stated: "If he could get back to the
missions, he would have gone the next day."[53] From September

1950, when a physician recertified McCauley physically ready to return, this thought was primary in his mind.[54] Stating, "I have always been and continue to be deeply interested in all that pertains to our mission work," McCauley began in 1951 to enter into dialogue with the provincial, Theodore Mehling, C.S.C., about returning to Bengal. He was most interested in assisting with the new mission at Notre Dame College in Dacca. Mehling admitted that McCauley had been cleared to return and was most eager, but he also realized his value with the Foreign Mission Society on the begging circuit.[55] In May 1955, McCauley renewed his call to return to Bengal:

> Because it has not been mentioned since this time last year, it may be assumed that I have given up my desire to return to Bengal. Nothing could be farther from the truth. In spite of my advanced age—I believe it is the same as yours—I am convinced that I have a few years of usefulness left. Though it will soon be eleven years since I returned from the missions, I have always wanted to go back and take this opportunity of reminding you. Please do not look on this as any more than the expression of a desire. I would not want to give the impression that I am not satisfied where I am, or that I want favors. It is rather, that I am not quite ready to be counted out mission wise, and thought I would let you know about it.[56]

Vincent McCauley's intense desire to return to the missions was rekindled significantly when he was sent on a mission fact-finding tour in February 1958. During his trip he visited Bengal and reconnected with many Holy Cross missionaries and Bengalis, especially those associated with Little Flower at Bandhura. He left Bengal and rendezvoused with Father Arnold Fell, C.S.C., in Rome.[57] Little did McCauley know that soon his whole life would change, including a return to the missions, but not where he ever dreamed.

Summary

A missionary at heart, Vincent McCauley spent the period from 1944 to 1958 on the back lines in an integral yet supportive role to those on the mission front. Returning to the United States broken in body, but never in spirit, McCauley spent almost a year in recovery before settling down at the Foreign Mission Seminary in 1945. After one year as assistant superior, McCauley was appointed superior of the Bengalese in 1946. For the next six years he formed Holy Cross missionaries in ways that were forward-thinking for his day. He favored a more open, less restrictive formation program that emphasized equality and trust in the individual, a system that was attractive to all, including those seminarians in residence at Holy Cross College. In 1952, McCauley took a full-time position as procurator of the missions, spending the majority of his time on the road "begging" for the ministry that lay at the core of his being. However, he never lost his ambition to return to the missions. Unbeknownst to him, that opportunity literally lay in his immediate future.

CHAPTER 4

Superior of the Uganda Mission: 1958–1961

Vincent McCauley's missionary spirit of adventure and service, as manifest in eight difficult years in Bengal, was to be exercised again as 1958 dawned. The Congregation of Holy Cross had been a missionary society from its inception, not only to Bengal, as previously described, but in its failed attempt to Algiers in 1840, its foundation at Notre Dame in 1842, and its arrival in Canada in 1847.[1] McCauley had served with great joy and fervor in Washington, D.C., as rector of the Foreign Mission Seminary and procurator of the missions, but it was always his desire to continue his vocation as a missionary to proclaim the gospel message in foreign lands. The opportunity came quite unexpectedly when a plea was received from western Uganda to assist in the Diocese of Mbarara.

The New Mission Discovered

The post–World War II period was a time of great expansion in the American missionary front. Historian Angelyn Dries, O.S.F., states: "In the 15 years between the end of World War II and Pope John XXIII's call for an Ecumenical Council, the US Catholic mission picture was redrawn in significant ways."[2] Missionaries worked to rebuild war-torn regions and many Americans returned to the mission fields with travel restrictions now lifted. American Servites went to South Africa to replace Italians who were needed at home. Divine Word Missionaries, priests and brothers, went to the nation of Ghana. The number of American missionaries going overseas almost doubled from 2,222 in 1940 to 4,123 in 1949.[3]

Mission associations began to blossom. In November 1949, the Mission Secretariat, organized through the National Catholic Welfare Conference (NCWC), was formed. It was an effort to encourage Church and business people to talk with each other in mutual support of the mission effort. The secretariat was functional by April 1950. Frederick McGuire, a former missionary to China, was chosen as secretariat director. In 1957, the Association for International Development was formed in Paterson, New Jersey, "to inform and form mature Catholics for assuming Christian responsibility and leadership through service at home and abroad."[4] In September 1950 (serving until 1966), Fulton Sheen was appointed national director of the Society for the Propagation of the Faith. This provided much visibility to the mission movement as Sheen was well known from both radio and television.

The 1950s were also the high tide of American anti-communism, which significantly impacted the missions. Sheen was the perfect person to defend the Church against communism. Douglas Hyde, in his book *One Front Across the World*, saw missionaries as the elites who were defending the world against communism. Sheen fought communism through a philosophical platform. He had written and spoken against it since the 1930s. Cardinal Francis Spellman of New York was another whose anti-communist stance was legendary.

Communism was not the only catalyst to the renewed mission drive. In 1957, Pope Pius XII issued *Fidei Donum* to draw attention to sub-Saharan Africa, a region virtually unknown to American Catholics. He stressed indigenous Church leadership, noting,

> It is not enough to preach the gospel as if this were the whole of the missionary's work. The present situation in Africa, both social and political, requires that a carefully trained Catholic elite be formed at once from the multitudes already converted. How urgent it is then to increase the number of missionaries able to give a more adequate training to these native leaders.[5]

Some American missionary presence in Africa existed before the war. The largest American concentration of missionaries in Africa in 1957 came from the Congregation of the Holy Ghost (the Spiritans). In 1932, the United States province had its own vicariate, covering the region of Kilimanjaro in Tanganyika. Other prominent congregations on the continent were the Sisters of the Holy Name from Albany, New York, the Oblates of Mary Immaculate, and the Brothers of the Sacred Heart, along with members of Maryknoll.

The pope's call to action prompted additional American religious congregations to respond. New arrivals in Africa were the Salvatorian Sisters in Tanzania and the Jesuits in Nigeria. The Society of Mary (the Marists) went to western Africa in 1957; Holy Cross brothers arrived in Ghana that same year. Lay missionaries also greatly increased, such as the Archdiocesan Lay Mission Helpers from Los Angeles. This group stressed personal holiness and a strong sacramental life as the foundation for mission work. The Grail was also prominent in its mission of educating women to prepare other women for service.

The Congregation of Holy Cross in the United States also began to feel the breeze of new mission life. Extant correspondence shows that community leaders were considering many possibilities for mission outreach, including a new foundation in Korea, but the call to East Africa was the most significant.[6] Thus, Africa's need for assistance and Holy Cross's openness to a new mission came together in April 1958 for what proved to be a new congregational commitment.

In early 1958, as mentioned earlier, Vincent McCauley and his Holy Cross colleague, Arnold Fell, director of the Holy Cross Foreign Mission Society, were sent on a fact-finding expedition to mission lands. The two men ended their journey in Rome, where they were presented with a new challenge. The superior general, Christopher O'Toole, C.S.C., told them that Propaganda Fide had requested Holy Cross to investigate a mission possibility in East Africa. Specifically, the procurator general of the White Fathers and Father Richard Walsh, assistant for the African Missions in Propaganda Fide, came to O'Toole seeking a "community to take over some of the work in Uganda."[7] The invitation came as a result of a petition from Bishop Jean Ogez, W.F., of Mbarara, Uganda (and his predecessor Bishop Francois X. Lacoursiere), who requested a division of the diocese.

In April 1958, McCauley, who admitted he did not even know the location of Uganda, and Fell traveled there for a ten-day examination of this mission possibility. After their arrival at Entebbe Airport, the party then traveled west to Mbarara to begin a 1,200 mile tour of the diocese with Ogez.[8] The bishop's idea was for Holy Cross to take over administration of the northern region of the diocese, which comprised the kingdoms of Bunyoro and Toro. The bishop gave four reasons for his request: (1) The physical size of the diocese, originally 400 miles north-south, was too large for good pastoral service. People in the northern regions (with the see city of Mbarara in the south) were being neglected. (2) Bishop Ogez did not have sufficient personnel to adequately staff such a vast area. (3) The division of placing Toro and Bunyoro together was natural. The two kingdoms were closely linked by heritage, a very similar language, and Fort Portal would serve as an excellent see city. (4) The opportunity for Church expansion was significant and the time was ripe. Ogez recommended that the Holy Cross contingent be led by a middle-aged priest with mission experience, as he would likely be made vicar and eventually bishop.[9]

The trip to Uganda, its possibilities for ministry, and Bishop Ogez himself were all well received by McCauley and Fell. It was clear to both men that Ogez needed assistance. McCauley wrote to the general, "Unless something changes our impression, this is the great opportunity for Holy Cross."[10] Additionally, he offered a very positive view of Ogez:

> He is observant, shows good judgment, can analyze total and individual problems quickly, is extremely energetic, moves quickly but with reason, and is not likely to be stopped easily. He is direct, practical and completely frank in admitting problems and deficiencies, even his own personal ones. If he doesn't know the answer, he admits it. He does not shy from decisions; usually makes them swiftly; has [an] adequate sense of humor.
>
> The most impressive characteristic is his universal, apostolic outlook. He is the very opposite of nationalistic, or "closed door" Catholicism. His one concern is to use everybody and everything to develop the Faith among all classes and peoples of his Diocese.[11]

Upon returning from Uganda, McCauley and Fell presented a detailed report of their findings and recommendations.

The report described the people of the region as "uniformly friendly and polite" and virtually without "evidence of any anti-European hostility." The local indigenous clergy were seen as "pro-African to the detriment of the universal outlook of the Church" and effective to the limits of their training. The possible Uganda mission would give the community a new direction and a welcome change after more than one hundred years in Bengal working to serve a small Christian community. Holy Cross would have "a stimulating opportunity to share in the making of a Catholic nation." The report went on to say that government assistance for schools, the economic ability of the people, and their traditional support for the Church, would make the mission basically self-sustaining. Spiritual returns also would be significant in this rapidly growing mission.[12]

The richness and possibilities of the Uganda mission seemed to be almost boundless. The McCauley-Fell Report stated, "Uganda is a potentially rich and rapidly progressing country. Its protectorate status promises the early achievement of independence. . . . Uganda's progress and position indicate that it will have great influence on other East African territories." Even more important was the strong evidence that the nation was ready for Catholicism. The report stated,

> With the exception of Protestants, and even some of these,
> . . . the people are highly susceptible to conversion. The
> problem is one of missionary manpower, and of finance
> to a lesser extent.[13]

The report also provided the provincial with recommendations of possible personnel to send. Ogez suggested Holy Cross start with five or six men, one of whom was more senior, and, if possible, add three religious annually, including brothers, who would be very important in staffing schools. McCauley and Fell also presented their views:

> He [the mission leader] would have to be physically fit for
> work and travel, be keenly observant, have particularly
> good judgment, be a good organizer, and be something of
> a diplomat who could get on pleasantly with all types of
> people. He and his confreres should forget nationalities,
> thier [sic] own as much as possible, and put into practice
> the universal outlook of the Church. This would not only
> be necessary for getting along with other missionaries
> from other countries, but especially for giving an example
> to the Africans themselves, who have a tendency to be
> African Catholics rather than universal Catholics.[14]

McCauley rejected his own participation, suggesting, "it [is]
a place for young men because it is a very active place."[15]
McCauley was, nonetheless, very excited about the Uganda
mission. In letters to his provincial and the superior general,
he expressed his great hope. He told Mehling,

> Both Father Fell and I think it is the opportunity of the
> century. It is the best of many offers received by Father
> General, and the one he wants to receive full consid-
> eration. . . . In Africa the mission spirit of the whole
> Congregation would get an encouraging "new lift." We
> would have a part in the making of a Catholic nation. We
> would be in the midst of the fastest growing part of the
> Church.

On the more practical side, he wrote to O'Toole: "The needs of
the Church and the advantages to Holy Cross are self-evident
to all who examine the proposal. We can make men available
and we have sufficient funds without additional burden to
other C.S.C. projects."[16]

McCauley's enthusiasm for the Uganda mission was shared
equally by his religious superiors. Christopher O'Toole,
C.S.C., liked the idea that the mission would be self-
supporting, stating that it "should bring God's blessings on the
Congregation." He told McCauley, "Do what you can to stir

up interest in Uganda."[17] Theodore Mehling, C.S.C., wrote to
O'Toole, "I am completely sold on this marvelous opportunity
to expand our foreign mission work."[18] Holy Cross religious at
the Bengalese believed a new foundation was an excellent idea
to generate more interest in the missions and offer an alternative to East Pakistan.[19]

While support of the possible Uganda mission was present
on all fronts, Holy Cross had also received instructions from
Propaganda Fide to investigate its potential participation in an
academic mission in Beirut. Bishop Eustace Smith, O.F.M.,
of Beirut, had invited Holy Cross to start an English-speaking
Catholic college to serve as competition for the Protestant
American college that was flourishing there. McCauley traveled to Lebanon after his return from Uganda in April 1958,
but he was not impressed. He did not feel it was a missionary
project, but more wholly educational. While admitting that
such a school would probably be successful, he did not recommend the project.[20]

The overwhelming support for the Uganda mission project
led Holy Cross in June 1958 to accept Ogez's offer to assist
him in Mbarara. The news was welcomed by all, save possibly
Archbishop Lawrence Graner of Dacca, who believed the new
foundation would take missionaries away from East Pakistan.
O'Toole, in anticipation of such a reaction, however, told
McCauley, "The biggest opposition I see to the Uganda project will come from Archbishop Graner. In any case we have to
look ahead to the future and not tie ourselves down too much
to present needs."[21] McCauley, while sympathetic to Graner's
need for personnel, responded to the general: "To postpone
starting in Uganda until we have men in sufficient numbers
will mean losing it—the best opportunity we ever had." He
went so far as to offer himself to Graner so the Africa project
could proceed:

Since I am somewhat familiar with the Dacca mission, perhaps the Archbishop would accept me as a replacement for one of the men you would need in Uganda. I feel confident that I have ten years of usefulness left, and by that time he will have more Bengali priests and ten or fifteen more from here.[22]

The new mission in Uganda needed personnel, especially a leader for the group. O'Toole recommended three men to Mehling: Robert Hoffman, C.S.C., Al Croce, C.S.C., and McCauley. The first two were also veterans of the Bengal mission, former students of McCauley, and approximately ten years his junior. In a subsequent letter, O'Toole suggested three newly ordained men to accompany the leader: Francis Zagorc, C.S.C., and Robert Hesse, C.S.C., from the Indiana Province, and Burton Smith, C.S.C., from the Eastern Province.[23]

Mehling believed McCauley to be the best man to lead the mission, but he was concerned about his health after some twenty surgeries to remove facial cancers.[24] Still he wrote,

I agree with you that the best man to be named as head of the new diocese[25] would be Father McCauley. I found as you did that Father McCauley is doing excellent work, is extremely well informed, and is well liked by all with whom he has dealings.[26]

After much consultation, Mehling informed McCauley, "We have decided to assign you as Director of the first group [of] missionaries to go to our new foreign mission in Uganda, Africa." He continued:

I know of your long-standing desire to return to the foreign missions. Therefore, I am sure that you will be happy with this appointment and we are sure you will do a wonderful job in establishing Holy Cross in this fine new foreign mission field.[27]

McCauley was overjoyed about his selection, but he also worried about his adequacy for the position. He wrote to Mehling:

> *Deo Gratias!* And my sincerest thanks to you for the appointment to Mbarara. I wish I could tell you how happy I am for the privilege of helping to start our new mission in Africa, with the three newly ordained priests.[28]

Despite his joy, the magnitude of the project began to weigh on him and he began to doubt his ability. He wrote, "It is obvious I lack many of the qualifications we [McCauley and Fell] suggested for the Director of the group. I presume, therefore, that you cannot at this time free such a man for the post."[29] One month later he wrote again to the superior general: "I feel suddenly very inadequate for the assignment, and realize more and more how much we in the new mission will have to draw on the spiritual resources of the Congregation."[30] O'Toole responded, noting with pleasure and confidence the appointment: "We are all very happy that you have been named to launch the new mission project in Uganda. Your experience will be invaluable."[31]

The three newly ordained priests chosen for the new mission, Francis Zagorc, C.S.C., Robert Hesse, C.S.C., and Burton Smith, C.S.C., were assigned with McCauley. All three had been originally slated to go to East Pakistan. Due to the lateness of the assignment their trunks had already been shipped to Dacca. The enthusiasm for the mission, demonstrated by McCauley, Fell, and others at the FMS, began to rub off on the newly ordained. Their original question, "Where is Uganda?" was transformed to excitement about the great possibility the mission held for Holy Cross.[32]

Christianity in East Africa

In the nineteenth century, Christian missionaries referred to Africa as the "dark continent" for several reasons. First, Europeans knew little about the area, which gave no indication of civilization. Dark also illustrated the many crimes perpetrated against Africa's peoples by Europeans and Arabs. Finally, the continent's inhabitants were black and lived in the darkness of ignorance of Christ. It was this latter reality that marked the continent and its people as prime for Christian evangelization.[33]

Some light began to dawn on this unknown region in the mid-nineteenth century through the explorations of Englishman David Livingstone. Livingstone became a folk hero through his book *Missionary Travels and Researches*, which chronicled his extensive travels across the continent between late 1853 and May 1856. He was convinced that the chief hindrance to the promotion of the gospel lay not in lack of individual effort, but rather in the great social evils that plagued the region—poverty, ignorance that generated much fear, and the mutual rejection of tribal groups, leading to much violence. It was the slave trade, however, which Livingstone considered the greatest evil and obstruction to Christianity. He believed the abolition of slavery "would only be accomplished by the impact of civilised and Christian society as a whole."[34]

Livingstone's work was the catalyst needed for Christian evangelization of Africa. In December 1857, he delivered a speech in the Senate House at Cambridge that focused English Christianity on Africa:

> I beg to direct your attention to Africa:—I know that in a few years I shall be cut off in that country, which is now open; do not let it be shut again! I go back to Africa to make an open path for commerce and Christianity; do

you carry out the work which I have begun? I leave it to you.[35]

It was Livingstone's death while on safari in 1873, however, which became the major springboard, giving energy to the mission effort. Historian Roland Oliver suggests it was Livingstone, not the Christian Missionary Society (CMS), which preceded the former by some ten years, "who set in motion the missionary invasion of East Africa."[36] Livingstone's contribution to the promotion of Christianity in Africa is summarized by historian Adrian Hastings:

> Livingstone, by the force of his character, his almost indestructible physical constitution, his most meticulous observations, climatic, botanic, and anthropological, relating to so much of Africa hitherto wholly unreported, his enormous and infectious sense of high purpose, both religious and humanitarian, so vastly reinvigorated the missionary scene that its post 1856 history takes, for a good quarter century, a decidedly post-Livingstonean character.[37]

Following Livingstone's lead, many Christian churches sent their missionaries to Africa. The Scottish Presbyterian Church was the first to organize a significant effort, beginning in May 1874. On May 21, 1875, a party actually left London and arrived at Lake Nyasa (present day Malawi) on October 11. This same year the CMS and the London Missionary Society organized new missions to East and Central Africa through the assistance of wealthy benefactors. These groups faced many hardships, including famine, disputes among tribal chiefs, and the diversity of languages, which mitigated their effectiveness. Nonetheless, in rather short order the missions became full-fledged economic political units, governed by missionaries.[38] Missionaries were seen as magicians, diviners, and workers of miracles, images they deliberately reinforced to maintain hegemony.[39]

Although these Christian missions faced many obstacles, many tribal chiefs welcomed the Europeans because of the benefits they brought. The wealth of the missionaries was a great attraction to the chiefs; they could provide many things not previously available. Also, Africans in missions generally lived free from famine, war, and slavery. Medical care far advanced to what local people knew was also provided. Above all, however, were the educational opportunities the Europeans brought, especially skills associated with trades and literacy.[40]

The advantages and advancements brought by Christian missionaries, and thus their acceptance by various tribal chiefs, raised a question on the motivation for acceptance of Christianity. Several historians believe most conversions during these pioneer mission days were for reasons other than an attraction to the faith. Roland Oliver sees most African converts of this early period as "Christians from circumstance rather than choice." Adrian Hastings similarly has commented, "For the most part, . . . early conversions came in other [than religious] ways—through employment, protection or just a desire to read."[41]

The European missionary movement in Africa was driven by three primary motives: Christianity, commerce, and civilization. While promotion of the basic biblical message may have initiated mission efforts, a resurgence of the medieval notion of civilization as a rationale cannot be ignored. This idea, along with commerce, became especially significant when conflicts arose between the Christian missionaries and Muslim traders. In order to place their message above that of Islam, Christians were forced to offer more than religion; attraction to Christianity could only be sustained by offering more than the Muslims.[42]

Uganda, a nation situated along the equator in East Africa, was rather unique in its creation and outside perception. Formed as a result of competition between imperial powers England, Germany, and France over control of the headwaters of the Nile, Uganda was carved from the African landscape based on geographic boundaries of rivers and mountains, not locations of tribal peoples. This created significant tension when tribes were split between nations. An amalgam of peoples, Uganda was, nonetheless, viewed by the English as "an orchid in a field of poison." Both Winston Churchill and explorer Henry Stanley called Uganda, "the pearl of Africa."[43]

Uganda experienced the European missionary movement within the context of two great conflicts: (1) Christianity against tribal religions, and (2) Catholicism versus Protestantism.[44] When Christian missionaries arrived in Uganda they found a religious system intact that was well organized and impressive. Ideas such as a supreme being, a day of rest, and recourse to prayer for intervention circulated among the people. Missionaries were struck by this religious sensibility. This rather unique environment generated a melding of Christianity with certain tribal religious ideas. Adrian Hastings comments:

> Christianity did not replace the traditional culture of Buganda. It merged with it, almost consecrating a commitment to tradition in regard to all sorts of things which elsewhere Christianity was more likely to challenge.[45]

The conflict between Catholics and Protestants (Anglicans) would color Uganda's religious landscape for many years, creating great competition and generating at times significant violence.

Anglicans from England arrived in Uganda in June 1877. In a famous October 1875 letter to the *London Daily Telegraph*, Henry Stanley spoke of the great possibilities for evangelization in the African interior. Inspired by Stanley's challenge and in response (it seems) to an invitation from Buganda's Kabaka (King) Mutesa I, members of CMS, led by layman Alexander Mackay, came to the north shore of Lake Victoria to begin their ministry. Mackay's knowledge of science and many practical matters made him an overnight sensation. With such an attractive resume, Mackay's Christian message was generally well received. Mutesa's welcome to the Christians was, however, more politically motivated than religious.[46] Historian Samwiri Karugire suggests that incursions from Egypt may have prompted the Kabaka to seek security from Christian missionaries.[47] The initial receptivity to the Anglicans was crowned with the first baptisms in 1882.[48]

Catholicism joined Protestantism in the contest for African converts. The condemnation of the slave trade by Pope Gregory XVI through *In Supremo Apostolatus* (1839) was the catalyst to Catholicism's entry into the African continent. During Gregory's reign, vicariate apostolics were erected at the Cape of Good Hope in 1837, Guinea (effectively Angola) in 1842, Egypt in 1844, and Sudan or Central Africa in 1846.[49]

Catholicism's arrival in Uganda was closely tied with the *Société de Notre Dame d'Afrique*, commonly known as the White Fathers, who were founded in 1868 by Cardinal Charles Lavigerie, the archbishop of Algiers.[50] Adrian Hastings has commented: "[The] White Fathers would provide the vanguard of Catholic participation in the missionary scramble for the centre of the continent around the great lakes."[51] Father Simon Lourdel, W.F., and Brother Delmas Amans, W.F., the leaders of a five-man party, arrived in Buganda on the north shore of Lake Victoria, near present day Entebbe, on February 17, 1879. Lourdel immediately met with the Kabaka, Mutesa I, who authorized that a Catholic mission be started.[52] The first Catholic baptisms were recorded in 1880.

Education was the centerpiece of the White Fathers' mission in Buganda. Less than one year after the mission's establishment a basic catechism in the vernacular (Luganda) language had been prepared. In the early 1880s a Luganda dictionary was prepared; by 1885 a primer for school-age children was ready. In 1883, Pope Leo XIII authorized the establishment of the Vicariate Apostolic of Nyanza, the first official foundation of the Church in Uganda.[53]

The initial success gained by Lourdel and his companions was short-lived, however, with tragedy looming just around the corner. In 1882, Mutesa, who had initially welcomed the White Fathers, turned against them, forcing a relocation of the mission to the south side of Lake Victoria. When Mutesa died in 1884, the White Fathers returned as his son, Mwanga, initially welcomed them by sending boats for their transportation. But in 1886, Mwanga, like his father, turned against all Christian missionaries in a violent way.[54] He began to execute Christians, with the culmination on June 3, 1886, when thirty-one Catholics and Anglicans were burned alive at Namugongo.[55]

Mwanga's murderous rampage caused Catholics, Protestants, and Muslims to come together to achieve his overthrow. Since many Buganda chiefs had converted to Catholicism, Mwanga's action generated a united front against him. The Kabaka was overthrown and his son, Kiwewa, was named in his place. However, in 1888, taking the advice of Muslims, Kiwewa, who was told of a Christian plot to remove him, moved against the Christians. For one year, 1888 to 1889, Muslims held power in Buganda, but eventually in 1890 Mwanga was restored to power through a united Christian drive. Under the circumstances, Mwanga once again took a favorable view of Christians. In an ironic comment, Adrian Hastings claims, "[Mwanga] may well have done more to save

Christianity in Uganda than the work of any of his former colleagues."[56]

The restoration of Christian hegemony did not bring peace in Uganda's religious picture, but rather set the stage for a full eruption of a clash between Protestants and Catholics. Rivalry between these two groups was strong, with each side making every effort to besmirch the reputation of the other. African theologian James Ndyabahika summarizes the situation:

> Both religions in an effort to win new converts tarnished and labeled each other as people who did not teach the true faith and whose followers were destined for hell. . . . The competition to win new converts was characterized by scanty respect [for] human rights and sporadic killings in the name of God.[57]

The Anglicans used the British flag as their symbol; Catholics used the crucifix to oppose British power. The conflict was taxing on both sides and beneficial to neither.

The hostility grew to a high point in 1892. On the Protestant side, the influence of Alexander Mackay was significant. Mackay, a Calvinist who worked with the CMS, believed Catholics were present in Uganda to fight Protestants, not convert Africans. He saw the White Fathers' mission as an intrusion into areas already "claimed" by the CMS.[58] In a scene reminiscent of the turf wars of the Counter Reformation era, the Uganda conflict grew into armed conflict when war broke out between the two sides on January 24, 1892. The "war" destroyed three missions at Rubaga, Ssese, and Buddu, driving Catholics temporarily from the country. Historian Phares Mutibwa states, "Thus religion became a divisive rather than a unifying force right from the very beginnings of colonialism in Uganda."[59]

The brief Anglican-Catholic war did more than divide Uganda religiously. The conflict "established the principle that religious affiliation would henceforth be the basis of political association and action."[60] Competing religions were associated with competing nations: French Catholicism versus British Anglicanism. No similar situation linking religion and politics was present in East Africa. After a visit there in 1907, Winston Churchill stated about the "civil war":

> It would however be unfair to charge the missionaries with having created the feuds and struggles which convulsed Uganda twelve years ago. The accident that the line of cleavage between French and English influence was also the line of cleavage between Catholics and Protestant converts, imparted a religious complexion to what was in reality a fierce political dispute.[61]

One of the important lessons of the 1892 war was the need to broaden the view that Catholicism was solely associated with France. Thus, while the White Fathers continued to be at the forefront of the Catholic mission, other religious congregations joined the mission to broaden the Catholic base politically. In 1895, the British Mill Hill Fathers came, working mainly east of Kampala. One year earlier, by decree of Propaganda Fide, the Nyanza Vicariate (which comprised the whole of Uganda) was divided into three sections. The north and northeast sections were entrusted to Mill Hill; the south and southwest areas were given to the White Fathers.[62] Additionally, the Comboni or Verona Fathers, who had been ministering in southern Sudan since 1894, came south into Uganda in 1904, establishing a mission at Bahrael-Ghazal.[63]

The religious expansion of this period included congregations of women. Female religious associated with the three principal male orders in Uganda, White Sisters, Mill Hill Sisters (known in Africa as the Franciscan Missionaries of St. Joseph), and Verona Sisters came to support their male counterparts. Additionally, beginning with the Daughters of Mary

(Bannabikira), founded in 1910, several groups of indigenous women religious formed, including the Daughters of St. Therese, Sisters of Our Lady of Good Counsel, Sisters of Mary Mother of the Church, and Sisters of Mary Immaculate.[64]

The turn of the twentieth century was a time of great expansion for the Catholic mission in Uganda. In 1900, the North Nyanza Vicariate, renamed Vicariate of Uganda in 1915, the region of the White Fathers, had thirteen missions; Mill Hill had established three missions with three more in preparation. A survey in 1927 listed over 225,000 Catholics in Uganda.[65] This explosion of converts came about through a combination of devotion to the Uganda martyrs, greater disposition of the people to conversion, the faithful work of lay catechists, and the intense efforts of missionaries.

One significant barometer of Catholicism's rise was the career of Henri Streicher, who became bishop of Masaka in 1897. For the next thirty-six years his leadership brought great growth to the region. The number of Catholics increased tenfold to over 300,000, clergy rose from 2 to 46, and 280 women religious were present in the diocese. Adrian Hastings comments: "He [Streicher] did in fact establish the model to which everyone else in Africa had perforce to conform. For sheer effectiveness as well as for length and single-mindedness of commitment it would be hard to find a rival."[66]

The Catholic missionary zeal and growth was aided by additional factors. The promotion of a method of inculturation, an appreciation of the local traditions and culture, drew many to the missionaries. Father Francis Libermann, "Second Founder of the Spiritans," articulated this idea in November 1847:

> Empty yourselves of Europe, of its manners and mentality; make yourselves blacks with the blacks, then you will understand them and they should be understood; make yourselves blacks with the blacks to form them as they

should be, not in the way of Europe, but leaving them what is their own; behave towards them as servants would behave to their masters, adapting to the customs, attitudes and habits of their masters.[67]

The ability for priests and religious to master all the vernacular languages was also a great attraction. Dictionaries, catechisms, and other written materials were prepared in these languages.

Just prior to World War I, missionary influence in Africa reached its zenith,[68] but then began to retreat. Many missionaries, both from Mill Hill and the White Fathers, were called home to serve as chaplains during the war. The growth of nationalism, which pitted Germans against British and French missionaries, was another major setback for the mission. Historian Roland Oliver captures the position of Christianity in Africa during this period:

> After the First World War, with the setback suffered by conventional Christianity in the West, and with the impetus given to colonial development by the economic impoverishment of Europe, the missionary factor was gradually but steadily outpaced by secular forces, although by reason of its established interests it was able to participate in development and in some measure to influence its course.[69]

The twentieth century Catholic expansion was also manifest in an explosive growth of native clergy. The reorganization of Propaganda Fide and official documents by Popes Benedict XV and Pius XI helped promote indigenous clergy.[70] Almost from their arrival, Catholic missionaries understood and began to promote native vocations. A preparatory school for the training of priests was set up in Uganda in 1891, but the first two priests, Bazilio Lumu and Viktoro Mukasa Womoraka, were not ordained until 1913. However, numbers picked up rapidly so that by 1946 there were 208 Ugandan priests with another 385 in their last stages of initial formation.[71] Oliver comments, "With the steady flow of Africans into the clerical ranks, African Christianity began to acquire a momentum of its own."[72]

The Ugandan Church continued to expand throughout the twentieth century. The first African congregation of brothers, the Brothers of St. Charles Lwanga,[73] was formed in 1927, with first profession made by four men in November 1929. Orders of women religious continued to expand their numbers and ministerial influence. The Church organization continued apace as well; by 1950 the original two vicariates in Uganda were now six. The Diocese of Masaka, led originally by Henri Steicher, received the first African bishop in modern times with the appointment of Joseph Kiwanuka in 1939. Historian Adrian Hastings describes the significance of this event:

> Kiwanuka represents an age in which Catholicism had moved to the centre of African Christianity in a way that was not at all the case in the nineteenth century. . . . He proved [to be] a model bishop who worked with the laity, pressed forward with the education of the clergy, gave sage political advice, and tempered Episcopal autocracy with basic democracy through the development of elected parish councils and school parent associations. Few missionary bishops achieved so much.[74]

The physical growth of the Church was even more dramatically demonstrated through education, which was described as "the most outstanding contribution of the Church" in Africa.[75] Education was integral to the mission movement; it was considered indispensable to the spreading of the gospel message. Schools were built as fast if not faster than parish churches. Historian of African education, Brother John Paige, C.S.C., states:

In the work of the missions in Africa . . . school and
Church went hand in hand. The missionaries almost
everywhere began to instruct the young without lengthy
reflection as to whether they ought to do so. In the vast
majority of cases the school sprang up soon after the arrival of the missionaries. It often happened that the number
of schools increased much more quickly than did the
number of parishes, and the number of pupils was much
greater than that of the baptized Church members.[76]

By the end of the nineteenth century, the British colonial
government was actively encouraging missionary education
for its pragmatic value. Indeed, "there is little doubt that the
colonial government viewed the missionaries as collaborators
in building a viable protectorate."[77]

Education was the vehicle used by missionaries to enter
more completely into African society. Winston Churchill
commented about Christian education efforts:

Apart from their spiritual work, which needs no advocacy here, the missionaries have undertaken and are now
maintaining the whole educational system of the country.
They have built many excellent schools, and thousands of
young Baganda [citizens of Buganda] are being taught to
read and write in their own language. Technical education is now being added to these services, and in this, it
is hoped, the Government will be able to cooperate. I do
not know of any other part of the world where missionary
influence and enterprise have been so beneficially exerted,
or where more valuable results have been achieved.[78]

Education provided the chief tool for evangelization. The
desire for literacy was the initial hook, but many were then
drawn to Christianity. One African so influenced explained,

Many boys came to instruction to learn to read and write,
things to their advantage. Then behold! In the midst of
the craving to read and write, the Word of God, in their

reading books overwhelmed them. . . . They became Christians, saved by Jesus, children of God. So it was with me.[79]

The technological superiority of Christians also drew many to the missions; it indicated to tribal peoples that the Europeans' religion was superior. Historian Elizabeth Isichei claims, "It was the missions' near monopoly of education that was the single most effective way of attracting new Christians."[80]

One of the most significant evangelical initiatives of Christian missionaries was the use of lay catechists. First, the need was so great that sufficient priests and religious could never be generated. More importantly, however, is the powerful witness the African lay catechists gave to their own people, serving as a catalyst to their own learning and conversion. Indeed, many Catholic missions had over 150 lay catechists assisting Europeans in the mission effort.[81]

The efficacy of the Christian missionary effort was noted on several fronts. In 1924, the Phelps-Stokes Commission, noting that Catholic missions were only marginally supported financially by the British Protectorate, commented,

> An even more important element in the demand for educational re-organization is the need of mission societies for assistance [in order] to continue their achievement in education. Missionaries have maintained practically all the educational activities which exist up to the present time.[82]

Sir Hesketh Bell, first governor of Uganda, extolled the Church's efforts in a 1926 letter to *The Times* of London:

> Though not a member of the Church, [I] would like to offer my testimony to the admirable work which the Roman Catholic missionaries . . . have done and are doing in our African Protectorates. . . . The contribution that these devoted men are making to the cause of

education and to the uplifting of the native population in Africa should always be remembered when account is being taken of the admirable efforts of [the] missionary enterprise in the outer parts of our Empire.[83]

British Rule in Uganda

British interests in East Africa in the mid-nineteenth century were most concerned with the abolition of the slave trade, yet colonialism and its ramifications cannot be denied. Adrian Hastings describes the situation:

> By the 1870s Africa was then, in principle, becoming conquerable by Europe in a way it had not been previously. Indeed the contrast between power and powerlessness was now so huge that conquest was not only possible, but almost inevitable.[84]

The power of the British government and its white hegemony created a situation that often led to the subjection of African people and their culture. Inequality and division only seemed to grow greater as time progressed. Indeed, Alexander Mackay, a powerful witness for the CMS, commented in 1889: "In former years the universal aim was to steal the African from Africa. Today the determination of Europe is to steal Africa from the African."[85]

The move toward British control of Uganda began in a formal way with organization of the British East Africa Company in 1886 by Sir William MacKinnon. Its purpose was to explore British resources present in Africa. Additionally, England wanted Uganda for strategic purposes: (1) to safeguard India by securing all possible routes to it, and (2) for raw materials that might be used in British factories.[86] This latter idea was an important catalyst to the construction of the Mombasa Railway, which ran all the way to Kasese in western Uganda.

The formal division of lands of East Africa among the European powers came from the Heligoland Treaty of July 1, 1890. This Anglo-German agreement recognized the British as the controlling agent for the region defined today as Uganda. The British East Africa Company immediately dispatched Captain Frederick D. Lugard to Buganda as its representative. Lugard's presence, especially during the 1892 "civil war," gave the Anglicans a sense of hegemony they would hold for the next seventy years. On May 29, 1893, a provisional agreement was made with the Kabaka, Mwanga, who seems to have accepted the agreement believing the British would bring more stability between the rivaling Protestants, Muslims, and Catholics. On June 18, 1894, the British formally accepted Uganda as a Protectorate.[87] The region was an amalgamation of thirty cultural groups, divided into three major subgroups: the Nilotics, the Hamitics, and the Bantu.[88]

The British Protectorate system governed Uganda for the next seventy years. Initially, a sense of equality between British officials and tribal chiefs reigned, but when the Europeans began to fear the rising power of the Africans, a sense of control was applied to the local people. Historian Jan Jorgensen writes:

> While rudimentary social equality between African chiefs and European administrators might have been a necessary part of the initial "pacification" of Uganda, it jarred the European vision of the "proper" racial order in East Africa as a new generation of British administrators filled the ranks of the civil service of the Protectorate.[89]

There was close association between the Anglican Church and the British Protectorate government, yet at least initially the missions were not an arm of the government. Still, Elizabeth Isichei states, "The missionaries on the whole supported the colonial regime."[90]

The Holy Cross Mission
in Uganda Begins: 1958–1961

While Catholic White Father missionaries arrived in Buganda in 1879, it was not until 1893 that Bishop Jean-Joseph Hirth decided to send men west to the tribal kingdoms of Ankole, Toro, and Bunyoro. On November 16, 1895, Auguste Achte, W.F., arrived in the region, pitching his tent on a hill which gave him a view of the snow-capped Rwenzori mountains. The spot became known as Virika, a derivative of *ebirika*, meaning "snow" in Rutoro, the local tribal language.

When Achte arrived he was not given a welcome reception. Kasagama, the king of Toro, had come under the influence of the CMS and was, therefore, a devoted Anglican. He had witnessed the bitter war in Buganda between Catholics and Anglicans. Therefore, because he wanted peace, Kasagama ordered all his subjects to profess one faith. The situation is described by Fort Portal historian, Thomas Kisembo: "For a time therefore, the Protestants looked at the Catholics as second rate citizens. The Catholics were the 'dirty group,' and the Protestants were the Royalists and the 'Decent Lot.'"[91] Ironically, as in Buganda, Christianity, a religion oriented toward unity, divided the people, creating an uneasy atmosphere for some time.

As the twentieth century dawned, however, a shift in attitude was apparent. Père Pierre Van Weiss complained to the British Commissioner, Sir Harry Johnson, of injustices perpetrated against Catholics by Kasagama, leading to reconciliation. In 1900, Kasagama and the British government signed an agreement for religious tolerance. Winds blew more favorably for Catholics after this. Kisembo comments, "From this moment onwards, the Roman Catholic Church began to spread its tentacles far and wide throughout the Kingdom [of Toro]."[92]

The Church in Fort Portal began to establish itself through parishes and schools. Besides Virika, the central location for the White Fathers, Butiiti Parish, twenty-three miles west of Virika, was founded in November 1904. However, growth in the Catholic community was slow, due in large measure to the hegemony of the Anglicans and their influence on the Toro monarchy. In fact, Virika and Butiiti were the only parishes in the region until the mid-1930s.

Besides parishes, it was recognized at an early date that schools were necessary, especially as a vehicle for evangelization. Père Achte opened the first school, Virika Boys Day School, in 1903. In 1911, Bishop Henri Streicher in neighboring Masaka described the need: "We need schools, real ones and no caricature but the same value as the Protestant schools." Education was reserved for boys. Streicher articulated the prevailing attitude:

> When a girl of ordinary social condition obliged to work in order to earn her livelihood begins to handle the pen experience shows that very soon she gets disgusted with the hoe.[93]

As with Uganda in general, Fort Portal's educational needs, especially religious education, were in large measure handled through dedicated lay catechists. These men were leaders of local Christian communities who often worked without compensation. This fact was problematic at times when local tribal chiefs, hearing of the situation, offered catechists some salary, leading many to leave their ministry to the Church.[94]

The Church in western Uganda was formally established in May 1934, when by a decree from Propaganda Fide the Vicariate of Uganda (originally Nyanza, but named Uganda in 1915) was split. The western region, comprising the kingdoms of Bunyoro, Toro, Ankole, and Kigezi, was established as the Vicariate of Rwenzori, with Father Francois Lacoursiere, W.F.,

as vicar apostolic and Mbarara as see city. At the time there
were twelve missions and over 92,000 Catholics in the new
vicariate.[95] In 1954, the Vicariate of Rwenzori became the
Diocese of Mbarara with Lacoursiere appointed as bishop. In
1957, Jean Ogez succeeded Lacoursiere.

The Holy Cross mission to Uganda began with a grand
departure ceremony on October 15, 1958. Some 400 guests
were feted at the Commodore Hotel in New York, with Monsignor Vincent Jeffers as the principal speaker. The next day, the
three newly ordained priests, Francis Zagorc, Burton Smith,
and Robert Hesse (together with George Pope, C.S.C., who
was destined for East Pakistan) left the United States aboard
the *S.S. United States* bound for LeHavre, France. Members
of the Foreign Mission Society, including McCauley, Al Neff,
and Thomas Fitzpatrick, bid them *bon voyage* from the dock.
Eventually the three bound for Uganda arrived in Rome where
they met with McCauley, who had traveled to the eternal city
by plane. The group stayed in Rome two weeks during the
transition between the death of Pope Pius XII and the installation of his successor, John XXIII.[96]

The Holy Cross team arrived in Entebbe, Uganda, on
November 4, 1958, and was greeted by Bishop Ogez and three
other White Fathers. After a bit of "sight-seeing," courtesy calls
on Bishops Joseph Cabana, W.F., of Rubaga (the cathedral in
Kampala) and Vincent Billington, M.H.M., of Kampala, and
registering at the American embassy, the four journeyed west
to Mbarara where as guests of Ogez they were given "the royal
treatment."[97] McCauley almost immediately went to Butiiti
to teach at St. Augustine's Teacher Training College (TTC),[98]
but the others stayed at the Nyamitanga mission near Mbarara
for six weeks. The delay in initiating the mission confused the
Holy Cross team, who began to wonder if a plan existed for
the new arrivals.[99] Nonetheless, Ogez was very grateful for the
congregation's presence in Uganda:

> I am grateful to you for sending me such fine missionaries; they have the right spirit and will give a great impetus to the evangelization of this little corner of Africa. I am sure we will work well together for the greater glory of God. Thank you for giving me such wonderful help; I have now great hopes for the future.[100]

Ogez, who was very impressed with the "friendly spirit and enthusiasm" of his guests, decided that they be sent to Butiiti, twenty-three miles east of Fort Portal, to begin language school. While the superior general, Christopher O'Toole, C.S.C., felt the delay and assignment to Butiiti (as opposed to Fort Portal) complicated things, McCauley responded, "This is a much better place to start off."[101]

While the younger priests were in full-time Rutoro study, McCauley decided to forego formal language training and immediately began to teach at St. Augustine, where the medium of instruction was English. McCauley described his schedule:

> I teach in English (nine hours per week) all the religion classes at the Teachers' Training College, have an instruction for the Junior Secondary School on Friday, and [I] am moderator for three of the College societies.[102]

McCauley, who also taught history at St. Augustine, was considered "an exceptional teacher," was kind and devoted to students, and was "deeply religious and upright."[103] He realized that he was behind his fellow Holy Cross religious in learning the vernacular language, but his duties at the TTC and other responsibilities interfered with language study. As was noted by all who knew him, Vincent McCauley never understood nor spoke Rutoro well, yet, surprisingly, as will be described later, it never inhibited his ability to minister or his efficacy as bishop.

McCauley had plans for Holy Cross and St. Augustine's
TTC. In September 1959, three Holy Cross Brothers, John
Harrington, Christian Stinnet, and Cyrinus Martin, came to
Uganda to join the congregation's mission and were assigned
to the TTC at Butiiti. McCauley wanted the brothers to take
charge of the school, with Robert Chaput, W.F., initially
remaining as headmaster, allowing the brothers to get adjusted.
Bishop Ogez, however, wanted Chaput to remain. Recent conflicts with the Brothers of Christian Instruction, who worked
at St. Leo's Secondary School in Fort Portal, influenced his
thinking. O'Toole was not pleased, telling McCauley, "I am
sure in your own diplomatic and discreet way, you will be able
to communicate this idea to Bishop Ogez."[104] McCauley, who
lobbied strongly for the brothers, proposed that Holy Cross
take over both schools. Eventually in December 1961, Holy
Cross Brothers took control of St. Augustine's. One month
later, in January 1962, at the invitation of the Brothers of
Christian Instruction, Holy Cross took charge of St. Leo's in
Fort Portal.[105]

The Holy Cross mission in Uganda, an assignment geared
toward the establishment of the Church for the Ugandan people, was in operation with Vincent McCauley as the leader.[106]
As a fledgling foundation, McCauley placed a high priority on
keeping the Holy Cross religious together and fostering their
religious life. O'Toole wrote to McCauley on a regular basis,
placing strong emphasis on community unity. The general
worried, for example, about the possible separation of the
brothers from the whole:

> Under no circumstances should the Brothers be persuaded
> to take a school which will keep them out of contact with
> the Fathers. Our success in developing a section of the
> mission will certainly depend on staying together.[107]

He also advised him to shepherd his young priests:

> The young priests with you are of the first caliber, and I
> urge you to keep in close touch with them because this is
> so important in their first years in the priesthood.[108]

The first foundation by the nascent Holy Cross community
was Bukwali Parish in Fort Portal. Ogez believed Fort Portal
needed a second foundation after Virika. Thus, in 1960, when
Emmanuel Kaijakwamya donated land, the bishop instructed
McCauley and Robert Chaput, W.F., to start a new parish. The
new foundation gave Holy Cross a place for its headquarters
and provided the community the opportunity to work directly
with the White Fathers.[109]

The new Holy Cross mission in Uganda received significant
attention, as indicated by visits of community leaders. Only
a few weeks after the initial team had arrived, the provincial,
Theodore Mehling, C.S.C., visited in December 1958. His
visit was a major "shot in the arm" for morale and demonstrated to the local people the commitment of Holy Cross to the
mission. The superior general, Christopher O'Toole, C.S.C.,
made his initial visit in August 1959. He was very impressed
and congratulated McCauley: "In a short while you have done
a tremendous job particularly in getting Holy Cross known in
the area. Every priest I met spoke of you in the highest terms."
A few months later, speaking of the Bukwali foundation, he
thanked McCauley, but cautioned him: "You are doing a magnificent piece of work. My only fear is that you will do too
much and wear yourself out too soon."[110]

The Holy Cross mission was less than one year old when
McCauley celebrated his silver jubilee as a priest. McCauley
best describes the event:

> Surprisingly my 25th Jubilee was quite an occasion here.
> Our young priests decided on a celebration and invited
> the priests in Toro. We were 18 for the Solemn Mass . . .

and for the buffet lunch. It was a perfect day. I even got a purse—shs 1000[1000 Uganda shillings]—from the priests of the Diocese (White Fathers and Africans). To me it is a sign that Holy Cross is really "accepted."[111]

The celebration ended in the evening with the screening of the film *Sun Valley Serenade*, an American Western.[112]

The congregation's acceptance in the new Uganda mission, as heralded by McCauley, was verified on all fronts. An Indiana Province visitation team reported in August 1959:

> Father Vincent McCauley and the three young priests with him, Fathers Burton Smith, Robert Hesse, and Francis Zagorc, have made an excellent impression on the Bishop of the Diocese, on the White Fathers and on the religious communities of Sisters and Brothers.

About McCauley specifically the report continued, "Father McCauley seems to be on good terms with everybody, and everyone has a good word to say for him."[113] He was seen as adaptable and one upon whom any and all could count.[114] An initial evaluation of the Uganda mission was very positive. After a year McCauley reported:

> We are no longer newcomers. Not only we, but everyone in Western Uganda looks on the Holy Cross Fathers as part of the Catholic Church, and takes for granted that we are here to stay. I'm sure we are. Anything less is unthinkable.[115]

McCauley admitted that he and Holy Cross still had much to learn, but all, including McCauley, were surprised at the community's ability to be so effective so swiftly.[116]

The optimism was tempered somewhat with a dose of reality. Political instability in Uganda and neighboring countries made McCauley somewhat cautious about expanding too swiftly. He wrote to his family:

The uncertain political situation tends to make us cautious in regard to expansion, but we hope to get some of the basic needs started at least. Then, if there is improvement later on, we can step up the pace without loss.[117]

Even with the caution, McCauley, and Holy Cross in general, were very impressed with the new Ugandan mission and pledged their full support. McCauley admitted the assignment was possibly more than he anticipated, but concluded, "Uganda continues to be the most interesting place I've seen." In another forum he stated, "I haven't been more content in years. And to think that in my 25th year I am just a beginner again. But I love it."[118] When the community could not send men to the mission who had been previously promised, he wrote, "Although we are disturbed by the turn of events, we are far from discouraged, and are willing to fight for a Holy Cross mission in Toro and Bunyoro."[119] Other community members and Africans pledged their loyal support for the Uganda mission. From the very outset Christopher O'Toole, C.S.C., was behind the project:

I know that yourself [McCauley] and the priests with you are going to do excellent work because you have the zeal and intelligence and enthusiasm needed. Be sure that I will be supporting you in every way possible.[120]

Support also came from East Pakistan. One missionary wrote to the superior general:

I was so thrilled to hear about the new mission that is to open in Uganda that I thought I would write to tell you how pleased all the Fathers were over here at the news. I am sure that your decision in this matter will be most fruitful for Holy Cross.[121]

The African diocesan clergy also welcomed Holy Cross. One typical letter read:

The stay of the Holy Cross Fathers with us in Toro and
Bunyoro is welcome! Every secular priest in this part is
joyful. We shall try to make our dear Father feel at home,
and cooperate for the greater glory of God in our
country.[122]

During the first few years of the mission the Holy Cross
presence expanded slowly, forcing McCauley, as local superior, to attend to various personnel issues. Between 1959 and
1962, besides the brothers formerly mentioned assigned to
St. Augustine, those who joined the mission included Fathers
Louis Meyer, John Keefe, James Stupfel, George MacInnes,
Tom Fotusky, Lou Rink, James Donohue, Robert Malone,
and Robert Murphy, and Brothers Joseph Gerstle and James
Gulnac. After new men were trained in the vernacular and
clergy had successfully passed a test to hear confessions, they
were assigned to parishes and schools. One important element
of parish life that McCauley mandated was the integration
of Holy Cross religious with White Fathers and local diocesan clergy. In order to accommodate the White Fathers and
to maintain a harmonious working relationship, McCauley
insisted that Holy Cross religious follow the White Fathers'
rule. This caused some problems, as Holy Cross was more
autonomous and members felt restricted by the more fixed
schedule of times for prayer and other common community
exercises. This policy was even more important for the White
Fathers, who could only have communities of three or more.
Thus, the question arose, could White Fathers and Holy Cross
members who followed the White Fathers' rule create an
acceptable mixed parochial team?[123] Because of their experience, White Fathers often served as mentors for the young
Holy Cross men. Despite the tensions and differences in life
style, Robert Malone, C.S.C., concluded, "Generally speaking,
although there were stormy times, I think we did quite well
getting along with each other, in respecting each other."[124]

McCauley met frequently with the Holy Cross religious assigned to the mission. Regular meetings, generally monthly, provided a forum for information flow, swapping of stories, and recreation among members. Religious appreciated McCauley's efforts, describing him as "always very positive."[125] McCauley was very pleased with his religious and their good faith effort. He wrote to the superior general, "The spirit of the men here is excellent and we are trying to maintain it."[126] McCauley's appreciation for his people was reciprocated. Father John Keefe, C.S.C., has commented, "McCauley was good to us; he treated us well."[127]

McCauley was appreciative of the support he received and grateful to his priests and brothers; nonetheless, he was often frustrated by what he perceived as a lack of cooperation in securing men for the mission. In February 1960, he voiced his concern to the superior general:

> Father Mehling has been our main source of encouragement. He is one man who is willing to make sacrifices to get the mission going. Fr. Deprizio could. Brother Ephrem won't.[128]

McCauley was even more concerned about his lack of personnel when he learned from Bishop Ogez, who had spoken with the apostolic delegate, that a division of the diocese would come very soon. He vented to the general:

> What is going on over there . . . a conspiracy to dump Uganda? Whatever has gone wrong it better be fixed, . . . and soon. Rome is ready to move, and move us. We had better get those anchor weights up on deck or we'll never clear the dock. Although I am not conscious of causing this apparent distaste for Uganda, you can—if it's true—correct the situation in a minute. Just replace me with someone acceptable. I'll welcome it. But please don't

abandon the mission. It can be and should be one of Holy
Cross' finest assets.[129]

The problem with available personnel could not negate the
fact that it was Ogez's desire from the very outset to have Holy
Cross take responsibility for the northern region of Toro and
Bunyoro as fast as possible. Actually, the White Fathers had
made an earlier attempt to obtain assistance but had failed. In
1955, Bishop Francois Lacoursiere, W.F., and Louis Durrieu,
W.F., superior general of the White Fathers, made contact with
the Salvatorian community, seeking their assistance in Mbarara. A deal was struck in principle, with the Salvatorians agree-
ing to send seven men to assist, five priests and two brothers.
However, due to resistance on the part of the White Fathers in
Uganda, who did not want to move and abandon their missions, the agreement fell through.[130] Despite the setback, the
general aim of seizing the opportunity to develop Uganda into
a Catholic country remained. A 1958 report from the Diocese
of Mbarara stated, "If we had the manpower, we could 'steal'
this district . . . province . . . country from the Protestants, and
develop a really Catholic country for the future."[131]

The arrival of Holy Cross reignited the desire by Ogez to
split his ecclesiastical responsibilities. To initiate the process,
Christopher O'Toole, C.S.C., insisted that some formal agreement be placed in writing between Holy Cross and the White
Fathers. While not formally set, Holy Cross had hoped to send
five new religious each year to the mission so that in five years
sufficient personnel would be present to adequately administer
the region and serve its people.[132] While this "dream" never
materialized, the future reality of Holy Cross control was easily visible and thus formal steps to prepare became even more
urgent. Mehling told McCauley, "Father O'Toole seems to be
very insistent about drawing up definite agreements." He was
confident that McCauley, as the Holy Cross point man for
the mission, was best qualified to speak in the congregation's

name: "I believe that you are in the best position to draw up an agreement in its final form. . . . I shall only be too happy to see such an agreement and to give it my approval."[133]

A formal agreement was signed in the fall of 1959. Under the pact, Holy Cross agreed to minister in the region until December 31, 1963. If by this date no decision had been made by the Holy See with respect to the establishment of a diocese, "Holy Cross [would] consider its obligations to the Diocese of Mbarara as terminated." It was also less formally agreed that should Holy Cross take responsibility for the northern region of Mbarara, the White Fathers would remain until sufficient American personnel were present.[134]

Although the formal agreement spoke of a five-year initial commitment, Ogez continued to push for a division of the diocese as quickly as possible. One principal reason for the urgency, besides Ogez's personal desire, was the receptivity of the people to such a move at the time. One report commented,

> The division should be made before too long. The reason for this is that, at the present time, both the African priests and the people are ready to accept another foreign community to head the diocese. However, if we wait too long, the nationalistic spirit will have a greater chance to develop and there will be a great pressure for an African bishop whereas in the Toro area there does not seem to be any African priest capable of taking up the problems present.[135]

Ogez re-echoed his earlier rationale to act now: the size of the present diocese, increased Catholic population, and the desire to challenge Protestant hegemony.[136] Additionally, he felt that Holy Cross control in the north would make his own position in Mbarara (in the south) more secure.[137]

McCauley sensed Ogez's desire and felt his not-so-subtle pressure for division. He wrote to Mehling, "It is quite evident that he [Ogez] is concentrating on the two districts (Ankole and Kigezi) which he will keep, and that he is putting off matters pertaining to our territory until we decide to move." However, McCauley was in no rush to take complete responsibility. He had told Ogez that Holy Cross was "too new and too few," but the bishop responded that the White Fathers had fewer resources when they started.[138] Yet, McCauley was pragmatic, admitting:

> I talked it over with Fathers Meyer, Zagorc and Smith. Reluctant as we are to assume responsibility for Toro & Bunyoro, it looks as though nothing much will be done until we do. If we wait much longer it it [sic] will become increasingly difficult to manage when we do take over.[139]

Mehling concurred with McCauley's conclusion:

> I certainly agree with you that, if we had a choice, we would delay this major step until we had more men in Uganda and until we had more experience. However, if circumstances make it necessary to go ahead with this known and anticipated division, I suppose we will have to take some action.[140]

Even with the "handwriting on the wall," caution was the continual theme and advice. O'Toole warned McCauley that before any agreement was made, "the matter must be thought out and planned carefully." He wrote to Mehling, "We do not want to go into this project unless we are properly prepared for it and unless we are ready to set aside a sufficient number of men to carry it on."[141] Mehling agreed with caution, but pragmatically stated,

> Naturally, all of us would like to wait until we were better established and until we had more men and experience. However, if the Holy See insists on a division in the near future, we shall have to try and meet the manpower needs as you list them, including a firm agreement with the

Bishop to retain the essential White Fathers for a given period of years.[142]

As the end of 1960 drew near, however, McCauley, understanding the eventuality, pressed for Holy Cross to act. He argued that the territory was too much for the White Fathers, that this division was precisely why Holy Cross came to the area, and the local priests and people expected it. Demonstrating a leap of faith and seemingly discarding his previous cautious attitude, he wrote,

> Although we realize the pressing need for more personnel and for large sums of money, we think it advisable to assume responsibility for the mission territory as soon as possible, even though the men and the money may not be forthcoming immediately.

In December 1960, O'Toole was still cautious but informed Propaganda Fide:

> If the Holy See decides to confide the new area to the Congregation of Holy Cross, your Eminence may be sure that we will do our best, with the personnel and resources at our disposal, to carry out the wishes of the Sacred Congregation of the Propagation of the Faith.[143]

While the decision to create a new diocese continued to circulate, Holy Cross did formalize its mission in Uganda according to its constitutions and statutes. O'Toole informed Mehling that sufficient Holy Cross personnel were present in Uganda to form a district, should the provincial wish to erect one. Mehling took the hint and began to dialogue with McCauley on possible councilors. He wrote, "I do think that the establishment of a District in Uganda is the most practical method of establishing proper constitutional jurisdiction."[144] Eventually, in August 1960, the District of Uganda was formally erected with Vincent McCauley appointed as superior.[145]

Summary

Possessed by an intense missionary spirit, and having experienced both the exhilaration and the suffering of the missions in Bengal, Vincent McCauley spent half of his priesthood in preparation for his time in East Africa. From his first experiences of the region and its people in his 1958 fact-finding mission with Father Arnold Fell, McCauley knew that East Africa was the place where Holy Cross could make a major impact and he could fully utilize his talents to proclaim the gospel message. From the outset of the mission in November 1958, progress toward the establishment of diocese under the jurisdiction of Holy Cross was under way. Bishop Jean Ogez's invitation to come to western Uganda and the Diocese of Mbarara was extended to promote the expansion of the Church in a region where evangelization was bearing much fruit. After three years of settling in, establishing institutions, and growth in the region, Holy Cross and Vincent McCauley were poised to take the eventual step toward autonomy through the establishment of the Diocese of Fort Portal.

CHAPTER 5

Bishop of Fort Portal—
The First Years: 1961–1969

The foundation of the Holy Cross Ugandan mission in 1958 expanded the congregation's horizons on the missionary front. The confidence expressed by Fathers McCauley and Fell in their May 1958 report that recommended the mission be accepted was borne out over the first three years of its life. Starting with only four men, the mission quickly expanded in personnel and apostolates. The foundation of Bukwali Parish and Holy Cross personnel assisting White Fathers and African diocesan clergy in other parishes, as well as educational institutions, were important additions to the mission effort. Additionally, an agreement was finalized between Holy Cross and the White Fathers clarifying their joint ministerial responsibilities. It was, however, clear to all almost from the outset that Bishop Jean Marie Ogez of Mbarara was interested in ceding control of the northern

sectors of his diocese, the kingdoms of Toro and Bunyoro, as
soon as possible. While Holy Cross came to assist, and realized
the basic plan for the turnover, the timing was a bit swift for
McCauley and his Holy Cross superiors. Nonetheless, plans
were rapidly moving toward the erection of a new diocese at
Fort Portal and, therefore, the need for a new bishop. Vincent
McCauley, who had been appointed superior of the Holy
Cross Ugandan district, stood ready to begin his greatest and
possibly most challenging days in ministry.

The Diocese of Fort Portal Established

Since it was clear that authority for Bunyoro and Toro
kingdoms would be transferred to Holy Cross, the need arose
to discuss candidates for bishop. In support of a policy of
Africanization, Archbishop Guido del Mestri, the apostolic
delegate in Mombasa, suggested that an African bishop be
named for Fort Portal. Ogez, believing an appropriate African
candidate was not present, strongly disagreed and traveled to
Rome to argue against such a plan. McCauley too voiced his
disagreement with the delegate. In a forceful and pragmatic
tone he wrote:

> It is evident that the Apostolic Delegate is catering to the
> independence movement in Africa. Taking the broad view
> and in spite of the considerable risks involved, there may
> be some merit in his policy. But as applied to the Western
> Provinces of Uganda it seems from here to be unwise.
> Of the 30 African priests in Mbarrara Diocese, 17 are
> in Toro-Bunyoro. Five are in charge of mission stations;
> none is outstanding; three are too old to work; several have
> been tried and found wanting. How such a small group of
> incompetent priests can carry on the work of ten mission
> stations—to say nothing of building up ten new missions

that are needed—is beyond comprehension. Humanly speaking it would be disastrous for the Church.[1]

McCauley suggested both qualifications and names for a future bishop. Comically, yet realistically he wrote to Mehling, "See if you can find an organizing genius who is also a saint, and who will come to us accompanied by fifteen priests, and have at least $250,000.00 in his pocket."[2] He gave the superior general four names: John Harrington, Edmund Goedert, Robert McKee, and James Martin. He was most positive on McKee, but "would welcome any other choice you might make, except myself." He did say, however, "I think, . . . I could be of help to the new man, and am anxious to remain."[3]

While McCauley tried to deflect attention away from himself, others disagreed. An internal Holy Cross report on the Uganda mission, made in August 1959, stated, "It appears that, after a year or two, we will have to be ready to suggest candidates to the Holy See for the bishopric. If his health holds out, Father McCauley seems to be the logical choice since he is acceptable to everybody."[4] McCauley, however, stood aloof. He wrote, "I pity the poor C.S.C. that will get the job, since I am safely out of the picture."[5] As late as January 1961, McCauley was still trying to divert attention away from his candidacy: "I again urge that you remove me from consideration and select a really capable administrator."[6]

The discussions concerning a qualified man to be the local ordinary were concurrent with the establishment of the Diocese of Fort Portal. In October 1960, McCauley heard from Ogez that the apostolic delegate had authorized the new Diocese of Fort Portal and that official word from Propaganda Fide on its establishment was expected soon. In late February 1961, O'Toole informed McCauley of the diocese's erection and his appointment as bishop: "This morning his Eminence Cardinal Agagianian told me that the new Diocese of Fort Portal has already been erected and that you have been named as the first Bishop." McCauley hoped that O'Toole's letter was a mistake, but eventually responded:

> Today's mail brought word from the Apostolic Delegate that no change can be expected. Since it is a matter of obedience and not of choice, I must accept. God's will be done, and may His Divine Providence and His mercy be both abundant and unfailing for Fort Portal, for Holy Cross and for me.

He informed the general that he would come to Rome "to be instructed, coached, and all else that is necessary to make a Bishop out of a bush missionary."[7] The diocese was canonically erected on April 19, 1961. O'Toole informed Agagianian, Prefect of Propaganda Fide,

> Your Eminence may be sure that the Congregation of Holy Cross will do everything possible to plant the Church as securely as possible in this new ecclesiastical territory which has been confided to its care.[8]

McCauley traveled to Notre Dame where he was ordained as bishop in Sacred Heart Church on May 17, 1961. The principal consecrator was Cardinal Richard Cushing of Boston, who was joined by co-consecrators Archbishop Gerald T. Berigan of Omaha and Bishop Albert Cousineau, C.S.C., of Cap-Haitien, Haiti. Bishop Leo Pursley of Fort Wayne–South Bend gave the sermon and eight other bishops, including two from Africa, were present. McCauley took as his episcopal motto, *Mariam Sequens Non Devias*, "If you follow Mary, you will not stray."[9]

After a few weeks with family and ever-necessary fundraising, McCauley returned to Uganda for his formal installation as bishop of Fort Portal. The event was held on July 2 on the football pitch of St. Michael's secondary school in Fort Portal. Archbishop Guido del Mestri presided at the Mass; Bishop Francois X. Lacoursiere, retired Bishop of Mbarara, preached the sermon. Also participating in the installation were Bishop Ogez, Christopher O'Toole, C.S.C., the regional superior of the White Fathers, provincial of the Brothers of Christian Instruction, and representatives from the Archdiocese of Kampala. A luncheon for 250 guests was held at St. Leo's College after the installation Mass. McCauley received several gifts, including a Zephir car from the Christians of the new diocese, a substantial check from the Kingdom of Toro, several cows as personal gifts, and furniture for his residence from local school children.[10] Del Mestri commented at the installation that this was

> the culmination of a long and studious preparation by the Holy See, and the result, too, of an intense pastoral activity on the part of Bishop Ogez (of Mbarara) and his key predecessors, of the White Fathers who first worked here, and of the Fathers of the [sic] Holy Cross to whom this diocese has now been entrusted.[11]

It did not take McCauley long to begin his work as administrator of the diocese. As one of his first formal acts, the new bishop consecrated Fort Portal to the Immaculate Heart of Mary.[12] He saw his task as preparing for the future, to set up foundations and institutions, as he fully believed his successor would be an African. He appointed Harry Heyes, W.F., as vicar general, Robert Chaput, W.F., as chancellor and treasurer, and Francis Zagorc, C.S.C., as secretary. Still, he realized the difficulty of his task, especially noting that neither he nor any of his chosen administrative assistants had any experience working in a chancery office or in any positions such as vicar-general. In the end, however, he concluded, "Our main concern is still people. It [our mission] is to establish the Church on a solid foundation among the people of Uganda that we have come here [to serve]."[13]

Church and State in Uganda in the 1960s

The formal establishment of the Church in Fort Portal came at a time when Uganda was reaching the climax of a political struggle that would lead to independence from Britain. The post–World War II demobilization saw a growing number of Ugandans disgruntled by the British colonial government. Several small political parties, including the Bataka (1946), Abaganda Abakopi (Baganda Peasants, 1947), and Uganda African Farmers' Union (1947), led other smaller groups in a series of mass protests beginning in 1949. While the protests were squelched, certain reforms, especially in economic areas, were implemented. Eventually the protests led to the reforms of colonial structure under Governor Andrew Cohen (1952–1956). Unfortunately, Cohen's insistence upon the unity of Uganda proved highly problematic for Buganda, the most powerful and significant kingdom, which was pushing for more autonomy and freedom. A gulf was created between Cohen and the ruling Kabaka, (King) Mutesa II, leading eventually to the latter's exile to England in October 1953. When Mutesa returned two years later, however, his position was strengthened and relations between Britain and the protectorate's other kingdoms grew more strained.[14] At the dawn of the 1960s, one Ugandan political leader was quoted:

> Uganda is like the United States in the year 1850. We'll see more progress in this century than we have in the previous 19 centuries. It is our fervent hope that it will be orderly and intelligent progress so that we can join the community of nations with respect and dignity.[15]

The conflict between Cohen and the Kabaka provided the perfect environment for the generation of several political parties that governed Uganda's history during the period of independence and the nation's early sovereign years. Ignatius K. Musazi formed the first genuinely national party, the Uganda

National Congress (UNC), in 1952. The party, which was dominated by Protestants, and found its strength in Buganda, trumpeted the theme, "self-government now," through its ability "to inculcate the concept of single-nationhood in the multifarious tribes of the Protectorate."[16] The Progressive Party (PP) was formed in 1955 with the express purpose to bring Protestants and Catholics together. The party's domination by Buganda and Protestants, however, raised red flags to Catholics, who were wary of membership. Partially in response to the "failure" of the Progressive Party to attract Catholics, Matayo Mugwanya formed the Democratic Party (DP) in 1954. It was strongly Roman Catholic in inspiration and membership, with an agenda to promote Western Christian values, including democracy, as well as racial partnership and harmony. Catholics claimed the need for a political face in Uganda for two primary reasons: (1) Discrimination against Catholics in public office was rampant due to Protestant control, and (2) Catholic priests had long seen themselves as political as well as religious figures. While the party claimed independence as one of its reasons for foundation, some found it a contradiction with many expatriate members. Africanization of the civil service, "based on truth and social justice," was a primary policy of the DP.[17]

As the 1950s waned, additional parties began to appear on the Ugandan political scene. In July 1957, a group of intellectuals broke away from the Uganda National Congress to form the United Congress Party (UCP). In late 1958 and early 1959, the Uganda People's Union (UPU), one of the first parties not to have a strong Buganda base, was formed. Additional anti-Buganda elements, including Milton Obote and other UNC members, joined with the UPU to form the Uganda People's Congress (UPC) in March 1960. Ugandan politician Grace Ibingira describes the coalition: "The two parties agreed to merge with the object of consolidating party politics in Uganda in order to present to the people a common programme for the immediate attainment of complete independence."[18] However, local patrons fared quite well while national issues took a back seat. Still, the UPC, together with the DP, were the two political rivals with sufficient members and power to achieve control in the forthcoming independence showdown.[19]

The issue of Buganda's independence in the overall question of Uganda's freedom struggle with the British led to the launching of still another party. The Kabaka Yekka or "Kabaka only" (KY) was formed in 1961, "as a tactical maneuver in support of Buganda's drive to maintain its identity in the face of approaching independence." The nascent group saw the DP as its enemy, and "no holds were barred" in its effort to assure Catholics were removed from office.[20]

The political landscape of Uganda was one where religion, as the nation's history had earlier demonstrated, brought significant division as the nation moved toward independence. Ibingira comments, "The use of religion as a basis for political action and organization either through conviction or as an expedient, was unmistakable." Since religion was used as a basis for identity, it also, due to a significant past antagonistic history, became a source of disunity. Protestants and Catholics argued among themselves and together, at times, worked against the Muslims. The result was "detrimental of national unity."[21] Historian Frederick Welborn aptly concludes, "Certainly it [Christianity] had failed to provide the integrating force which was needed if Uganda was to pass from tribalism to modern nationhood."[22]

The disunity that religion brought to Uganda's political process was deepened by a strong anti-Catholic sentiment that perdured and was associated with anti-independence elements. The large number of expatriate Catholic missionaries created in the minds of many the notion that Catholicism was foreign and thus anti-unity. Yet, historian William B. Anderson claims that this situation made Catholics more politically active than Protestants. Thus, Catholics saw the independence period as an opportunity for a reassessment of the status quo. In religious terms this meant the opportunity for Catholics to at last share in greater equality the fruits of the political kingdom.[23] The situation was not lost on Vincent McCauley, who astutely assessed the situation:

> These are days of frothy living in Uganda. The political pot is boiling and everyone is interested in the stew that the fires of independence are cooking up. Without a ladle we are nevertheless concerned, for the enemies of the Church are stirring frantically on the other side of the stove. Last week they came out in open opposition to the Church.[24]

The lack of unity in politics and religion did not, however, stop the drive for independence that reached its first great milestone in the Spring of 1961. The first national election in Uganda, held on March 24, was presaged by a Catholic clergy blitz on behalf of the Democratic Party. Priests transported DP supporters, planned and financed campaign efforts, and preached in support of DP candidates. The Catholic campaign was accompanied by a basic boycott of the election by the Baganda, who rejected the independence effort as it sought national unity at the expense of Buganda's autonomy. The Kabaka was so successful in keeping his people away from the polls that the DP won nineteen parliamentary seats in Buganda. This coupled with twenty-four additional seats throughout the country gave the DP a forty-three to thirty-five-seat victory over the UPC.[25] The party's leader, Benedicto Kiwanuka, was thus slated to become Uganda's first prime minister.

The victory of the DP in the March 1961 election solidified the forces opposed to Catholicism. Ibingira states:

> If the victory of the DP gave impetus and greater hope to
> the Democrats inside and outside the government, it cor-
> respondingly served a tremendous role in drawing closer
> all the anti-DP forces, eventually consolidating them into
> a powerful and united opposition.[26]

The opposition against Catholics, led by the UPC, greatly
feared that a Catholic-dominated government might take over
after independence. Thus, it was imperative in the minds of
many to dismantle the DP before independence. The desire
to keep power away from Catholics was the prime motivation
behind the formation of a coalition between the UPC and the
KY, with Milton Obote as its leader.

The political alliance forged against Catholics shared the
political spotlight with the question of Buganda and its persistent desire for autonomy. A conference was held in London
from September 18 to October 9, 1961, to review the Buganda situation and seek a solution that would bring unity to the
protectorate as it neared independence. A compromise of sorts
was achieved whereby Buganda's relation with the central government would be on a federal basis, but allow the kingdom
to retain its monarchical institutions. Buganda was given some
concessions in the agreement that, with minor adjustments,
was accepted.[27]

The political situation continued to be volatile as 1962
dawned. McCauley recognized that the situation was tense,
but he believed his role was to stay out of the fray. He wrote,
"So the bishop is going to stay put until after independence,
confident that the prayers of his people and his friends back
home will enable us to ride out the situation and prepare for
better days the Lord will send."[28]

The UPC-KY political alliance led to a political turnaround
in the final April 1962 elections. The coalition successfully
painted the DP as anti-Kabaka, thus generating a shift in the
Baganda vote for Obote. The transfer was so great that the DP

leader, Benedicto Kiwanuka, lost his seat in parliament. On a more positive note, from the perspective of national unity, the aftermath of the election saw a dampening of the rigidity between the competing forces.[29] McCauley reported the post-election situation to the general administration in Rome:

> Conditions in Uganda are still in a state of flux. I am more optimistic then a few months ago, for the political leaders seem to be developing a saner sense of realism. The ideal-istic talk has a different tone now that they are coming to grips with the practical problems of running an independent country. There is still a strong core of opposition to the Church, but it does not seem to be so out-spoken of late. We know that it will not easily subside, but we are in hopes of strengthening our Catholics to meet whatever comes. That is a tremendous task and it will take every man and every resource we can muster.[30]

With the parliament set, the final piece necessary for independence was a national constitution. The document was drawn up in a month-long conference held in London, beginning on June 12, 1962. The compromise document gave Buganda a privileged position because of its past history and the excessively pro-Buganda British colonial government. Milton Obote, who would soon take the reins as Uganda's first prime minister, later called the document divisive: "The Independence Constitution did not become an instrument for nation-building but a document and an edict whose objective was to keep as far apart as it could allow the Regions and tribes of Uganda."[31]

The independence drive in Uganda was part of a larger picture throughout the African continent. In 1958, Ghana became the first black African republic to achieve independence. In September 1960, France sponsored the admission to the United Nations of twelve independent black African republics, from Senegal to the Congo. In October 1960,

Nigeria gained its autonomy. The movement then spread east with Tanganyika winning independence in 1961, Burundi, Rwanda, and Uganda in 1962, and Kenya in 1963.[32]

With a constitution in place and elections completed, Uganda became the thirty-third independent nation on the African continent on October 9, 1962, with Milton Obote as prime minister. While internal politics, as described earlier, had been contentious, "the independence campaign in Uganda was not characterized by insurgency, violence or bloodshed, and the transition to independence was orderly and relatively harmonious."[33] Nonetheless, the seeds of future discontent and problems had been sown deeply. Historian Phares Mutibwa says of Obote's task to meld the multiple Ugandan sects, groups, and tribes into one: "No other East African Commonwealth leader faced such an unenviable task at independence."[34] In a prophetic statement, Church historian Adrian Hastings, speaking on the threshold of Ugandan independence, writes, "Uganda is here on the doorstep, and if her independence does not result in internal chaos it may involve instead an external chain reaction of enormous consequences."[35]

The predictions of problems in Uganda became manifest almost immediately after independence. The primary hurdle was Buganda and its insistence upon a place of special rank within the new nation. Political historian Terence Hopkins aptly posed a question at the time: "What place should Buganda, its *Kabaka* [emphasis Hopkins], and its people the Baganda occupy in the emerging national state?"[36] Independent Uganda was not ready nor willing to accept Buganda overrule any more than the British system from which the nation had just been released. Buganda's rather elitist attitude toward others placed it in opposition to many Ugandan peoples. Thus, the kingdom's citizens feared loss of their autonomy, especially the possible backlash from other tribes and kingdoms.

The constitution's differentiation in status among the various kingdoms and groups was another initial problem. Buganda was given federal status and the kingdoms of Ankole, Bunyoro, and Toro received semi-federal status. Other regions, however, received no similar recognition. This system created pockets of power within the nation. The mixed nature of the constitution—half federal and half unity—was, thus, problematic and created factions amongst Uganda's peoples.[37] Related to this differentiation in status was the so-called "lost counties" issue that muddied the political waters further. At the close of the nineteenth century, these lands had been taken by the British from Bunyoro and given to Buganda as a reward for the latter's assistance in subduing the region to British rule. These "counties," in which were located the burial tombs of many Bunyoro kings, were not returned at independence, adding fuel to the growing fire of discontent.[38]

The shaky political alliance between the UPC and the KY, as well as the persistent tensions between Catholics and Protestants, also served to destabilize Uganda from the outset. The original political coalition had been one of convenience to defeat the Democratic Party. Thus, after the election, with the coalition's seat of power outside Buganda, the party's unity began to break down. At the same time, the ever-present religious tensions were manifest in Obote, a Protestant, matched against a Catholic opposition that was gaining power in the decline of the UPC-KY coalition. None of these problems were unique to Uganda, but the presence of this combination so soon after independence exacerbated an already problematic situation. Vincent McCauley offered a note of hope based on faith:

> The challenges we face are great but not insurmountable. Just the sociological impact of Western society on the simple ways of a tribal society will pose great problems. When the values of the old society break down, they must

128

be replaced by something just as firm and even firmer. Thanks to the great missionaries who have gone before us, and the dedicated missionaries of the present, the faith continues to grow in this part of God's garden, and we are striving with all our energy to help the people keep their faith.[39]

McCauley's ideas extended to a more general understanding of the relationship of church and politics. The bishop stressed cooperation with the prevailing government, so long as it allowed religion the freedom to practice and operate. Yet, McCauley proclaimed that the Church had the right—even the duty—to make critical comments when necessary to assure justice for all peoples. He worried, however, when comments made in a positive sense were misconstrued as harsh or negative. Commenting on how tribal fears feed a negative sense of nationalism, he stated,

> This fear is shown in the extreme sensitivity of some African politicians to any sort of criticism—even very constructive criticism. It is shown in the trend toward one-party rule—a rule that sometimes suppresses such basic rights as freedom of religion, free speech, free press, the right of assembly. In these turbulent times in Africa the Church, which, paradoxically, has educated, mentally and spiritually much of Africa, comes under attack from nationalists.[40]

Similar fears threatened the future of Christian missions. Speaking of the tribal wars at the time of independence, McCauley wrote: "In the meantime our program continue[s] and since none of the tribes are hostile to missionaries, we are hopeful that we will be able to carry on."[41] Still, McCauley never allowed his political opinions to sway his judgment, especially on church matters.

McCauley strongly and repeatedly stated that priests and religious should not get involved in the political process. In his first quinquennial report to the Vatican, he stated,

> Fortunately no priests in this diocese will ever interfere in political matters. It is not so much as ordered by the Diocesan Authority, but rather as a spirit that has developed over the years. We are grateful to all our clergy for their clear understanding that cooperation with Government does not mean interference in politics.[42]

The close association of the DP with Catholics brought pressure upon McCauley to show more visible support for its candidates and ideas, but he remained aloof, to the dismay of some. In a 1978 interview he stated,

> We stayed out of the whole thing much to the consternation of some of the other bishops and a lot of priests [who felt] we were letting the Church down by not sponsoring the Democratic Party. . . . But we refused to get involved in the political.[43]

He believed that support of one party over another would compromise the Church's role to serve all people.[44]

While the Church remained outside the political arena, Milton Obote, the leader of the UPC-KY coalition, began his tenure as Uganda's first independent leader. Obote rose to leadership in the UPC through his acceptance by Ugandans and British colonial authorities. Although when he assumed the position of prime minister many problems beset him and the nascent Ugandan nation, he was widely respected, especially by the Baganda, who appreciated his ability to achieve a peaceful and relatively smooth government transition.[45]

Obote's regime, however, quickly ran afoul of many constituencies in Uganda, foreshadowing a bleak initial future for the fledgling nation. The prime minister's plan for governance was the transformation of political independence to economic independence. The strategy was, in the opinion of historian Jan Jorgensen, flawed in two of its basic assumptions: (1) the idea that the UPC was a party of the masses, and (2) that the dependent Ugandan economy could be made on a par with the outside economy on reform alone.[46] The political landscape moved closer to a one-party system, a situation that appealed to Obote but was contrary to the majority opinion. He unabashedly stated the UPC's goal: "We have decided to follow a socialist line of development. Consequently socialist principles must inform, guide, and govern the basis, form, and content of all institutions of our society."[47] Obote moved gradually toward dictatorial rule. One historian has observed, "When political independence was won from Britain in 1962 . . . little did the people know that colonial domination would be replaced with indigenous dictatorship and ruthless administration under the first Obote regime."[48]

Obote exhibited a Janus-face attitude toward the relationship between church and state. On the one hand he asked for cooperation between the two great institutions: "I am convinced that it is impossible for us in government to work single-handed." He suggested, "None is better established than the Church organizations" for a possible partnership.[49] Yet, the Obote government hampered efforts to evangelize, especially those of Catholics and Muslims. Expatriate clergy were especially harassed by severe restrictions on missionary visas issued. In response, one of McCauley's advisory groups, the Board of Consultors, suggested, "It is imperative that something be done. The Church must be seen as an integral part of the nation and not the opposition to everything the government does."[50]

Obote's internal political fortunes also began to collapse. Almost immediately after the April 1962 election, the UPC-KY coalition began to falter. The UPC began to receive some defections from the DP, causing hardcore UPC members, who were not Buganda based, to feel little need for the KY. More division arose between the UPC and Buganda over Obote's insistence that the "lost counties" be returned to Bunyoro, an idea that infuriated the Kabaka. Within the UPC itself, a "civil war" of sorts began to brew between Obote and Grace Ibingira, who ousted Obote loyalist John Kakonge as secretary-general of the party.[51]

The political ferment was problematic for the Holy Cross mission as well. Frustration at the situation was rampant. McCauley expressed his concern to his family:

> The opposition is organized and has muscle, while many of our people are disorganized and confused. No, things are not going the way we envisioned them when we first came. Even many of our hopes of a year or two ago have been blasted. But that's what we get for becoming missionaries. We asked for it.[52]

The turmoil of the Obote administration reached its apex in the constitutional crisis of 1966. In essence, the predicament was the result of personal conflicts between Obote, Ibingira, and Sir Edward Mutesa II, the Kabaka in Buganda. Obote and Ibingira argued over control of the UPC; Obote and Mutesa sparred over the lost counties and other Bugandan autonomy issues. The prime minister further accused the Kabaka of planning a government coup.[53] On February 22, 1966, fearing the rising instability, Obote ordered the arrest of Ibingira and other cabinet members and suspended the 1962 constitution, "in the interest of national unity and public security and tranquility."[54] Obote further justified his move as a "revolution of the masses against the forces of federalism and tribalism whose design was to divide Uganda into personal domains with the aid of imperialist forces outside Uganda."[55] Still, political commentators and historians have suggested less altruistic reasons for Obote's wresting of power. Phares Mutibwa states:

> To Obote peace, tranquility and, hence, development,
> depended on the total abolition of kingship, the con-
> centration of all political and administrative powers at
> the centre under his direct control and, later, placing the
> destiny of Uganda and Ugandans in the sole hands of the
> single party that had brought these changes about.[56]

It is clear that blame for the 1966 constitutional crisis is
abundant and widespread. Obote and his lieutentants were
certainly culpable, but Ibingira was equally ambitious for
power. The misguided ideas of Edward Mutesa and his activities in seeking assistance from outside government entities
added to the problem. The British government, which did
little to bring the various tribes and kingdoms together, can
also share blame, at least to some extent.

On April 15, 1966, Obote issued an interim constitution
that was passed by parliament without debate. The slogan of
the new order was: "One country, one parliament, one government, one people led by an executive, Milton Obote."[57]
On September 8, 1967, the new final constitution was issued.
The document emphasized centralization. Kingships were
removed; the kingdoms of Buganda, Ankole, Bunyoro, and
Toro were removed from the map. The post of prime minister was abolished and Obote took the title "president." The
position of the military was greatly strengthened under the
command of Idi Amin, who was promoted to the position of
major general. The Ugandan Air Force was founded.[58]

The Church's reaction to the crisis was rather muted. Three
months prior to the release of the 1967 constitution, McCauley, writing on behalf of the bishops of Uganda, stated in a
rather resigned tone:

> Because of our belief in the ultimate authority of God
> and our Christian understanding of human nature we
> welcome those provisions of the Constitution which
> safeguard justice for all, and we urge that both those who

govern as well as those who are governed should not be outside or above the rule of law, in order that the power which is necessary for the well-being of the nation may not be abused.[59]

Administration of the Diocese of Fort Portal

Central to the administration of Bishop Vincent McCauley were his concept of mission and the related notion of Africanization. Basic to his belief was the need to love the people he served. McCauley loved Africa and Africans and promoted their cause at every opportunity. His successor as local ordinary of Fort Portal, Serapio Magambo, spoke of McCauley as America's "greatest ambassador to Uganda and East Africa." As an ambassador of faith and good will, he was "interested in our total development—body and soul." He summarized McCauley's affection for the continent and its people:

> Africa and Africans had become his life blood. He breathed Africa, thought Africa, dreamt Africa and the Africans and did all he could to advance the cause of Africa and of the Africans at national and international meetings and organizations.[60]

McCauley lived so profoundly for the people of Africa that he felt one with them. In one of his last recorded sermons, he stated, "I am an old man . . . but I am a Mutoro, a man of this district."[61]

The basic concept of mission, as lived throughout history and as practiced in McCauley's time, was the basis upon which he built his vision of apostolic work. Historian Adrian Hastings has outlined four epochs of missionary history: (1) 30–1900—the period of the village, (2) 1900–1920—the age of the catechist, (3) 1945–1960—the age of schools, and (4) 1960 and forward—the age of independence. More recently, he suggests, institutions are far less important for evangelization when compared with preaching and popular liturgy.[62]

The 1960s saw the transition from mission to young churches in promotion of the faith and the development of the institutional church. New thinking could only negotiate this shift. Joseph Blomjous, bishop of Mwanza, Tanzania, described the needed shift:

> It seems that with the growth of the new nations in the non-western world (which is de facto the old "missionary world") and with their new awareness of their own dignity and responsibility, the formula of the "young churches" has far more chances of being for the good of the Church than the old formula of "mission territories" (which emphasizes their departure from the West), even where these young Churches would still be very weak.

For Blomjous the mission transition was a time of crisis. He articulated several tensions between old and new views of mission that needed to be recognized and corrected. Additionally, he suggested that a middle of the road response be given, thus avoiding the extremes that would either deny the problem or exacerbate it so much that no solution could be found. He also did not believe Vatican II and its "Decree on the Church's Missionary Activity" (*Ad Gentes*) was a panacea, but rather an avenue to articulate contemporary problems and recommend solutions.[63]

As a veteran of the missions in two locations, Bengal and Africa, Vincent McCauley had sufficient experience and depth of understanding to form his own concept of mission, yet he was very traditional in his views. He saw his basic role as one who "implants the faith."[64] This is first done by cooperation with the established Church. He explained,

> We are missionaries. We are not "do-gooders" working for the appreciation of others. Nor are we salaried servants of

the government. However much we must cooperate with the established authority and help promote the welfare of the country, our main purpose must never be lost sight of. That is to establish the Church, to raise up a People of God in Uganda, to educate our African brethren to understand Catholic living, a people who will love the Church, strengthen it, expand it.[65]

Also central to this implantation of the faith was the need to assist Africans to assume their appropriate responsibilities. Again he explained:

The objective of a foreign missionary must be to assist the Africans among whom he works to assume the responsibility for their Church. In order to reach this objective the missionary must be satisfied to do the training and to help his African fellow priest, Brother, Sister, or lay-man to advance as quickly and thoroughly as possible.[66]

Lastly, he believed missionaries must assume the attitude of servants in all aspects of their ministry. He wrote:

Our missionaries should be encouraged with greater emphasis to develop the mentality of "servants." . . . To be specific: the missionary must be well trained before he is sent out to control the project in which he is engaged or the parish. . . . A self-seeking missionary is a contradiction. The missionary is and must be a servant.[67]

McCauley's vision of mission extended to his understanding of the qualities and methods of missionaries themselves. He strongly promoted his belief that missionaries must be Catholic and not nationalistic or tribalistic. Too often personal and national agendas interfered with the ideas of the Church universal. McCauley fostered the ideas of Vatican II as articulated in *Ad Gentes*, especially the need to see missionaries on a par with all other church ministers. He wrote, "While the Pope and Propaganda Fide have attempted to implement the

ideas of *Ad Gentes*, too often efforts center about collecting
funds for 'our poor missionaries.'" He continued, "Much yet
needs to be done to consider missionaries as equal partners in
the whole Church's apostolate. Until this goal is reached missionaries will continue to be beggars."[68] Adaptability to the
local environment and to personnel who share the apostolate
was another critical quality for the missionary. He explained:

> The mentality of our [Ugandan] people is very different
> from what we are accustomed to and in order to get along
> with them we must cultivate (positively, not just in theory)
> a willingness to adapt ourselves to their ways. Our man-
> ner and our speech must reflect a love and a respect for
> them and their country, an interest in their problems, and
> a helping hand (more than financial assistance) in their
> needs. There is nothing that will arouse their animosity
> quicker than an attitude of superiority and a dominating
> manner.[69]

McCauley summarized his ideas on the mission and its ministers in a spirit of humility:

> Granted that not all our African priests are as well trained
> as those from other countries, we still have the duty of giv-
> ing them the responsibility gradually as soon as they can
> accept it. This will involve working under those who[m]
> we ourselves have trained. . . . I am convinced that our
> modern missionaries must more and more make the
> motto of St. John the Baptist their own: "he must increase
> and I must decrease." They are here to serve and assist and
> not to dominate.[70]

Citing mission tradition since the time of St. Francis Xavier
in India and Japan, McCauley was a firm believer in the value
of inculturation. He expressed this belief in a 1976 address to
the chapter of the Indiana Province of Holy Cross:

> We no longer use the term "adaptation." The suspicion
> is that "adaptation" implies putting African clothes on
> European and foreign interpretations of Christ's message.
> To the African Church the message of Christ is universal
> and, therefore, should be presented to the Africans as
> God's message to Africans. It must be something that can
> be understood and put into practice in Africa, and not
> be Europeanized or Americanized to be understood and
> practiced. . . . The Gospel, the Church, must be incar-
> nated in the African culture in which we live.[71]

Inculturation must be implemented in varied ways. Above all,
McCauley believed in caution and prudence when dealing
with local peoples and customs. His former colleague Bishop
Joseph Mukwaya once commented, "Whatever he [McCauley]
said or did had importance for the people. Thus, he was very
careful in his words, his movements, and his plans. He was
very respectful of local culture."[72] McCauley promoted inculturation through liturgy, especially local music and dance. He
additionally suggested that religious must adapt their rule of
life more to local custom so as not to be seen as foreigners who
live apart from the local peoples.[73]

Promotion of the local church was also integral to Vincent
McCauley's missiology. First and foremost in this area was
the need for stability, a goal that was strongly pushed when
peace and security were present. For autonomy, the local
church needed to operate on its own resources. He stated, "It
is becoming daily more clear that the Church in Africa must
deepen more and more its own resources. The key words heard
more and more frequently are: self-governing, self-propagating,
and self-sustaining."[74] Additionally, he firmly believed the
local church must be African, not European or American. He
opined:

> It seems clear that we cannot demand that the Church
> in Africa be run by Europeans and on European lines simply

because Christ first chose us. He chose the apostles, but
He did not make His Church Jewish. In Africa why
should it be European? Why should Europeans control it?
Why should Europeans prevail, etc., etc.?[75]

McCauley also believed local participation in the Church was
critical to the advancement of its mission. He described his
view:

Conditions that prevail throughout the world and especially here in Africa emphasize our need to do everything
possible to establish the Church firmly by raising up from
the People of God here in Africa, those to whom the
destiny of the Church may be safely entrusted.[76]

McCauley proposed several ways to strengthen the local
church. Primary was the need to build the local clergy, which
he did through the establishment of St. Mary's Minor Seminary
shortly after he assumed the position of bishop. The ranks of
religious were strengthened through his promotion of African
congregations of women, most notably the Banyatereza Sisters, and the invitation in 1964 to the Sisters of the Holy Cross
to join the diocese. In the spirit of Vatican II, McCauley was
also a great champion of lay leadership, especially catechists,
who were instrumental to education on the parish level.

McCauley's support for the local church was noted by many
of his contemporaries in Uganda. John Croston, C.S.C., who
worked closely with McCauley for several years in Uganda and
Kenya, writes:

He was quick to assess a situation and perceive the needs
in missionary work. His foresight and ability to plan for
the future were keen. He was content to fill a position
of need but always aware that it was temporary and that
the local Church must take the initiative and supply the
leadership as soon as possible. Convinced that a true

missionary was to step down for the local Church, he always followed that principle.[77]

Joseph Mukwaya claims that McCauley's enduring legacy and greatest achievement was "making the Church local and having it run by locals."[78]

The advance of the local church was strongly contingent on the creation of a well trained and significantly numerous indigenous clergy. Indeed, for McCauley it was the highest priority to the mission and the buildup of the local church. He realized, however, that for some time expatriate clergy would be needed in Uganda, but the life span was limited. Therefore, greater dependence on Africans for the mission was necessary to attain the goal of a self-sustaining local church. McCauley summarized his ideas:

> Uganda is a developing country. The Church is struggling for a place in the National Structure. Unless we can get a better-qualified local clergy there is little hope of the Church realizing her potential. Africanization is demand[ed] in Uganda. Foreign priests (and Bishops) are tolerated for the time being. But our day is waning. Soon—within the next decade—the Church must depend on native African Priests (and Bishops) to sustain Her.[79]

As he suggests, McCauley fully realized the increasing emphasis on Africanization and how this was related to building the local church and the promotion of indigenous clergy. Pressure from the Ugandan government was not always subtle in this area. Indeed, McCauley presented a warning,

> The handwriting is on the wall and we do not even need a Daniel to read and interpret it for us. Africanization is here to stay. Foreigners "in authority" over Africans will be tolerated only long enough to negotiate their replacement without destroying the positive value of what they have contributed to the country. If we have the "Good of

the Church" at heart we will make the best arrangements
we can, before a solution concocted by biased politicians
is imposed on the Church . . . as in Sudan, and Guinea.
The result . . . almost total paralysis.[80]

In response to this growing movement, which was certainly
fueled by and a natural outgrowth of the earlier independence
drive, McCauley suggested the Church make a measured but
clear change from its former dominant attitude over local
peoples. He rejected those who refused to alter their position:

> Any institution run by Foreigners is bound to be in the
> category of "the opposition." Until the Catholic Church is
> considered "ours," it will not be integrated into the hearts
> and minds of the thinking African or of the African who
> lives by instinct as a follower. Christ wants to share the
> whole life of His African people. Many Africans think we
> foreigners stand in His way. We are too bossy, too superior
> in attitude and manner. We are efficient, we can organize,
> [and] we do have the money and the technology that
> Africa needs to develop. But . . . we insist on our Euro-
> pean way of doing things. They don't like it. They don't
> want it. For a century we have tried to change Africa to
> our way. It hasn't worked. The only way the Church can
> remain in Africa is to become African-run as opposed to
> non-African.[81]

McCauley promoted Africanization, but believed it should
be done gradually and with the right intention, namely the
good of the Church, not simply to satisfy the more xenopho-
bic and jingoistic elements of Ugandan society. He summarized his position:

> The Africanization policy is a natural and expected result
> of the successful struggle for independence. Rather than
> oppose it we should try to develop the Church in accor-
> dance with its requirements in so far as these are just,
> practical and morally good. To be successful one should

not go "overboard" and Africanize simply for the sake
of Africanization. Neither should we approach it with a
biased mentality, the mentality that repeats the shibbo-
leth: "The Africans are not ready to take over" or "We can't
in conscience turn the Church over to incompetents."[82]

The indigenous clergy of Fort Portal supported McCauley's
measured response to the Africanization issue. Fort Portal's
diocesan clergy were willing to and ready to take up their
responsibility, but they realized expatriate priests were necessary. In a 1969 memorandum addressing the issue, the priests
stated:

> A challenge has been thrown and in no way are we dis-
> mayed; we welcome it; we, however, recommend that the
> Government's noble policy of trying to Ugandanize all
> the sectors of the life of its citizens be gradually adopted
> in our diocese. We have no doubt that, with due calcula-
> tions the policy of Ugandanization will eventually lead to
> prosperity and self reliance as far as Uganda personnel are
> concerned. Whereas we realize the importance of Ugan-
> danization we nonetheless implore the government to
> grant our expatriate missionaries a longer period of time
> to stay in the diocese.[83]

McCauley verified this stance in his first quinquennial report
to the Vatican: "The tendency to Africanize many posts is
noted. . . . There is no strong pressure from our clergy as they
are perfectly aware of the fact that the Bishop will without
hesitation Africanize whenever it is possible to do so."[84]

McCauley's plan for effecting Africanization in the diocese
and the Church in Uganda was manifest in multiple ways. He
always spoke of his willingness to Africanize. He did believe
some ideas and demands were premature or inappropriate,
but he concluded, "Never-the-less Africanization is a continuing process. It is a reality that we must be concerned with. To
direct its progress in matters relating to the Church is a very

important consideration for the African Bishops and their collaborators."[85] He believed that Africans must increase, while expatriates should decrease in authority. Generally, McCauley appointed African priests as pastors (parish priests) and placed expatriates as curates. More specifically, he appointed Africans to positions of authority in the diocese as soon as it was practicable, but he never jeopardized the foundations that had been laid. This was manifest in April 1965 when he appointed Emmanuel Wandera as his vicar general to replace Harry Hcycs, W.F., who had held the position since the foundation of the diocese.[86]

McCauley's motivation for his Africanization stance requires some exploration. As a missionary in Bengal, especially as rector of Little Flower Seminary, he was a strong supporter of indigenous clergy and the local church. While Bengal was more of a country in need of evangelization than Uganda, nonetheless, McCauley, through word and action, promoted local people to assume authority as much as possible. Similarly in Uganda, McCauley was a strong promoter of local church in every respect. However, one cannot deny the significant impact of the independence movement on the Church. When McCauley replaced Heyes with an African, he admitted, "You are well aware of the pressure I have been under to appoint an African V[icar] G[eneral]. I felt it necessary to make the move now. . . . In preparation for future developments I thought it best to Africanize now. I do hope you agree since it had to be done."[87] Contemporaries of McCauley disagree on whether the bishop's comment was an aberration or a more true indication of how he felt. William Blum, C.S.C., believes pressure was present and it was not so subtle. However, Robert Hesse, C.S.C., feels nationalistic pressures were not a factor with McCauley in his decisions.[88] John Keefe, C.S.C., believes that pressure was present, but it came more from changes in Church policy than nationalism or the drive for Africanization.

Vincent McCauley took his understanding of mission, local church, and Africanization and made them tools for his administration of the new Diocese of Fort Portal. Beginning from ground zero, McCauley realized his initial task would be to set up a system of operation and set of offices and institutions that would allow the diocese to serve its people. He wrote to the Holy Cross general administration in Rome, "We are making no attempt this first year to tackle the much needed expansion and development of the mission. We have concentrated on organizing the diocese and on consolidating our inheritance." As with his Africanization policy, he resolved to go slowly, but soon realized "some things could not be put off," including construction of a chancery, his own house, and renovations of a few key buildings.[89]

The new bishop possessed talent as an administrator and was a man of great vision. Beyond the basics of organization, McCauley was "a man who followed his faith and his nose" in a pragmatic approach to task accomplishment. He looked toward the future, always having another project in mind. Francis Zagorc, C.S.C., has commented, "Bishop McCauley was a good administrator in the sense that he could foresee things that had to be done and things he wanted to accomplish." This vision was never limited. Cornelius Ryan, C.S.C., characterized McCauley's vision, "If you reach your goal it isn't big enough."[90]

McCauley's personality and vision were effectively utilized in working with people to accomplish personal and diocesan goals. George Lucas, C.S.C., states:

> His great gift was to get people together and get them talking. He wasn't a great theologian, a great thinker, a great orator, but he was certainly a man who knew that bringing people together and sharing their resources would be helpful in building the local Church.[91]

He was a "hands-off administrator," placing full trust in his fellow priests and religious and giving them freedom to carry out his ideas as they believed was best. He realized that people on the local level had a much better feel for how a general teaching or particular policy could best be implemented. He often told his treasurer, John Croston, C.S.C., "Keep your eye on the money and when you get dangerously low tell me and I'll go and get some more." Because he trusted people on the local level he was able to find solutions to problems more quickly and permanently.[92]

The bishop's trust in his priests and religious was also expressed in consultation and collegiality. McCauley was never overbearing in his administrative style, but rather dialogued with individuals and groups, seeking consensus whenever possible. At times such a policy was costly, but it was worth it for the bishop. He wrote to a friend,

> . . . collegiality, cooperation and common effort of various kinds exact a heavy price but do on the whole help to make the Church in Africa participate more intensely in the life of the universal Church.[93]

He was always diplomatic and possessed the ability to listen; he was a man of great energy and zeal. Still, he clearly understood that the good of the Church was paramount and, thus, when necessary, made decisions and promulgated policies with which many disagreed.[94]

If McCauley had an Achilles heel as an administrator, it was that sometimes he needed to be more forceful. Several Holy Cross religious have commented that there were times when the bishop needed to take a firmer stand and refused. Too often he allowed situations to proceed without resolution. His pastoral sensitivity, seemingly always to say "yes" to various projects, was also at times problematic.[95] In some instances, religious believed the bishop did not use good judgment in his personnel appointments; missionaries felt he was "filling slots." Yet, McCauley never took offense at what might be said; he took criticism very well.[96]

As administrator of the local church, McCauley had significant interaction with the Toro government. He had excellent relations with the Toro king, George Rukidi II, who had served the region since 1929. When the king died suddenly on December 21, 1965, McCauley offered condolences and pledged the loyalty of the Catholic faithful to his son and successor, Patrick Olimi III, who ascended the throne on March 3, 1966:

> As Catholic Bishop of Toro I offer you the homage of all the Catholics in your kingdom. As a spiritual father of my flock I offer you the assurance of our prayers to God for your spiritual welfare, for good health, for the wise and fruitful reign of many many long years.[97]

McCauley regularly visited the Toro monarchs, celebrated national holidays and festivals with them, and worked with them toward achieving good church-state relations on all fronts.

Besides his association with the king, McCauley was also engaged in government efforts to assist Toro citizens. In July 1962, McCauley was called to chair the Toro Joint Welfare Advisory Committee, a group of local religious, business, and government leaders. In its constitution, the nascent body stated its purpose as a charitable organization to coordinate efforts by church, government, and business peoples in varied social programs.[98] The members agreed to meet at least three additional times annually, including a December session to assess needs and seek solutions to local social problems. McCauley remained associated with the group throughout his time in Fort Portal, although he resigned as chairman in March 1966, "due to many other commitments."[99]

Besides the Welfare Advisory Committee, McCauley was active in the local community on many fronts. Education was always central to his thinking and activity. Writing to the Bunyoro Minister of Education he stated:

> I declare once again my often repeated statement that as the Catholic Bishop of Bunyoro and Toro, it has been and continues to be my policy to foster education in the country at any level. It was to implement this policy that the Catholic Church built and conducted schools for many years on her own initiative. This policy was followed in cooperation with Government Authorities ever since there was an Education department in Uganda. Before Independence and after, our willingness to cooperate in the advancement of education is a matter of record.[100]

Before erection of the diocese, McCauley formed an American-style citizen's committee of business, labor, and British government officials to address problems associated with abandoned children. In March 1965, he threw his support behind an effort to raise government minimum wage standards, stating, "Our support of the principles of social justice is unqualified and deeply sincere."[101] McCauley continued his efforts even when Obote's national government threw many roadblocks in his way. With regard to the Church, he wrote to a benefactor:

> The pressure from local authorities is still plaguing us. Judging from recent events from some of the public pronouncements, we will have to exercise our ingenuity to the full in order to cope with the opposition to the Church, which is becoming more and more open in some circles.[102]

While McCauley's achievements in the secular community were many and noteworthy, he clearly concentrated his efforts on Church business and administration. As a local ordinary,

especially in his efforts to initially organize a missionary diocese, he was often pressed to raise money. Fortunately, his previous experience in Washington as procurator of the missions
was invaluable in this often unpleasant yet absolutely necessary
task of his office. He based his development efforts on the
goodness of people and the redemption brought by Christ. In
a lecture at Creighton University he stated,

> As a missionary who has had some experience of revolu-
> tions and of famines and of wide-spread natural disasters,
> I can still retain a strong basis of hope. I admit that my
> hope is supernaturally founded, but it is a hope that
> extends to my fellow man as well, because I believe that
> God does watch over His people. I believe that God will
> help us restore the balance that should exist among the
> families of nations, if we do our utmost in cooperation
> with Him to right the obvious wrongs that oppress mil-
> lions and millions of our fellow men. This will mean a
> long struggle, but if we can generate enough good will in
> the cause of justice all is not hopeless.[103]

McCauley unabashedly and even proudly declared himself
a beggar on behalf of others. He possessed wide contacts as
sources of revenue, especially European foundations such as
Misereor, Missio, and various Vatican offices, as well as individuals in the United States. He was successful through his
skill and personality, but also because donors saw the fruits of
their contributions in buildings and programs.[104] His fellow
Ugandan and East African bishops often tapped McCauley's
expertise as a fundraiser.

Organization of the priests of Fort Portal was an especially
important task for McCauley. Based on the teaching of Vatican
II's *Presbyterorum Ordinis* (Decree on the Ministry and Life of
Priests—December 7, 1965), McCauley established a board of
consultors and senate of priests. The Consultors, an appointed
group of priests and religious, sought to further "collegiality,

subsidiarity and shared responsibility as expressed in the Vatican Council." McCauley expressed his hope for the board:

> The tone of the Board should be unity, which is not the same as uniformity. Each [participant] should feel free. Each should feel free to express himself and his opinions though charity should rule as absolute and essential in the discussions. Together, we should seek the good of the Church, of our people and of those working for God, and seek the best means of sanctifying his people.[105]

The board received mixed reviews from its participants. Some believed it was helpful, both to advise the bishop and to allow varied opinions to be aired publicly. Others suggested that McCauley generally had already decided issues brought to the board. Thus, the board either supported the bishop or it was ignored.[106]

The senate of priests was organized in late November 1966, but did not receive its formal name until the fifth meeting one year later. The body consisted of all priests in the diocese and, like the consultors, met to discuss diocesan issues and make recommendations to the bishop. The senate met regularly (five times in the first twelve months), and generally without the bishop present. McCauley expressed his hopes for the senate:

> This meeting of the priests of the Diocese has a collegial significance that to me is extremely important. It is my hope that all the priests will look upon it as an opportunity to effect the closer collaboration with their brother Priests in our common apostolate.[107]

Like the Consultors, the senate received mixed reviews by its participants, but generally was seen as less effective than the former. On the positive side, the meetings, held without McCauley present, provided a good forum for discussion, and brought a sense of renewal to the local clergy. Most, however, believed the body accomplished little of significance.[108]

Fort Portal Diocesan Administration

Bishop

Vicar General

Priest Senate   Consultors   Diocesan Past. Comm.

Pastoral Zones

One of the more innovative administrative ideas McCauley initiated came in March 1969 when he established "pastoral zones" in the diocese. The proposal was to provide a forum for the discussion and resolution of various diocesan issues through discussion in smaller pastoral units. Introducing the program, McCauley wrote, "It seems by facing problems together we can better pool our energies and work toward solutions together." Six zones were established, four groups of parishes in close geographic proximity, and two groups of religious, one of brothers and another of sisters.[109] Zones met with some regularity (although not fixed), reporting their deliberations to McCauley, who used the input in his collegial style of decision making.

In 1965, McCauley submitted his first quinquennial report to the Vatican on the status of the Diocese of Fort Portal. The report provided statistical information with regard to numbers of Catholics, clergy and religious, parishes and various diocesan institutions. More importantly, however, he expounded on the problem created as a result of insufficient clergy and parishes. He stated:

> Our clergy is [*sic*] generous, hard-working and devoted to their work. There is no idleness and most of the missionaries and local religious are overworked. Parishes are much too large and distances are great. . . . The "*operarii pauci*" is the real problem of the diocese. Parishes should

be divided, but personnel is [*sic*] not available, not to
mention finances.[110]

Propaganda Fide was pleased with the report and responded:

> Under your Lordship's pastoral guidance, the Diocese
> continues to make significant progress, and I am confi-
> dent that, in the future, all will be encouraged to maintain
> the high degree of apostolic zeal which has produced such
> fine results so far.[111]

Lack of clergy and a rapidly expanding Catholic population were catalysts in the erection of the Diocese of Hoima in
August 1965. Originally, the Diocese of Fort Portal encom-
passed the kingdoms of Toro and Bunyoro, a vast land with
scattered groups of Catholics. The basic logistical problem of
meeting the pastoral needs of this area with very limited personnel and financial resources was exacerbated in December
1964 when the "lost counties" were unceremoniously returned
to Bunyoro. Overnight the Catholic population of Fort Portal
increased by 48,000.

The situation was complicated through tribal divisions,
which raised several different issues. More than one-half dozen
major tribes were present in the Fort Portal diocese alone, each
with its unique culture and language. Often members of one
tribe would not accept clergy from another, creating major
pastoral concerns. One significant manifestation of these tribal
tensions was seen in the attempt to reintegrate peoples of the
lost counties after their split from Baganda. Citizens of these
lands had not been pleased to be part of the Rubaga diocese,
but as Bunyoro people they equally rejected being associated
with Toro, which comprised half of the Fort Portal diocese.[112]
Tribalism colored many issues, either directly or more oblique-
ly, throughout McCauley's tenure as bishop in Fort Portal.

Pastoral need and practicality pushed McCauley to suggest that a new diocese be formed, with its see at Hoima. He wrote to the archbishop of Rubaga, Joseph Kiwanuka:

> Because, as I see it the annexing of Buyaga and Bugangaizi [the "lost" counties] will not be an acceptable solution, I propose rather that a Diocese be erected in Bunyoro with Hoima as the new see. This would give a third residential African bishop to Uganda, would be in line with the Holy See's policy on Africanization, would be acceptable to the Central Government, and would delight the Government, clergy and people of Bunyoro.

Additionally, he suggested it was not politically sound to increase Fort Portal, the territory of an expatriate bishop, while shrinking Rubaga, the region of an African bishop. With 80,000 Catholics, twenty priests and seven parishes, Hoima would be in about the same condition as Fort Portal at its formation in 1961. McCauley informed the regional superior of the White Fathers and his superior general, Germain Lalande, both of whom supported the idea.[113]

Pope Paul VI officially erected the Diocese of Hoima on August 9, 1965. The diocese was formed from the western extension of the Archdiocese of Rubaga and the northern part of Fort Portal. Bishop Cyprian Kihangire was named the first local ordinary.[114] McCauley, as expected, exulted at the new foundation: "The severing of this territory from our diocese is a blessing to me, for now we'll be able to use our limited resources to build up our numerous mission stations in the Kingdom of Toro." On January 9, 1966, the Feast of the Holy Family, Kihangire was installed as the first bishop of Hoima.[115]

The erection of Hoima, coupled with significant administrative accomplishments and progress in Africanization, had placed the Diocese of Fort Portal on the road to success. In

the blink of an eye on Palm Sunday, March 20, 1966, fortune
turned to disaster when a severe earthquake struck the region
at 4:45 a.m. The three-minute tremor, the most severe ever
recorded in Africa, struck when McCauley was at Bundibugyo,
an outstation west of Fort Portal. The bishop's initial reaction
was to help rescue schoolgirls trapped in the rubble of their
dormitory. Then he organized the few priests and religious
present, along with some of the still-stunned local residents, to
provide relief services for those injured in the quake.[116]

When McCauley returned to Fort Portal, he discovered the
magnitude of the loss of life and damage. The human toll was
high—104 dead, 510 injured, and 60,000 homeless, 200 children under the age of fourteen left orphans. Church institutions were crippled. The cathedral was a total loss; the bishop's
residence, St. Ann's Secondary School, St. Mary's Minor Seminary, and the convents for the White Sisters and Banyatereza
Sisters were badly damaged and not serviceable until repaired.
The estimated property damage was $237,000.[117]

The damage was severe and, thus, McCauley almost immediately shifted to his fundraising mode, realizing that the
money needed could not be secured in Africa. Within a week
of the disaster he launched his drive. Initially he wrote to the
superior general in Rome,

> I am sending appeals to all my friends and to several agen-
> cies. I would appreciate it, however, if you can find a way
> to enlarge the scope, for we are going to need every bit of
> help we can get.[118]

He informed his Holy Cross superiors that while he wanted
to be present to supervise reconstruction efforts, it was
more urgent for him to travel to the United States to obtain
funds.[119]

McCauley thus traveled to the United States, spending six
months in a whirlwind effort to raise money for his troubled

diocese. His previous contacts from Washington proved very helpful, both by their own contributions, and assisting McCauley to beg for funds from their associates and business colleagues. When he returned, he concentrated development efforts with European foundations: Misereor in Germany and the Pontifical Work of St. Peter the Apostle in Rome.[120] Repairs were slow, but progress was made, allowing religious to return to their residences and students to attend school.

On a practical level, the need to repair residences and schools was paramount, still the symbolic value of the loss of the cathedral was a severe blow to McCauley. Thus, he placed special emphasis on the design and construction of a new church that would be symbolic of the diocese's recovery. While in the United States, McCauley appointed Father James Rahilly, C.S.C., as "clerk of the works" to oversee the cathedral project. Besides McCauley's personal development efforts, a special cathedral fund was established. Parishes held various fundraisers, such as raffles, fairs, and film showings.[121] The architecture firm of Hughes and Polkinghorne, under the supervision of Thomas Watson, was hired and plans were ready by early June 1966.

Construction of the new cathedral, Our Lady of the Snows, began with the laying of the cornerstone on May 14, 1967. Delays in construction, due in large measure to lack of proper construction materials, forced postponement of the originally scheduled dedication date of February 18, 1968.[122] Two months later on April 21, the new cathedral was dedicated with great fanfare and celebration. Cardinal Laurean Rugambwa of Tanzania presided over the Mass that was concelebrated by eight other bishops. Approximately 10,000 people attended the event, including two national government ministers, Toro government officials, representatives from the Church of Uganda (Anglican) and many other dignitaries.[123] McCauley was happy and proud, but certainly relieved to have the project and the earthquake behind him. He told his provincial, "It was a great day for Fort Portal."[124]

Summary

Having successfully guided the Holy Cross mission in Uganda during its infancy, it was only natural for Vincent McCauley to continue his leadership as the first bishop of Fort Portal. Ordained at Notre Dame in May 1961, he was installed two months later and immediately began to organize his new diocese. The independence movement in Uganda played an important and immediate role in McCauley's initial actions. He organized his diocese using the basic principles of mission theory that had guided his hand twenty years earlier in Bengal, namely inculturation and the promotion of the local church and indigenous clergy. These same principles were used by McCauley to organize the diocese administratively and to set a tone for pastoral ministry in the service of God's people.

CHAPTER 6

The Pastoral Missionary: 1961–1973

Gaudium et Spes, "The Pastoral Constitution of the Church in the Modern World," the final document issued by the fathers at Vatican II, and the only one generated completely from the floor of the Council, symbolized an important element in the Church's new direction. In general, the Constitution fulfilled the principal rationale given by John XXIII when he called the Council on January 25, 1959. Pope John called for an *aggiornamento*, an updating, by opening the Church to the thought and issues of the mid-twentieth century. He did not see the Council as being dogmatic, like Vatican I and its proclamation of papal infallibility, but rather pastoral, setting guidelines for the Church, both for its members and in its relationships with the greater world community. This would allow better interaction with the rapidly changing and increasingly global and more technological world. Included in this new thinking was the inculturation theme so prominent in the work of many missionaries,

including Vincent McCauley, and a more collegial, less central-
ized vision of the Church, both on local and universal levels.
This important pastoral element of the Council was manifest
in *Gaudium et Spes* by addressing specific issues of family,
war and peace, development of culture, economic and social
life, and the political community. Other documents, such as
Lumen Gentium, the Dogmatic Constitution on the Church,
addressed pastoral concerns by speaking of the Church as "the
people of God."

While many of the ideas present in Vatican II were, as has
been shown, part of the personality and ministry experience of
Vincent McCauley before the Council, it is certainly not coin-
cidental that McCauley sought to bring the pastoral sense of
Vatican II to his diocese at a time contiguous with the Council
sessions between 1962 and 1965. Ever the hard-working and
well-organized administrator, McCauley never forgot that his
vocation was to proclaim the gospel message as a pastoral minister. This consistent spirit, influenced by current events in the
Church, was brought to his work as bishop of Fort Portal.

A Pastoral Bishop

When Vincent McCauley assumed the reins of the new
Diocese of Fort Portal there were many administrative tasks
necessary to get the operation going, but the new bishop was
at heart a pastoral priest who enjoyed people. McCauley possessed the rather unique ability to mark all that he did and said
with a sense of gentleness and consideration. Father Thomas
Smith, C.S.C., remarks, "I always think of him placing the
face of kindness on the church. The common people found
him approachable; he made them feel comfortable being in
his presence. He was never perceived as distant, but rather
approachable and kind."[1] He was always supportive of others
who worked for him; he never flagged from trying to help others.

Even when he denied a request, people could walk away in a good frame of mind, knowing they had been heard. The bishop possessed a smile that was both attractive and inviting; he was never seen as standoffish.[2]

One of McCauley's greatest personal qualities was his adaptability. His missionary experience on two continents during different time periods and under varied conditions taught him this necessity. Referencing the spirit of Vatican II, he explained his understanding to the apostolic delegate:

> A new orientation in the pastoral approach of our ministry is necessary. . . . The Bishop of this diocese realizes the necessity of the "*aggiornamento*." . . . More than once, in the priests' conference, in his pastoral letters and in his personal advice, he has tried to bring home very forcefully to all the religious and to the people of the choice that the Church in the world today must re-adapt herself to the problems of the hour and seek the answers in a closer contact with God and the re-organization of the Church works to meet the needs of the time.[3]

McCauley persistently demonstrated his pastoral presence in the diocese through visitations, concern for the poor, and his consistent desire to work for others. On a regular basis McCauley went on safari to isolated locations to visit more than 125 outstations serviced by the diocese's various parishes. After his installation as bishop he spent several weeks visiting parishes, remote chapels, and schools. He wanted to be visible to the people.[4] McCauley never failed on his visits to seek out the poor and do what he could to help, even if that meant only listening. Louis Rink, C.S.C., has commented, "When he first arrived he asked to be taken to the poorest outstation. He had great concern for the people's daily needs."[5] In general, McCauley was a pastor who desired to be with his flock in solidarity and to walk their road.

McCauley's pastoral presence even allowed him to trans-
form what on the surface might have been a liability into
something positive. McCauley never learned Rutoro, the Toro
tribal language, well. The combination of age, a hectic work
schedule, and lack of opportunity prohibited this. Possibly
describing himself, he explained, "What headaches these various languages can bring to a young missionary who can hardly
understand one of them! And it is not an easy task for the
older priests to learn a new language."[6] Amazingly, however,
his inability to verbally communicate well with his people
never seemed to be problematic. In fact, most who observed
McCauley interacting with the local people suggest that people
loved him possibly more because he could not speak or understand Rutoro well. Stephen Gibson, C.S.C. , has commented,
"The effort he made endeared him to people in a way that far
exceeded what he would have been able to accomplish even if
he were fluent in the language."[7] He was never self-conscious
about his inability, but unhesitatingly went to villages and
intermingled freely with the people. His magnetic personality
was infectious; he won the people to his side by his honesty,
caring nature, and dynamism in ministry.[8]

When pastoral necessity required McCauley to use the
vernacular, he prepared long and hard for the event. Confir-
mations, large public Masses, and similar celebrations found
McCauley practicing his homily aloud, often for an hour or
more. His sincere effort was noted by the faithful, who drew
closer to him. While verbal means of communication may
have been difficult, the people noted his sincere efforts on their
behalf. The message Vincent McCauley had for his people was
clearly and joyfully welcomed and received.[9]

Bishop McCauley's pastoral presence was exhibited shortly
after his installation when a fellow Holy Cross religious, Father
Patrick Peyton, invited him to participate in his well-known
rosary crusade. During the 1950s, Peyton became an

international Church celebrity by promoting family prayer and the rosary through radio and television and a series of rosary rallies that touched every continent, including an extensive campaign in Africa in 1955.[10] Knowing the community connection between McCauley and Peyton, several East African bishops petitioned the former to obtain from Family Rosary, Peyton's organization, copies of the popular films on the fifteen mysteries of the rosary. Peyton, however, would only allow use of the films if he could be assured that catechists, trained by Family Rosary staff, presented the films to the faithful. While having some misgivings about his loss to the Uganda mission, McCauley was willing to allow Francis Zagorc, C.S.C., to go to Latin American for three months of training.[11] The superior general was pleased that a deal could be struck:

> Personally I am happy to know that you have decided to accept Father Peyton's offer. Because the Bishops in East[ern] Africa are so interested you can and should expect some substantial help from them.[12]

The proposal fell through, however, when Peyton insisted that the films could only be part of the entire rosary crusade.[13] This change in requirements, which greatly increased the commitment of Eastern African dioceses to Peyton's program, was not acceptable to McCauley. He described the change in plans to the general administration in Rome. Assistant general, Bernard Mullahy, C.S.C., supportively responded:

> Father Peyton's all absorbent zeal is certainly admirable, but I think that others have found in the past that there are occasions when we must stand firm in dealing with him. You are certainly in the best position to know what is fitting and appropriate, and even possible for your diocese and the surrounding dioceses of Uganda at this particular time.[14]

A more successful pastoral program, the 1967 "Year of
Faith," was launched in solidarity with dioceses throughout
the world. The celebration was called to mark the 1900th anni-
versary of the martyrdom of Saints Peter and Paul. McCauley
inaugurated the year appropriately on June 29, the feast day
of the two great saints, by calling for spiritual exercises and
retreats throughout the diocese. Mission teams of priests, religious, and catechists were sent to various parishes and outstations "to deepen the Faith of our people."[15] McCauley was very
pleased with the progress of the year-long celebration:

> The "Year of Faith" programme . . . has been one of the
> bright lights of our mission apostolate in recent months.
> It has been hard work for all concerned but the results
> have been so encouraging that we hear no complaints at
> all from the Fathers. In fact, many are now saying that this
> programme has been such a boon to the spiritual life of
> the missions that we should plan a repeat if not next year,
> at least the year after.[16]

The most extensive pastoral outreach program sponsored
by Fort Portal during McCauley's tenure as bishop was ministry and assistance to refugees. In 1961, the Bahutu Revolution
in Rwanda[17] drove many Banyarwanda refugees from their
homeland into Ankole Province, along the border regions of
Uganda. In 1963, the Ugandan government relocated these
people, the Banyarwanda, into southern Toro, and, thus, into
the ecclesiastical domain of Vincent McCauley. Approximately
80 percent of these 30,000 refugees were Catholics, raising a
significant pastoral issue for the bishop.[18] Writing to his family,
McCauley described the "monumental new problem in trying
to care for them spiritually and materially with our limited
manpower and resources."[19] The refugee problem became a
national issue.

In the mid-1960s, the refugee problem grew more intense when peoples from the Congo and Sudan joined the Banyarwanda. The Congolese refugees were in two groups: government supporters and nationalists. Some of these people found accommodation with family members and thus "d[id] not bring many problems."[20] However, a smaller group in refugee camps, where conditions were described as "appalling," exacerbated the present situation. A Catholic Relief Services report described the camp conditions:

> Their conditions of living are bad. They complain of insufficient food, inadequate housing and poor medical attention. The hygienic conditions of these camps are far from being good. The Congolese are not friendly, and the entry to their camps is not easy. They are not cooperative and have in mind to return to their country.[21]

In the mid-1960s, Sudanese refugees entered the Diocese of Fort Portal from the north. In April 1967, McCauley reported the situation for some 3,000 Sudanese:

> They are in a pitiable condition having been harassed more than a year and left in the middle of the bush with little or no means of support. The sickness among them is appalling and the poverty is the worst I have seen in a long time.[22]

McCauley immediately recognized the magnitude of the refugee problem. Speaking on behalf of the Uganda Episcopal Conference (UEC), he commented, "The Church is now faced with the problem of cooperating with the Government for the permanent settlement of the Batutsi [Rwanda refugees] in Uganda."[23] Frustrated that he could not do more, McCauley lamented:

> We must try to do what we can for them and make every effort to preserve and nourish their faith. They have nothing but the few rags they wear, and their ever-present

cattle. The job [of caring for them] is a forlorn and discouraging one, for we just do not have the man-power,
nor funds, at present, to aid them as we should like.[24]

McCauley did the best he could to meet the immediate
physical and spiritual needs of the refugees, but he realized a
long-range solution was necessary. Such a plan must have two
important elements. First, the refugees must have, for three to
four years, a guaranteed market with a fair price for their cash
crops while they get back on their feet economically. Second,
each refugee camp needs an executive committee to make
certain living conditions are conducive to a future productive
life.[25]

McCauley was fully engaged in the refugee issue and led
many efforts to assist these people. He once wrote, "My interest in and concern for refugees remains . . . just as keen and
just as deep as it was."[26] He supported the "hands-on" efforts
of individuals, such as his secretary, Brother Orlando Gozdowski, C.S.C., who each Sunday traveled south to Kasese,
bringing food and any other supplies he could find. As one
fellow missionary stated, "He took anything that was useful to
aid the people."[27] McCauley also blessed group efforts in the
refugee camps. Teams of religious and lay catechists worked
directly with refugees. He wrote the regional superior of the
White Fathers, Richard Walsh, W.F., seeking his community's
assistance in this effort.[28]

The spiritual needs of the refugees were met in large measure by the establishment of two parishes dedicated primarily
to this ministry. In 1963, at the prompting of McCauley,
Fathers Burton Smith, C.S.C., and Robert McMahon, C.S.C.,
established Kahunge Parish in Kibale District, approximately
thirty-five miles south of Fort Portal. The parish served 20,000
Batutsi refugees who lived in the region. George MacInnes,
C.S.C., came to Kahunge in 1965. An expert in languages,
MacInnes quickly became enmeshed in the ministry. One

Ugandan contemporary suggests that MacInnes was almost omnipresent: "They depended on MacInnes for everything."[29] Later, he started a school and became the champion for many people abandoned by their native land.[30]

In March 1966, Father Robert Hesse, C.S.C., was sent further southwest of Fort Portal to explore the need and possibility for a second parish for refugees. After some investigation by Hesse, and the recommendation of the board of consultors, McCauley founded a new parish at Kitagwenda. The groundbreaking was held on October 1, 1968, and the parish church opened on June 8, 1969, with Hesse as parish priest.[31]

Besides his own resources, McCauley organized the efforts of several other agencies to assist the refugees. Shortly after his installation, the new bishop began to elicit assistance from the British Red Cross to coordinate the humanitarian relief effort to the refugees.[32] Beginning in 1962, McCauley made numerous requests of Catholic Relief Services. He wrote, "85% of the Refugees are Catholic. But they are a discouraged, destitute and desperate lot. Quite understandably they accept help from whatever source they can get it."[33] McCauley also petitioned the Propagation of the Faith, seeking $25,000 for the relief effort. Some of the many agencies that assisted in this humanitarian drive were the International Red Cross, Lutheran League, World Council of Churches, Muslim Relief, OXFAM, and Swedish Peace Corps.[34] Additionally, McCauley authorized "sacramental safaris" into regions such as Bwamba where Congolese refugees were numerous. This continued until he deemed the situation too dangerous for missionaries.[35]

Bishop McCauley's pastoral presence and concern, as manifest in his work with refugees, was exhibited with equal or greater fervor in his relationship with his priests. He was not a micro-manager, but rather, trusted his clergy to carry out their duties and his programs to the best of their ability in a way that fit the local situation. He was always encouraging and served as their principal cheerleader. He was proud of them and what they accomplished. He once wrote, "The spirit of our missionaries is excellent and I am very proud of them and feel that it is a privilege for me to be here in the missions with such an excellent group of zealous missionaries."[36] McCauley was very concerned about the excessive work ethic of his priests. He wrote to the superior general:

> It worries me greatly that there are so very few of us for these multiple tasks. After the long Lenten safari I saw so many tired missionaries that I was tempted to declare a moratorium on all mission activity for fear many would collapse. A few I had to force to rest and others to slacken their pace. We simply can't afford to lose a single man, for every mission is under-staffed—and still the work grows.[37]

Working with the Holy Cross local superior in the same vein, he opined, "How many times have both you and I had to insist that these men take time off to rest?"[38]

McCauley made significant efforts to assist his priests through special opportunities and various programs. Several African priests were sent to Europe for additional education. In 1971, he instituted a "Priests Aid Fund" in the diocese. Each parish was "taxed" annually to raise revenue to finance special programs, workshops, and other events attended by the clergy for their professional development.[39] The bishop held regular meetings with his priests to discuss issues and demonstrate his solidarity with their concerns. He also made an effort to recreate with clergy and religious, hosting an annual post–Christmas open house to celebrate "African life and spirituality."[40]

McCauley sponsored regular clerical conferences as a means to educate and bring greater unity to the Fort Portal clergy. He described the purpose of these conferences:

I would not want this conference to become static. I do not want it to be a mere echo from the Bishop's office. I would hope that it manifests the spiritual dynamic of dedicated, intelligent, experienced missionary servants whose meeting is one of minds and hearts for the purpose of promoting the best interests of the Church in Fort Portal. Your bishop is here to participate, not to dominate; to get your views not to impose my own; to stimulate and to coordinate your efforts, not to stifle them. I hope to learn much from these exchanges and to use them as the basis for decisions that must be made by me in exercising my office and in promoting the welfare of the Church in the days ahead. I hope that all of you will also learn something to your profit and that of your apostolate.[41]

Topics for these conferences ran the gamut, including African families and marriage, role of the priest in Africa, education, catechetics and catechists, Sunday worship without a priest, schools, and parish finances. The main area of concentration was Vatican II and all of its varied ramifications in areas such as liturgy, celebration of the sacraments, the lay apostolate, fostering inculturation, and the role of the priest in the post–Vatican II Church.[42]

McCauley worked tirelessly to bring unity to the priests of the diocese. The need to bring together three diverse clerical groups, Holy Cross, the White Fathers, and the African diocesan clergy, made his task more difficult. He inherited a situation where division was often the case between expatriate and local clergy. The Katwe Catholic Council, a group of concerned Fort Portal Catholics, wrote McCauley on several occasions asking why African and European clergy ate separately. The group asked, "Are we to understand that the priests were given [the] option and after good consideration chose at their discretion to keep separate halls and feed on different diets?"[43] There is no extant response from the bishop, but he clearly was concerned about the situation and made every effort to break down barriers and bring unity.

McCauley's ability to negotiate this difficult road of clerical unity requires some comment. Robert Hesse suggests that McCauley believed his first priority was to gain acceptance from the White Fathers, whose territory Holy Cross had been given in 1958. While McCauley's charm, inviting attitude, and friendly demeanor endeared him to all, still tensions between the two expatriate religious communities brewed just below the surface. Robert Malone, C.S.C., one of the early arrivals to Uganda, has commented: "We didn't hate them [the White Fathers] or dislike them, but we were not comfortable with them. They had different customs, different ways of doing things." William Blum, C.S.C., noting the age difference between the groups, says general respect prevailed, but little if any interaction was present save professional association.[44]

The subsurface tensions between Holy Cross and the White Fathers were, in some ways, to be expected from the history of the transfer of authority in the diocese. Some veteran White Father missionaries felt usurped by Holy Cross. This sentiment was most apparent when, as a result of the transfer of power, changes came in personnel assignments and diocesan policies.[45] The tension was noted by the White Fathers in a comment about the growth of Holy Cross in the region:

> The White Fathers cannot help noticing that the H[oly] C[ross] Congregation is building a magnificent rest home for its members at Saka. We have noticed and decided that it was better for us not to make use of this house even if invited. An occasional visit for a couple of hours would be enough to keep up relations.[46]

McCauley worked hard to bring and maintain unity in the group. Although not intended, but understandable under the circumstances, some suggested that McCauley went out of his way to avoid partiality toward Holy Cross religious. More difficult personnel assignments were often given to Holy Cross religious.[47] The bishop almost exclusively created "integrated" parishes where Holy Cross and the White Fathers ministered together, often with Ugandan diocesan clergy as well. Holy Cross religious were asked to follow the "rule" of the White Fathers, a life much more regimented in strict times for common prayer and similar communal exercises.[48]

McCauley depended on the White Fathers and regularly praised their efforts in the diocese. He wrote the community's superior general:

> May I take this opportunity to express my personal satisfaction with the cooperation shown by the White Fathers assigned to the Diocese of Fort Portal. You have undoubtedly received reports from Father Braun [regional superior] and others regarding the harmonious cooperation that has existed between the White Fathers and the Holy Cross Fathers, and between the White Fathers and the Bishop in the Diocese of Fort Portal. . . . The White Fathers stationed here have adapted very well to conditions as they have evolved in Fort Portal and have exhibited an excellent spirit of cooperation. So far as I am concerned, and so far as the Holy Cross Fathers are concerned, we have no regrets whatever that the White Fathers have agreed to remain in Fort Portal as an integral part of the missionary effort of the Church here. It is our prayerful hope that this collaboration of the missionary effort of the Church in Fort Portal may not only continue but be expanded.[49]

In a reciprocal manner, the White Fathers held McCauley in high esteem. In a 1964 report issued by the White Fathers on their mission in western Uganda, surprise was expressed in how smoothly things ran in the new diocese:

> I found the confreres happy and zealous. I had expected to find more frictions between the three groups [White

Fathers, Holy Cross, and Africans secular clergy], which form the clergy of the diocese. There are some frictions, of course, but they come from individuals and not from groups as such: there is no group opposition.[50]

McCauley's desire to use all personnel for the good of the Church was also evident to the White Fathers' visitation team:

The Bishop himself does all that he can to foster the spirit of unity among his priests by his own impartiality and also by encouraging free mixing at meetings, visiting neighboring missions, and the courtesy call if he happens to be passing.[51]

While McCauley expended time and energy to build relations among the three groups of clergy, he worked equally hard on recruiting additional personnel for the mission. The bishop constantly made appeals for more personnel. In a typical letter, he implored the superior general for consideration:

So with no increase in Holy Cross Fathers, with six veterans no longer active, along with the loss of three Africans, and the illness of a young Holy Cross Father, our man-power situation is critical. If there were some way to lighten our burden on the active men, I would welcome it. But the contrary is the fact.[52]

The dream to send five Holy Cross religious per year did not materialize, but, nonetheless, a steady stream of religious to Uganda was maintained. During the early to mid-1960s, many Holy Cross religious who would make a great impact on the mission arrived, including John Keefe, John Croston, Thomas Keefe, James Rahilly, James Ferguson, William Blum, Orlando Gozdowski, Cornelius Ryan, Richard Wunsch, Richard Potthast, Walter Foley, and Tad Las. In 1968, fifty-two Holy Cross religious (priests, brothers, and sisters) were serving in Fort Portal. They were joined by seventeen White Fathers and nine African priests.[53]

. The bishop also petitioned the White Fathers for more missionaries. In communications with the community's leadership he pleaded that priests not be taken from the mission: "You have yourself visited us recently enough to know the acute shortage of manpower in this long neglected part of Uganda."[54] He also requested more personnel, suggesting that, because many religious were sick, on home leave, or limited in capacity due to age, the statistics showing available missionaries were very misleading: "Unless we get more priests soon the future looks bleak." He continued:

> My concern is for the Fathers. Many are greatly over-worked. They have too many people to care for—in too many outposts—too far away. . . . As a result of inadequate staffing, the Fathers are often tired; many of them are always tired. Still, they work on, regretting only that we do not speak of trying to expand the Church. That is but a dream.[55]

McCauley continued to appeal for more missionaries over the years, stating, "We are expecting too much of too few in demanding daily heroic dedication for so long a time."[56]

Insufficient personnel was a perpetual concern for McCauley that demanded much of his time. He wrote to a friend, "Our shortage of personnel is a perennial headache, and it has got to the point now where I am looking all over the world trying to get some priests to help us."[57] McCauley lamented his situation to the apostolic delegate and the prefect of Propaganda Fide. The latter offered no real assistance, commenting in a resigned tone: "As your Lordship indicates, the missionaries are scarcely adequate in number. . . . But it is clear that what they lack in quantity is amply compensated by their excellent quality."[58]

Clearly McCauley pushed for more Holy Cross personnel, but his more general pastoral concern was the welfare of each religious. Thus, when it was obvious that the Uganda mission was not the proper place for a religious, McCauley supported the individual over the mission. Writing to the Eastern Province provincial, Father Richard Sullivan, C.S.C., McCauley explained:

> We who are so short of priests in the growing work of the Church here in Uganda are sadly reluctant to see one of our own priests withdraw from the missions. Nevertheless, I feel a responsibility for the priests and their happiness in their work.[59]

Maintenance of the dignity of each individual, manifest through compassion for them, was paramount to Vincent McCauley.

Leader of the Diocese

As bishop of Fort Portal, Vincent McCauley had responsibility toward all institutions, religious and priests, and laity, but as a Holy Cross priest his relationship with the congregation and its members was of great significance. From the very outset of his episcopal tenure he made it clear that religious life in Holy Cross was an integral part of his responsibility as bishop: "Be assured that I will do my best to maintain and stimulate the Religious Life among our missionaries." McCauley received complete support in his role from the superior general:

> I am very grateful to God for the splendid work you are doing for the good of the diocese. I know that you are totally and unreservedly committed and dedicated to the establishment of the Church in every corner of the territory entrusted to you. At the same time, however, I cannot

but encourage you to take care of your health for the benefit of the diocese and of our men working with you.[60]

McCauley demonstrated confidence in the Holy Cross religious with whom he served and made every effort to assist them. Francis Zagorc, C.S.C., was appointed treasurer of the diocese in December 1961; in 1966 he was appointed chancellor. He realized that virtually all his Holy Cross priests were young and inexperienced and, thus, he invited his former Bengal colleagues, John Harrington and Edward Massaert, to join the Uganda mission.[61] As more missionaries arrived, the bishop made arrangements to construct a community residence for rest and relaxation. In 1962, a house with a picturesque view of Lake Saka was opened.[62]

Regardless of his significant episcopal responsibilities, all agree that Vincent McCauley was the consummate community man. His close friend and long-time colleague, John Croston, C.S.C., once wrote:

> He may have served as Bishop of Fort Portal or Secretary General of AMECEA, in apostolates outside the community, but no matter what position he held, he always stressed he was first and foremost a Holy Cross Religious. Holy Cross was his "family" and not merely in a nominal sense.[63]

There was no one who wanted to be present with Holy Cross religious more than Bishop McCauley. When he was in Fort Portal he almost always came to the community residence at Saka on Sunday afternoons to recreate with the parish ministers who regularly went there for rest and relaxation after Sunday Masses were completed. While there, he never came across as an authoritarian, but rather played bridge (his favorite card game) and enjoyed a beer or a drink. Still, he was cautious not to use his association with Holy Cross to play favorites and possibly alienate White Fathers or African priests. At times strained relationships were present between McCauley and individual Holy Cross religious, but he never held a grudge. For McCauley, religious could disagree but still be brothers.[64]

Bishop McCauley's love for Holy Cross could not prevent conflict in the local community that arose in the latter part of the 1960s. Members of the congregation were pitted against each other and the bishop in a struggle that simmered below the surface but was clear and felt by the missionaries. The conflict arose over how various religious understood the congregation's role in the Diocese of Fort Portal. Some perceived that McCauley intentionally subjugated Holy Cross religious to other clergy in the diocese. This was most visible in the assignment of parish priests as more and more African priests were selected for these positions over members of Holy Cross. Certain members did not feel McCauley was moving swiftly enough in implementing the changes of Vatican II. These voices were pitted against those who believed the bishop's policies and actions were proper for the congregation and the Diocese of Fort Portal. Additionally, a split was present over the understanding of poverty, with some feeling rising personal autonomy and economic prosperity were highly detrimental to the community and its mission.[65]

Extensive interviews with Holy Cross religious in Uganda at the time suggest that the split was the result of different ecclesiologies of men theologically trained before and after Vatican II. Those educated prior to Vatican II were basically content with McCauley's policies and his progress in implementing the teachings of the Council. Those trained after the Council seemed less at ease with what they experienced. The result was less unity in the congregation's ministerial effort. One missionary explained, "We weren't pulling together. We weren't thinking of how we could be there as Holy Cross and to serve the Church in Fort Portal. I felt we were drifting from what was our real purpose."[66]

The rift in the community was manifest in a few important ways. Negative attitudes toward McCauley were present. Some of his opponents labeled him as "inept," using "any argument *ad hominem* to prove their point."[67] A sense of apathy and a feeling of failure were additional expressions of this split. In November 1968, a community meeting was held at Saka to discuss: (1) the aim and mission of the congregation's apostolate in Uganda, (2) what Holy Cross might do better to fulfill its mission, and (3) the place of mission in the congregation's new (1968) constitutions. The meeting minutes reveal a sense of hopelessness. With respect to accomplishments, the participants stated, "There has been limited success." Speaking of the community's mission, religious stated, "Many felt we [we]re engaged in little more than a holding operation (perpetuating the system found), not really effecting [*sic*] the people by making religion something vital."[68]

The tension within Holy Cross in the late 1960s passed, but not without a few battle scars worn by religious. McCauley was hurt by the split, especially his perception that some of his own religious had turned against him. Several years later, some religious left East Africa to pursue other ministries, dissatisfied with the direction the apostolate had taken.[69]

Religious women were an essential component in the Uganda mission that Holy Cross initiated. The Daughters of St. Theresa of the Child Jesus, the Banyatereza Sisters, were an indigenous group that due to their size, local roots, and influence were very helpful to McCauley. The community, whose motto from their patron was "To love God and make Him loved," was founded in 1937 by Francois Lacoursiere, W.F., then vicar apostolic of the Rwenzori Vicariate. The sisters had achieved diocesan approval in July 1956 and an approved constitution in September 1957.[70]

The association of Bishop McCauley with the Banyatereza Sisters was marked by a sense of deep mutual love and respect.

The community's presence in the diocese was a significant boon to the bishop's strong support for the local church and his promotion of Africanization. The bishop appreciated the sisters' zeal and devotion to ministry, which would be the perfect vehicle to work with the clergy to spread the faith, especially in the outstation villages. Therefore, he worked closely with its membership, becoming in many ways a second founder to the order. He was very appreciative of the group's apostolic zeal, "making service of the people a practical manifestation of their service of God."[71]

Knowing that these religious women could play an integral role, McCauley guided the community to reach new heights by expanding its ministerial options. McCauley's successor in Fort Portal, Bishop Serapio Magambo, has commented:

> The Congregation of the Daughters of Saint Theresa of the Child Jesus (Banyatereza), though not started by him, was so dear to him that he left no stone unturned in search of ways and means of developing it both academically and spiritually.[72]

He encouraged the sisters to expand their horizons, moving beyond the domestic work, which had been their basic ministry, to embrace catechetical positions in parishes. To assist this evolution, McCauley encouraged and financially sponsored some members to complete degrees in higher education, often at Kampala's Makerere University.[73] Additionally, he brought Holy Cross sisters to Fort Portal for the express purpose to educate the Banyatereza at St. Maria Goretti Senior Secondary School.

The bishop's call for the Banyatereza to take positions in local parishes was a unique and bold move for the time. The dearth of clergy in the diocese necessitated innovative solutions and, thus, McCauley called upon the sisters. He once commented, "These are the ones upon whom I am depending to deepen the faith of the people in my diocese."[74] McCauley's program for the sisters was extensive. In three parishes, Muhorro, Kiryandongo, and Katoosa, the sisters were responsible for: (1) preaching the gospel, including presiding at a Sunday communion service and religious education for catechumens and children; (2) sacraments, including distributing communion at Mass and taking viaticum to the dying when no priests were available, preparing all for the sacraments of baptism, first communion, confirmation, and marriage, baptizing in emergency situations, and assisting couples with troubled marriages; and (3) animating the Christian community, including visiting homes, assisting lay associations, going on safari to outstations, and meeting with catechists.[75]

McCauley's "experiment" with the Banyatereza Sisters was well received by local people and missionaries. Henri Valette, W.F., who worked closely with McCauley and Holy Cross religious for many years, wrote:

> The experiments of Muhorro, Kiryandongo, and Katoosa are a sign of the vitality of the Church, which tries new solutions to new problems. . . . The Sisters' contribution could be the running of smaller units with all the independence and competence required, while the priests would be in charge of the spiritual help and giving the sacraments.[76]

McCauley was also instrumental in a canonical reorganization of the Banyatereza order. In general, he encouraged the order to exercise greater self-governance. In this light, he helped the sisters set up structures within the community, including the separation of the novitiate community from the motherhouse. Working with Edward Heston, C.S.C., in Rome, McCauley directed the sisters' efforts to rewrite their constitutions in light of the Second Vatican Council.[77]

The Banyatereza Sisters were highly significant, but only one of a few orders of religious women who served the Diocese of Fort Portal. The White Sisters had assisted their brother religious in the diocese for many years, serving as educators in schools and as nurses at Holy Family Hospital near the cathedral. In 1963, McCauley welcomed into the diocese the Ladies of Mary, who were assigned to the Kinyamasika Teachers Training College.[78]

It was the loss of significant numbers of White Sisters and the community's inability to continue its ministry at Holy Family Hospital (renamed Virika Hospital in 1968) that forced McCauley to search for replacements for this vital diocesan function.[79] As early as 1958, McCauley had initiated correspondence with Mother Benedict, superior general of the Medical Mission Sisters, asking her to consider Uganda for her community's future plans. Dr. Anna Dengel had founded this religious order in 1925 at Philadelphia. Its stated objective was "to bring the benefits of modern medicine to the medically less-developed areas of the world. The Sisters are to manifest Christ's charity by the example of their lives and work among the sick and poor."[80]

McCauley's initial contact with the community bore fruit in 1962. In March, Mother Benedict visited Fort Portal to formally investigate her community's possible assumption of the hospital ministry. Impressed with her experience, an agreement was reached and the first Medical Mission Sisters arrived in September 1962. On January 1, 1963, they officially took responsibility for Holy Family Hospital. Additionally, when sufficient personnel arrived, the sisters' mission expanded to include medical safaris on a weekly basis to Bukonjo, Bwamba, and Bugombwa.[81]

The Medical Mission Sisters' apostolate took a giant leap forward beginning in 1964 with their introduction of a nurses training program. The bishop was elated with this news: "As there is not one training center for nurses in the whole of Western Uganda, this surely will be a most welcome and important work in the future health and growth of the country."[82] Supportive of the project from the outset, McCauley worked diligently with architects and contractors on the construction of the nurses' training center. He immediately made contact with possible donors, most especially Misereor, the German episcopal body known to assist mission foundations.[83] The bishop informed Misereor officials, "The project can be started within one month of the date on which we receive your final approval. I have an experienced builder ready and waiting."[84]

McCauley's enthusiasm and strong support for the project could not obviate the many problems that plagued the center's construction. Due to funding difficulties, design inconsistencies between architects and contractors, and slow communications, the project was not formally approved by all sides until August 1965, with a contract signed in November. Under the direction of Hughes and Bilkinghorne, architects, and Associated Builders and Technicians, contractors, the project formally started in December; the building was blessed by McCauley and opened on September 13, 1966. Classes began the next month.[85]

The essential role of religious in the life of the Diocese of Fort Portal was complemented by an active lay apostolate that Vincent McCauley strongly supported. He differentiated roles in the Church while affirming the importance of all peoples:

> We priests by our selection and ordination have the privilege and the duty of being dedicated servants, especially commissioned to *praedicare, sacrificare, baptizare, et regere* in the Church; as the Ordination Ceremony puts it. But others also have their part to play. These are important parts, they are indeed essential parts. Without them the Church and the Body of Christ will not function properly.[86]

In the spirit of Vatican II, McCauley believed that the laity must be involved as much as possible and have a voice in the operations of the Church. Therefore, he made every effort to uplift their spirits and empower them to take responsibility for the apostolate.[87] In supportive of this effort, McCauley sponsored several lay men and women in advanced education. Also, he recognized the efforts of the laity through the awarding of the *Pro Ecclesia* medal.[88]

All did not share McCauley's strident support for the lay apostolate. While completely supportive of Vatican II's call for greater lay participation, differences of opinion were present on adequate qualifications for personnel. Some missionaries believed in general that Africans were not good leaders; they preferred to be followers. As one man put it, "They [the laity] rarely took things into their own hands." It was acknowledged that many fine catechists had carried the faith to the remote villages for generations, but some saw this as the exception, not the norm.[89]

The most visible manifestations of the lay apostolate in Fort Portal were the rise and efficacy of various lay organizations, both diocesan sponsored and more generally under the rubric of "Catholic Action." Two diocesan bodies were formed. On March 3, 1966, the Diocesan Council of the Lay Apostolate was founded. This group was originally formed as the Catholic Council by Bishop Ogez in the 1950s, but later disbanded. The body, headed by a central staff of three (parish) priests and three laymen, oversaw the work of ten committees.[90] The council functioned primarily as the vehicle to organize local parish councils, thereby giving the laity more voice. Additionally, the council raised money for reconstruction of the cathedral after the 1966 earthquake, aided parishes with local celebrations, and fostered associations for women and girls in the parishes.[91] The Diocesan Pastoral Commission was another significant lay apostolate in Fort Portal. With the bishop, priests, religious, and laity as members, the commission's stated purpose was "to advise the Bishop and the Central Administration on pastoral needs and to suggest ways and means of meeting these particular needs."[92]

Catholic Action, manifest in groups formed earlier in the twentieth century[93] was the other main branch of the lay apostolate. McCauley assigned Henri Valette, W.F., to supervise Catholic Action in the diocese.[94] Several groups were present, but the most active were the Catholic Council, Young Christian Students, Young Christian Workers, and a series of eighteen local women's clubs. McCauley admitted that the lay apostolate was progressing slower than he anticipated, but nonetheless reported positively, "We note with interest the full cooperation of many priests and an elite of parishioners who are unanimous in their decision to work for the recognition of the Church in Ugandan society."[95] McCauley realized that the lay apostolate was very important, for increasingly, the Church was in a fight to keep the laity in the fold. He once wrote:

> When the population had no other interest that [sic–than] their village life, the Church was welcome as one of the most interesting factors in their progress. Nowadays, when the influence of the outside world is reaching the remotest hill of the country, it seems that theinfluence [sic] of the Church is on the decline. Material progress is replacing God in many aspects of the life of our people.[96]

As his promotion of the Banyatereza Sisters illustrates, Bishop McCauley held great respect for women, which included the laity. He saw "women as an effective power in the Church." He encouraged them to serve in the Church. Despite Ugandan tribal customs and church norms, he challenged women to assume roles considered progressive for the day, such as eucharistic ministers, lay catechists, and general leadership. He often met with women's groups to demonstrate his solidarity with their desire to advance and make a full contribution to church and society, based on their talent, not their sex.[97]

McCauley made great strides in his work with religious and the laity, but his greatest contribution came in the area of ecumenism. The historical antipathy present in Uganda between Anglicans and Catholics, with the added dimension of the Muslim presence, made ecumenism (and interfaith dialogue) of utmost importance in the progress of church and society. Old ideas of division between peoples of faith were passed from one generation to the next; people were taught to dislike each other. Historian Adrian Hastings accurately describes the religious environment in Uganda in 1960:

> In many places Catholics and Protestants have been taught to see each other as open enemies and far more than in most European countries they present two rival groupings struggling for every position of power and influence.

Ecumenism, the natural antidote to such a situation, had taken no root in Africa. Again Hastings comments:

> The ecumenical spirit has developed far more in Europe and North America, in fact in large parts of Africa it has made almost no impact at all within the Roman communion and even forward-looking priests can still set it aside as "inopportune."[98]

Many Holy Cross religious have verified the almost palpable tension in the religious separation. One missionary commented, "The reality of the separation was clear."[99]

The pervading hostility toward ecumenism, however, began to diminish as a new breeze of Christian unity began to blow during the Second Vatican Council. In Uganda, three factors converged to assist the ecumenical process. First, Pope John XXIII presented an inviting presence to all people. He was someone who was well respected, especially in calling Vatican II with its *aggiornamento* theme. Second, the attempt by the government to take over management of denominational schools prompted an alliance between Anglicans and Catholics to resist this move. Third, the two hierarchies started to communicate and became friendly.[100] Historian Adrian Hastings synthesizes the transformation: "Today . . . Africa may be said to stand on the verge of great ecumenical developments."[101]

Vatican II was the watershed event that broke the dam and allowed the waters of ecumenism to flow. Indeed, Hastings comments, "Into the world of ecumenical thinking Catholics have now to enter. The Decree on Ecumenism published in the third session of the Vatican Council (1964) leaves them no alternative." Ecumenism meant much more than merely cooperating with non-Catholics in the social and civil sphere and replacing latent hostility with friendliness. It meant to work "for the complete ecclesiastical unity of eucharistic communion."[102] On practical levels this could be manifest through biblical and theological discussion.

Vincent McCauley was very positive on the Vatican II's document on ecumenism, especially as it corrected many misconceptions. He wrote to the faithful in Fort Portal, challenging them to make ecumenism part of their everyday faith:

> Many are not yet familiar with the principles of ecumenism. Others have confused ideas about it. Prejudice and ignorance have stifled the spirit of Ecumenism in the minds and hearts of many Catholics. Historical divisions, political rivalries, imported European dissensions have prevented the full understanding of the Gospel message of Jesus Christ and the teaching of His Church. It is for this purpose of rectifying the prevalent erroneous attitude that the Church now issues her extremely important, practical and timely document on Ecumenism. I commend it to everyone, not only as a matter for study, but much more for practical application in your daily efforts to bring all

into union with our Lord in His Holy, Catholic, [and] Apostolic Church.[103]

He further told his flock to "always show respect and consideration" for non-Catholics. He concluded, "Although they may not understand the value and the beauty of the Catholic Faith, one must show towards them a Christlike [*sic*] charity at all times."[104]

McCauley further expressed his views on the nature of ecumenism and how it might be manifest. He agreed that a better environment was present; hostility between denominations was on the decline. He believed there was no one definition of ecumenism and, therefore, the Church should not bind itself to a detailed program that might be outdated or ineffective. However, the bishop clearly voiced his view on what ecumenism demanded of the churches:

> Ecumenism is not merely high-level theological dialogue where fruits gradually filter down to the grass roots. Ecumenism is more than the replacement of prejudice and suspicion among Christians by a mutual understanding and esteem. Rather, the continuing missive of the Gospel insists that Ecumenism mean for us unity through renewal. The total message of the Gospel to say nothing of the specific words of Our Lord, demand that we assume the obligation to draw all Christians together in a re-vitalized spiritual life within the churches.[105]

On a more pragmatic level, McCauley had several general ideas to build a more ecumenical religious environment. Realizing that theological agreement was a future hope, he encouraged joint participation in areas of charity, publicity, social work, medicine, and economics. He reported to the superior general, "It is here we are striving to often work hand in hand with our non-Catholic friends. It is not an easy task, but already the atmosphere has been cleared . . . and the spirit of dual co-operation grows month by month."[106] The bishop believed compromise was necessary and that solutions to disagreements must be supra-denominational and supra-national. The attitude and the charity of Christ must prevail.[107]

McCauley moved from generic ideas to specific tasks, events, and programs. He realized that the Church in Uganda was only a beginner in the field of ecumenism, and thus had no "highly developed program." Still, specific efforts were manifest. The bishop encouraged the efforts of George MacInnes, C.S.C., who led the team that translated the New Testament into Rutoro for the use of all Christian churches. One missionary commented, "The new translation of the Bible into Rutoro was a major ecumenical step; it was a great gift to the Church of Toro."[108] McCauley fostered ecumenical prayer services. In December 1970, he invited Erica Sabiiti, Episcopal archbishop of Uganda, to help him plan an ecumenical prayer service slated for the following January, to be celebrated at the Virika Cathedral. Later in December 1971, McCauley preached at the opening of an interdenominational chapel at Kyanjaki, calling it a "great occasion."[109] In a letter to an academic at Makerere University in Kampala, McCauley wrote:

> May we hope that the continuation of the dialogue will bring greater understanding among the Christians in Uganda and be a means of implementing our Lord's prayer to the Father: "That all may be one as Thou, Father, in me, and I in Thee."[110]

While McCauley's efforts were many and noteworthy, they must be understood in the context of his day and the resistance he faced. One major problem was the lack of enthusiasm and support from the African clergy. Generally speaking, they were not interested in dialogue with non-Catholics. Additionally, several missionaries have commented that ecumenism was making some inroads on the top level, but local grass roots efforts bore little fruit. The relevance of dialogue with non-Catholics could not be appreciated by ordinary Catholics, who were pressed on many fronts with issues that touched their daily lives.[111]

McCauley's ecumenical efforts were noted by many. He was described, along with Archbishop Joseph Kiwanuka (Kampala) and Anglican Archbishop Leslie Brown (Uganda, Rwanda, Burundi, and Boga-Zaire), as "one of the fathers of ecumenism in the region." Most believe he was more ecumenically minded than his fellow Catholic bishops, possibly due to his personality and the "baggage" that others brought from the past. Some believed he was moving too fast in his suggestion "to mix with others."[112]

Unquestionably Bishop McCauley's greatest contribution to ecumenism was his faithful participation in the Uganda Joint Christian Council (UJCC).[113] During the period of independence, power struggles were common. The churches were not excluded from this situation. Thus, leaders of the Church of Uganda and the Roman Catholic Church were anxious to calm the situation. On several occasions, Archbishops Joseph Kiwanuka and Leslie Brown (Anglican) conferred on matters of common interest, seeking to extricate the churches from the political frenzy and rhetoric. Other bishops and clergymen did likewise. In this spirit, Anglican Bishop Lucien Usher-Wilson of Mbale, under the direction of the Church of Uganda, invited Kiwanuka to send a representative of the Catholic hierarchy to formulate a program of cooperation between the churches that would include all the bishops of Uganda. McCauley was Kiwanuka's choice. On August 30, 1963, he was joined by Victor Ravensdale, education secretary of the Church of Uganda schools, and Father Stanley Lea of the Uganda Catholic Secretariat as conveners of a conference at Mbale. The meeting, chaired by Usher-Wilson, produced a report and a draft constitution for the proposed Uganda Joint Christian Council. The report was transmitted to Kiwanuka and Brown who, after consultation with their bishops, approved the foundation.[114]

Under the guidance of Vincent McCauley, who was elected chair, the UJCC organized itself. Membership consisted of all Catholic and Anglican bishops, plus an elected clergyman and layperson from each diocese. The nascent body agreed to meet three times annually, approximately in March, July, and November. A committee structure was established over time to broaden the reach of the UJCC and its possible efficacy.[115]

The aims and basic creed of the UJCC were found in its constitutions. The body sought "to provide means of joint consultation on matters of common interest based on Christian principles, and to make recommendations for action to member churches."[116] The constitution continued:

> Whatever may be our differences, we are claiming to be followers of One Lord. It is a common experience among Christians of different churches that when they start by cooperating together in practical ways, they soon find themselves making friends, appreciating one another's ways of following Christ, and wanting to ask other deeper questions about their disunity.[117]

In a practical dimension, the creed was "to demonstrate that Christian charity [could] be operative and practiced among Christians of Uganda."[118]

The initial results of the UJCC were favorable. The council started slowly but began to have an effect through its committee system and periodic joint meetings, developing some common programs and creating an atmosphere of trust to replace the past persistent animosity. The future ecumenical picture for Uganda appeared bright.[119]

Bishop McCauley contributed significantly to the UJCC over a long period of time. He was the organizing chairman of the group and served as its leader until 1968, providing the guidance and direction necessary for the nascent body to become rooted and to grow. He reported to the superior general concerning the UJCC:

> Our local ecumenical effort shows steady progress. The Uganda Joint Christian Council was set up only last August but there are many indications that it has already united Catholics and Protestants in common projects to the benefit of all.[120]

The UJCC met challenges from the government in a bold manner. The forced expulsion of missionaries from Uganda during the administration of Milton Obote forced McCauley and the UJCC to respond. They denounced the government's actions in a strongly worded statement:

> The Uganda Joint Christian Council . . . regrets the unprecedented action by which ten Catholic priests were forced to relinquish their ministry among the People of God in Uganda and to leave the country. . . . The Christians of Uganda . . . look upon the mass expulsion as an act seriously injuring religion. While regretting this unfortunate and unhappy incident, we call upon our Government and trust that they will give assurances by word and deed that the exercise of Religious Freedom, guaranteed by the Constitution of Uganda shall be maintained.[121]

At the suggestion of McCauley and the UJCC, Idi Amin, upon usurping power in 1971, set up a channel of communication between the government and organized religion through the Religious Affairs Desk in the Office of the President.[122]

The UJCC was also instrumental in the promotion of dialogue on sacramental and social issues. Discussions led to the adoption of a common baptism formula in the vernacular for Anglicans and Catholics. Excitedly, McCauley wrote:

> This is a significant step in the direction of closer unity, which derives from the prayerful cooperation of the churches and of a common study in the depth of the essentials of Christianity.[123]

The issue of monogamous marriages, a significant problem in African society, was also a major topic for discussion and debate. On the social front, the UJCC addressed alcoholism and the refugee problem, among others.[124]

McCauley was very pleased with the progress of the UJCC and the ecumenical drive. He sensed a greater drive in organized religion to responsibly seek unity. The barriers of separation had been breached; now it was time to continue toward further progress. He wrote:

> Let me say that I am encouraged by the spirit of cooperation shown so far by the members of the sub-committees and I hope that this spirit not only continues and grows, but that it extend more widely and more deeply into the minds and hearts of our laity.[125]

Health Issues

The many efforts McCauley made in ecumenism and his pastoral ministries in general were conducted while constantly battling personal health issues. Health concerns in Bengal once forced him to change ministry locations and apostolates, and eventually drove him from that region in 1944. McCauley battled with facial skin cancer as a result of his Bengal experience for the rest of his life. His condition was never life threatening, but required constant vigilance and numerous surgeries. These were generally done at the Mayo Clinic, beginning while he was rector of the Foreign Mission Seminary. He dealt with his condition bravely and never spoke about his health, save in a joking manner. His numerous facial surgeries (as many as fifty) disfigured him, but he used the situation to call himself "scarface." He never allowed his pain and suffering to dampen his love and zeal for ministry and people. He gained great respect from all when they observed how he handled the situation. When eulogizing McCauley, Father Theodore Hesburgh, C.S.C., stated:

> Vince McCauley was afflicted with very real painful illnesses all his priestly life, but neither did he worry about being sick nor did he allow these painful afflictions to interfere with his zeal, his concern for others less afflicted than himself, his deep sense of priestly service to the kingdom and all God's people. Not only did his spirit transcend his bodily ills, he did it with a comical sense of serenity and equilibrium.[126]

Summary

The Second Vatican Council's significant emphasis on the pastoral nature of the Church was a strong influence on Bishop Vincent McCauley. While he labored to set up administrative structures and place the new Diocese of Fort Portal on firm financial ground, he was equally concerned with the everyday pastoral aspects of his ministry as shepherd of his people. In the mid-1960s, this was manifest most strongly in his strong advocacy for refugees who began to pour into the Toro region from Rwanda, the Congo, and the Sudan. McCauley seized the moment to bring the face of God, through material and spiritual assistance, to thousands of refugees who had been abandoned by their own countries. He was also a man who worked diligently and closely with his fellow priests in an effort to bring together a group of clerics who were diverse in age, culture, nationality, and race. The constant and long-standing disagreements between tribes were another source of tension that McCauley was forced to endure. But as with others, he masterfully brought peoples together in a common effort. Additionally, he fostered the advance of orders of religious women and promoted their movement into new areas of ministry. Most especially, Bishop McCauley was instrumental in the promotion of the laity and ecumenism, the latter within a rather hostile environment created over decades of animosity between various peoples of faith. All of this was accomplished despite his personal suffering, a condition that never slowed his spirit nor his achievements for others. One of his greatest accomplishments was in the area of education.

CHAPTER 7

An Educator in the Faith: 1961–1973

The educational component that was integral to the work of those pioneer missionaries to East Africa, and many other lands, was part and parcel of the apostolic philosophy of the Congregation of Holy Cross. The Brothers of St. Joseph, a teaching order of French lay religious, were united with auxiliary priests of the Diocese of LeMans, France, to form the Congregation of Holy Cross on March 1, 1837. Educational institutions have, throughout the history of the congregation, been an indispensable element on all levels. In the United States and mission territories, Holy Cross religious have migrated to the academic apostolate in great numbers. Education, both formal and informal, has thus been a strong tradition. The present constitutions of the Congregation of Holy Cross refer to the community as "educators in the faith."

This strong tradition and his previous experience in Bengal provided the catalyst for Vincent McCauley to champion the cause of education in East Africa. The period brought many successes, but also one of the most significant conflicts of his time in Fort Portal. Vincent McCauley parlayed his organizational expertise and his "Midas Touch" for financial development into creating a highly developed, educationally sound, and well-respected series of schools, both on the secondary and graduate seminary levels.

Educational Ideas in Fort Portal

Education was always central to the mission of Catholic evangelization, especially in Africa. Schools were a significant attraction to the indigenous peoples as they could easily see the value in education for advancement in society. Additionally, religious education was imperative for the promotion of indigenous vocations. In Uganda, the White Fathers' school system (along with that of the Church of Uganda) was extensive and used by the British colonial government as its vehicle for state education. Speaking of the educational system of the European missionaries, the first African cardinal, Laurean Rugambwa, of Tanzania, stated, "What the missionaries have done for the material progress of the African can only be surpassed in importance by what they have done for his soul."[1]

Vincent McCauley was a great promoter of education, as his days both in Bengal and Washington, D.C., demonstrated. His theory of mission education, patterned after that of Theodore Hesburgh, C.S.C., president of the University of Notre Dame, was rather simple, yet profound: "Don't bring the man to education; bring education to the man."[2] Thus, for him the construction of parish schools and appropriate educational facilities was critical for the mission effort. Additionally, sufficient and proper training of educators was necessary. In short, as his colleague Bishop Joseph Mukwaya stated, "He promoted it [education] and showed people how to use it."[3]

Knowing the value of education, and realizing that he would never have sufficient priest teachers, McCauley strongly advanced the idea of catechist training. Noting a clergy/laity ratio of 1 to 5,000, McCauley told his priests that his top educational priority was catechist training and their proper and efficacious utilization. He wrote:

> Our educational problem over here is more a question of trying to find a place for all our youth who want to improve intellectually. From a religious standpoint one must educate more intensely our catechists, and lay leaders, for we must depend more on them in promoting the Church, and its moral ideals, etc.[4]

Richard Potthast, C.S.C., who worked for many years in Butiiti parish, echoed the bishop's ideas on the critical role of catechists: "Catechists do everything except baptizing and witnessing marriages. In fact they are the 'priest' of their region. They are the heart and soul of the Church."[5]

McCauley linked his ideas of education with promotion of the local church. He actively supported the idea that catechists were the ticket to unifying a local community. He wrote:

> We are trying to build up a sense of community in the villages that will promote responsibility among the people for their own Church. . . . We are convinced however that unless our African catholics [sic] take charge of their own welfare in religious matters as well as others, the efforts of the foreign missionaries will be ineffective.[6]

Integral to the development of a cadre of catechists was the need for local communities to take the responsibility both to recruit and financially support parishioners for this ministry. He challenged his flock in a pastoral letter:

> My dear Christians, all of us need catechists and good catechists. We need more; and we need those who are already catechists to continue working as catechists. We do not

want them to leave nor do we want new candidates to
shy away from being catechists. The main reason for this
seems to be our catechists are not appreciated sufficiently,
and are not given a sufficient gift. Let us all work together
to help and do what we can to support our catechists.[7]

He understood the difficulty that local parishes (actually the
Church in general), experienced in adequately compensating
catechists. Thus, he sought some assistance from the Holy
Cross mission procurator in Washington. Noting the problem
of raising money, he concluded, "In the long run we should
be better off and have better coverage, even with slightly
increased costs."[8]

The important role of catechists was also evident in the
extensive training program that McCauley developed for
them. Three catechist training centers operated. A one-month
refresher program for present catechists had been open for
some time. McCauley added two new facilities, a six-month
program at Mugalike for candidates with better educational
backgrounds (operated jointly with the Diocese of Hoima)
and a two-year program at Ibanda (Archdiocese of Mbarara)
for a select few who had completed secondary education.[9]

As with many aspects of the mission, McCauley's most significant problem with catechist training was its cost. In June
1967, when local and Holy Cross funds were inadequate, he
turned to Propaganda Fide to establish the aforementioned
training facilities. McCauley was grateful for a $20,000 sub-
sidy and explained, "We will never catch up in a generation
with the number of priests that are required and so the need
to employ more and more religious and local people is [the]
only answer."[10]

Educational Institutions in Fort Portal

St. Augustine's Teacher Training College (TTC) was the first educational institution that Holy Cross religious supported. McCauley taught there immediately after his arrival in 1958. In September 1959, three Holy Cross brothers, John Harrington, Christian Stinnett, and Cyrinus Martin, arrived to teach at the school. While Martin returned to the United States almost immediately, Brother John Stundon, C.S.C., replaced him. Additional brothers, including James Gulnac, C.S.C., and Walter Foley, C.S.C., were added in the next few years. The school served the people of Butiiti Parish and the local environs, preparing them to take positions as elementary-level school teachers. John Harrington, C.S.C., commented on the student population: "I was always impressed myself with the desire to learn on the part of the Africans, simply because they saw [education] as a means to an end. And there was no lacking of their wanting to learn."[11]

The mission at St. Augustine TTC was noted for harmonious relations between the priests and brothers of Holy Cross who worked there. McCauley supported the idea of a brother as headmaster of the school, an idea that Bishop Ogez rejected at the outset. Recalling an April 1963 visit to Uganda, the brother's provincial, John Donoghue, C.S.C., described "the much better spirit I found between the Fathers and Brothers."[12] Possibly due to its rather isolated location in the far eastern portion of the diocese, St. Augustine was able to avoid many intra–Holy Cross battles that would arise later in schools closer to Fort Portal.

St. Leo Senior Secondary School in Fort Portal was a second significant educational mission tackled by Holy Cross. Founded in 1921 by the White Fathers as an elementary school, St. Leo was elevated to a middle school in 1926 and became a full-fledged junior secondary school by 1936.[13] In

1938, the White Fathers ceded control of the school to the Brothers of Christian Instruction from Canada. In July and October 1961, Holy Cross brothers came to Fort Portal specifically to work at St. Leo's. On January 1, 1962, Holy Cross took responsibility for the institution, which served some 250 boys from across the country.[14]

In June 1963, St. Leo's became the scene of the first of several problematic situations that Holy Cross encountered in its educational mission. As a consequence of the still-emerging independence movement, both in Uganda and more generally in Africa, and closely allied with the desire for Africanization, many secondary schools experienced student strikes in the early 1960s. On June 3, students at St. Leo's refused to attend class. By June 7 the school was ordered closed. Learning about the situation while on one of his many United States "begging tours," McCauley rushed back to Fort Portal, arriving on June 13. Immediately he met school administrators to assess the situation and find a solution. He gave his full support to the brothers, who understood the strike action to be directed toward them. Realizing the resentment was against expatriates in general, McCauley discussed with the headmaster, Brother Lewis James, C.S.C., the possibility of obtaining Africans as a chaplain and lay teachers. James agreed if qualified personnel were available. McCauley informed the superior general on June 17, "The condition is still not settled at the school."[15]

McCauley sought answers concerning the strike's causes. He sensed a strong anti-American sentiment, led by communists, behind the strike. He wrote to the superior general:

> The disturbance follows a pattern very well known wherever the Communists operate. We should not be surprised they attack us; in fact, in a way, it is a compliment they aim first at us. We hear much anti-American talk here in the country and I would not have you believe that this incident is directed entirely against the Brothers or that

they are to blame in any way. It is a program to disorga-
nize the Church in Uganda and is aimed at the Americans
now.[16]

In a letter to the provincial, Howard Kenna, C.S.C., McCauley elaborated on the anti-Catholic aspect of the protest, foreseeing "a long campaign of antagonism by the avowed enemies
of the Church":

> We knew there were many in the country who were
> against our Catholic missions. However, I did not know
> they were quite so strong or so well organized. Frankly I
> am surprised at the rapidity with which they have swept
> the country with their anti-Catholic propaganda. The
> resulting riots in schools and the opposition to our Catho-
> lic school system is [sic] but one phase. We will have to
> watch very closely and work together to offset this well
> planned anti-Catholic program.

He went on to lament this situation in light of recent progress
with Holy Cross "just beginning to reach the peak of efficacy."[17] After punishments were given to student strike leaders,
classes resumed on July 1.

In a case of *déjà vu*, another student strike occurred during
July 6–8, 1965. Whereas the "Chronicles of St. Leo's" refers
to the incident as "a relatively minor disturbance," McCauley
told the brothers' provincial, John Donoghue, C.S.C.: "It
was a serious affair. Our Brothers were threatened. The police
had to be called."[18] While peace was restored in a few days,
the Uganda Ministry of Education set up a "commission of
inquiry" to review the events, ascertain causes, and recommend solutions.[19] The Commission had found, two years earlier, that the strike was generated by outsiders, but with more
force. Threats of physical violence against brothers made many
question their mission vocation.[20] Donoghue reported that the
brothers were "disgusted," concluding, "Our mission at St. Leo

is pretty far gone."[21] He told McCauley that the essence of the problem was the classroom. He suggested, "I would be most happy to have all our Brothers go out to 'bush' schools and live in great poverty and want *if* [emphasis Donoghue] they could have some feeling of success."[22]

McCauley again backed the brothers, but he also hinted that their training for apostolic work in Africa did not adequately prepare them for the cultural divide they experienced. He wrote:

> In my opinion the Brothers have not failed. They have, indeed, been confronted with a difficult mission beginning. It will take courage, cooperation, adaptation and a strong community spirit to overcome the initial handicaps. I have full confidence in them to do so. We are doing all we can to help them, and will continue to do so, as they are our Brothers. They know that their problem is also our problem.[23]

The superior general echoed McCauley's call for better training for missionaries:

> I insist that our men get the best possible preparation before they are sent to the missions. This period of training should not end with their departure from America but last until they have somewhat taken root in the country to which they are sent. . . . I feel that, eventually, we will simply have to face the necessity of giving our men one solid year of training before they leave their land and another solid year of formation in the country to which they are sent, after their arrival there. Such intensive training, I feel, is a must for our missionaries, priests and brothers.[24]

In a sense of resignation, Donoghue admitted that the "report card" on the brothers in Uganda "is horrible" and the desire for their departure was strong.[25]

Donoghue's disappointment led him to consider a withdrawal of the brothers from Uganda, prompting McCauley to respond. He told the provincial that he often felt rejected and not wanted, but since no qualified African was ready to take the episcopal reins, he would continue to serve. He wrote Donoghue, "Take no drastic action until we have a chance to talk it over." McCauley offered to come to the United States, if necessary, to speak with him. He concluded:

> It remains my firm conviction, however, that our Brothers can weather this storm and the problems of the future. Given the right men, the right motivation, the convictions of Religious, and missionary ideals (including a willingness to adapt to mission conditions), there is no reason what-so-ever why they should not continue. I lived with Holy Cross Brothers for six years through strikes, famine, riots, and political upheavals in Bengal. I know they can take it.[26]

The superior general seconded McCauley's advice, telling the brothers to stay on the job. He suggested that other events, including the recent independence movement, must be factored into the equation as causes for the strike.[27]

Vincent McCauley's promotion of Catholic education also extended to women, especially religious who served the diocese. Additionally, he was always looking for additional missionaries to join the Uganda missions. He combined these two desires by recruiting Sisters of the Holy Cross to teach at St. Maria Goretti Senior Secondary School at Virika, with special emphasis on advancing the education of the Banyatereza community.[28]

In late 1964, McCauley's drive for women's education was formalized by inviting the Sisters of the Holy Cross to join the Uganda mission. In December it was announced that Sister Mary Olivette, C.S.C., would journey to Uganda "to determine if and when Bishop McCauley's request for sisters should be realistically considered."[29] In April 1965, Sister Olivette spent one week in Uganda investigating the mission possibility. An initial report on the visit suggested McCauley would welcome the sisters, and the field was wide open for apostolic work. Yet, due to tribal warfare and the generally unsettled environment, the report concluded, "The work in Uganda should be undertaken on a technical assistance basis for the Church in Uganda and not with the idea of setting up permanent establishments for Holy Cross."[30]

However, on July 29, 1966, the sisters agreed to accept McCauley's invitation. Initially two veterans of the missions, Sister Catherine de Ricci, C.S.C., and Sister M. Madeline Patrice, C.S.C., were slated to initiate the mission. Sister Olivette joined the initial group.[31] McCauley was elated and commented, "We will have the red carpet ready."[32] On February 13, 1967, the three sisters arrived at Entebbe and were greeted by John Croston, C.S.C., and Sister Marie Pouliot, W.S., superior general of the Banyatereza Sisters. Due to the 1966 earthquake, the sisters' convent was not ready. Thus, they stayed with the Medical Mission Sisters until February 28 when their home was set for occupation. While Sister Olivette stayed only a short time, three additional Holy Cross religious, Miriam Josephine Schuk, John Miriam Leahy, and Mary Louise Wahler, joined the group in July.[33] McCauley continued to express his joy in a report to Mother Olivette:

> Even you would be surprised at the extraordinary spirit
> of cooperation that exists between the Holy Cross Sisters
> and the White Sisters at Maria Goretti. What a blessing
> and what a delight.[34]

The sisters came to teach as part of McCauley's plan for the advancement of the local church. He explained his rationale: "Our main objective is to help the African Sisters raise their standards and become qualified for the needs of the Church here in Uganda."[35] In January 1967, Sister Gaetane Marie, W.S., principal of St. Maria Goretti School, reported twenty-five students in Senior I and thirty-five in Senior II, all of whom were Banyatereza Sisters.[36]

Administration of St. Maria Goretti School was ceded to the Sisters of the Holy Cross on January 1, 1968. Catherine de Ricci, C.S.C., was appointed headmistress. In September additional sisters arrived, both to assist in the school and also to initiate the Holy Cross apostolate of health services, a ministry that had deep roots and many manifestations with the Sisters of the Holy Cross.[37] McCauley was very appreciative of the sisters' ministry, lauding their accomplishments:

> The Holy Cross Sisters in Fort Portal are doing magnificent work. Sister Catherine de Ricci is a tremendous missionary. She and the other sisters have brought up the Maria Goretti School to a high standard in a very short time. We are all pleased and delighted with the work they are doing; not only for our Banyatereza Sisters and the aspirants, but also for the young women of the region.[38]

From the perspective of Bishop McCauley, the most significant Fort Portal educational endeavor was St. Mary's Minor Seminary. Three important and persistent ideas concerning mission came together in this project: (1) his belief in the need for education, (2) support for the local church, and (3) need for indigenous clergy. In February 1959, only three months after the start of the Uganda mission, Bishop Ogez asked McCauley for three Holy Cross brothers to work in St. Michael's Junior Secondary School at Virika.[39] The bishop's plan was to develop the school into a minor seminary. McCauley wrote to the superior general, seeking support for the plan:

> The minor seminary is another position for which we should prepare a C.S.C. priest. It started only this year and is far from being the "seminary" we want. If the

Brothers would take St. Michael's Junior Secondary
School one of our priests could run the seminary, which
is attached to it.[40]

Ogez's request and McCauley's enthusiasm for the project
did not begin to bear fruit until 1964. In January, St. Mary's
Minor Seminary, a senior secondary school that replaced St.
Michael's, was opened, administered by White Fathers, with
four Holy Cross brothers as teachers.[41] McCauley continued
to negotiate with the Holy Cross brothers to take over administration of the seminary, both due to an insufficient number
of White Fathers and his desire for greater Holy Cross influence in the diocese. Additionally, some tensions were present
between the brothers and White Fathers, based primarily on
different educational ideologies. One Holy Cross religious
described his experience: "The White Fathers seem cold and
do not seem to want to make friendships."[42] The bishop's hope
was fulfilled in January 1966, when the brothers took official
responsibility for the seminary.

McCauley's interest and support for St. Mary's were high
and constant throughout his tenure as local ordinary. He was
very interested in the quality of education and made every
effort to improve it. He demonstrated his enthusiasm through
regular visits to the school, playing table tennis and other
games with the seminarians, attending athletic contests and
other school events, and generally showing his support.[43] He
also was the principal fundraiser for the institution, seeking
assistance on many fronts, but especially through the Pontifical Work of St. Peter the Apostle in Rome.[44]

At the outset, the St. Mary's apostolate ran well in all
observable ways. McCauley was very pleased with the participation of the brothers in this effort. He wrote, "The mission
zeal and generosity of the Holy Cross Brothers is making
the development of our Seminary possible."[45] An academic
government inspection gave the seminary very high marks. It

reported, "The Seminary is well staffed, and we felt that the members of [the] staff were devoted and working hard." The teachers' pedagogy was also praised:

> We were impressed by the satisfactory and effective teaching we saw and we noted that this was quite outstanding, compared to an assessment of the average teaching we see day to day in the course of our work.[46]

The positive impressions reported by McCauley and the government were only the lull before the storm of conflict that would envelop St. Mary's for several years. The "Chronicles of St. Mary's Seminary" describe "trying times for the Bro[ther]s," as they "didn't know where they stood."[47] The problems arose on several fronts. As mentioned previously, differences in educational philosophy created tension between the brothers and the White Fathers, especially Father Emile DeSorcy, the rector. DeSorcy was more of a traditionalist who disagreed with the more liberal policies of the post–Vatican II Church. The vice regional superior of the White Fathers agreed that the conflict was "significant." John Croston, C.S.C., the diocesan treasurer and McCauley's confidant, placed the situation in proper perspective:

> The situation in the seminary here at Virika has not been ideal. The Holy Cross Brothers and the Rector, Father DeSorcy, have not hit it off too well. The Brothers aren't unjustified in some of their complaints but neither is it all a one-sided affair.[48]

The solution suggested by a visitation team was for a Holy Cross religious to be appointed rector.[49]

The conflict with the White Fathers masked even deeper and more widespread problems between the brothers, McCauley, and the Holy Cross priests on at least three fronts. The provincial administration of the brothers pressed McCauley to pay their religious at St. Mary's the same stipend as those teaching at St. Augustine's TTC and St. Leo's College. McCauley was rather stunned at the request. He explained to his friend Arnold Fell, C.S.C.:

> I can't quite see how I can, in conscience, accept the new conditions that have been presented by the Provincial Administration. We do need the Brothers and we are quite happy with the work they are doing in the Seminary. But it is quite a shock to us to find out that [what] was supposed to be free has now become the most expensive item we have. . . . I have been willing all along to support the Brothers in the Seminary, but on a missionary basis. Since I was not asked to support them[,] but was to have them as a gift, no figure was mentioned until recently. Hence, my offer to give them the same as the highest paid missionaries we have, that is the White Father Brothers. Even that would be a heavy expense in view of the fact that they were [supposed to be] a gift.[50]

This conflict was part of a wider problem in securing a contract between the bishop and the brothers for their services at St. Mary's. The "Chronicles of St. Mary's" report that the bishop ridiculed a contract proposal of the brothers that was akin to one used at the Vincentian Institute in Albany, where Holy Cross religious had taught since 1935. The chronicles suggest that the bishop strongly pressured the brothers to accept a contract as he stipulated. Only in January 1968, two years after Holy Cross took administrative responsibility for the seminary, was a contract signed between McCauley and the brothers' provincial.[51] McCauley explained his understanding of the contract difficulty to the superior general:

> How much of the background of this particular contract you are aware of, I have no way of knowing, but I do assure you it has been a most difficult undertaking for me. After all these years in the Community, I have only recently come to appreciate the diffirence [sic] between the

school mentality and the mission mentality. It is my hope and my prayer that all of us in the missions will acquire a mission mentality to interpret, supplement and bolster the school mentality that is absolutely necessary but not exclusively viable.[52]

The third and most complex problem was an authority question between Holy Cross priests and brothers. The recommendation of the 1966 Parish Visitation Team to assign a Holy Cross religious as rector did not resolve the problem. The arrival of Thomas Fotusky, C.S.C., as rector in 1969 only seemed to exacerbate the problem. Personality clashes, lack of trust, and vastly different understandings of mission between Fotusky and the brothers grew into a serious conflict. A report filed by Brother Francis Ellis, C.S.C., at the request of Elmo Bransby, C.S.C., the brothers' provincial, suggested the problem, at its root, was a failure to communicate, leading to a breakdown in discipline on all fronts. He suggested to McCauley a weekly meeting between the headmaster and rector. [53]

Brother Francis's intercession and suggestion "clear[ed] the air" toward the end of 1969, continuing through 1970.[54] James Rio, C.S.C., a teacher at St. Mary's, wrote his provincial, Elmo Bransby, C.S.C.:

> Everyone seems to be quite happy—and I even heard a compliment from some of the priests saying that the relationship of the priests and Brothers at the Seminary are [sic] the best they have ever seen it. That made everyone quite pleased to say the least.[55]

Bransby happily responded: "It must be a great sense of peace for you (and all those) now that the relationship of the priests and Brothers are [sic] so very good."[56]

The conflict between the brothers and priests came to the front again in the Spring of 1971. In March, Hugh McCabe,

C.S.C., the Eastern Brothers' provincial, and William Reiser, C.S.C., the educational supervisor for the Eastern Brothers, made a visit to Uganda. The visit raised other issues: (1) lack of cooperation and understanding of the priests as to their obligations in teaching and supervision, (2) priests' insistence on having a day off, and (3) the problem with communication between the headmaster and rector.[57] The brothers felt McCauley was too heavy-handed in his suggested resolutions and personnel assignments.[58] Sensing an extremely volatile situation, McCauley took control to settle the issue.[59] In March 1971, he relieved Fotusky as rector[60] and replaced him, on a temporary basis, with Bonaventura Kasaija, a Fort Portal priest who had been involved with education for many years, including recent experience at St. Mary's. James Rio, C.S.C., was appointed headmaster.[61] McCauley told Kasaija that he lamented "the tension that has unfortunately existed in the Seminary," but that Kasaija would receive his full support. McCauley encouraged him to proceed as he thought best:

> These lines are written only after long and prayerful consideration. It is my hope that they will help you and your staff reconstruct in our Seminary the spiritual atmosphere of fraternal cooperation that must prevail if our Seminary is to succeed. Yours is the most important institution in the Diocese. Your task is to give us "other Christs" for His people. May the Divine Master . . . the First Priest . . . be with you always to assist, bless and approve all you and your staff does in His Name.[62]

Besides the personnel changes, McCauley's solution to the seminary conflict included placing authority at the school under one man. Thus, the position of headmaster was eliminated and a new "director of studies" created to oversee academic programs. The rector would be in overall control of the seminary. The bishop reasoned that personality and authority conflicts between the headmaster and rector would be eliminated by his suggested move. He informed the superior general of his plan, stating that it was acceptable to St. Mary's personnel. Since Kasaija had found acceptance and was doing a commendable job as the acting rector after Fotusky's departure from the position, McCauley was prepared to name him permanently.

Reaction by the brothers against McCauley's plan was swift and strident. The brothers' provincial, Hugh McCabe, was frustrated with the bishop's solution as it violated the contract between the brothers and the diocese. Brother Thomas Keefe, C.S.C., rejected both elements of McCauley's solution:

> It seems a shame that this problem has gotten as far as it has. . . . I am firmly convinced that the only ones who can handle the Headmaster[']s job is [sic] the Brothers. I do not see us given [sic] it up if we are going to remain. We fought too hard in the past to put our policies in operation. I can see Africanizing the job but there is no one available at the moment who could fulfill that role as there is an acute shortage of African Priests in the Diocese.[63]

James Rio, C.S.C., was critical of McCauley's perceived bias against the brothers:

> Everyone talks about harmony and being able to work together as one, etc., etc., but when is this all going to take place[?] The Bishop takes a stand with the priests, especially the two Holy Cross priests at the seminary, and never has he once backed the Brothers on any issue— the priests are always right, and the brothers, well they are necessary "things" to get along with. . . . I wish the Bishop would for once stop listening to those two one-sided men.[64]

McCauley defended his decision on Africanization to Hugh McCabe, C.S.C.:

> As a policy arrangement there is nothing new in my pro-
> posal. This is what is being done all over Uganda and in
> the neighboring countries. The Holy See has been advo-
> cating it for years. In the other twelve minor seminaries
> in Uganda there are African Rectors; we are the last to
> Africanize.[65]

McCauley told the superior general that Africanization was
already complete at Butiiti (St. Augustine's TTC), and that St.
Leo's was on this same trajectory. He believed the in-process
program in Fort Portal should augur well for his proposal at
St. Mary's.[66]

McCauley's strong sense that Holy Cross was in East Africa
to serve the local church colored his thoughts and actions on
Africanization. Possibly somewhat naively, he believed all Holy
Cross religious believed as he did that it was necessary to go
anywhere, do anything, and live anywhere for the good of the
common goal. It was hard for McCauley when others could
not see what seemed so obvious to him.[67]

McCauley's solution continued to draw fire from several
sides. Brother James Nichols, C.S.C., explained that the director of studies position would be almost untenable if a disagreement arose between the rector/headmaster and the director.[68]
McCabe wrote the superior general:

> I feel it is important that the General Administration see
> both sides of this issue and not merely that represented by
> Bishop McCauley. . . . I must quite frankly say that I find
> the Bishop's sudden enthusiasm for the Africanization
> started by the Brothers as quite strange in view of my past
> exchanges with him concerning St. Leo's. It is difficult to
> sort out the truth.[69]

McCauley remained fearful that the brothers would leave
the seminary. Thus, he continued to proclaim his support for
their work at St. Mary's:

> We have some very fine Brothers here who are really dedicated to their mission apostolate. I continue to have great respect and admiration for our brothers in spite of Brother Hugh's opinion of me. I state categorically that I wish to have the Holy Cross Brothers remain at St. Mary's Seminary to educate and to train candidates for the Priesthood.[70]

The permanent appointment of Bonaventura Kasaija as rector/headmaster was eventually accepted, and the conflict ended. McCauley continued to provide his rector with the needed support:

> We are determined to do our utmost to provide you with the personnel who will collaborate whole-heartedly in carrying out this policy and in creating an atmosphere of harmony among the staff, the Seminarians and throughout the Diocese.[71]

The conflict was one of mismatched strong personalities and incomplete or inaccurate perceptions of people and the rationale for their actions. The common wish of McCauley and the superior general, Germain Lalande, C.S.C., that brothers work under the tutelage of a priest was rejected by Donoghue and McCabe, as well as the brothers at the seminary.[72] Philosophical differences between brothers and priests in the day-to-day religious life were also problematic, leading to conflict.[73] In the end, securing a staff with compatible personalities was the proper formula that allowed St. Mary's to move forward and help McCauley fulfill his dream for an indigenous clergy.

Vincent McCauley's vision for seminary education and the promotion of an indigenous clergy for Uganda could not be confined to the limits of Fort Portal. In 1964, the Uganda Episcopal Commission (UEC) "agreed that the final aim of the Uganda Hierarchy is one National Seminary with an African Rector for all candidates to the priesthood."[74] At the

time three major seminaries were in operation, each sponsored
by a religious order with long ties to the country: Katigondo
(White Fathers), Gaba (Mill Hill Fathers), and Gulu (Verona
Fathers). McCauley viewed the national seminary possibility
as an avenue to bring unity to the bishops in their efforts to
build the local church.[75] He explained:

> It should be obvious, therefore, that in pressing for a
> National Seminary in Uganda, my insistence and persis-
> tence has not had a mere personal or Diocesan basis. It is
> the Church in Uganda and not only the Diocese of Fort
> Portal that needs a National Seminary.[76]

It was clear to the bishops that some new facility was necessary as the facilities at Katigondo were inadequate. Realizing
his connections with benefactors, both European foundations
and many United States contacts, the bishops asked McCauley to chair the episcopal building committee for the national
seminary, which included Bishops Adrian Ddungu of Masaka
and James Odongo of Tororo. Appointed on February 9,
1966, the committee's first task was to consider two possible
sites for the seminary, Nsambya and Gaba, both in Kampala.
After a review of several architects' reports for both sites, Gaba
was chosen with Hughes and Polkinghorne hired as the project
architects.[77]

From the outset, the project was plagued by financial
problems. The original design bid of USh 450,000 ($1.28
million) was immediately rejected by the UEC as too costly.
A second bid, based on a scaled back design, was received at
USh 365,000 ($1.04 million). McCauley submitted this figure
to the Pontifical Work of St. Peter the Apostle in an attempt
to fund the project. The Roman foundation was unanimous
in its desire to assist with the project, but told McCauley the
requested funds were "beyond the Secretary's extraordinary
resources." It was requested that the project be scaled back and

new plans and costs submitted.[78] A third design, scaled back even further, was bid at USh 293,000 ($837,000). McCauley was later informed by the apostolic delegate that USh 200,000 ($571,000) was available for the Gaba Seminary project.[79]

McCauley was very concerned that the severe restrictions on funding would not allow construction of the necessary facilities. He voiced his alarm to Cardinal Peter Agagianian, prefect of Propaganda Fide:

> Your Eminence will now appreciate that drastic reductions have been made during the progress of the project and it has been a laborious struggle to preserve our main objective and to maintain the basic design with its finely calculated functional features.

Claiming, "We have pared the cost as much as possible," McCauley asked Agagianian to intercede with the Pontifical Work of St. Peter the Apostle for the lowest bid of USh 293,000 ($837,000).[80]

In a dilemma, McCauley sought advice from his fellow committee members, Bishops Ddungu and Odongo. Possible scenarios included seeking a new architect, have Hughes and Polkinghorne submit a design for USh 200,000 ($571,000), or keep the present plans and find ways to raise the additional USh 92,000 ($263,000). It was decided to ask for a fourth design from the present architect.[81] The redesign, however, was in McCauley's mind inadequate for a national seminary. In a letter to Uganda's bishops, he gave some specifics. The chapel had only one altar, no side altars. The dining room, assembly hall, and library were all drastically reduced in size. McCauley described the sixty-five square feet given each seminarian for a room, "satisfactory nowhere except in an ancient prison."

Having heard nothing from his earlier request from Propaganda Fide, and with the support of the UEC, McCauley re-petitioned the Pontifical Work of St. Peter the Apostle, stating that the maximum allowed grant of USh 200,000 was simply inadequate. Receiving no satisfaction, McCauley decided to resign his position as chair of the special committee. Convinced the project was not viable under the constraints imposed, he wrote to Archbishop Antonio Mazza, Secretary of the Pontifical Work of St. Peter the Apostle:

> Our need in Uganda is, therefore, to develop a well-trained modern clergy, capable of competing with the University-trained leaders of Uganda. To attempt this 1970 need of the Church in 1940 accommodations is impossible. Because this impossibility is so clear to me, I cannot in conscience assume responsibility for what I know will be inadequate for the Church's need in Uganda. Since I cannot do what I see clearly must be done, and since I have been unable to persuade you and the Supreme Council, I reluctantly withdraw in favor of others who may have better success in obtaining for Uganda a Seminary adequate to her needs.[82]

Despite McCauley's frustration, his resignation was rejected by the UEC. He wrote, "The Bishops of Uganda . . . insisted that I try to reach a solution that will enable us to build the Theologate at Gaba."[83]

In July 1967, an agreement was finally reached on funding for the Gaba Seminary project. Mazza accepted McCauley's final design for USh 201,250 ($575,000), to which was added USh 5,000 ($14,300) for a sisters' convent. It was decided that the funds ($600,000) would be distributed in two equal amounts in 1967 and 1968. In the meantime, however, the architects, who had been UEC employees for three years without compensation, began to press McCauley for payment. Since UEC funds were not available, McCauley dipped into his own Fort Portal earthquake restoration fund. Rather sarcastically he wrote to Mazza, "I have restored the credit rating of the Uganda Bishops, but I hope that of Fort Portal is not ruined."[84]

In February 1968, with financing secured, construction of the national seminary began. Brother Casimir Brampton, M.H.S., was the overall supervisor of the project, which was scheduled for completion in eight months. McCauley met almost monthly with the architects and contractors on the project to keep abreast of progress.[85] As the construction went forward, however, it was clear that the $600,000 promised for the project would not be sufficient. New taxes and higher costs since the time of the original bid necessitated an additional $140,000. Thus, McCauley again petitioned the Pontifical Work of St. Peter the Apostle for the additional funds.[86]

A negative response to the request led McCauley to again vent his frustration concerning the entire project. He told Mazza that students in the first two years of theology were slated to move to Gaba in January 1970. Without the money, he wrote:

> We will have a building without the furniture and equipment; a chapel without an altar or pews; a kitchen without stoves; a dining room without tables or eating utensils; a library without books; classrooms without desks and dormitories without beds, desks, chairs, etc.[87]

He insisted that without the additional funds, the project was in serious jeopardy. In a rather callous response, Mazza wrote, "I think it advisable to do the best Your Excellency can with what you have and let a touch of poverty be part of the proposal."[88]

Disappointed, McCauley worked to cut costs while seeking other sources of revenue. While cutting design and construction to the bare minimum, McCauley determined $65,000 was necessary to complete basic necessities. He held hope that more money could be found to adequately complete the

project. Gratefully, McCauley unexpectedly received a generous gift "from the good people of Germany [that] will enable
us to complete our Uganda National Seminary at Gaba."[89]
Despite the good news, the long years of frustration were evident when McCauley wrote to a fellow Holy Cross religious
in February 1970:

> For five years this National Seminary project has been one
> of my particular headaches. We just moved in, although
> the construction workers are still on the job. The begin-
> nings for such an undertaking are hectic in any country,
> but in the missions where we have to scrape and save and
> improvise (to say nothing of the constant begging), the
> situation is magnified many times.[90]

Increasing construction and material costs, even with the
recent input of funds, forced McCauley to go to his fellow
Uganda bishops for funds. He lamented that cost increases
"have forced us to leave unfinished our Library, Assembly
Hall and Kitchen equipment."[91] On August 1, 1970, a special
meeting of the Uganda Episcopal Conference was held to
"discuss matters that needed urgent action." McCauley told
the bishops that a "stop order" on construction at Gaba was
imminent unless $20,000 could be raised immediately. If con-
struction were halted it would cost more in the end to resume
the project. The UEC unanimously agreed to the request, with
the proviso that when promised funds were received from
Rome members would be reimbursed.[92] In a vote of confidence, Archbishop Emmanuel Nsubuga, Chairman of the
UEC, wrote McCauley:

> Your Lordship, believe me, since the Uganda Episcopal
> Conference put all trust in you for the building of the
> Gaba National Seminary, you have done wonderfully.
> Without your indefatigable effort and skill, the

construction of Gaba National Seminary would not be
what it is now.[93]

After six years of planning, fundraising, and construction,
Gaba National Seminary was dedicated on October 21, 1970.
Among the many dignitaries present for the event were Milton
Obote, president of Uganda, Archbishops Nsubaga and Mazza,
and the new rector, Father Paul Mukasa. Due to transportation
problems, McCauley missed the dedication Mass, but arrived
in time to address the assembly. Despite their sometimes testy
exchanges in correspondence, McCauley praised Mazza for his
effort in making the seminary possible:

> Msgr. Mazza struggled under great difficulty and against
> almost insurmountable odds to make possible this Semi-
> nary for the Church in Uganda. Except for Msgr. Mazza's
> skill, persistence and patience and wise guidance we
> would not be here today. The greatest patron of the clergy
> in Rome is Msgr. Mazza and thanks to him we in Uganda
> have our Gaba National Seminary.[94]

In March 1971, the seminary was operating with eighty
students, but construction was still ongoing. Additional subsidies were still necessary to complete the project and pay
all concerned. McCauley continued, therefore, to ask Mazza
for funds. Grateful for what was received from the Pontifical
Work of St. Peter the Apostle, McCauley nonetheless pressed
for more, saying recent grants covered only the debt, not costs
to be incurred in the completion of the project.[95] Eventually
in early December 1971, McCauley received a $28,500 grant
from Misereor in Germany and the Pontifical Work of St.
Peter the Apostle. In gratitude he stated, "We will at last be
able to complete the Construction of the Uganda National
Seminary at Gaba."[96]

Summary

Vincent McCauley, an educator in the faith in the line of his congregation's founder, Basil Moreau, was ever diligent in raising the educational level of his people so as to become full players in world society. McCauley's six years in Bengal, and his involvement with the education and the formation of future priests, prepared him well for his years as bishop of Fort Portal. His experience was instrumental in his promotion of the local church and the formation of indigenous clergy, who would one day take the leadership roles in the Eastern African Church. During his time in Fort Portal, McCauley significantly expanded his horizons in the educational domain. While he continued his care, oversight, and devotion to St. Mary's minor seminary, he expanded his endeavors to include other venues. Having initiated his Uganda ministry at the St. Augustine Teacher Training College, he was very interested in the promotion of Catholic secondary education. His association with the Banyatereza Sisters and desire for Holy Cross religious in the diocese led to the formation of St. Maria Goretti Senior Secondary School as a training base for religious women. Additionally, McCauley was asked by his fellow Ugandan bishops to oversee the development and construction of a new national seminary at Gaba in Kampala. The new theologate was one of the crowning jewels in Vincent McCauley's episcopal role as an educator in the faith.

CHAPTER 8

An Influential Bishop: 1961–1973

Vincent McCauley led the Holy Cross mission to Uganda in 1958 and was appointed the local ordinary of Fort Portal in 1961, but his influence could not be contained within this rather limited purview of a religious community and a small diocese. As stated previously, many who lived and worked with him described McCauley as a man of great vision. Not only did he see what needed to be accomplished and have the expertise to put in place programs to achieve his ends, he also had a far-reaching vision of what the Church in Uganda, Eastern Africa, and the world could become. Thus, almost from the outset of his episcopal ministry, Vincent McCauley began to apply his multiple and significant gifts for organization and leadership in broad strokes. The 1960s, and most especially the Second Vatican Council, 1962 to 1965, provided the impetus and catalyst to McCauley's energy and the opportunity to apply his gifts to the world Church. The Council's promotion of collegiality among bishops on national, regional, and worldwide levels, its emphasis on liturgical renewal, and its view of the Church as "the people of God," became the bases upon which Vincent McCauley ministered throughout the 1960s.

The Second Vatican Council: 1962–1965

In the history of Roman Catholicism, ecumenical councils have been called for two basic reasons: to root out perceived or acknowledged heresy and to define significant Church doctrine or dogma. The first council, held in Nicaea in 325, served both purposes. First, it condemned the theology of the priest Arius, who viewed Christ as a *tertium quid*, one not fully human or divine. Second, the council formulated the Nicene Creed, which was modified into its present form at Constantinople in 381. Vatican I, the twentieth council, held during 1869 and 1870, defined the dogma of papal infallibility in its document *Pastor Aeternus*. In the interim, eighteen other councils, including the famous gatherings at Constance in 1415 that ended the Great Western Schism, and at Trent (1545–1563), which presented the Catholic response to the Reformation, gave direction, corrected abuses, and defined teachings in the Church.

Pope John XXIII called the Second Vatican Council in a speech at St. Paul's Outside the Walls on January 25, 1959, the last day of the annual week of prayer for Christian unity. John had been elected just months before his announcement, and partly because of his advanced age of seventy-six, was considered an interim pope. Thus, his dramatic announcement came as a great surprise to the entire world, especially the Catholic Church. The pope called for a diocesan synod for Rome, a revision of Canon Law from the 1917 Code, and an ecumenical council of the world's bishops. He also stated the Council's three principal purposes: to promote ecumenism, to bring the Church into the modern world (he used the word *aggiornamento*), and to be pastoral in nature and work.

Preparations for the Council began almost immediately when the pope asked over eight hundred theologians, the hierarchy, heads of male religious orders, and the faculties of thirty-seven Catholic universities worldwide to provide suggestions for what the Council should address. A relative oasis of calm in the midst of secular Cold War upheaval, combined with a Church seemingly free of both heresy and uncertainty about doctrinal matters, indicated that there would be minimal response to the pope's call for action. However, over two thousand individuals and institutions provided ideas for possible study by the Council. Cardinal Alfredo Ottaviani, prefect of the Holy Office, was assigned the task of organizing the Council. He was a strong theological conservative and thus wary of modernization in any form. He used his influence and position to "pack" the preparatory commissions with only "safe" theologians who would not move the Church from the position it had maintained with barely an inch of movement since the time of Trent. The twelve commissions that were established wrote seventy schemas on such topics as revelation, moral order, the deposit of faith, family, liturgy, the media, and Christian unity. The schema were to serve for possible debate by the Council fathers. All of these draft documents were neoscholastic, juridical, and moralistic in tone and content.

The Council was formally convoked with the document *Humanae Salutaris* of December 25, 1961. In this document, Pope John used the terms "signs of the times" and *"aggiornamento,"* expressions which would prove significant for the future direction of the Council's work. The pope's comments reversed the long-standing edict proclaimed at Lateran V (1512–1517), which said, "men must be changed by religion" to "religion must be changed by men." On October 11, 1962, shortly after the first session of the Council opened, the bishops voted, with the pope's concurrence, to move away from the rather staid tone of the preliminary schema, and substituted a more open view that would allow the bishops themselves to determine the Council's direction. Ottaviani and his conservative forces had been routed at the outset, setting the tone that would be carried through to the Council's conclusion on December 8, 1965.[1]

The four sessions of Vatican II produced sixteen documents that were divided into three areas of descending significance. Four constitutions, including documents on liturgy, revelation, the Church, and the Church in the modern world, were the Council's crowning achievement. Nine decrees, including important treatises on ecumenism and the lay apostolate, and three declarations—including one document with a distinctively American tone, the Declaration on Religious Liberty—were also published. The net effect of these important documents was the emergence of a new self-understanding for Roman Catholicism, exemplified most significantly in the rise of collegiality, the increased role of the laity, ecumenical dialogue, and a complete updating of the liturgy, including the use of vernacular language. The importance of Vatican II in the history and direction of the Church might best be stated in the work of Jesuit theologian Karl Rahner. In his division of Church history into epochs, Rahner provides three: the apostolic era, 30–49; the era of the Church, 49–1962; and the era of Vatican II, 1962 to the present.[2]

Although very junior in the ranks of the episcopacy, Vincent McCauley played a significant role among the African bishops at Vatican II. He was the driving force in organizing the bishops, especially in Eastern Africa, to make their voice heard at the Council, especially in the areas of mission and ecumenism, issues that were more pressing to their region of the world. He attended all four sessions, initially residing at the Holy Cross Generalate. After session I, however, he organized all the Eastern African bishops to stay together, so that issues could be more readily discussed and they could speak as a united voice.[3] McCauley described his day-to-day activities during the sessions:

> The Council pace is a killer. If it were only the morning sessions it would not be so bad, but I get stuck for many chores concerning Uganda operations. We have two conferences—study sessions on topics being discussed in the council, plus an ITEBEA [Interterritorial Episcopal Board of Eastern Africa] board meeting, plus all the contacting of other bishops' conferences. Its [*sic*] a merry-go-round.[4]

As alluded to earlier, McCauley served as the catalyst to organize and, thereby, give voice to the African bishops. He quickly gained the respect of his fellow bishops through his administrative skill, including convincing them to reside together at the Medici Hotel.[5] John Croston, C.S.C., has commented: "He gave them [the Eastern African bishops] the organizational power that they needed so they could begin to work together."[6] McCauley gave the bishops a sense of dignity and purpose. Simply because Christianity was in an infant stage in Africa did not mean it had nothing to offer. On the contrary, the African bishops were in the unique and powerful position to bring insight in certain areas that other, more established churches could not provide. Arnold Fell, C.S.C., explained McCauley's efficacy:

> At the time of the Second Vatican Council Bishop Vince was the prime mover in organizing the East[ern] African hierarchy. They discovered for the time that they had a collegial identity and a voice that was heard in the Council.[7]

He had the ability to lead the bishops and make them heard without any overt direction or sense of domination. Without realizing it, McCauley was setting the stage for his later career when he would work (1973–1982) directly with the Eastern African hierarchy as head of its regional conference.

McCauley's influence and assistance were clearly visible in the Council's work on ecumenism and mission.[8] McCauley was a leader in the ecumenical efforts in Uganda, through the Uganda Episcopal Conference and, most prominently, the Uganda Joint Christian Council, which he helped establish and chaired for its first fledgling years. McCauley's ideas on ecumenism were certainly sharpened by his contact with Edward Heston, C.S.C., who provided an important background and insight to this topic from a more universal perspective. Heston told McCauley that in the past, Catholics understood ecumenism strictly under the rubric of return—that is, non-Catholics must return to the fold. However, many denominations, not believing themselves in error, held no desire to return. Catholics had never understood that people could be born and raised in error, but still be of good faith. Appreciative of the insight, McCauley related that for Africans, ecumenism was a "hard sell" and thus was best dealt with on pragmatic levels. He spoke of relations with non-Catholics as a "practical necessity of doing business with them." Few Africans understood the term ecumenism, much less what it would entail for them personally or for the Church.[9]

As leaders of a mission church under the guidance and care of Propaganda Fide, the African bishops held great interest in the schema on mission. One concern raised at the outset was the need to review the 1919 Mission Instruction. Promulgated at a time when the local African church was not organized, the document granted far ranging powers and jurisdiction to superiors of religious communities operating in various African colonies and protectorates. McCauley believed that the emphasis on indigenous clergy and bishops required a review of this instruction and its present applicability. He wrote, "This instruction is not a conciliar matter, but will be in the background during the discussions and *must* [emphasis McCauley] be resolved soon."[10] McCauley was aware of the complaints of African clergy concerning expatriates and some religious communities. He wrote:

> On the whole . . . indigenous clergy indoctrinated with the anti-colonial sentiments prevalent in mission lands resent foreign domination. The likewise prevalent opinion that "the haves," i.e. foreigners, *owe* [emphasis McCauley] them stringless assistance in much greater abundance . . . in justice rather than charity . . . increases dissatisfaction with foreigners' control of funds, selection of priorities, curtailment of local aspirations and desire to do things the native way. Justification by foreigners of their imported policies and management rarely convinces.[11]

The schema on mission was formally introduced and discussed at the third session of Vatican II, November 6–9, 1964.[12] Cardinal Paul E. Leger of Montreal spoke first, emphasizing the message that missionary activity is the very essence of the Church. In the four days of discussion a total of twenty-eight Council fathers spoke on the schema, including nine from Africa.[13]

African ideas on mission and the Vatican II schema were diverse and asked many important questions. McCauley was a strong proponent of the traditional view of mission—planting the faith, raising an indigenous clergy, and in the end, "working oneself out of a job." He realized that such a view "could be the big battle ground for the proposed schema," foreseeing opposition from those who believed in "geographic penetration," a more intense form of evangelization.[14]

Bishop Joseph Blomjous, the expatriate ordinary of Mwanza, Tanzania, expressed his views on mission and the schema in a well-publicized talk. He initially asked a few probing questions. First, he inquired, if "missionary fatigue" had ended the traditional mission? Second, he stated that Europeans were asking themselves, "Was the mission worth all the effort?" Then, since the traditional view of mission, namely planting the faith, had been completed, what was next? Blomjous said the Church must face the ugly reality that, although it has been planted worldwide, the number of Christians was not increasing proportionally to the world population. He described this as "the uncomfortable failure of the missions." Lastly, in an age of ecumenism, religious liberty, dignity of the human person, and salvation outside the Church, to what length should one go in the process of evangelization? Can a traditional view of mission be held and simultaneously uphold the other modern principles raised at Vatican II?[15]

Besides his questions, Blomjous was concerned about how the mission schema dealt with the laity. He suggested that the draft document discussed at the third session addressed itself too much to the Western Church, without empowering the laity. As McCauley had consistently argued, the lack of indigenous clergy mandated the use of lay people in the promulgation of the faith. He suggested that responsibility for mission churches was equally if not more on the local people. He stated:

> If the schema had put itself squarely on the basis of the missionary task of the universal church (including first and foremost the African and Asian local churches), we would have had far more to say about the role of indigenous laity, apart from the short mention of the catechists and the lay apostolate organizations.[16]

In preparation for the fourth session of Vatican II, and its probable publication of a mission document, the African bishops began preliminary discussions. Between January 12 and 26, 1965, an African subcommission, consisting of bishops and *peritii*, met outside Rome to begin a redrafting of the mission schema. A report of the commission stated, "The aim of the commission with the new text is to provide a solid theological foundation to the schema by giving the reasons which support the missionary activity of the Church."[17]

In his role as chairman of AMECEA, McCauley led the East African bishops' efforts to redraft the mission schema. A study conference was scheduled for Nairobi in July 1965. McCauley wrote of his hopes for the meeting:

> What many of us would like to do at the Nairobi Study Conference is to dispose of as much of the controversial matter as possible, and to get some sort of agreement on a *modus agendi* for dealing with difficulties on a permanent basis.

As the spokesman for sixty-five bishops, McCauley sought to calm any possible rough waters by seeking input for the schema from many possible venues and doing his best to incorporate these ideas into the schema. He was pleased with the progress made to date on the schema's revision:

> I like the proposed schema on the missions. It is a big improvement over the four previous drafts I have seen and several satellite distances above the rejected "*propositiones.*" My guess is that there will be very few radical emendations.[18]

The Nairobi study conference on the schema on mission was held July 6–8, 1965. While McCauley felt the revised schema was "good from my point of view," he realized sufficient support was necessary, and thus a general review of the revised document was imperative.[19] Like McCauley, general satisfaction with the revised schema on mission was voiced, but the assembled bishops did suggest some changes. In total, twenty-seven specific emendations were requested, but the principal ones asked for further clarification between the mission of the Church and the missionary activity of the

Church.[20] The conference produced a draft with the intention of presenting it to the Council fathers in the fall.

Debate on the revised mission schema began in the fourth session of Vatican II on October 7, 1965. McCauley organized the bishops from Africa who would speak. First would be those commenting on the schema as a whole, and second those on specific points. McCauley himself voiced two concerns about the schema on the Council floor. First, he suggested that a reference to the Blessed Virgin Mary as exemplar, mother, and model to all missionaries, be added. Next, he spoke of the importance of the sacrament of confirmation. Since through this sacrament one gains greater obligation to work for the diffusion and defense of the Church, he asked that the mission document reflect its importance to missionaries and those they evangelize. The document was issued in its final form on December 7, 1965.[21]

When Vatican II concluded, McCauley was ready and eager to implement the Council's many changes, manifest in both the general direction of the Church and specific practices. Unquestionably, the Council was a turning point for the Church universal and, therefore, the Church in Fort Portal. Henri Valette, W.F., who worked closely with McCauley for several years, described Vatican II as a watershed event: "Before the Council we were trying to bring people into the Church. After the Council we wanted the Church to be light to the world—*Lumen Gentium.*" For Valette, McCauley, "was the right man at the time to make the shift from the old Church to the new Church."[22] John Keefe, C.S.C., remarked, "He [McCauley] was very much a proponent of it [Vatican II] and pushed it very hard."[23]

McCauley in general described the new directions the diocese must take. He told his priests that Vatican II was "an invitation to the whole Church to . . . up-date; and the Church under the guidance of the Holy Spirit must take the necessary steps."[24] He insisted that the mission status of Fort Portal did not in any way negate the need to implement the Council's teachings. The first priority was to know what the Council said. He stated, "As post–Vatican II missionaries it is our duty to know the documents of the Council. It is also our duty to develop the mind and the spirit of the Council."[25] Acting on this idea, McCauley quickly published and distributed an English version of the Vatican II documents. In the foreword he wrote, "The purpose of this volume is to make the official documents readily available for information, study, and implementation among the People of God in Africa." He further outlined his hopes for the post–Vatican II Church:

> It is my hope that readers will be inspired to continue in their daily lives the spirit of Vatican II. It is a spirit which strives for a more complete dedication to Christ in His person, His teachings and His Church; a spirit of Charity for the union of all in Christ; a spirit of zeal, of sacrifice, and of work for the Church of Christ; and finally a spirit that pleads with the Paraclete to make the love of God, and of neighbor, prevail among the people.[26]

McCauley supported his document translation with presentations and seminars by his friend and colleague, Edward Heston, C.S.C. In 1966, McCauley invited Heston to come to Uganda and give a series of short classes to various groups in his diocese about the Vatican II documents and their appropriate implementation. His purpose was to "initiate, implement and build an awareness of the Council and the documents."[27] Heston spent two months in Uganda and gave a series of five-day seminars in Fort Portal, as well as Katigondo Seminary (Masaka) and Kampala. He spoke to over 240 priests, 130 women religious, 40 Holy Cross and White Fathers, and 85 lay men and women. The presentations were well received. John Croston wrote the provincial, Howard Kenna:

From reports that have come back from the first course,
all were delighted with the presentations. I had thought
that with such a comprehensive topic he might step on
a few toes with some stands he might take, but my fears
were short lived after hearing the reports. All the Fathers
were most grateful to Holy Cross and Bishop McCauley
for arranging such a meeting.[28]

Heston's efforts were well appreciated. One White Father commented, "May I thank you again for 75 lectures given here and
for 2000 questions answered."[29]

After laying the foundation with his English translation of
the documents and Heston's presentations, McCauley pushed
forward with many changes in the wake of Vatican II. Administratively, he simplified diocesan offices and structures. As
mentioned earlier, he organized the board of consultors and
senate of priests. Additionally, he set up the Diocesan Pastoral
Commission to be "a consultative body to the Bishop, stress-
ing the role of the People of God in collaborating in the life
and work of the Church through participation."[30]

Consistent with Vatican II's strong emphasis on liturgical
renewal, McCauley began to implement changes in the celebration of the sacraments. He wrote to the clergy:

Since the Liturgical renewal is the first fruits of the Ecumenical Council and has been promulgated by Our Holy
Father, Pope Paul VI in the Council, it is incumbent on
all of us to cooperate in every way possible to implement
it.[31]

Celebration of the Mass, with special emphasis on inculturation, received primary attention. As in many parts of
the world, a sense of experimentation with the rubrics was
practiced by individual clerics. While McCauley was a strong
proponent of the Council and its spirit, he was equally strident
that any changes would come from his office. In an attempt to

stop abuses and set standards for the revised eucharistic liturgy, McCauley published prescribed rubrics for use in the diocese. In a strongly worded statement, he wrote:

> All changes *must* [emphasis McCauley] first be promulgated by the Bishop. The Bishops insist on unity for the whole of Uganda. Priests *may not* [emphasis McCauley] put into practice on their own initiative changes which they find in newspapers or reviews which may be duly promulgated in other countries.[32]

Two popular innovations that McCauley fostered, while insisting upon control, were the Saturday Vigil Mass for Sunday and the use of lay eucharistic ministers.[33]

McCauley's desire to control experimentation in liturgical renewal did not stop the practice in the diocese. He hoped that the instruction from the Sacred Congregation of Rites, to take effect on June 29, 1967, would bring unity and halt innovation. He wrote:

> It is my sincere hope and prayer that these changes will be received and implemented in the spirit with which they are sent to us, namely that our love for and participation in the Liturgy of the Church be enhanced, that personally and in communion with our brethren we give greater glory to God, and derive more spiritual advantages for ourselves.[34]

Unfortunately, McCauley was still battling for liturgical unity in mid-1972. He referenced an instruction from the Sacred Congregation of Divine Worship:

> Many options were given in order that the Liturgy might be adapted to varying needs and circumstances. There is no longer, however, the liberty of continuing personal preferences indiscriminately. Only what is allowed in the "Instruction and the *Ordo Missae* may be used.[35]

The direction of the African Church was altered greatly by Vatican II. George MacInnes, C.S.C., in an informative yet opinionated essay written in 1969, outlined several key points. He advocated the need for a new approach to the mission apostolate. Too much emphasis in earlier days on conversions created a mass of poorly educated and trained, and less committed, Catholics. He summarized the past errors:

> The obvious concluding observation is that we have over-extended ourselves. A too exclusive concern with conversions has produced the great body of uncommitted. Existing procedures and personnel can no longer adequately serve the People of God in Africa. With the tools at hand we have little hope of developing a mature laity, effecting their encounter with God, or improving their earthly lot. There are too many of them, too few of us. Our cleric-dominated, European-designed system is an inept and unattractive vehicle of salvation to Africa. It has been self-defeating in terms of the Vatican II task.[36]

The immediate problem, MacInnes suggested, was the need to adapt rites and procedures to the African context. The Roman structure "inspires no enthusiastic response in the heart of today's student." He called for "a system, which will work for us and not against us. We need a religious system which can interpret African history, explain the processes of African society, and provide a basis for an African vision of the future." He called for a mature faith, a new course centered about the local church. He concluded, "Only a truly African Church will be able to convert the hearts and engage the minds of an ever-growing legion of African converts."[37]

The Uganda Episcopal Conference (UEC)

Uganda's Catholic bishops began to formally organize in the early 1950s. The Uganda Episcopal Conference was formed in

1953; the Catholic Secretariat, the episcopal organizing and oversight body, was started in April 1959. The Secretariat was originally formed with six departments: secretary-general's office, Catholic Medical Bureau, Education secretary-general's office, Lay Apostolate, Secretariat for Information, and Social Services. In April 1961, a constitution for the Secretariat was accepted and implemented.[38]

From the very outset, Vincent McCauley was integrally involved with the Uganda hierarchy. He expressed his sense of integrity and personal involvement with his fellow bishops in a letter to the apostolic pro-nuncio in Zambia:

> Each day brings us an increasing sense of the responsibility for the welfare of the Church on the part of the Bishops and the need to foster fraternal cooperation in order that the best interest of Christ among the people of God be promoted, deepened and extended.[39]

McCauley played a key role in systematizing the Uganda hierarchy. Bishop Joseph Willigers of Jinja called McCauley "the main thrust in shaping the new Uganda Episcopal Conference." He continued, "From the beginning it was obvious to me that Bishop McCauley was a major organizing power amongst the Uganda Bishops."[40] Bishop Paul Kalanda (local ordinary in Fort Portal from 1991 to 2003) wrote, "Bishop MacCauley [sic] played a very big role in organizing the Uganda Episcopal Conference."[41] Not only was McCauley highly regarded for his organizational skills, he was equally well respected for his advice. Bishops from many areas came to Fort Portal to seek his counsel in many matters, most especially the initial organization of a diocese. McCauley's fellow bishops held him in high regard.[42] He was never considered a threat, but always a wise and considerate father who was present to help. McCauley's long-time colleague and trusted friend, John Croston, C.S.C., remembered:

His relationship with other bishops was extremely good. I don't think they ever saw him as an outside threat to their power. They always knew he was there temporarily. He would set up the diocese and then prepare to leave.[43]

McCauley was thrust into positions of leadership in the UEC from the very outset. In October 1961, while attending his first meeting of the conference, he was appointed recording secretary. Still, his humility was ever apparent, as indicated in a letter to the chairman, Archbishop Joseph Kiwanuka: "Since this is my initial appearance at your meetings, I'll keep to my beginner's role for the present and let the veterans propose matters for the agenda."[44] McCauley served as vice-chairman of the conference on three different occasions and was also a member of its executive committee.[45] As mentioned previously, the bishops were well aware of McCauley's fundraising ability. Thus, he often served as the conference's representative requesting funds for the Secretariat and various other UEC commissions and departments.[46] In 1970, he served as chairman of the UEC's Social Services Commission and was a member of the Ecumenical Commission.[47]

McCauley was extensively involved with two of the UEC's commissions, Social Communications and Medical Bureau. As chairman of the former from 1966 to 1972, he was a strong advocate of training Africans for communications positions. He wrote to his friend Edward Heston, C.S.C., president of the Pontifical Commission for Social Communication:

> Communications happens to be my portfolio in the Uganda Episcopal Conference and of considerable concern on the AMECEA level. During the past two years, we have stepped up our emphasis on training of Africans for Communications in several fields. Although we are by no means "Pros," there has [sic] been impressive advances throughout Eastern Africa.[48]

McCauley's efforts were concentrated in the areas of journalism, radio, and television. In this vein, he met and worked closely with Joseph Mukwaya, who succeeded him as chairman of the commission and years later as secretary-general of AMECEA in Nairobi. His support for printed communications bore fruit with the establishment of a central publishing house that, by his initiative, was staffed by the Daughters of St. Paul.[49] Additionally, using foresight, McCauley called for an upgrade to the communications systems and hardware to meet future needs: "We need to use modern techniques and devices in communicating our ideas in order to counteract slants which distort the message of Christ, with the correct message."[50]

From the very outset, McCauley was also a major participant in the UEC Medical Bureau, which was established in 1957. At his first meeting with the hierarchy, McCauley was assigned as chairman of the Medical Bureau, a position he held until 1971. He saw his role as one of support, not control.[51] He wished the bureau to work with other UEC commissions and the Ugandan government to provide more medical facilities and better-quality service to the nation's citizens. In this spirit he reported,

> I could point out ways in which the medical apostolate can contribute much to the ecumenical movement. Suffice it to say, briefly, that I hope all of our medical missionaries are aware of the necessity of cooperating—in a positive way—with their non-Catholic neighbors and fellow professionals.[52]

He encouraged cooperation between all church-related medical work, "so that . . . they might be able to contribute more effectively towards establishing an overall health care system in this country."[53]

The Visit of Pope Paul VI to Uganda—August 1969

The Ugandan Church came of age in a special way in August 1969 with a visit from Pope Paul VI. While attending the 1967 Synod of Bishops, Archbishop Emmanuel Nsubuga had extended an invitation to the pope to visit the site of the twenty-two Ugandan martyrs whom Paul had canonized in 1964. In an address to pilgrims on March 19, 1969, the pope accepted the invitation:

> We have often been earnestly invited by numerous bishops and faithful to pay a visit to Africa, more precisely to Uganda where work is progressing on a new Shrine where an altar has been erected in honour of the African martyrs whom we had the privilege of canonizing. It is desired that we preside over the consecration of the altar at a ceremony to be attended by the African Bishops and faithful whose response to their Christian vocation is well known. We have accepted the invitation; . . . we shall go to Kampala.[54]

Besides consecrating the altar, Pope Paul also stated his desire to attend the All Africa Episcopal Symposium, which eventually came to be called the Symposium of Episcopal Conferences of Africa and Madagascar, or SECAM. It was hoped as well that the pope would consecrate several new African bishops, attend an ecumenical prayer service (or at least meet non-Catholic religious leaders), and bless the cornerstone of the new Gaba National Seminary.[55] The pope's planned visit, the first by a pontiff to the African continent, was viewed as "recognition of all that ha[d] been accomplished" toward the growth of the Church in this region of the world.[56]

McCauley played a significant role in the pope's visit as a member of the episcopal committee responsible for all preparations. At a March 6 meeting of the UEC, a steering committee was formed to work out the many details for the pope's visit.

As a member of the steering committee, McCauley worked with Archbishops Nsubuga and Amleto Poggi (Apostolic Delegate), and Killian Flynn, O.F.M. Cap. It was decided that the pope would attend the SECAM closing session and visit the Anglican martyrs' shrine (adjacent to the Catholic shrine) at Namugongo, the latter request coming with the strong suggestion of McCauley.[57]

The pope visited Uganda between July 31 and August 2, 1969. During this time, he spoke of the universality of the Church that must be lived through multiculturalism:

> Your Church must be first of all universal—that is, Catholic. . . . The expression, that is the language and mode of manifesting this one faith, may be manifold; hence it may be original, suited to the tongue, the style, the character, the genus and the culture of the one who professes this one faith. From this point of view a certain pluralism is not only legitimate but desirable.[58]

He encouraged the African Church "to be missionaries to yourselves," a challenge to enhance indigenous vocations.

The pope visited several places during his stay. He traveled west of Kampala to Mityana to visit the site where one of the Ugandan martyrs died. He returned to the capital and made a pilgrimage to Namugongo to visit both the Catholic and Anglican martyrs' shrines. At the latter site, Leslie Brown, the Anglican archbishop, welcomed the pope. In a frank but hope-filled message the archbishop stated,

> In recent years many steps have been taken to strengthen the bonds of friendship between the Roman Catholic Church and the Church of Uganda, Rwanda and Burundi; and in many places we rejoice to see a good spirit of co-operation and mutual concern, and not the least in the Uganda Joint Christian Council. But the story of the relations between our two churches in Uganda has not, it must be frankly and honestly admitted, always been

a happy one. Our members have even fought and killed each other, and in some places there still remain feelings of suspicion and hostility. But now is the time for us to strengthen the spirit of friendship and co-operation which has been growing and, at the same time, to examine together any hardness, any darkness which is still in our hearts.[59]

The pope additionally visited Rubaga Hospital. As chairman of the UEC Medical Bureau, McCauley was part of the official greeting party at the hospital.

Symposium of Episcopal Conferences of Africa and Madagascar (SECAM)

The collegiality experienced by the African bishops at Vatican II generated action for some form of permanent episcopal association, linking all African countries. The 1967 Synod of Bishops in Rome provided the opportunity to call a meeting of representatives of the various African Episcopal conferences. The Association of Member Episcopal Conferences of Eastern Africa (AMECEA) was tasked with organizing this possible symposium. Cardinal Paul Zoungrana of Ouagadougou, Upper Volta (today Burkina-Faso), was chosen as organizing chairman, but McCauley, as chairman of the AMECEA, was charged with the actual organization of the initial meeting in Kampala.[60] The body's membership was National Episcopal Conferences of Africa and Madagascar, the cardinals from Africa and Madagascar, and African members of the Council of the Sacred Congregation for the Evangelization of Peoples.[61]

"Conceived as an instrument of unity and solidarity and of the symbol of the common identity of the Catholic Church in Africa," the Symposium of Episcopal Conferences of Africa and Madagascar (SECAM) proclaimed its three primary objectives. First, to effect and maintain liaison between the episcopal conferences "in order to promote and safeguard their higher value"; second, to facilitate intercommunication between episcopal conferences through their secretariats; third, to serve as the coordinating agency for studies and other forms of collaboration.[62] The nascent body saw its primary pastoral challenge as the formation of the clergy, especially at a time when the magisterium was under constant attack and ridicule.[63]

The initial SECAM meeting was originally scheduled for April 13–15, 1969, but the pope's announced visit to Uganda forced a change in plans. With the hope that the pontiff would attend the closing session, a late July meeting was suggested. McCauley, chairman of a planning meeting, championed the effort in the rather routine necessities of transportation, finances, and schedules. More importantly, he also asked some of his episcopal superiors to get involved. He invited Sergio Pignedoli, the secretary-general of the Propagation of the Faith, to attend a planning session on April 13–15, 1969, to discuss the proposed late July and August meeting. He wrote, "This could be an excellent opportunity for your Excellency to outline to all Africa some of the new features of mission policy envisioned by the Holy See." He also asked the guidance of Archbishop Amleto Poggi, apostolic pro-nuncio in Uganda: "I would appreciate any help that you would be willing to give us for this all-African conference."[64]

The inaugural meeting of SECAM opened on July 28, 1969, at the Gaba Pastoral Institute in Kampala. The bishops welcomed Milton Obote, president of Uganda, to the opening session. Obote's opening comments were followed by talks by Cardinals Laurean Rugambwa of Dar es Salaam, Tanzania, and Paul Zoungrana of Ouagadougou, Upper Volta. The bishops elected a standing committee to guide the fledgling body: Zoungrana as chairman, Archbishop J. K. Amissah of Cape

Coast, Ghana, as first councilor, and McCauley as second councilor.[65]

The meeting addressed several pertinent topics. The bishops' first order of business was to agree that SECAM should be a permanent body. Meetings were to be held every two years, save the second meeting to be held in 1970. General topics raised at the open sessions of the three-day Kampala meeting included: seeking better communication between the Holy See and local bishops, as well as between members of the episcopacy; financial needs for formation of the clergy and pastoral work; personnel shortages in local apostolates; problems with formation of catechists and the laity. Particular emphasis was placed on personnel needs, especially recruitment and formation of the clergy.[66] Two declarations were issued by this initial session. A statement on peace condemned all racial discrimination and the abuse of tribalism. Peace, the statement concluded, must be founded on justice that guarantees the rights of all people. In a declaration on development, the bishops spoke of the grave problem of poverty, hunger, disease, and illiteracy, and stressed the need for all to seek answers to these pressing needs.[67]

The meeting concluded on July 31 with the pope in attendance. Two days later, while visiting the Ugandan martyrs' shrine, he commented on SECAM. Echoing the theme of ecumenism, he spoke favorably of the efforts of the Uganda Joint Christian Council. He also praised SECAM in its initial efforts: "May the Lord bless the work of the All-Africa Christian Conference, as it bends its efforts towards the unity of all Christians."[68]

McCauley's interest and enthusiasm in SECAM were apparent from the outset. He was very pleased with the cooperation and collaboration that the 1969 SECAM meeting generated. Realistically, McCauley knew that a new organization would have some problems, but he wrote, "Please let me assure you that my interest in SECAM is as great as ever, and I want to do everything possible to cooperate."[69] Others noticed McCauley's drive, and acknowledged his contribution. Joseph Osei, who became secretary-general of SECAM, wrote McCauley:

> I know the difficulties and the sacrifices you have borne and made for SECAM, but I am more conscious of your great love for this organization. As the saying goes—every beginning is difficult, but I know that you Americans say, "we shall overcome."[70]

SECAM chairman Cardinal Zoungrana was pleased to work with McCauley: "I am happy that you were chosen to help me, and it gives me confidence. Through you I shall know better the Church of East Africa."[71]

Preparations for the second SECAM meeting in 1970 began almost immediately. The standing committee met three times: in Rome, and in Cape Coast and Kumasi, Ghana. In Rome, in October 1969, the committee agreed that the second SECAM meeting would be held August 18–24, 1970, in Abijan, Ivory Coast.[72] McCauley proposed two business topics for the next session: acceptance of a constitution for the nascent body, and naming and locating a permanent secretariat. Possible topics for the meeting—priesthood, marriage, the lay apostolate, or catechists—were discussed. The choice was narrowed to two: clergy and catechists. To "prime the pump" for discussion, White Fathers Theo van Asten and Alyward Shorter were engaged to prepare position papers on the clergy and catechists, respectively.[73]

On May 27–28, the standing committee met at Kumasi for its final preparations. Influenced strongly by McCauley, the committee selected priesthood as the plenary session's primary discussion topic, "because . . . the question of the clergy was of primary importance all over the world."[74] McCauley was pleased with the meeting, most especially because he met Joseph Osei. He commented:

> The SECAM Conference in Kumasi, Ghana went off better than expected. The new Secretary General, Father Joseph Osei, looks very good. He is a brilliant young man who speaks five European languages as well as the local Ghanian languages and with a little more experience in organizational work should fill the post quite capably.[75]

SECAM's second plenary session was held August 18–28 in Abidjan. The position papers of van Asten and Shorter were presented and discussed. Additionally, the bishops initiated dialogue on an overall program for development, justice, and peace.[76] Most importantly, the bishops also agreed to form a permanent secretariat at Accra, Ghana. Plans were immediately initiated to petition Misereor in Germany to financially assist the construction effort. McCauley volunteered to assist in this endeavor. He wrote to Osei, "You can be sure that I will inquire and urge him [Monsignor Goetz of Misereor] to come to the rescue of SECAM."[77]

Following the originally agreed-upon two-year periodicity for SECAM plenary sessions, the third general meeting was scheduled for August 1972 in Burundi. However, in June 1972, with political unrest present in Burundi, the standing committee asked Archbishop Nsubuga if he would host the session in Kampala.[78] The change in venue placed McCauley in charge of the plenary's organization. At the meeting, held August 13–18, the bishops voted overwhelmingly to establish a Committee for African Internal Affairs (CAIA). The task of setting up and specifically defining the function of CAIA was assigned to the standing committee. At its December 4–7, 1972, meeting, the standing committee formally inaugurated the CAIA.[79] At this same meeting as well, McCauley resigned his position as second councilor and was replaced by Archbishop Jean Zoa of Yaounde, Cameroon.[80]

Bishop McCauley's formal association with SECAM ended in December 1972, but he continued to give assistance to the organization when asked. While secretary-general of AMECEA, McCauley wrote to his SECAM counterpart, Joseph Osei, "It is good to know that you have us on your mailing list and that we will be cooperating regularly in the future. After all, we are in the same business—serving the Church in Africa."[81] On several occasions McCauley arranged for translation services for SECAM meetings.[82] In 1978, he was actively involved with the planning for the SECAM plenary held in Nairobi, including arranging for a position paper on marriage to be submitted and read at the meeting.[83] Osei was very grateful to McCauley, calling him "an inspiration":

> I should like to thank you and through you the AMECEA Secretariat for the invaluable contribution made to the meeting of the Secretaries-General of the various Conferences. It was indeed a great help devotedly rendered in the service of the Church and Africa.[84]

Summary

Bishop Vincent McCauley was never a man with limited vision; on the contrary, if he reached his goals, he believed they were too shallow or insufficiently challenging. Thus, from the outset of his time as bishop of Fort Portal, McCauley branched out in various ventures that involved the Church more broadly, in Uganda, the African continent, and the world. McCauley was an active participant in the Second Vatican Council, leading the organizational efforts of the Eastern Africa bishops and convincing them of the important collective voice they possessed. That voice was heard in the creation of the "Decree on the Church's Missionary Activity." Returning from Rome,

McCauley, a bishop who lived the *aggiornamento* spirit of Vatican II, implemented the Council's ideas and teachings throughout his diocese, not only in liturgical renewal, but additionally through promotion of ecumenism and the advance of the laity. During this same period, McCauley was engaged with the Uganda Episcopal Conference, serving the body as vice chairman and being very active in the medical and social communications commissions. Moving beyond Uganda, McCauley capitalized on Pope Paul VI's visit to Kampala in July and August 1969 and helped organize the Symposium Episcopal Conference of Africa and Madagascar (SECAM). He continued to shepherd this all-Africa conference through its infancy years, and even continued his assistance for several years after his formal association ended. The many relationships that he held with bishops would continue in more significant ways a few years later after his resignation from Fort Portal.

CHAPTER 9

Transition and Resignation: 1969–1973

As bishop of Fort Portal, Vincent McCauley had made great progress in his goal to establish his missionary outpost. He had forged an infrastructure of institutions, especially parishes and schools, made measurable inroads in relationships with the local tribal government, established pastoral programs for refugees, and aided efforts to promote the growth and sustenance of the local church through the fostering of religious congregations and diocesan clergy. Additionally, he brought the teachings and spirit of Vatican II to his diocese, especially through his promotion of ecumenical groups and the advancement of the laity. Not content to serve only the local Fort Portal church, McCauley answered the call to assist the Uganda Episcopal Conference in significant leadership roles, and was instrumental in the foundation of SECAM, which sought to serve the collective African Church. As the 1960s began to wane, a period of transition came to the Church in Fort Portal. Feeling he had done what he could do,

McCauley, in the spirit of Africanization in which he strongly believed, prepared a successor, eventually resigning and moving to Nairobi, where he could serve the Eastern African Church more broadly.

Grooming a Successor

For Vincent McCauley, the concept of mission was basic: prepare the local church for the eventual departure of expatriates. McCauley manifested this idea during his days at Little Flower Seminary in Bengal, as well as in his leadership of the Fort Portal church. However, he was equally strong in his conviction that the local church and its members needed sufficient and proper training to adequately handle the educational, administrative, and pastoral necessities that would arise; he did not want the local church to fail. Thus, for some time at the outset of the mission, there was a need for expatriates to fill critical administrative posts. In Fort Portal, he initially used White Fathers and Holy Cross priests to serve as vicar general, chancellor, and director of diocesan schools.

McCauley's certain belief that his role in Fort Portal was to initiate and organize the local church so it could be run by Africans led him to constantly be watchful for an appropriate candidate to succeed him as bishop. The bishop found his man in Serapio Magambo, a Fort Portal priest.[1] He described him to a Holy Cross confrere as "a highly capable ecclesiastic, an excellent speaker, and a great credit to his native land, where he is beloved by his people, and unsparing in his work among them."[2] McCauley prepared Magambo by sending him to Oxford for additional education. Upon his return in 1966 he was appointed Vicar General of the Diocese.[3]

In the spring of 1969, Magambo was appointed as auxiliary bishop in Fort Portal. McCauley excitedly wrote to the diocese:

EAST AFRICA

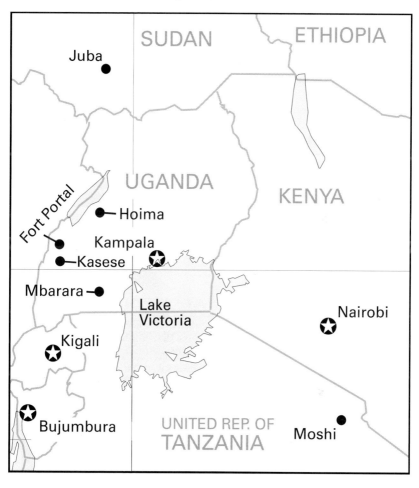

SUDAN

ETHIOPIA

Juba

UGANDA

KENYA

Fort Portal

Hoima

Kampala

Kasese

Mbarara

Lake
Victoria

Nairobi

Kigali

Bujumbura

UNITED REP. OF
TANZANIA

Moshi

⭐ = Capital
● = City

Young Father Vincent McCauley, C.S.C. (ca. 1934).

Father Vincent McCauley, C.S.C. (right), with three other Holy Cross religious (ca. 1936).

Father Vincent McCauley, C.S.C., Father Burton Smith, C.S.C., Father Francis Zagorc, C.S.C., and Father Robert Hesse, C.S.C.: the first Holy Cross missionaries to East Africa (1958).

Bishop McCauley after a celebration in Fort Portal, Uganda (1960s).

Bishop McCauley receives first blessing from a newly ordained African priest, Father Thomas Kisembo (ca. 1967).

Father John Croston, C.S.C., Bishop Serapio Magambo, Bishop McCauley, Father Robert Gay, Fort Portal, Uganda (ca. 1969).

Cardinal Laurean Rugambwa and Bishop McCauley at the dedication of the new Virika Cathedral, April 21, 1968.

Virika Cathedral, Fort Portal, Uganda (1968).

Bishop McCauley with Pope John XXIII (ca. 1962).

Bishop McCauley with Pope Paul VI (ca. 1975).

Bishop McCauley with Pope John Paul II (1979).

> We are overjoyed by the announcement that our Holy
> Father has appointed Msgr. Serapio Magambo as Auxil-
> iary Bishop of Fort Portal. Most warmly do I congratulate
> Bishop-elect Magambo and the people of Fort Portal
> Diocese.[4]

On August 1, 1969, Pope Paul VI ordained Magambo and
eleven other African bishops in an open-air Mass held during his visit to Uganda. McCauley, the SECAM bishops,
and Archbishop Sergio Pignedoli, the secretary-general of the
Propagation of the Faith, concelebrated the Mass with the
pope.[5]

Magambo's appointment fed rumors that McCauley planned
to leave Fort Portal. John Croston squelched the gossip in correspondence to both White Fathers and Holy Cross officials.
Immediately after Magambo's ordination, Croston wrote:

> Bishop McCauley has no plans for departing from Fort
> Portal that I am aware of. However, he felt it was time to
> think about the future and have someone who can step
> into his shoes. I would imagine that much would depend
> upon his health. He appears to be well, although we can
> never slow the man down. He has boundless energy which
> he must use.[6]

By January 1970, Croston admitted, "Bishop Magambo is
taking over a bit more of the work load." However, he added,
"There is no indication that Bishop McCauley is intending to
leave in the near future."[7]

McCauley and Magambo held great mutual respect profes-
sionally, and became friends on a more personal level. John
Croston, C.S.C., summarized their bond: "The two had a
remarkable relationship, trusting in one another and loving
one another." McCauley extolled Magambo both administratively and pastorally. He wrote:

> Bishop Magambo is grand. He is taking on more and
> more of the work in Fort Portal and also on the national
> scene particularly in Social Services and National Service
> fields. Everyone is delighted with the way [in] which he
> is operating.[8]

On another occasion he noted, "Bishop Magambo continues
his fine pastoral work among the people. He usually has a line
up outside his door daily, people seeking advice and help."[9]
Magambo was equally appreciative of McCauley. After the latter's death he commented:

> Without speaking Rutoro well, he was loved by everyone,
> even those of other faiths, in the diocese of Fort Portal.
> He insisted on being positive. You could hardly get him
> to pass a negative remark on someone else. He knew well
> the value of positive thinking and acting.[10]

McCauley prepared Magambo for his future in Fort Portal
by introducing him to many of his international contacts,
especially those capable of assisting the diocese financially.
Thus, beginning in April 1971, McCauley traveled with
his auxiliary to Europe and the United States on one of his
familiar "begging tours." He wrote to the head of Propaganda
Fide, "It is time, now, to introduce to my states-side contacts
our Auxiliary, Bishop Serapio Magambo—the Holy Father's
gift to Fort Portal when he visited Uganda."[11] In Rome, the
two met privately with Pope Paul VI. In Germany, McCauley
introduced his auxiliary to officials at Misereor, Missio, and
other agencies that had assisted him in numerous fundraising
efforts during the previous decade. During May and June, the
two traveled through the United States. While there, on May
2, McCauley gave an address at Creighton University titled,
"The Church and Development in Africa."[12]

Church and Politics in Uganda: 1969–1973

From the time of independence in October 1962, the Catholic Church and the Ugandan government had experienced a rather unsettled peace. Since the constitutional crisis of 1966, Milton Obote had become a virtual dictator. As economic problems grew, so too did opposition to his administration. The president responded harshly to opposition by restricting liberty, including the freedom for churches to operate. This political situation, combined with some reticence on the part of local churches to adequately and properly adapt to the precepts of Vatican II, generated a strong negative effect on the Church in general. In 1969, Adrian Hastings commented about the Church in Uganda:

> The Church in Uganda still has great possibilities: not only an extraordinary numerical growth, but a truly indigenous christian [sic] life deeply rooted in some areas, the much appreciated tradition of the Martyrs, the flexibility potentially present in what is still a young Church. But there is no country in Africa today where reluctance to face up to the inadequacies of the established system and the need for re-orientation is beginning to have more disastrous effects upon the whole quality of the Church's life.[13]

The church and state situation in Uganda took a radical shift in January 1971 with the rise of Idi Amin Dada to power. Amin was born on January 1, 1928, in northern Uganda near the Sudan and Congo borders. He received little formal education, but possessed the ability to learn. He joined the army in 1946, and by the time of independence held the rank of captain. His assistance in suppressing dissent against Obote in 1964 and 1966 gained him presidential favor and promotion to the position of deputy commander of the army. However, with increasing time, Obote and Amin grew far apart.[14] By

October 1970, each man was making plans for the elimination of the other.[15]

On January 25, 1971, Amin initiated a coup. Obote was away in Singapore at the time of his overthrow. At 3:45 p.m. of that day, Radio Uganda announced Major General Idi Amin's assumption of the office of president. The coup was relatively peaceful, although two White Fathers, Gerard Perreault and Jean-Paul Demers, were accidently killed.[16] Amin wrote in consolation to Archbishop Nsubuga:

> As your Grace knows, we are very dedicated in our cause towards God, therefore, we naturally fully appreciate the work of the Missionaries in Uganda. I personally have full admiration for the sacrifices made by the missionaries and, therefore, the accidental loss of the two priests is a great blow to Uganda.[17]

Uganda seemed ripe for political chaos when Amin acted. The British were very upset at Obote's policies. Four days after the coup, the *London Daily Telegraph* commented, "With Obote . . . out of the way, Britain could pursue the course of her strategic interests lightened of one mill-stone."[18] Israel and Sudan also had expressed the desire that he be removed. Internal dissension was also present, with the elite particularly worried about Obote's increasingly more socialist political stance.[19] Many withdrew their support; some even sought to frustrate the president's policies. Most historians agree that Amin's motivation was personal, not political. One historian claims:

> The coup was a pre-emptive move on the part of Amin and his faction in the army, aimed at forestalling further corrosion of the major General's power and ensuring his personal safety.[20]

Amin's rise to power was welcomed both by those in Uganda and the international community. He drew his popular support from the Baganda, who hated Obote from his earlier struggles with the Kabaka. For many in the region, Amin was a savior. One typical comment after the takeover stated:

> You and your brave officers and men of the Uganda Army have saved the honour, integrity and freedom of our country. Uganda, Africa and humanity owe you a deep and irreparable debt of gratitude. The whole country is behind you, our redeemer.[21]

Western governments were generally pleased, believing Amin would be tough on communism in the ongoing Cold War.[22]

Amin's takeover was generally well received by the churches in Uganda as well. He made several attempts toward reconciliation with various groups. He freed many political prisoners, set up a secretary for religious affairs to bring greater unity to the churches, and most prominently arranged that the body of the last Kabaka, Edward Mutesa II, be returned for a state funeral.[23] Churches rejoiced that Amin ended socialism. The Joint Religious Council, an interfaith group in Fort Portal, congratulated Amin for "taking over the reins of government and saving the country from total destruction to which it was exposed." The letter continued:

> Your attitude towards God and religion has mightily restored our confidence. We see great hope in the new ministry, namely the SURVIVAL of RELIGION and PEACE, TRANQUILITY, and PROSPERITY of our nation.[24]

The *Uganda Drum*, an internal Holy Cross publication, was grateful that Amin had praised missionaries and expatriate teachers for their efforts in the development of Uganda.[25] Francis Zagorc, C.S.C., echoed this general idea. With the vision of hindsight he stated:

> Sure the military takeover was the turning point, but certainly not in the beginning. We thought it was a turning

point for the better because there was a lot of enthusiasm and a lot of excitement.[26]

Vincent McCauley, like the rest of Uganda, was very optimistic concerning Amin. Writing to friends a few months after the coup, he stated:

> [Due to] the stunning and successful military coup of January 25th Uganda has since dissolved into a peaceful and progressive era. Inflation is being combated. Religious freedom remains undisturbed. The missionaries continue their daily labors, and are welcomed by the people. Travelers come and go unmolested. And overall the new Government appears to have the approval of the vast majority of Uganda.[27]

One year after the coup, McCauley was still very positive on the new regime. He commented:

> President Idi Amin Dada, a Moslem, encourages and endorses religious participation by all. This, of course, is a vital and gratifying fact, for it enables all religious congregations to go about their pastoral work freely and safely.[28]

Five months later McCauley was still impressed, stating, "We continue to enjoy full freedom of religion, and movement, and I'm quite optimistic that both privileges will remain undisturbed."[29]

The support given the Amin government, from church and state, both within and outside Uganda, turned sour after a brief honeymoon period. In July 1971, Amin visited Israel and Great Britain, securing agreements for financial assistance from both. Still, Amin claimed that his was a caretaker government until a civilian system could be created.[30] However, the support he received gave him new ideas. Historian Phares Mutibwa explains:

> Essentially . . . this adulation and excessive praise gave
> Amin a confidence that he had previously lacked, arous-
> ing ambition and a sense of destiny which he probably did
> not have at the outset of the coup.[31]

Opposition arose in 1972 when some of Obote's supporters invaded Uganda from Tanzania. The attempt failed, but the incident led Amin to begin to systematically eliminate all possible enemies, including the nation's chief justice, Benedicto Kiwanuka, and the vice-chancellor of Makerere University, Frank Kalimuzo.[32] In four separate massacres in July 1971 and February, June, and September 1972, Amin removed all military opposition to his rule. When Western governments rejected his request for aid, assistance, and armament, Amin turned to Libya and Colonel Muammar al-Gaddafi. Amin became a Moslem crusader in Christian Uganda.[33]

A second coup attempt came in March 1974. While it failed, it still nearly succeeded, thus shaking Amin's confidence. He took greater personal control, molding the army into an instrument to consolidate his personal power. He became more and more ruthless in his attempts to hold power at all costs.

Amin's new direction created an immense economic downturn in the nation. Massive military spending was one significant problem. In 1972, Amin nationalized several British companies and usurped British properties in Uganda. England retaliated by cutting off aid to its former protectorate.

The most significant factor in Uganda's economic demise was Amin's expulsion of all Asians (Indians and Pakistanis) in 1972. Between 1896 and 1901, a large contingent of Indians came to East Africa to work on the Mombasa-to-Lake Victoria railway. Over time, many of these people created a successful business subculture in Uganda, "holding a very privileged income position in relation to the African population."[34] Their success was a boon both to Uganda and to the individuals. Political economists Bert Adams and Mike Bristow comment,

> Whatever the economic growth that was achieved during the colonial regime, it had obviously enriched the immigrant communities and their descendants far out of proportion to the benefits that accrued to the great majority of indigenous people.

While the Asians claimed economic power, they were politically vulnerable. The Asians were British citizens but enjoyed only second-class status in society.[35]

Amin credited the Asians with their assistance on the railway, but he raised several "red flags" about their presence in Uganda. First, he claimed that while these people had been trained in Uganda, few supported Uganda's interests. Secondly, he chided the Asians for their business practices, especially their tendency to undercut African traders with unfair competition. He further claimed that Asians kept all business in the "family circle" and avoided paying their required taxes.[36] Amin gave the Asian community of eighty thousand only ninety days to leave.[37]

Amin's expulsion of the Asians had an immediate deleterious effect on the Ugandan economy. Uganda's middle class evaporated almost overnight. Many of the nation's critical industries fragmented and died. Revenues from business taxes plummeted 38.6 percent. High unemployment hit the nation. Massive shortages in many of the basic necessities (e.g., food stuffs, kerosene, and similar household items) were the day-to-day experiences of the people.[38]

In general, the churches reacted negatively to Amin's action against the Asians. In a cautious statement that did not question the expulsion order, Cardinal Emmanuel Nsubuga asked Amin to consider two questions: (1) the idea that people would be allowed to find a new home before expulsion, and

(2) if sufficient time had been allowed for people to prepare for their departure. The statement concluded:

> We realize that they [Asians] are not Ugandan Citizens, and we do not question the directive that they leave the country. But we are very anxious that the decision, which naturally affects the lives and futures of many thousands of men, women and children, should be carried out with as much care and consideration for their welfare as possible.[39]

During his regime, Amin demonstrated a significant evolution in his religious thought and the role of religion in the state. Initially, he portrayed himself as a non-participant in religion. He exploited the traditional animosity between religious groups, acting as a peacemaker. He sought to influence the leaders of various religious groups by providing them with cars and cash gifts. Muslims, Protestants, and Catholics all benefited from his actions. Over time, however, religion became more politicized, to the point that Muslims were automatically presumed to be Amin supporters and Christians, especially Protestants, his opponents.[40] Amin clearly favored Muslims, although he was never coercive in forcing citizens to embrace Islam. On the other hand, he did suppress all Protestant denominations save the Church of Uganda.[41] The confused religious picture did not allow a united opposition front to be presented to Amin. Historian Kevin Ward believes that churches seemed relatively unconcerned with the fate of their sister churches so long as Amin's policies did not negatively affect them. He comments further:

> Many opportunities to present a united front against the evils of the Amin regime were neglected. The churches seemed to lack the will for any common action. They had lapsed back into the mentality of the earlier period of disengagement.[42]

As mentioned previously, the 1972 and 1974 coup attempts forced Amin into a defensive mode, including his association with churches. In November 1972, he ordered a census of missionaries and then promptly began to expel expatriates with little or no rationale. Visa restrictions were also used by Amin to hamper the missionaries' efforts. Reporting the expulsion of sixteen Verona Fathers, one Mill Hill priest, and one White Father from Uganda, McCauley wrote:

> Although no reason was given on the external broadcast from Uganda, the Acholi broadcast told the people in the North of Uganda that there were too many Catholics and that it was not fair to have more than a reasonable proportion of Catholics in Uganda.[43]

The nadir of Amin's actions came in February 1977 when he ordered the murder of Anglican Archbishop Janani Luwum.[44]

While the period of Idi Amin's regime was a trying time for Uganda and its churches, it was also a decade that found Holy Cross in a quandary over its East Africa mission. The negative feelings and factionalism within the community continued to grow. Several Holy Cross members began to feel that the congregation no longer believed in the Uganda mission. The closing of the Foreign Mission Seminary in 1968 and the almost complete evaporation of new missionaries, combined with the national question raised by Amin's tyrannical regime, forced the congregation into a significant period of introspection.[45] Additionally, anti-American rhetoric in Uganda led to the closure of the American embassy in 1973, adding more fuel to the fire.[46]

With this context as background, the 1973 East Africa District Chapter met as scheduled in January to discuss the congregation's mission in Uganda.[47] In a vote of ten yes, six no, and three abstentions, the chapter recommended that the

Uganda mission be terminated. Recommendation 5 of the chapter legislation read:

> The chapter recommends that the Holy Cross Community's contractual agreement with the Bishop of Fort Portal be . . . terminated in a minimum of eight and a maximum of ten years from January 1973. This would leave room for individuals within the community staying longer at the request of the Bishop for specific tasks.[48]

However, when the Indiana Province[49] Chapter, which had ultimate governing authority over the district, met that same summer, the district's recommendation was rejected. The legislation read, "The province reaffirms its commitment to the Diocese of Fort Portal as long as its services are necessary to the extent that its members and other resources are available."[50]

In 1976, however, due certainly to the flat rejection of its 1973 recommendation, and possibly a broader perspective on the present situation in Uganda, the district reversed course. The District Chapter, which opened on January 1 with a Mass celebrated by Bishop McCauley, actually recommended an expansion of the congregation's East Africa commitment. Three specific goals were set: (1) to investigate other opportunities to serve the local church without prejudice to present commitments in Fort Portal, (2) to develop a formation program to accept African candidates, and (3) to develop a program to allow Holy Cross seminarians to come to Uganda as part of their pre-ordination formation.[51]

Later that year, at the invitation of the provincial, William Lewers, C.S.C., who succeeded Howard Kenna, C.S.C., McCauley addressed the Indiana Chapter with a strong defense of the congregation's role and mission in East Africa:

> In 18 years Holy Cross has not yet become firmly established in Africa. It is a young, growing Church. In what country did we become self-sufficient and self-reliant in

18 years? My request is that this chapter not drop Africa after an 18-year experiment. Those speaking of phasing out should be answered. I would like to have a commitment from this chapter in support of the men working in the Fort Portal diocese and elsewhere in the Uganda mission. Africa is still a land of opportunity for Holy Cross. Far from retrenching we should look for opportunities to reach out. We were founded as auxiliaries—this was even our name. Let us now show that we are truly auxiliaries by considering the many opportunities of service offered by Cardinal Otunga in Nairobi as a start.[52]

Resignation as Bishop of Fort Portal

Vincent McCauley had always seen his role in Fort Portal as an organizer and initiator; he never viewed his role as permanent. Thus, as his time in the diocese continued, and his task of systematizing its operations was more complete, he looked for the proper rationale and opportunity to tender his resignation. His first overture to resign came in 1968. During the high point of Milton Obote's nationalism drive, McCauley, who clearly believed in Africanization, was prepared to step down. John Croston, C.S.C., wrote to the provincial:

> The Bishop himself feels that the best interests of the Church might be served with his bowing out of the picture. . . . The pressure is coming from the Government and is in line with the policy of greater Africanization of the top spots.[53]

McCauley submitted his resignation to the Holy See, but he reported, "My resignation was not accepted." He was happy, however, that more African bishops had been appointed in Uganda.[54]

In 1970, McCauley again hinted that resignation was possible. He wrote the superior general indicating he was open but not eager to step down:

> Propaganda Fide has given me no indication how long they want Bishop Magambo to remain an Auxiliary in Fort Portal, but it would not be surprising if they decide that I am now redundant. There have been rumours of requests for my services (strange at my advanced age) in other positions, but so far nothing definite has been proposed. I very definitely am not encouraging the moves. I like it very much here in Fort Portal and as long as I am considered useful I hope to stay here. Nevertheless I would be most willing to step down if it is for the good of the Church; I am not at all worried about the future.[55]

In April 1972, McCauley informed the bishops of the UEC that he desired to resign the see of Fort Portal through a formal request to the Vatican. Almost immediately, Cardinal Nsubuga, Chairman of the UEC, wrote to the prefect of Propaganda Fide requesting that McCauley be allowed to continue to serve in Uganda, even if his resignation was accepted. He wrote, "The work Bishop McCauley has done in our country, for the Church, has been invaluable, and the service he has rendered during his four years as Vice-Chairman of the Episcopal Conference, have really made us appreciate his worth."[56]

In early December, McCauley received news that his resignation had been accepted and of Magambo's selection as local ordinary. While the clergy and people of Fort Portal were saddened by the news, they did take heart from the fact that he had agreed to take the position of secretary-general of AMECEA in Nairobi.[57] He congratulated Propaganda Fide for selecting an African as his replacement: "I really think that is best for the Church at this particular time in this particular case."[58] In a farewell letter, McCauley expressed gratitude for his time in Fort Portal: "I treasure as a blessing from Heaven my years among you, my collaboration with you in the Lord's work and our friendship in Christ which has been so pleasant."[59]

News of McCauley's resignation generated tributes from many fronts. The UEC spoke of his "tremendous contribution to the spiritual and material well-being of Uganda."[60] Possibly the greatest accolade came from Thomas Kisembo, chairman of the Fort Portal senate of priests:

> Your Lordship, the problem is not to find out what to thank you for, but how to thank you for what you have done for Fort Portal Diocese in particular and all Africa at large. You have taken it as a point of special concern to provide both the material and spiritual nourishment for us. . . . Your sincere and cool diplomacy with which you face the various situations is another inspiration to us. It is indeed frivolous to entertain you with heaps of praises; it is enough to say a hearty THANK YOU FOR ALL YOU HAVE DONE.[61]

Vincent McCauley's resignation as bishop of Fort Portal requires some explanation and analysis. Opinions vary, but most likely a combination of factors led McCauley to resign at this time and move to another locale and ministry. McCauley's strong support for Africanization and the need to provide the local church with indigenous clergy was certainly a major factor in his decision. He intentionally groomed Magambo for his position and often commented about the benefit an African bishop would be to the diocese and the Church in general. John Croston, C.S.C., once commented, "McCauley's idea was that sooner or later an African would take over— the sooner the better."[62] Thomas Smith, C.S.C., claims that McCauley was comfortable with Magambo and moreover realized that such a move "would be favorably interpreted by the Ugandan government."[63]

Were nationalism and direct pressure from the Amin government more of a factor than Smith indicates? As mentioned previously, Amin expelled many missionaries and threatened or pressured others to leave the country. Fellow bishop Joseph Willigers, M.H.M., believes that Amin's expulsion of the Asians raised red flags for McCauley: "For Bishop McCauley this was a sign that it was time to go."[64] Religious of Holy Cross and the White Fathers, who believed McCauley felt threatened by Amin, support Willigers's opinion.[65] The *Rwenzori Echo*, a local magazine, commented, "In December 1972 Bishop McCauley submitted his resignation because it seemed that expatriates might be forced to leave the country."[66] On the other hand, other Holy Cross religious do not believe government pressure was a factor in McCauley's decision. John Croston, C.S.C., states, "He was not intimidated by Idi Amin. His only concern was for local Christians, his priests and sisters."[67]

Pressure from the Holy Cross community must also be considered as part of the resignation equation. The aforementioned fracture in the community in the early days of the 1970s was a considerable cross to McCauley. One religious stated that McCauley told him he felt "run out of town" by those Holy Cross members who believed his episcopal leadership was not sufficiently proactive in instituting change. Another priest stated that McCauley's resignation was premised on "disenchantment with the [Holy Cross] Community."[68]

This biographer agrees with the conclusion that many factors contributed to McCauley's decision to resign, but its timing was forced by the pragmatic realization that his contribution to Fort Portal had ended. Clearly, as seen both in Bengal and Uganda, McCauley believed in the local church and indigenous vocations. His concept of mission almost mandated expatriate influence end when local people could handle the need adequately. McCauley groomed Serapio Magambo, but this does not adequately explain why in April 1972, after two earlier rejections, McCauley's resignation was accepted. While no extant correspondence gives us the mindset of McCauley at the time, the combination of a hostile government and a significant division within Holy Cross was the perfect pretext to act when he did. He had effectively organized and guided Fort Portal from its birth; there was little more he could do. Additionally, as one Holy Cross religious stated, "Bishop McCauley had bigger fish to fry in East Africa."[69] The last ten years of his life in Nairobi validate this statement.

The acceptance of McCauley's resignation placed Serapio Magambo at center stage in Fort Portal. Pope Paul VI officially appointed him as bishop on November 16, 1972. Archbishop Belloti, the papal representative in Uganda, presided over Magambo's installation on December 31. At the Mass, attended by numerous dignitaries, including Idi Amin,[70] Magambo praised his predecessor for his efforts in the diocese, especially catechetical efforts with seminarians, religious sisters and brothers, nurses, catechists, and lay leaders. He proclaimed:

> To us Catholics he [McCauley] was a real priest, a pastor, a faithful servant of the Church obedient to God and loyal to the Sovereign Pontiff and the Holy See. To me personally he's been a counselor, a friend, a companion and benefactor.[71]

Vincent McCauley's legacy in Fort Portal was assured. He was responsible for transforming the religiously unsettled kingdoms of Toro and Bunyoro into an organized diocese of parishes and administrative offices. Working with insufficient personnel and constantly begging funds, he managed to overcome every obstacle, including the devastating 1966 earthquake, to build a Church institution that was ready to be operated by local clergy. This was done within the context of political independence that generated a shaky government that was less than friendly toward organized religion. At the same time, McCauley was leading the Uganda Episcopal Conference in many of its key positions and projects. He served as chairman of the Medical Bureau and Uganda Joint Christian Council, championed the effort to build the Gaba National Seminary, and presided over the formation of the Diocese of Hoima. Additionally, he served in leadership roles with SECAM and AMECEA, bringing his expertise and influence more widely to the African Church as a whole.

Summary

Vincent McCauley and three newly ordained Holy Cross priests established the Uganda mission in 1958, unaware of what the future would hold. Led by McCauley's broad vision of the Church and his classic understanding of mission as the promotion of the local church, Holy Cross's project soon blossomed in many and varied ways. The establishment of the Diocese of Fort Portal, with McCauley named as bishop, brought some permanence to the initial endeavor. McCauley immediately established an administrative structure of institutions and personnel, most especially for the formation of the clergy and religious, that placed the diocese on firm footing. All of McCauley's efforts were pointed toward the goal of transferring control of this mission church to Africans. After ten years of service, McCauley believed that time had come. Although his initial overture for transfer was rejected, eventually, through a combination of events beyond Africanization, including Ugandan government pressure, friction within the local Holy Cross community, and the perception that he might extend his influence beyond western Uganda, Vincent McCauley resigned as local ordinary in December 1972. His episcopal career and contribution to the African Church had not ended; on the contrary, it took a significant turn toward a broader scope with the bishops of Eastern Africa. Vincent McCauley was ready and able to "fry a few bigger fish" in the mission fields of the Church.

CHAPTER 10

Chairman of AMECEA: 1964–1973

From the outset of his ministry as bishop of Fort Portal, Vincent McCauley moved beyond the geographic confines of his diocese to serve the Church more broadly in Africa. He was immediately recognized by his fellow bishops in Uganda as a leader, and aided the growth and enrichment of the Uganda Episcopal Conference. At Vatican II, he was again called upon, now by the bishops of Eastern Africa, to become their organizer and spokesman. Through his leadership, the Eastern African hierarchy had a voice, especially in the editing of "The Decree on the Church's Missionary Activity." Even with the responsibilities of organizing a new diocese and his many activities with the UEC, McCauley continued to look outward. The opportunity came immediately after his ordination as bishop when an effort was initiated to organize the Eastern African bishops in order to address issues pertinent to the region and its missionary churches. Vincent McCauley, entering on the ground floor, would very soon be raised to a position of leadership in this nascent episcopal body and would continue to serve it in various capacities for the remainder of his ecclesiastical career.

Interterritorial Episcopal Board of Eastern Africa

In the years just prior to World War II, when colonialism reigned in the African continent, the bishops of Eastern Africa began to meet in Uganda in informal ways. These prelates, all expatriates, discussed issues such as the formation of the African clergy, pastoral issues, and especially Catholic education, which, as we recall, was so vital to the mission effort. At the time no formal organization of the episcopacy was considered.[1]

In 1960, the bishops of Tanganyika met in plenary session with the apostolic delegate, Archbishop Guido del Mestri. The delegate expressed his conviction that the establishment of some organization of English-speaking bishops of Eastern and Central Africa would be constructive in bringing joint action to the region. He envisaged not only an exchange of ideas and information, but a forum for true cooperation and common ground to establish policies on many important issues pressing on the African Church. He suggested that the bishops of Tanganyika take the initiative to call a regional meeting of ordinaries to explore such a possibility.[2]

The Tanganyikan bishops expressed their willingness to explore del Mestri's proposal. An initial meeting of the secretaries-general of the colonial episcopal conferences in Eastern Africa favored the idea and asked the delegate to float the idea with the archbishops of Nairobi, Kampala, Blantyre, and Lusaka, seeking their opinions and ideas. In September 1960, del Mestri and the metropolitans agreed that some formal body for regional cooperation between countries should be initiated. As a first step, del Mestri called a formal meeting of the secretaries-general of the episcopal conferences of Tanganyika, Kenya, Zambia, Uganda, and Malawi to meet in Dar es Salaam in February 1961. The representatives suggested a "study conference" of local ordinaries to exchange views in an attempt to find uniform policies and actions. The proposed theme was "The Future of the Church in Africa." Formal plans for the proposed conference were delegated to a steering committee, chaired by Bishop Joseph Blomjous of Mwanza, Tanganyika.[3]

The preliminary meetings led to a conference, July 17–26, 1961, at the Cathedral of St. Joseph in Dar es Salaam. Forty-seven local ordinaries, including Vincent McCauley, attended the meeting, under the title Interterritorial Episcopal Board of Eastern Africa (ITEBEA).[4] Although del Mestri was the overall coordinator, the bishops chose their own leadership. Archbishop Adam Kozlowiecki, S.J., of Lusaka, Zambia, was elected chairman and Father Killian Flynn, O.F.M. Cap., was appointed secretary-general. Cardinal Laurean Rugambwa was appointed honorary president for life.[5] An executive board was also formed with bishops from each of the five founding nations: Tanganyika, Zambia, Malawi, Uganda, and Kenya.[6]

The Dar es Salaam meeting provided opportunities for the presentation of professional papers and discussions on a whole host of issues present in the Eastern African Church. Nine position papers were presented, ranging in subject from indigenous clergy to church-state relations to cooperation between national hierarchies.[7] The bishops' discussions were even more wide-ranging, with some 130 topics raised in the ten-day conference. Using the future Church as the focus, the areas of indigenization and episcopal cooperation dominated the common sessions. The bishops decided to establish the ITEBEA as a permanent body. The executive board would meet at least annually; plenary sessions would be held every three years. The nascent body described its mandate:

Its task would be to pool information concerning the
views and actions of the five Episcopal Conferences, and
to carry out projects of common interest and seek solutions to common problems, when so requested by the
national Episcopal conferences.[8]

The bishops also agreed to finance their organization by each
nation donating annually 10 percent of its anti-slavery subsidy, an annual stipend from the Holy See to assist the local
churches. This was verified at an executive board meeting held
September 12–14 in Nairobi.[9]

The Formation and Growth of AMECEA

The Second Vatican Council provided the opportunity for
ITEBEA to meet. With McCauley now representing Uganda,
the Executive Committee met in November at San Anselmo
College to discuss how the ITEBEA Episcopal conferences
would divide costs—locally, inter-diocesan, and internationally. Each representative presented a one-year development
plan as part of an overall five-year arrangement.[10]

The ITEBEA's internal financing plan, namely to use the
anti-slavery fund, was not adequate for the organization's
needs, especially for funding new and possibly costly programs
and institutions. Thus, overtures were made to Misereor, the
development agency of the West German hierarchy whose
mission was to provide financial support for the Church, especially in developing nations. Founded in 1959 for the specific
purpose of combating hunger and disease in the world, Misereor was very interested in assisting the Church in developing
regions such as Africa.[11] At a meeting held on November 20,
Monsignor Wilhelm Dossing of Misereor was invited to speak
to the ITEBEA board and explain its mission and possible
assistance to Eastern Africa. The secretary-general of Misereor wrote to McCauley, "I may assure you that our Society

[Misereor] as well as the German Bishops are interested in preserving and advancing the image of the African Church."[12] McCauley lauded the German bishops for their efforts:

> Your zealous and organized approach has been an inspiration to us in Africa and we are deeply grateful for the truly magnificent help you and the people of Germany have given to the Church and to the new countries of Africa.[13]

At this same meeting the executive board appointed Benedict Kominiak, O.S.B., to represent the ITEBEA before Misereor.

In 1963, at the second session of Vatican II, the ITEBEA Executive Committee met once again. The bishops were disappointed to learn that their one-year national development plans had been rejected by Misereor, as the requested funds far exceeded monies available. Not deterred, the board asked the national representatives to revise their plans. Additionally, discussions were held about securing a central office site with a permanent secretary-general, and the establishment of a retreat and treatment center, operated by the Paracletes, in Tanzania for alcoholic religious and priests.[14]

The third session of Vatican II provided the environment for a transformation and rebirth of ITEBEA. Beginning in the second session, the bishops of Eastern Africa physically came together, residing as a group in the Hotel Medici. Closer and more regular contact outside the council venue provided more opportunities for the bishops to discuss, both formally and informally, issues pertinent to them. This enhanced prospect bore fruit at the third session in the fall of 1964 when the ITEBEA held its second plenary session.

The transformation of ITEBEA into a more permanent organization began in August 1964. That month an official office was established in Nairobi and Killian Flynn, O.F.M. Cap., temporarily appointed secretary-general at Dar es Salaam,

was made permanent.[15] Major changes happened in early
November 1964 when a plenary session of limited scope was
held in Rome.[16] The bishops admitted that ITEBEA,

> was essentially weak in that it was a gathering of represen-
> tatives of widely separated Episcopal Conferences, stem-
> ming from no parent plenary body to direct it from time
> to time, and depending solely on occasional recommenda-
> tions from individual national conferences. ITEBEA as it
> stood could not satisfactorily accomplish the task given it
> in Dar es Salaam, viz. "The sharing of information and
> experience; inter-consultation; and combined action in
> great spheres."[17]

In order to rectify this situation the ITEBEA reformed itself
under the title Association of Member Episcopal Conferences
in Eastern Africa (AMECEA)[18] with a new more comprehensive constitution. A new executive board was elected with
Vincent McCauley selected as chairman.[19] Almost immediately, the association began to offer study sessions on Council
matters, both for its own members and in conjunction with
other groups.[20]

McCauley's election as chairman of AMECEA demonstrated the rapidity with which his fellow bishops had discovered his leadership ability and the trust they placed in him.
He was re-elected to this post in 1967 and 1970. Over the
years it became clear that his fellow prelates greatly depended
on him. In 1970, for example, fearing that both Flynn and
McCauley might step down from their positions, Cardinal
Laurean Rugambwa wrote Maurice Otunga, the archbishop
of Nairobi:

> Bishop McCauley now has an auxiliary and could be
> persuaded to continue as chairman of AMECEA until
> a co-chairman or deputy-chairman has become familiar
> enough with the work to assume the position.[21]

McCauley realized that his responsibilities at AMECEA "could be a full time job," but he was grateful for the opportunity to assist. He explained his role as chairman:

> The idea of a common approach to the needs of the Church among the 73 Bishops of Eastern Africa has been growing for the past three or four years. My job as Chairman [of AMECEA] is to keep the pot boiling.[22]

During this initial transformation stage, the AMECEA bishops sought to more clearly and precisely define their role and the aims of the organization. At the November 1964 plenary session the bishops agreed that the 1961 theme, "The Future of the Church in Africa," was still valid, but more formal and concrete proposals for action were required. Specific ideas discussed were implementation of new liturgical decrees; review of ecumenical policy and practices; training of appropriate canonists for the region; revising and updating a curriculum and orientation for seminarians; and supplying an English version of the Vatican II documents.[23] Study and implementation of the conciliar decrees was considered a must. The bishops also agreed to hold a more formal plenary session, along the lines of Dar es Salaam in 1961, in 1966 or 1967, possibly in Nairobi. Additional possible topics for discussion could be Christian education, seminary formation, lay apostolate, ecumenism, catechetics, mass-media communications, re-orientation and updating of the clergy, and relation of lay associations with AMECEA.[24]

The 1964 session also more clearly articulated AMECEA's objectives. Foremost was to promote intercommunication and cooperation between local churches in Eastern Africa. Next, the body sought ways to support the apostolate in light of the new conciliar documents. Also, the bishops wished to study problems of common interest in Eastern Africa and find solutions. Lastly, the association hoped to render services in a collaborative effort to meet the needs of the people of God.[25]

Following Vatican II, with a new constitution and a permanent home, AMECEA began to assert its influence and fulfill its objectives through various projects. In general, the nascent body sought to be at the forefront of Church leadership. Father Joseph Kelly, C.S.S.p., one of the leading figures with AMECEA in its early years, stated, "Forward-looking concepts epitomized AMECEA's birth and much of its later development."[26] In 1965, AMECEA published the first Catholic Directory of Eastern Africa. Between December 1966 and January 1967, a conference on priestly formation was held at Katigondo Seminary. Representatives from nine major seminaries in eastern Africa participated. McCauley was very pleased with the effort: "I think nothing has 'put AMECEA on the map,' so successfully as this . . . meeting of the Episcopal Conferences and of nine major seminaries."[27] The bishops also studied and redrafted the 1919 "Instruction of the Propagation of the Faith," *Maximum Illud*, which was deemed inadequate and certainly outdated.[28]

Significant time and work was placed on the aforementioned project to open a retreat and counseling/rehabilitation center for alcoholic priests to be administered by the Paraclete Fathers. The executive committee had discussed the project in 1962 and 1963. St. John's Corner opened in 1964 near Iringa, Tanzania. Almost from the outset the project began to falter, "primarily because of the lack of support by the Bishops."[29] Additionally, the facility's location was not optimal. Eventually the Paracletes abandoned the facility in 1966. Trappists from Lumbwa, Kenya, were asked to take the project but declined. Despite the failure, McCauley was sanguine in his 1967 report to the bishops:

I . . . am of the opinion that a Retreat Center of this nature situated more suitably is an essential service in a region where there are no monastic or similar establishments for the specialized care of the clergy.[30]

More positively, AMECEA sponsored a highly successful Vatican II information project. British theologian Father Adrian Hastings was engaged by the bishops to write fortnightly commentaries on all the Vatican II documents. These summaries, composed between July 1966 and May 1968, were very well received and distributed to 3,400 priests in Eastern Africa. Hastings's effort was eventually published in a two-volume work. McCauley reported, "Many expressions of satisfaction at the value of the Bulletin have been received."[31]

On a more personal level, McCauley used his position and the formation of AMECEA in an effort to assist people in the United States to better know and appreciate Africa. In his 1967 chairman's report he wrote:

The U.S. Hierarchy . . . complains that all they know about Africa is the wars and rumours of war prevailing; they are unaware of the steady build-up and development of the Church . . . in Africa.[32]

Thus, in July 1967, he wrote to William G. Connare, bishop of Greensburg, Pennsylvania, and chairman of the U.S. Episcopal Commission on Missions, about the possibility of forming an African Bureau with the United States Catholic Conference of Bishops. The idea was to increase awareness and information and improve the image concerning African missions in the United States and coordinate mission appeals.[33]

The third AMECEA plenary session was held at St. Mary's School in Nairobi from September 5 to 11, 1967. In response to the decision made in Rome in 1964 to meet in plenary session every three years, this full meeting of the AMECEA bishops was originally scheduled for Dar es Salaam in July, but political unrest necessitated a change in venue.[34] The bishops decided to formalize their gatherings with a more strict regimen. Each plenary would be divided into business and pastoral sections. Approximately two days would be dedicated to business matters, with the remaining time given to discussion of some prearranged topic, with position papers prepared in advance to stimulate the sessions' discussions. Appropriately, for the 1967 plenary, the theme was "Pastoral Perspectives in Eastern Africa After Vatican II." Seven position papers were presented, generating much discussion.[35]

By the conclusion of the 1967 plenary meeting, it was clear that AMECEA had matured significantly and was poised to be a permanent episcopal association for Eastern Africa. Basic administrative rules mandated that plenary sessions be held every three years, at which an executive board, with a chairman and vice-chairman, be elected. The board was to meet at least annually. Additionally, the functions of the general secretariat were now clearly defined.[36]

AMECEA also expanded its operation by creating departments to work with the secretary-general and chairman to meet the needs of the Eastern African Church. The first such department, social communications, was formally erected by the bishops at the 1967 plenary session. Actually established in 1968, with Father Joseph Healey, M.M., as its director, the department coordinated social communications between member nations in areas of training, research, production, and collaboration with similar organizations in electronic and traditional media. McCauley's experience with social communications in Uganda prompted him to support AMECEA's efforts fully, especially by providing sufficient funds to assure that a professional press office was present at all plenary sessions.[37] Beginning in 1970, the department began to make a significant contribution by offering social communications workshops in broadcasting and journalism.[38]

Associated with the social communications department was the AMECEA Documentation Service (ADS). A common concern was found that older churches knew very little about the younger developing churches. Additionally, a vehicle to promote communication within the Eastern African Church was necessary.[39] In an effort to remedy this situation, an extensive feasibility study was conducted. In 1973, the AMECEA bishops approved the initiation of a documentation service for better communication. The ADS was given two objectives:

> To serve the Church in the five AMECEA countries by sharing pastoral experiences of the Church in one place with all the other jurisdictions of Eastern Africa.

> To offer the universal Church a share in the on-going picture of the developing local Church in Eastern Africa with its initiatives, successes and problems.[40]

Joseph Kelly, C.S.S.p., was appointed director of ADS with headquarters at the AMECEA offices in Nairobi. McCauley was very positive on the new addition, asking full cooperation from the bishops:

> The new service is essentially a sharing of partoral [*sic*] situations and initiatives between dioceses in the AMECEA countries. However, there can be no sharing unless the Service receives the necessary information from the diocese. We ask, therefore, to give Fr. Kelly your full cooperation in this regard.[41]

Vatican II's "Pastoral Constitution on the Church in the Modern World," (*Gaudium et Spes*) led to the establishment of the Pontifical Commission for Justice and Peace, which held its first plenary session April 18–25, 1967. Inspired by the action of the Holy See, McCauley invited Joseph Gremillon, secretary of the commission, to address the AMECEA bishops at their 1967 plenary session.[42] Similarly motivated, the bishops decided that AMECEA should start a local version of the

justice and peace commission. The formal proposal described
the objective:

> There should be an organ of the Church in East[ern] Afri-
> ca to focus on the problems of poverty, hunger, develop-
> ment and social justice within the area and to show [the]
> concern of the Church in all aspects of the development
> of the area and the developing nations within it.[43]

Despite the good intentions, the commission did not take root
at this time, due in large measure to poor response from the
bishops.[44]

Following the rubric set up in 1967, the AMECEA executive board prepared for the next plenary session, scheduled for
1970. As chairman, McCauley was concerned by the decision
of SECAM to hold its second plenary that same year, only
one year after its inauguration during the visit of Pope Paul VI
to Uganda.[45] Despite his reservations, planning went forward
with several venues considered: Nairobi, Dar es Salaam, or
Lusaka, Zambia. At the plenary, held August 4–10, 1970, at
the Dominican Convent School in Lusaka, the participants
discussed "The Priest in Africa Today." Because of the topic,
one hundred priests joined fifty-six bishops for the sessions
that were guided by the presentation of five position papers.[46]
The plenary concluded with the election of a new executive
board, with McCauley again asked to serve as chairman.

Between the 1967 and 1970 AMECEA plenary sessions,
McCauley was making significant efforts to promote ecumenism. Recall that in Fort Portal he had been integrally
involved from the outset with the Uganda Joint Christian
Council (UJCC). Now, through his position with AMECEA,
he sought to enlarge his vision to the whole of Eastern Africa.
One of the position papers at the 1967 plenary, dedicated to
pastoral aspects of Vatican II, was "Ecumenism in Africa."
McCauley hoped that this would be the catalyst to the creation

of a commission on ecumenism in Eastern Africa, something along the lines of the UJCC for the whole region.[47]

The initial overtures in 1967 became more concrete in 1970. The Secretariat for Christian Unity in Rome queried the episcopal conferences of Eastern Africa on the feasibility of an ecumenical seminar in the region. Receiving positive feedback, Fathers Tom Stransky, C.S.P., and Jerome Hamer, O.P., of the secretariat, asked AMECEA to organize the meeting for January 12–16, 1970, at Langata Seminary in Nairobi. Position papers for presentation were assigned to *periti*.[48] The All Africa Conference of Churches (AACC), the Kenya Christian Council, and the UJCC were invited to attend the last day of the meeting and discussion.[49]

A combination of circumstances forced a postponement of the planned conference.[50] However, the seminar was held March 31–April 4, 1970, at the original Nairobi venue. McCauley chaired the seminar, which featured thirty-five delegates from seven countries, plus three non-Catholic observers.[51] The seminar's stated purpose "was to study the basic principles of ecumenism and to try to find means for closer collaboration between the churches."[52] Some of the topics discussed were ecumenism and mission, baptism and common worship, mixed marriages, ecumenism on diocesan and national levels, and ecumenism in catechetics and higher education.[53] The seminar participants reached some very significant agreements. First, it was agreed that ecumenism must be based on theological foundations. Next, churches must find a realistic solution to mixed marriages. The participants also agreed on the need for diocesan and national ecumenical committees. Possibly most significant, it was suggested that a common syllabus for religious education in all secondary schools be created and implemented throughout Eastern Africa.[54]

The success of the Langata seminar was hailed on several fronts. McCauley reported in August to the AMECEA plenary session, "The general consensus was that the venture was a real success and could well stimulate ecumenical efforts on a wider basis in the future."[55] Cardinal Willebrands of the Secretariat for the Promotion of Christian Unity offered his congratulations on the seminar's success:

> Please convey to the chairman and members of AMECEA my appreciation of what is being done to integrate the ecumenical dimension into the rapidly expanding life of the Church in South [sic–Eastern] Africa. The zeal and loyal obedience of the African Church in making its contribution to the current renewal is indeed an inspiration and example to many other parts of the world.[56]

At this same time, AMECEA began to look more seriously at development programs and how efforts in this area might be advanced through ecumenical cooperation. In December 1970, a three-day conference chaired by McCauley was held at Limuru, Kenya, to discuss numerous issues related to this topic.[57] A consensus report issued at the end of the conference stated in part, "In its work for development, the Church must be prepared to cooperate to the fullest with men of other Christian religions as well as with those of other faiths."[58]

The growth and expansion of AMECEA and its success in moving forward in important areas, such as ecumenism, could not mask the reality of the association's growing financial crisis. As mentioned previously, in 1961 the bishops agreed at Dar es Salaam to fund the ITEBEA (later AMECEA) through the *Pro Afris* or anti-slavery fund, a subsidy of 10 percent of the annual grant given by Propaganda Fide to national episcopal conferences to operate their secretariats. This agreement was reconfirmed at the AMECEA executive board meetings in Nairobi in 1966 and Kampala in 1967. The system initially worked well as regular funds were received. Yet after 1967 the practice began to break down as apostolic pro-nuncios, who distributed the funds, received mixed information concerning *Pro Afris* and payments were made irregularly through various sources.[59] The bottom line from McCauley's perspective as chairman was that the association was not financially solvent.

McCauley's first move was to request assistance from Propaganda Fide. He was told in response that AMECEA could not be supported: "The Council consistently votes against the provision of running expenses for such bodies."[60] Speaking of the extensive program AMECEA planned for 1970, McCauley wrote to Propaganda Fide in a rather exasperated tone:

> All of this will be stopped and the AMECEA office will probably have to close unless we find funds . . . funds which we should have received last March, 1969, nine months ago.[61]

He lamented to the AMECEA membership:

> The very existence of AMECEA is now at stake. The reason, to put it briefly is: *AMECEA is broke* [emphasis McCauley]. This situation has come about at a time when AMECEA has proved not only its value to the Church in Eastern Africa, but its potential for increased service on the broader scope recently outlined at Gaba (28–31 July) and the Synod in Rome (11–27 October). At this time when the Holy See and the African Episcopal Conferences are encouraging "Regional Groupings of Episcopal Conferences," AMECEA with its eight years of regional service in Eastern Africa is in danger of folding up. The sole reason is: NO FUNDS.[62]

By 1970, AMECEA's financial crisis had become severe. McCauley was still confused why the *Pro Afris* fund no longer functioned properly. He wrote to the apostolic pro-nuncio in Nairobi: "Whatever happened to the missing AMECEA funds is still a mystery to me."[63] At the August AMECEA plenary session, McCauley reported the situation to the bishops. For the

past two years, AMECEA had operated on borrowed funds.
The *Pro Afris* fund was not functioning and additional funds
were needed as AMECEA operations had expanded greatly
since the association was founded in 1961. More than twenty
letters sent to the apostolic pro-nunios and other officials had
not rectified the situation.[64] Thus, he petitioned Propaganda
Fide for a one-time grant of $15,000 "to meet the emergency."
The subsidy was received in June.[65] Forthrightly, he assessed
the situation and offered a possible solution:

> AMECEA cannot continue on a deficit-spending basis.
> Had it not been for the ingenuity of our penny-pinching
> (of necessity) Secretary General, AMECEA would have
> been out of business a year ago. I strongly recommend
> that a guaranteed income based on an annual budget be
> set up by the AMECEA Bishops. The indirect, insecure,
> varying 10% of *Pro Afris* Funds are [*sic*] not reliable.[66]

In September, he called an emergency meeting of the executive board to consider options for the association, including,
if necessary, its dissolution. McCauley reported that he had
received many sympathetic replies from the pro-nuncios in
Lusaka, Nairobi, and Kampala, as well as a letter of encour-
agement from Archbishop Pignedoli of Propaganda Fide.
AMECEA's executive board, meeting in emergency session,
seemed somewhat optimistic:

> The Board members present on behalf of their conferences
> rejected any suggestion of discontinuing the regional
> association, which had pre-dated the recommendations
> of Vatican II, had given to date almost nine years of
> beneficial service to the constituent Episcopal Confer-
> ences, and would prove, moreover, of benefit to the whole
> continent in the organization of the All Africa Bishops'
> Symposium.[67]

McCauley's suggestion at the 1970 AMECEA plenary session of levying a tax on each member episcopal conference took time to develop. The inability of some conferences to pay their share kept the association on very tenuous financial ground.[68] Thus, in 1971, McCauley was again forced to beg funds from Propaganda Fide. He understood that it was not Propaganda Fide's policy to fund episcopal conferences, but nonetheless he pleaded, "Unless AMECEA is given financial support it will surely die. With its demise a valuable means of effective collegial collaboration will cease. . . . another victim of mission poverty."[69]

McCauley explored his European options as well. He discussed with Killian Flynn the possibility of petitioning *Cor Unum*.[70] He wrote:

> "*Cor Unum*" might (??) consider that a service organization for five African countries with the variety of assets AMECEA represents should be worthy of assistance. The petition would have to be carefully drawn up with stress on the proven values of AMECEA services, and the potential for even greater benefits to the Church in our Developing Countries.[71]

McCauley also petitioned his longtime financial ally, Missio, in West Germany. Grateful for a significant grant of 113,000 shillings ($323,000) to "keep AMECEA's door open,"[72] he wrote:

> May I on behalf of the seventy-three Bishops of Eastern Africa (Kenya, Malawi, Uganda, Tanzania, and Zambia) express our deep appreciation to the Bishops of Germany for their fraternal concern and generosity. For more than ten years the services of our Association (AMECEA) have been growing in scope and importance for the Church. We have, however, been constantly hampered by lack of finances. There was a danger a year ago that AMECEA would have to close. Thanks to Monsignor Wissing, who

made a personal investigation, and to the gracious recommendation of all at Missio, the Bishops of Germany
have saved AMECEA. Although I cannot possibly convey
to you all that your generosity means to the Church in
Africa, I do assure you that all of us are deeply and prayer-
fully grateful to the Church in Germany. Only the Lord
can reward you fully. It is our prayer that He will.[73]

The 1973 AMECEA plenary provided the forum for a final
resolution to the association's financial crisis. Although still in
existence, the *Pro Afris* fund was not viable, nor was voluntary
taxation of the member episcopal conferences. McCauley told
the bishops:

AMECEA has been existing for 10 years on hand-outs.
These unreliable sources of livelihood have made our sub-
liminal subsistence level so precarious that positive planning is next to impossible. It is true that we are still alive
after several miraculous rescues from bankruptcy, but we
are not yet in a sound financial condition.

Thus, as a permanent "fix" to the problem, he suggested the
bishops set up a financial committee or administrative board,
composed of a chairman and four expert financial consultors
from the five AMECEA nations. This body would be responsible to the executive board for the construction of an annual
budget. Each country would be assessed and contribute equally to the approved budget. The implementation of McCauley's
plan finally ended the crisis and placed the association on the
path for future accomplishment.[74]

The Gaba Pastoral Institute

The post–Vatican II era provided the environment for the
bishops of Eastern Africa to review and renew catechetical
training, especially in the light of the advancement of the lay
apostolate. In February 1966, acting in response to a meeting

of religious superiors in Lusaka the previous December, the AMECEA executive board initiated discussions on how the association could respond to the new catechetical challenge before it. One memorandum from the board read: "There is an increasing awareness of the need for more thorough training in catechetics according to the new catechetical approaches [for] both missionary personnel and African lay and Religious teachers." The board realized that schools were available for such training in Europe and the United States, but funding for travel and maintenance of students in such locales was not feasible. Additionally, the board spoke of "the need for a specifically African orientation of such a course."[75]

These initial discussions continued later in the year with significant progress made toward the formulation of a plan of action. A meeting of the regional superiors of the White Fathers, held in June 1966, proposed a catechetical center whose "primary aim . . . would be to train experts in catechesis, pastoral liturgy, and applied theology."[76] In September, the executive board met to discuss the idea proposed by several of the member episcopal conferences and various communities of religious to establish a catechetical institute. The board commissioned Killian Flynn, O.F.M. Cap., secretary-general of AMECEA; Adrian B. Smith, W.F.; Ton Simons, W.F.; and Alden M. Pierce, M.M., to study and write a report on the possibility of establishing a *Lumen Vitae* type of catechetical institute to train clergy, religious, and laity for teaching religion and supervising this teaching.[77] The institute was to be an English-medium residential college that would emphasize catechetical theory and practice.[78] The institute listed its aims:

> The purpose of the Institute shall be to give selected persons a thorough and specialized training enabling them to promote a more efficacious apostolate in their home dioceses or appointed spheres.

[The] secondary purpose of the Institute shall be to
serve as an information center and provide coordinating
facilities for national and regional pastoral centers and
commissions.[79]

A positive report from Flynn's committee sent the project
in search of logistical support. As chairman of AMECEA
and a strong proponent of catechetical education,[80] Vincent
McCauley petitioned Archbishop Emmanuel Nsubuga of
Kampala for permission to use the old and underused Gaba
seminary buildings for the proposed institute. Nsubuga agreed
to the request, but with stipulations concerning the housing
of seminarians and ownership of the facility.[81] With facilities
secured and a clear desire for the institute, the AMECEA plenary session of 1967 gave its official approval of the project.[82]
Ton Simons, W.F., who was released by the White Fathers to
assist, was appointed by McCauley, in the name of the executive board, as director of the Gaba Pastoral Institute.[83]

Although facilities had been procured and all were in agreement for the institute's inauguration, the ever-present reality
of financing such a project loomed large. AMECEA's elected
leaders, Flynn and McCauley, were tasked to secure the necessary funds. Propaganda Fide, through the intercession of the
Apostolic Delegate, was the target of the development effort.
Extant records show that a total of $30,000 was secured for the
renovation of the old Gaba seminary along the lines necessary
for the pastoral institute.[84]

The AMECEA Gaba Pastoral Institute officially opened
on February 1, 1968. Its ten-month program, divided into
two parts, was available to priests, religious, and the laity.[85] In
order to obtain a full complement of students, each bishop of
AMECEA was asked to send one student. McCauley, however,
sent five to make up the shortfall from some who failed to send
a representative.[86] Faculty in the areas of African anthropology,
methodology, and scripture were secured. A board of

governors was also appointed.[87] Lastly, a management committee, headed by McCauley, was responsible for maintenance
of the institute and recruiting students.[88]

In support of Gaba's vital function of training educators for
the Eastern African Church, the Pastoral Institute expanded
its horizons. McCauley sought to upgrade the institute's academic recognition by having its certificate diploma accepted
by Makerere University, the leading institute of higher education in Uganda.[89] Besides its program of catechesis, Gaba conducted research studies to advance the work of AMECEA. In
August 1971, the AMECEA executive board decided that the
Gaba Institute would take oversight for the *African Ecclesial
Review*.[90] Joseph Healey, M.M., voiced what many thought
of the project: "Gaba was a winner; it put AMECEA on the
map."[91]

After three years of operation, the Gaba Institute conducted an internal critique of its operations and service to the
African Church. The director's report in 1971 highlighted the
institute's many good works and projects, but bemoaned the
fact that there was such an ancillary association with AME-
CEA. This disconnect was made manifest most strongly in the
perception that Gaba was forcing its projects and their fruits
upon the bishops. The director, Ton Simons, W.F., stated:

> We are sometimes faced with the anomaly that some
> bishops seem to think that we are trying to force certain
> things on them . . . while as a matter of fact we are simply
> producing these things at their own request and at the cost
> of much extra work, headache and expense, in an effort to
> fulfill the mandate they themselves gave us. The Gaba staff
> would have a much easier life if they did not take these
> mandates so seriously. But would we then be answering
> the expectations the AMECEA bishops had when they
> established the Institute?[92]

He went on to suggest that the rather tangential association Gaba held with AMECEA needed to draw closer. The triennial AMECEA plenary sessions were hardly sufficient contact with the bishops. Simons reported, "The ordinaries are entitled to more frequent contact with their Institute, to a better and more direct knowledge of our problems and difficulties, as well as the successful outcomes of some of our undertakings."[93]

Africanization was also on the mind of Simons in his report to the bishops. He stated:

> From the beginning and until now the Gaba staff has been entirely expatriate. We have made several attempts to get some African members released for appointment to the Gaba staff, but up till now with very little result. Future staff members should be well qualified and such people are either hard to find or, once found, hard to get released. We would like to ask in the course of the coming three years some capable Africans be appointed to Gaba in view of a gradual takeover.[94]

Simons felt strongly that the Africanization program should begin with his position of director:

> It is particularly important that *"the function of Director* [emphasis Simons] of the Institute" be taken over by a capable African priest in the near future. All the rectors of major seminaries in the AMECEA countries are now Africans. Gaba stands out as the one exception. If this is allowed to continue longer than necessary it will have an adverse effect on the name and influence of the Institute.[95]

Simons's insistence that a capable African be appointed to his position prompted him to state his intention not to renew his contract, which was slated to end in December 1971. In a letter to McCauley, he gave three reasons: (1) the need to Africanize his position, (2) his belief that negative attitudes of bishops and episcopal conferences toward Gaba persisted, and (3) personal reasons.[96] McCauley accepted Simons's resignation, but reported that he was leaving due to ill health.[97] With no qualified African candidates available, McCauley was thus forced to find another expatriate. McCauley explained the dilemma he faced in his desire to appoint an African, but finding no suitable candidate:

> We are trying harder than ever to train Africans for the needs of the Church in all our countries. Time is short. We do have a majority of African Bishops, but even they cannot ordain incompetents to the priesthood. Three of our AMECEA countries (Kenya, Malawi, and Zambia) are woefully weak in African clergy . . . 250 priests in their 31 dioceses. So . . . self-reliance is still years away.[98]

After consultation with Robert Chaput, W.F., the White Fathers' regional superior, McCauley appointed John Lemay, W.F., as the new director of the Gaba Institute.[99]

During the dictatorship of Idi Amin, the Gaba Institute's problems grew far greater than the Africanization question and the need of a new director. With increasing severity, Amin restricted entry visas to Uganda and travel outside the country for citizens. Although John Lemay, W.F., tried to allay fears,[100] it was clear by 1975 that Gaba had become another victim of Amin's regime. Staff and students felt the pinch of these restrictions. In 1975, only thirty-eight students entered the program, down twelve from a full complement. At the same time, the Ugandan bishops informed AMECEA that there was a need to house thirty-two first-year seminarians at the Gaba site due to overcrowding at Katigondo and Gaba seminary facilities.

The combination of Amin's negative influence and the need to return the Gaba Pastoral Institute facilities to the Archdiocese of Kampala forced McCauley and AMECEA to find a new home.[101] Several possibilities arose, but the best offer came from the Sisters of Loreto in Eldoret, Kenya, who offered their convent school. In June 1975, three representatives from the Loreto Sisters and four from AMECEA, Cardinal Maurice Otunga of Nairobi, Bishop John Njenga of Eldoret, (later archbishop of Mombasa), McCauley, and Lemay, met to finalize plans. Lemay believed the facility would work well with some $25,000 in renovation costs.[102]

After the last Gaba Ugandan graduation on October 19, 1975, the move to Eldoret began on December 16. Due to the move, it was decided not to offer the program in 1976. On January 23, 1977, the chairman of AMECEA, Bishop James Odongo, welcomed fifty-two participants for the ninth AMECEA Pastoral Institute program. The institute formally opened the next day with a Mass celebrated by Otunga with McCauley and others as concelebrants.[103]

Vincent McCauley offered profuse praise for Gaba and defended its work and reputation against all detractors. In 1969, when informed that some bishops had offered less-than-favorable comments about Gaba, he wrote the Uganda Episcopal Conference:

> The Gaba Pastoral Institute has proved, not only highly satisfactory to the Executive Board of AMECEA, but has received distinctive commendation from Bishops who have visited the Institute during the visit of the Holy Father and by many other knowledgeable people from Africa and abroad who have taken the trouble to investigate its operation, experience, even briefly, its spiritual vitality, consulted its students and staff, examine the content of its course, etc.[104]

One year later, McCauley reported, "In my opinion our Gaba Institute has been the outstanding achievement of AMECEA. . . . Gaba has proved its worth far beyond our expectations. Its soundness and its value to the Church are now well established and almost universally recognized."[105]

The Gaba Institute continued to evolve and offer more programs and services to the Eastern African Church.[106] The most important evolution was the creation of the Gaba research department, a wing of the institute designed for long-term study of significant pastoral questions. Launched at the time Gaba was founded in 1968, the department, under the guidance of Aylward Shorter, W.F., started its first major study in 1971. Titled the "Churches Research on Marriage in Africa" (CROMIA), the study was a theological and sociological investigation into all the aspects of marriage, from the viewpoints of Church and society. The study's report, "African Christian Marriage," published in 1977, was considered a seminal work on the subject.[107] Other projects conducted by the Gaba research department included "Attitudes and Initiatives Toward Christian Unity," (1975–1979) and "The Role of the Priest in the Christian Community," both under the direction of John Mutiso-Mbinda.[108]

Summary

The geographic limits of the Diocese of Fort Portal were too confining for the talent and energy of Vincent McCauley. From the outset of his tenure as local ordinary, McCauley was integrally involved with the organization and promotion of the work of the Eastern African bishops, first through the Interterritorial Episcopal Board of Eastern Africa (ITEBEA), and then the body's more mature form, Association of Member Episcopal Conferences in Eastern Africa (AMECEA). In 1964, during the Second Vatican Council, McCauley became chairman of the nascent body. As chairman, McCauley organized the bishops to present a voice at Vatican II, guided the association through its first three triennial plenary meetings, and set up the basic organization of AMECEA and its varied departments. Along with the body's first secretary-general, Killian Flynn, O.F.M. Cap., McCauley rescued AMECEA from impending financial insolvency by using his fiscal skills and placing in operation a more secure financial system of operation. His crowning achievement as chairman was the establishment of the Gaba Pastoral Institute, which provided year-long catechetical programs, and, through its research department, initiated several significant long-term studies on pastoral issues for the African Church. McCauley's association with AMECEA did not end in 1973, however, but only grew greater through his appointment as secretary-general.

CHAPTER 11

Secretary-General of AMECEA: 1973–1979

V atican II's promotion of the concept of collegiality
was manifest in varied and multiple ways throughout
the Church. On an international level, regular synods
of bishops were called by the reigning pontiffs to discuss and
receive input on pertinent issues in the Church universal.
National episcopal conferences, such as the Uganda Episcopal
Conference, blossomed as effective tools in the promulgation
of the teachings and ideas of Vatican II as well as providing a
forum for the discussion and resolution of concerns present in
local churches. In a similar way, AMECEA, born just prior to
the Council, grew through the 1960s from a fledgling organization on rocky financial ground to the best-known and most
well-respected of all African regional episcopal organizations.
Vincent McCauley's leadership as AMECEA chairman from
1964 to 1973 was instrumental in this process of maturation

and rise to international status. Thus, it was only natural when McCauley retired as bishop of Fort Portal that he would be called upon to minister more closely to the organization with which he was so closely associated from the outset. As McCauley came to the summit of his episcopal career, he moved to Nairobi to lead AMECEA and the bishops of Eastern Africa to new heights in service to God's people.

Secretary-General of AMECEA

Killian Flynn, O.F.M. Cap., who had served as secretary-general of AMECEA since the association's inception, made clear his desire to retire and transfer his position to a qualified African. In 1967, he communicated this message to McCauley and the executive board. McCauley realized that AMECEA's top position was becoming progressively more complex, and, therefore, an assistant might be necessary. Others, as well, had noticed that Flynn was slowing down: "When the rush is on, he can hardly cope."[1] Still, the AMECEA executive board supported him while a search was initiated for a qualified African candidate.[2]

Flynn's desire to retire came at the same time as discussions about his being consecrated a bishop. In 1968, the AMECEA executive board raised the idea that Flynn should be put forward as a bishop candidate. A straw vote was very favorable toward such a move, but the Kenyan bishops were unanimously opposed. With AMECEA headquartered in Nairobi, McCauley wisely and prudently suggested that the board not move forward with the suggestion.[3]

The inability to find a qualified candidate forced Flynn to stay on the job. In 1970, however, he again asked to retire, noting the need for an African. While sensitive to the issue, Cardinal Laurean Rugambwa was more pragmatic in his response:

> Regarding proposals for a new Executive Secretary of
> AMECEA, the stress should be put on "competence"
> rather than African. It would not be wise to push some-
> body just for the sake of Africanization. What we need is
> a competent administrator and it means little whether he
> is European, African or anything else.[4]

McCauley in turn asked the AMECEA bishops to submit
names for consideration. When no candidates were offered, he
lamented his frustration to the AMECEA membership:

> Unless the Bishops do come forth with [an] exception-
> al Secretary-General, the continuing development of
> AMECEA cannot be assured. May I ask therefore that
> in the Episcopal Conferences this matter be given serious
> consideration and effective implementation.[5]

The need to find a new secretary-general for AMECEA was
pressed further when Flynn's religious community, the Irish
Province of Capuchins, asked him to return to Ireland to take
a position assisting in the formation of young friars. The situation prompted McCauley to petition Rugambwa, permanent
honorary president of AMECEA:

> You will remember how hard we tried to get an African
> priest for the position, but without success. It would be
> fatal to put any but a top-notch man in the job, and so far
> no AMECEA Bishop is willing to part with "the best he
> has." In any case, even a qualified African priest will need
> some "inservice training" in order to familiarize himself
> with the many faucets [sic] of the AMECEA operation.
> But who is the African priest? Until we find him we must
> make an interim arrangement.[6]

The circumstances forced McCauley to suggest that Joseph
Healey, M.M., director of the social communications department, be appointed as "acting secretary-general." In August, the

executive board followed McCauley's proposal and appointed Healey to the post.[7]

Shortly after his return to Ireland and the celebration of his golden jubilee, Flynn died of inoperable stomach cancer on December 3, 1972. Flynn's death generated an outpouring of praise for his efforts on behalf of AMECEA and the Eastern African Church. Joseph Healey, M.M., remembered Flynn for his contributions as administrator and educator, but even more as priest and religious:

> The search for and training of Africans—priests, religious and lay people—for work in the fields of communications, catechetics, social activities, urban development, etc., was his constant endeavor. Nevertheless with all his administrative and detailed duties performed with remarkable proficiency and dedication, Father Killian Flynn was always first and foremost the Capuchin priest. Wherever he went and whatever company the priest in him stood out in strong relief.[8]

McCauley credited Flynn with building AMECEA and its many accomplishments. He wrote:

> I feel certain that any bishop would insist that we record and publicly express our heartfelt gratitude. To many, Fr. Flynn became known as Father AMECEA. He even had letters so addressed to him. Fr. Flynn watched over AMECEA from its first days. He coaxed it through a sickly infancy, encouraged its youth during Vatican II years, [and] nursed it through a financial crisis in 1969 and 1970. AMECEA has arrived at its present stage of development largely because of the selfless dedication of the exceptionally competent Fr. Flynn.[9]

Killian Flynn's tragic death came, nonetheless, at an opportune time for AMECEA and Vincent McCauley. The bishop's resignation at Fort Portal had been accepted and thus he was "free" to take the secretary-general position, at least temporarily. McCauley wrote, "Since the death of our beloved Father Killian Flynn on the 3rd of December, there has been a void at AMECEA Headquarters. The Executive Committee wants me to try to fill the gap."[10] On January 15, 1973, the AMECEA executive board confirmed McCauley's appointment. McCauley agreed to serve until the next plenary session scheduled for December 1973. The board echoed the earlier call of Flynn for an African to take the position:

> Africanisation of this position, Secretary General, is an AMECEA priority and must be filled as soon as possible by a man of integrity, responsibility and administrative ability, who would be acceptable to the bishops.[11]

McCauley concurred with this idea, seeing its fulfillment as part of his responsibility. He wrote to friends, "As has been the objective up to now, my new job will entail the training of an African to take the post of Secretary General of AMECEA."[12]

While the Africanization move was clear in the minds of expatriates, it is important and interesting to note how Africans viewed this question. McCauley's AMECEA colleague, Joseph Healey, M.M., suggests that Africans were delighted to have Americans in the local hierarchy. They realized that Americans were efficient and had the ability to get things done. Thus, when it was clear that McCauley was free to take the secretary-general position, the Africans were glad to have him. Unlike McCauley, they were not insistent that an African be named.[13]

McCauley's transition to the position of secretary-general was rather natural, especially considering his long association with AMECEA. Bishop Joseph Willigers commented, "It seems to me that this was really a job that suited him and he worked hard to forge this association of bishops into

a working reality."[14] Fellow Holy Cross Archbishop Charles
Schleck echoed similar sentiments:

> He gladly undertook this task and quickly developed
> this Regional Conference of Bishops that involved much
> of Eastern Africa (English speaking) into the best such
> regional Conference in the entire continent.[15]

Again, Joseph Healey, M.M., has commented that McCauley
possessed a special talent to get bishops to work toward a
common cause. McCauley told Healey, "Unity is strength. By
working together we can achieve more."[16] McCauley moved to
Nairobi and immediately dove into his new work.[17]

The secretary-general post made McCauley responsible to
the executive board for many functions. He was to direct and
supervise the activities of the central secretariat in Nairobi and
its departments, keep the association informed of the secretariat's activities, prepare and arrange with the chairman and the
executive board the plenary meetings (including transportation and accommodations), and be responsible for the minutes
of all meetings and keeping the archives.[18] McCauley commented on his busy schedule: "Some people think that I am a
retired bishop with nothing to do. Actually, there has been of
late more pressure at AMECEA than at Fort Portal."[19]

Vincent McCauley was a natural fit for the AMECEA top
post in other ways. After many years in the region, he understood and could practice well an "African style" in accom-
plishing goals. He became adept at less formal ways to gain
information, answer questions, and achieve results. He set a
hospitable and congenial tone in the AMECEA offices. His
concern for those with whom he worked and their families
was clearly manifest. In return, people gave their best, yielding
significant results for AMECEA.[20]

One of the first items that needed McCauley's attention
was the association's membership. From the outset, AMECEA

(originally ITEBEA) comprised five nations: Kenya, Uganda, Tanzania, Zambia, and Malawi. At the December 1973 plenary meeting, Sudan was granted membership. At this same plenary, the Episcopal Conference of Ethiopia submitted a request to initiate contact with the association. Eventually, in 1979, Ethiopia was also granted membership.[21]

McCauley's move to Nairobi prompted action on the outstanding need for a permanent home for the association. The original headquarters building was a forty-year-old home, "picked up cheap during a real estate slump." It had five rooms—four offices and a dining room; the kitchen was separate.[22] As early as 1970, McCauley, in his Chairman's Report, described the AMECEA offices at 47 Gitanga Road as "totally inadequate." He suggested at the time, "Unless the proposed Catholic Centre progresses beyond the planning stage, AMECEA must build."[23] In October 1973, the executive board authorized McCauley to seek the advice of an architect to draw up plans for a new and permanent AMECEA office and residence facility. Eventually, with architects and contractors in place and permission secured from the Nairobi municipal government for a new building on the same site of the original residence and office, construction began. Misereor and Missio were the primary funders of the project, while McCauley raised 35 percent of the revenue himself.[24] Although there were some delays in construction, the offices opened on July 1, 1975. The residence opened two months later on September 1.[25] McCauley was happy that the new headquarters would assist AMECEA's mission:

> The AMECEA residence has been a valuable asset. It is "home" for our Bishops when they are in Nairobi, as well as the AMECEA staff. We expect our bishops to make it their Nairobi headquarters.[26]

AMECEA Plenary Meetings—1973 to 1979

Even before he assumed his new position as secretary-general, plans were well underway for the triennial 1973 plenary meeting. Although Dar es Salaam and Makerere University in Kampala had initially been proposed as venues for the plenary, the meeting was actually held December 14–21 at St. Thomas Aquinas Seminary outside Nairobi. The conference theme, "Planning for the Church in Africa in the 1980s," was supported, as in the past, by the presentation of position papers.[27]

The plenary session theme led the bishops to a series of intense debates on the local African Church. Discussions related to personnel planning, the Christian family, religious education, integral social development, and specialized apostolates were held. These issues, it was observed, would be the agenda for AMECEA in the 1980s and 1990s. The bishops initiated a discussion on Small Christian Communities (SCC), a topic that would be addressed formally in future AMECEA meetings as well as serve as a basis for development in the African Church. While Bishop Patrick Kalilombe was the architect, McCauley was a great supporter of the concept:

> Our main pastoral priority in the 85 dioceses of Eastern Africa is the "Building of Small Christian Communities." For this we have several training programs for the clergy, the Religious and the Laity. Hopefully, well established Christian Communities will be better able to assist the poor and the refugees who are and will be with us.[28]

Concerning the African environment of dispersed people and insufficient clergy, the bishops were clear on their endorsement of SCC in building for the future:

> We are convinced that in these countries of Eastern Africa it is time for the Church to become really local, that is:

self-ministering, self propagating and self-supporting. Our planning is aimed at building such local Churches for the coming years. We believe that in order to achieve this we have to insist on building Church life and work on basic Christian communities in both rural and urban areas. Church life must be based on the communities in which everyday life and work take place: those basic and manageable social groupings where members can experience real inter-personal relationships and feel a sense of communal belonging, both in living and working. We believe that Christian communities at this level will be best suited to develop real intense stability and become effective witnesses in their natural environment.[29]

The 1973 plenary also brought a change in AMECEA leadership. Now serving simultaneously as the permanent secretary-general and chairman, McCauley, after nine years in the latter position, needed to be replaced. Bishop James Odongo of Tororo, Uganda, was elected as McCauley's successor. He praised his predecessor for his accomplishments and long tenure as chairman:

It must go down in history that not only has Bishop McCauley always played the part of priest and Bishop, but more so as a father to AMECEA. . . . It is the hope of all AMECEA Bishops, that now as our Secretary General, Bishop McCauley will continue with the same spirit to serve and direct AMECEA with the advice of a Grandfather.[30]

With the AMECEA leadership fixed, formal planning for the 1976 plenary session began in earnest in March 1975. The executive board made a formal request to the Malawi Episcopal Conference to host the session. Possible seminar topics were also proposed: "Position of Religious Sisters and Brothers in the Church," "Family," "Role of the Laity in the Church," "Christian Communities," and "Building Christian

Communities."[31] When the bishops of Malawi reported that
they could not host the conference, the Tanzanian hierarchy
was asked. Again a positive response was not forthcoming:
"Sorry that Malawi has not been able to host the AMECEA.
It may be impossible in Tanzania as well, then . . . Zambia or
Kenya will have to host it!!!"[32] Eventually, AMECEA returned
to St. Thomas Aquinas near Nairobi, the venue of three years
earlier.

The plenary session, with the theme of "Building Christian
Communities in Africa," was held July 13–23, 1976. At the
business meeting, James Odongo was re-elected chairman.[33]
This session, like three years previously, focused its attention
on the local church. The formation of small Christian communities was considered a "key pastoral priority," for the Eastern
African Church. In fact, the AMECEA documentation service
reported that 75 percent of the AMECEA bishops believed,
"Building Christian communities has been recognized today
as the highest pastoral priority in the AMECEA countries."
The bishops stated in the session legislation:

> The Christian communities we are trying to build are sim-
> ply the most local incarnations of the one holy Catholic
> and apostolic Church. . . . The task of building Christian
> communities is more creating and developing awareness
> of what our renewed vision of the Church means in prac-
> tical terms and relationships, than one of building new
> structures.[34]

With this mandate, each diocese was asked to formulate a plan
for implementation of this vision.

While the 1976 plenary session had been a success, it
took its toll on the secretary-general. McCauley wrote to his
family:

> The past two weeks—64 Bishops and 144 other
> participants—saw the 6th Triennial Plenary of AMECEA

at the Major Seminary here in Nairobi. The affair taxed the abilities and stamina of our staff and co-opted helpers . . . including "Mzee," i.e. the old man. I don't think I was ever so glad to say "kwaheri" (goodbye) to Cardinals, Archbishops, clergy, religious and lay visitors from 18 countries. Thank the Lord it will be three years before the next gathering of that magnitude.[35]

While McCauley's duties associated with AMECEA were significant and time consuming, he nonetheless found time for other episcopal responsibilities. The regularly scheduled Synod of Bishops was called for September 1977.[36] Bishop Adrian Ddungu of Masaka was scheduled to attend as the Ugandan representative. However, this, as we recall, was a period when Idi Amin placed significant restrictions on travel. Thus, Ddungu asked McCauley to attend the Synod in his place.[37] The Synod theme, "Catechesis for Youth and Children," was of great interest to McCauley as evidenced by his promotion of Christian education, both as ordinary in Fort Portal and now as secretary-general of AMECEA.[38]

As AMECEA moved forward and matured during the 1970s, the need for some self-reflection was clear. Thus, after the conclusion of the 1976 plenary, the executive board began to review past conferences and look at other possible formats for the triennial meetings. Some ideas that arose were a formal seminar for the bishops, a formal retreat format, and a combination of these two. Thus, in 1977, the executive board proposed that the 1979 plenary be a meeting for bishops only, and that the format include small group sessions and retreat days. Each episcopal conference was asked to provide feedback on this proposal.[39] Additionally, as part of this self-reflection, the board agreed that the seminar topic would be a review of the 1973 and 1976 study conferences. The aim was to see what had been implemented, what still needed to be done, and what, practically speaking, was possible for the future.[40]

Unlike past plenaries where changes of venue were common, in 1979 two countries, Uganda and Malawi, vied for the privilege to host the conference.[41] Although Uganda's bid was based on celebrating the centenary of Catholicism in the country, Zomba, Malawi, was selected to host the association.[42] For the first time, Ethiopia attended the plenary session as a full-fledged member.

The 1979 plenary session made great strides in reviewing AMECEA's past while charting a course for its future. McCauley, who for the first time gave a position paper at the plenary session, spearheaded the bishops' movement into the future. His paper, "Commission for Integral Human Development," was a call for the Eastern African bishops to look at issues of justice and peace. McCauley suggested that once national episcopal conferences had addressed the issue, it then would be possible for AMECEA to make recommendations for the whole of the region.[43]

The official theme, "Review of Institutions, Problems and Progress Experienced by the AMECEA Countries in Implementing the Recommendations Made at the 1973 and 1976 AMECEA Plenaries," led the group in 1979 to focus on the clarification of Small Christian Communities (SCC). Through a review of the past, the bishops agreed to recommit themselves to greater implementation of this pastoral priority. A summary document read:

> This policy represents the most appropriate way of expressing the mystery of the Church as a communion of faith, hope and love, as well as being an excellent means of involving all the members of the People of God in the common task of continuing the reconciling mission of Christ in the world.[44]

The study conference stressed that SCC were the best way to develop African Christianity:

Small communities also seem the most effective means of making the Gospel message truly relevant to African cultures and traditions. By participating in the life of the Church at this most local level, Christians will foster the gradual and steady maturing of the young Church.[45]

At the 1979 plenary, it was necessary for the bishops to bid farewell to Benedict Kominiak, O.S.B., who had well and faithfully served AMECEA as its representative to Misereor since 1962. Kominiak had told McCauley in December 1978 that the Father Archabbot of the Benedictines had appointed him secretary-general of the Benedictine Community at St. Ottilien in Germany. He was given permission to stay with AMECEA until a suitable replacement was found. McCauley found two possible candidates, Fathers Theobald Kyambo of Tanzania and Emmanuel Kibirige of Uganda. After consultation, Kibirige was selected. McCauley was appreciative of Kominiak's work, telling him that he had served "a very valuable mission . . . in helping the development of the Church . . . in Eastern Africa."[46]

The Apostolic Programs of AMECEA

During McCauley's tenure as secretary-general, AMECEA expanded its operations by initiating several programs designed to improve the educational, social, and religious fabric of Eastern African society. At the July 1973 AMECEA plenary session, the bishops discussed the need for some training program for Church personnel in accounting. Expanding Church roles and revenues necessitated greater accountability for funds and their disbursement. Thus, in January 1975, a one-year diploma program in accounting was initiated by AMECEA at the Social Training Center in Nyegezi, Tanzania. The Episcopal Conference of Tanzania administered the program with

Brother Fred Cosgrove, C.S.C., as director. It welcomed seventeen students that first year.[47]

The program's initial success was tempered with several concerns. McCauley reported to the executive board in February 1977 that poor communication between the program director and the secretaries of the national Episcopal conferences was raising concern. Additionally, some worried that the qualifications of some sent to the program were insufficient to properly benefit from it. By 1979, McCauley's trepidation was high enough to recommend the program shut down unless it was better utilized. However, in 1980, after McCauley's retirement from AMECEA, the program continued to operate, to the delight of the executive board.[48]

In April 1971, AMECEA began to formally discuss the concept of an interdisciplinary and ecumenical training program for social and pastoral development of urban and industrial areas. Killian Flynn, O.F.M. Cap., referencing a memorandum from the Lutheran World Federation, told the AMECEA executive board, "The Catholic Church is in serious and urgent need of specialized structures in urban areas." He specified the need for pastoral programs and asked the bishops for advice "to continue to explore the possibilities in this [the Lutheran] proposal."[49] By August the executive board was voicing support for a one-year ecumenical seminar to be based at Nairobi University, beginning in September 1973. The aim of the seminar was "to train and equip Christian laity and clergy for serving God and men in the contemporary urban structures in Eastern Africa."[50]

The proposal, however, hit several obstacles. First, Nairobi University (and also Makerere in Kampala) rejected the offer. Additionally, while AMECEA acknowledged the need for such a program, the financial resources to support it were not present. Therefore, the project was scaled back and its start date rescheduled so that the problems could be rectified. With

McCauley taking the lead, AMECEA was eventually able to raise the funds necessary from a few different agencies. The opening was rescheduled from January to November 1974, with eight Catholic participants scheduled to attend.[51]

The Interdisciplinary Urban Seminar was held from February to October 1974 in Tanzania. The seminar had two main objectives: (1) to train and equip men and women in Africa for services to God and humanity in contemporary urban situations, and (2) to provide a basis for a human understanding of urban life and to sensitize students and equip them with knowledge of such academic disciplines which would enable them to serve better in urban situations.[52] Twenty-five participants were present, with seven slots allotted to Catholics. McCauley, who had led the AMECEA effort in bringing the seminar to fruition, was asked to serve on the project's academic board, together with Father Joseph Donders, W.F., and two Protestant laymen. Some of the topics covered in the nine-month seminar were industrial mission, presence of the Church with youth, elderly citizens, destitute children, structures of the Church in urban centers, and secular efforts in areas where the Church's influence had not penetrated.[53] At the conclusion of the seminar, McCauley wrote the local ordinaries of each Catholic participant, evaluating the individual's involvement and making recommendations for how the person might use what was gained from the seminar.[54]

The 1974 interdisciplinary seminar was only the first of several programs and efforts geared toward ecumenical dialogue. One significant connection point was the All Africa Conference of Churches (AACC). Even before the seminar had concluded, McCauley received an invitation to send AMECEA representatives to the AACC assembly, scheduled for October 7–12, 1974. Joseph Healey, M.M., Joseph Kelly, C.S.S.p., and Joseph Mukwaya, all holding significant staff positions with AMECEA, were sent as observers. McCauley himself attended some sessions.[55] McCauley reciprocated by inviting the secretary-general of AACC, Sarwart Shebata, to observe the August 1979 AMECEA plenary in Zomba, Malawi.[56] Besides trading representatives at meetings, the two groups found connection through joint participation in a conference, "Attitudes and Initiatives Towards Christian Unity in Eastern Africa," held October 5–7, 1976.[57]

AMECEA's ecumenical efforts were also linked with the World Council of Churches (WCC). In September 1974, Cardinal John Willebrands, Secretary for Christian Unity in Rome, asked McCauley to assist with preparations for the 1975 plenary session for the WCC. McCauley responded in a very positive sense: "You will . . . find among the AMECEA staff several members who have had contact with the Kenya Christian Council and the All Africa Council of Churches. We will be at your service in whatever way our limited resources permit." As with the AACC earlier, AMECEA sent observers to the WCC assembly.[58]

Another ecumenical effort of AMECEA in the 1970s was the body's association with the Christian Organizations Research and Advisory Trust (CORAT).[59] In July 1974, G. S. Snell, director of CORAT in England, wrote to McCauley to inform him that CORAT planned to open a branch of its operation in Africa "to serve the many Christian organizations on the continent which have sought our assistance."[60] The announcement was welcomed by McCauley, as the Gaba Institute and the AMECEA headquarters had previously benefited from CORAT's services. Thus, he informed officials in Rome: "We have plans to collaborate with CORAT in setting up a training programme for auditors and a management course for Church executives."[61] Initial meetings in November 1974 eventually led to the incorporation of CORAT in Kenya as a charitable trust in March 1975. The first local training course, "Managing the Christian Organization," was held later that year from June 23 to 27.[62] McCauley was very pleased with CORAT's services to Eastern Africa:

> It is in the light of this that the importance of CORAT is increasing. They have already done very much for us in helping to train some of our key personnel, and their value to us in the future should be even greater.[63]

McCauley's association with CORAT continued for many years. From 1977 to 1981, only a year prior to his death, he served as a member of the CORAT advisory board. He was often consulted about possible workshops and course offerings and was sufficiently influential with the group to assist people he knew to gain positions within the organization.[64]

Vincent McCauley's strong drive for religious unity was matched by his efforts to assist religious women. His close and long-standing association with the Banyatereza Sisters in Fort Portal provided the experience and heightened his desire to assist these women through his position at AMECEA. In January 1973, the executive board went on record to promote "as a priority" the education and training of African sisters to minister in more wide-ranging apostolates. McCauley was the primary champion behind the foundation, later that same year, of the Association of African Sisterhoods, to study common goals, aspirations, and challenges.[65] The 1973 AMECEA plenary meeting recommended that a meeting for African women religious be held to open dialogue and to exchange experiences in order to assist congregations by identifying common weaknesses, problems, and offering recommendations to resolve them.[66]

Plans were thus initiated for a special study conference to be held in the latter half of 1974. A preliminary meeting was held in Nairobi, April 29 to May 4, 1974, to plan for the conference. Each of the AMECEA nations were granted funds to send four or five sisters to this initial planning assembly.[67]

The first study conference, titled, "The Role of AMECEA in the Service of the Church and the Participation of Sisters in the Same Service," was held September 8–13, 1974. McCauley, Joseph Healey, M.M., and AMECEA chairman James Odongo attended.[68] A second conference was held August 21 to 30, 1975, at the Generalate of the Assumption Sisters in Nairobi. McCauley was fully supportive of the sisters' efforts. He wrote:

> The AMECEA Bishops are concerned with the development of the potential of the African Sisters for greater service to the Church. . . . We at AMECEA have encouraged their efforts.[69]

He also noted how the study conferences had been helpful for the sisters to take charge of their own lives and be more assertive:

> It has been encouraging . . . to note that during the past couple of years, the Sisters themselves have become more aware of the need to deepen the religious formation of their members and to upgrade the Sisters for more responsible service to the Church.[70]

In response to the challenge, the sisters set up an academic scholasticate training center in Nairobi. McCauley was appointed by Cardinal Maurice Otunga to be chaplain to the scholasticate located at the Adams Arcade, a short distance from the AMECEA offices. McCauley responded:

> I highly approve of the programme of the scholasticate which endeavors to assist the formation of our African Sisters and their commitment to the work of the Church. . . . Its potential is very promising and as more and more of the African Sisters are trained at the scholasticate their dedicated service to the Church will become more and more evident.[71]

Education, another favorite interest of Bishop McCauley from his days in Bengal and Fort Portal, was another significant area for Africanization. McCauley's previous experience was influential in his drive to assist catechists in their ministry of Christian education. The catechists were the backbone of parochial religious education, especially in the bush, a fact that McCauley knew well. In fact, McCauley considered support for catechists to be second only to priests. Thus, AMECEA sought funds for both the training and maintenance of catechists. Local possibilities were insufficient, so, as was common, McCauley sought assistance from Rome. Additionally, he pushed for the problem to be discussed at the 1973 AMECEA plenary.[72]

AMECEA's most significant educational endeavor during McCauley's tenure as secretary-general was the "secondary school religious education syllabus project." The project was first conceived in June 1968 when a half-dozen representatives of the episcopal conferences of all five AMECEA nations met at the Gaba Pastoral Institute. The group decided that a standardized ecumenically acceptable secondary-school syllabus, and associated student and teacher texts, needed to be generated. Father Alden Pierce of the Gaba Institute was asked to head the project.[73]

Phase I of the project (1970–1974) concentrated on the materials for years one and two of the secondary education level program. Three full-time teachers worked with Pierce in the planning and composition of the syllabus and lessons. The 1970 AMECEA plenary at Lusaka confirmed the mandate of 1968 for an ecumenically based program, believing this to be the only possibility to gain adoption of the syllabus by various ministers of education. Added incentive was provided when the Non-Catholic Religious Education Committee for Kenya, Tanzania, and Uganda joined with Gaba in the preparation of the syllabus.[74] Published and promulgated in sections, the junior secondary-school syllabus, "Developing in Christ," was well received. The syllabus received a significant boost from Cardinal Nsubuga in Kampala, who strongly recommended the document be adopted by the Idi Amin government.[75] McCauley was pleased with the project's progress and trumpeted its usefulness: "The AMECEA SECONDARY SCHOOL SYLLABUS [emphasis McCauley] is important. It is not only a useful production for the Gaba Pastoral Institute. It is also a very necessary program for the Church in Eastern and Central Africa."[76]

Phase II of the project (1975–1979) saw its completion and distribution among the AMECEA nations. Eventually years 3 and 4, called "Christian Living Today," together with "Developing in Christ," were spread broadly, reaching twenty African countries by 1979.[77]

In a related education matter, the AMECEA plenary in 1973 spoke of the need for a secretary for religious education to join the departments already in place. The mandate was:

> That a qualified person be engaged for the post of AMECEA Secretary for Religious Education, who would live at Gaba Pastoral Institute. The Secretary would work with the Gaba Staff and be responsible for investigating and fostering the possibilities for cooperation among Episcopal Conferences and the ministries of education in the 5 AMECEA countries in a joint primary school Christian religious education programme.[78]

Christian Brother Richard Kiley, chief editor of the religious education syllabus, was appointed secretary of the new department, starting in January 1977.[79]

Clearly the majority of programs offered by AMECEA during McCauley's tenure were positive initiatives to meet forward-thinking needs, yet the reality of the volatility of Eastern African politics forced the bishops to react to an emerging and significant refugee problem. In order to understand AME-CEA's role, the political situation in Uganda in the latter 1970s must be understood. After 1972, three rebel groups sought to topple the Amin regime. The first was a group of pro-Obote soldiers who had escaped Amin's earlier purge and had reorganized in Tanzania. A second, the Front for National Salvation, mainly young exiles from western Uganda, looked toward Yoweri Museveni for leadership. The third cluster was the Save Uganda Movement, an underground group composed mainly of young academics.[80] These groups argued amongst themselves, but the president of Tanzania, Julius Nyerere, pressured them to meet during March 24 through 26, 1979. The meeting produced the Uganda National Liberation Front (UNLF). An eleven-man executive council was elected with Yusuf Lule as chairman.[81]

By mid-1978, Amin could see his power beginning to ebb and, thus, he reacted by attacking his enemies. When his attacks spilled over into Tanzania his fate was sealed. The Tanzania Peoples' Defense Force, united with the UNLF, counterattacked. The coalition force moved rapidly, taking Kampala in April 1979. Amin fled east, but eventually found sanctuary in Libya through his friend and national dictator, Muammar al-Gaddafi.[82]

The last years of the Amin regime created a huge refugee problem with thousands fleeing Uganda for safety, many to Kenya. McCauley described the general situation to a friend:

> We in this part of Africa are certainly "where the action is." . . . Here in Kenya we are very fortunate to be in a peaceful country. All around us there is turmoil that spills over the borders and gives concern to all of us. The hottest spots are Uganda and Ethiopia; it is hard to choose between them when it comes to evaluating chaotic situations. The oppression of the people in these two countries is almost beyond belief and everyday we offer special

prayers that the Lord will redress the wrongs they suffer
and bring them relief.[83]

McCauley was forced to walk a very fine line in his efforts to
assist refugees. He wrote:

> Over here in Kenya we keep a very "low profile." Although
> many know we give assistance to refugees, we do not pub-
> licise. The Kenyan government has willingly permitted
> refugees to come into the country but they have no pro-
> gramme to take care of them once they are here.[84]

McCauley was clearly concerned about the refugee situation,
but AMECEA was not in a position nor oriented to supply
such relief. He explained in greater detail the tightrope he
sought to negotiate:

> My name is not on any body's [refugee] committee. I have
> had to refuse to be a member of many of the refugee com-
> mittees here because the word gets back to Uganda the
> next day and it makes it impossible for me to deal with the
> friends of mine in Uganda or to go there when need arises.
> So far I have been able to go to Uganda when necessary,
> but if I were accused of training guerillas to overthrow Idi
> Amin, I would never be able to go to Uganda. I think you
> can see my point.[85]

McCauley's public disclaimer to his participation in refugee
relief allowed him to work behind the scenes and more directly
with individual cases. The fact that AMECEA had no official
refugee program did not impede requests for assistance. He
dramatically described the situation at AMECEA headquarters
to his family:

> Refugees—refugees—refugees. We are swamped. Two of
> the official refugee agencies have stopped functioning,
> so we and the White Fathers and Verona Fathers and
> Mill Hill Fathers who have missions in Uganda as well as
> houses in Kenya are hard pressed to cope with the influx.

I get from 350 to 400 a week at my door. We try to limit things so that we can deal with refugees only on Friday afternoon; otherwise they disrupt our regular business. Thanks to Christmas gifts and friends in U.S. and Europe we have been able to give small handouts, but do pray that the official organizations (United Nations High Commission for Refugees, All Africa Council of Churches, Joint Refugee Service of Kenya, Catholic Secretariat of Kenya) get back into the act.[86]

McCauley's care for the refugees is well illustrated in one incident related by Joseph Healey, M.M. One exceedingly busy day at AMECEA, some refugees had come to the office seeking assistance. The office secretary, seeking to shield McCauley from the onslaught, and knowing him to be busy, sent the beggars away. Later that day, the bishop heard what had happened and told the secretary to never turn away the refugees, for it may be Christ at the front door. A few weeks later a similar situation arose, only when the refugee came to the office, the secretary interrupted McCauley and informed him, "Christ is at the front door asking for you."[87]

McCauley used his magic touch to obtain funds to meet the immediate needs of the thousands who flocked to the front door at AMECEA. Since these refugees did not qualify for funds under the rubrics of the United Nations High Command for Refugees, McCauley sought other sources. McCauley acknowledged a $25,000 gift from the Maryknoll Fathers.[88] Funds were also received from Misereor in Germany. McCauley gratefully wrote,

Thanks to your generosity, we have been able to give a little assistance to these destitute people. We have told them of the help you gave us, and on their behalf I wish to thank you and all those who participate in Misereor's charity.[89]

Those who worked closely with him at AMECEA have acknowledged McCauley's personal initiative and dedication to the plight of the refugees who flocked to him. Joseph Mukwaya, who succeeded McCauley as secretary-general, commented, "The people lined up every day to get something from him. It was a problem for us, but he didn't care." McCauley's long-time assistant and confidant, Father John Croston, C.S.C., relates how McCauley sent him to the bank on a regular basis to obtain five-shilling notes. When the people came he gave one bill to each person. He gave almost without reservation. Croston admitted, "He was a sucker. He was so good he could not imagine anyone being a con man." McCauley felt impelled to assist others, even if he was "being taken." He always responded to those who worried, "That is what Christ would do."[90]

Closely allied with the work of McCauley and AMECEA in support of refugees was a new effort of outreach to nomads. When missionaries first came to Africa little effort was made to evangelize and assist nomadic peoples, due in large measure to scarce personnel and funds, as well as the itinerant wanderings of the people. By the mid-twentieth century, some initial efforts had been made, but the methods effective with sedentary peoples were ineffective with this new population. Thus, the more direct approach of building Christian communities among the people found some success.[91]

AMECEA's first formal outreach to nomads came through the 1976 plenary meeting. The bishops agreed to form an apostolate to the nomads to evangelize pastorless peoples of either nomadic or semi-nomadic lifestyles. Additionally, the bishops agreed that a conference was needed to discuss various questions and issues associated with this much-neglected segment of the African population. The meeting took place October 31 to November 5, 1977, at Karen College in Nairobi. The mind of the participants was that SCC would be the best vehicle for these people. Once evangelized, the faith could be continued at any location through these more intimate communities of prayer and faith sharing.[92] While AMECEA was concerned about this specific population, still the bishops, at least initially, were measured in their response.[93] A second conference on nomads, again held at Karen College, was sponsored by AMECEA January 29 to February 3, 1979.[94]

Holy Cross Expansion in East Africa—1973 to 1982

The years that followed Vincent McCauley's move to Nairobi were a period of great growth for the Congregation of Holy Cross in East Africa. This expansion, however, was not achieved easily, but initially evolved from the dark days that characterized the Idi Amin years in Uganda. Amin's decision in 1972 to expel all Asians was the direct cause of an increasingly more severe economic crisis, manifest most visibly in the lack of basic staples for food, transportation, and other general necessities of life. Holy Cross members, like all people in Uganda, local and expatriate alike, felt the crunch. McCauley, who continued to keep abreast of the situation, reported in April 1973 to the superior general, "The men are holding up well. The strain persists, and some are getting nervous."[95]

The situation in Uganda came to a critical point in February 1977. Angered by a statement of President Jimmy Carter, Amin ordered all United States citizens to a meeting in Kampala on Monday, February 28. No Americans were to leave the country before this meeting. The radio announcement of February 25 stated:

> The meeting on twenty-eight February should cause no alarm. . . . It is the intention of the President to thank all Americans for the excellent work they have been doing in Uganda since the closure of the American embassy in

Uganda in nineteen seventy-three during the Arab-Israeli War.[96]

The announcement's disclaimer of "no alarm" meant little to members of Holy Cross (and all others) gripped with fear, especially in light of Amin's general policy in recent years that placed severe restrictions on the movement and activities of all expatriates. On February 27, Holy Cross priests, brothers, and sisters celebrated the Eucharist together at the Medical Mission Sisters compound in Fort Portal. After the Mass, just prior to leaving for Kampala, Radio Uganda reported the scheduled meeting was delayed two days; on February 28 the meeting was cancelled. Still tension remained.[97] McCauley informed the new superior general, Thomas Barrosse, C.S.C., and his staff that things were looking better for Holy Cross, but many problems persisted:

> Although the heat is off for our missionaries . . . for the present, it is not so far for the Ugandan people. Prominent Ugandans of all tribes, but especially those of the Acholi an[d] Lango tribes are living in constant fear. Soldiers of "the Special Research Unit" (we call them "The Goon Squad") are picking up people every day. They are beaten when picked up, then tortured and few are ever seen again.[98]

When Amin was toppled, Uganda was in total disarray, yet McCauley still voiced a note of optimism to his family: "It will take years to recoup our losses, but the spirit of the missionaries and people have quickly revived now that the war is over."[99]

Even during the time of Amin, possibly the most critical and contentious issue for the congregation in East Africa was the question of accepting local vocations. The concept of promoting the local church was a general barrier to such action. Historian Elizabeth Isichei describes the prevailing mindset:

"Missionary Congregations insisted that Africans become diocesan clergy, rather than joining their own ranks."[100] From the very outset of the Holy Cross mission in East Africa, caution was advised toward native vocations. A 1959 report stated:

> As in Ghana, the question of recruitment must be studied carefully, and we must proceed slowly in the process of formation because there are many social and moral problems existing in Uganda as well as in Ghana.[101]

The issue became a source of significant debate within the congregation throughout the 1970s. Several former missionaries have stated that Holy Cross wanted to start a local formation program, but strong fears that the congregation would be ejected from the country and, thus, possible seminarians would be left unattended, were a significant barrier.[102] Additionally, the rather poor success rate experienced by other religious congregations and communities in their efforts to form candidates to perpetual profession and/or ordination raised another red flag for those voicing caution.[103] Also recall that Holy Cross in the early 1970s was debating its congregational commitment to East Africa and was not in the proper frame of mind to welcome new members.

Vincent McCauley was also rather wary of local vocations for several reasons. As we have seen previously, the bishop was a strong promoter of the local church and indigenous vocations to the local diocese. This was fundamental to his basic theology of mission. As local ordinary in Fort Portal, this view was strengthened as evidenced by his efforts for the construction of the new Gaba National Seminary in the late 1960s. The congregation's lack of roots in East Africa was another barrier for McCauley. The aforementioned fears of the community's status in the region and its ever-problematic lack of personnel made the possibility of formation work difficult at best.[104] After his transfer to Nairobi, McCauley was more open, but still voiced caution. Howard Kenna, C.S.C., the Indiana Province provincial, stated:

> Bishop McCauley was in the other day and he too discussed the matter saying that he was not opposed to the admission of Africans but that he would be afraid that some might seek to join for unworthy motives.[105]

Despite reservations, Holy Cross began to move toward the creation of a local formation program. In an August 1972 apostolic plan, members of Holy Cross related that the congregation's commitment was "seen in the more general terms of service to the Church in Uganda and more specifically to the People of God in the Fort Portal Diocese." The plan suggested a deeper and more developed commitment was needed. It concluded:

> The community feels its service is of value, [but] when it reviews that service in relation to the vastly increasing population, it feels the need to actively seek out and invite other members of the community who want to share in its work.[106]

William Blum, C.S.C., led the congregation's efforts to establish a formation program. In a general letter to the East African community, he related recent conversations with local ordinaries, both indigenous and expatriate, which strongly supported the idea of religious communities accepting local vocations. He wrote position papers that convincingly argued that the time was proper and the environment sound for the congregation to invite men to join their apostolate. Blum's passion was highly influential. In June 1977, a meeting of Holy Cross religious concluded, "It seems the Community is now positively enthusiastic about local vocations."[107] In June 1979, John Bashabora, a secular priest from Mbarara, was the first to enter the candidacy program for Holy Cross.[108]

The Holy Cross formation program shifted locations as the congregation's institutional commitments expanded east to neighboring Kenya. The deteriorating political situation in Uganda in the 1970s was a catalyst that led to the congregation's establishment of a new foundation in Kenya. Local discussions on various fronts prompted the 1976 District Chapter to recommend a new foundation. In June, the Indiana Provincial Chapter gave permission for an investigation to continue.[109] Thus, negotiations began with Cardinal Maurice Otunga in Nairobi about possible venues for a Holy Cross apostolate. Otunga suggested three sites, with Thika, twenty-eight miles outside Nairobi, as the greatest need. The decision was made, however, to take a parish assignment at Dandora, a poor district in Nairobi.[110] In early 1978, James Rahilly, C.S.C., and William Blum, C.S.C., arrived in Nairobi to inaugurate the new Holy Cross mission.[111]

The Kenyan foundation became fertile ground for the congregation's fledgling formation program. Under the direction of Thomas McDermott, C.S.C., native vocations were first formally invited to enter Holy Cross. A house of formation was opened adjacent to the Dandora parish in July 1982. Initially seminarians studied at Consolata Seminary and later at Hekima College. Growth was slow and frustrations were many, but with time the program began to bear fruit. In August 1991, Holy Cross celebrated the ordination of Fulgentius Katende, its first East African member.

Summary

Vincent McCauley's retirement as bishop of Fort Portal, concurrent with the death of his friend and AMECEA colleague, Father Killian Flynn, O.F.M. Cap., provided him the opportunity to easily transition to a new position in a new locale, with an institution he knew from its infancy. Taking

the reins as secretary-general of AMECEA in January 1973,
McCauley moved to Nairobi and immediately began to place
his stamp on the Eastern African episcopal association in ways
even more profound than earlier. He was responsible for the
day-to-day activities of the body, especially the organization
of the triennial plenary sessions, but more significant contributions were made. He championed the establishment of
an accounting program at the Nyegezi Social Training Center and fostered the work of CORAT, both of which aided
Church personnel with skills in administrative functions. On
a more pastoral level, McCauley led AMECEA's efforts toward
ecumenical development, promotion of small Christian communities, the generation of syllabi and texts for secondary
religious education throughout the African continent, and
increased training for religious women. Through personal
contact and institutional commitment he reached out to thousands of refugees and nomads who sought his assistance. Vincent McCauley stood ever ready to answer the call to service,
within his congregation and the Church universal. His hard
work and positive attitude would continue until his death.

CHAPTER 12

Retirement and Death: 1979–1982

Retirement is certainly a relative term in today's society. Some people consider sixty-five the "retirement age," while some organizations offer favored status as "senior citizens" to those over fifty-five. In the Catholic Church, local ordinaries are asked by canon law to submit their resignations, basically to formally retire, at age seventy-five. Some people literally never retire, preferring to "die with their boots on," perceiving retirement to be either a waste of time or inconsistent with their ethic of life. In 1979, Vincent McCauley formally resigned as secretary-general of AMECEA, having guided the organization, initially as chairman, since 1964. He was hardly through, however, with his work for the Church in Africa. On the contrary, ending his formal position of leadership provided him the time, consistent with his energy, to pursue other avenues and apply his significant talents. Before death would claim him, he worked long and hard on the establishment of an institution of higher education for Eastern Africa, as well as assisting in numerous other AMECEA projects.

Retirement as Secretary-General

Vincent McCauley strongly believed in the promotion of the local church, and manifested this conviction both in Bengal and Eastern Africa. As a young missionary, he was instrumental in the promotion of local Bengali vocations through his work at Little Flower Seminary and St. John's Apostolic School. In Africa, too, the education of seminarians was a high priority in his work. Additionally, he trained and groomed Africans to take leadership positions in the Diocese of Fort Portal, including his successor, Serapio Magambo. Now, as he entered the twilight of his life and ministerial career, McCauley continued to see his role to serve in leadership only so long as was necessary to prepare local clergy to assume responsibility. Having experienced a rather reticent attitude on the part of many bishops to release priests for service to AMECEA, McCauley in March 1975 began to press the ordinaries to consider their responsibility to the organization.[1]

McCauley's drive for Africanization of AMECEA became more personal in 1977. McCauley had agreed to fill the slot vacated by Killian Flynn only until a suitable replacement could be found. In November, a report circulated at AMECEA stated, "Bishop McCauley mentioned that he is anxious to find a replacement." The request, again voiced early in 1978, asked that a person be in place by January 1, 1979, so that he could be adequately trained for the secretary-general position prior to the plenary later that year.[2] McCauley's vast experience in Uganda and with AMECEA provided him insight to the nature and details of the secretary-general position.[3] Fellow Holy Cross prelate Archbishop Charles Schleck properly synthesized McCauley's belief and desire:

As soon as he prepared one whom he considered capable of taking over his office, he wished to turn this responsibility [secretary-general of AMECEA] over to the person and remain an advisor so long as this would be necessary. It was more than clear that he was in no way attached to authority and power. He was there to build up the local Church. It was because of his competence in administration and his humility and non-attachment to power and authority that he was considered not only a competent person for the task but a holy person as well.[4]

Finding McCauley's replacement began in 1976 at the AMECEA plenary meeting. In February 1977, Joseph Mukwaya, whom McCauley knew from his time on the social communications commission with the UEC, and who was presently assisting Joseph Healey, M.M., at AMECEA headquarters, was officially appointed assistant secretary-general. McCauley was pleased with the appointment and hoped that he would soon be relieved of his duties.[5] In order to advance this hope, McCauley began in earnest to train Mukwaya to take the helm of the AMECEA ship. As he had introduced Serapio Magambo, his successor in Fort Portal, to his European and American contacts, so McCauley took Mukwaya to Europe in November 1978 to meet AMECEA's financial backers and other influential people. During the two-week trip, Mukwaya met Missio and Misereor officials in Germany, attended an international meeting of communicators at The Hague, and met officials of the Sacred Congregation of Propaganda Fide, the Secretariat for Christian Unity, and the Secretariat for Non-Christians in Rome. They finished their trip with a private audience with Pope John Paul II.[6]

McCauley's proactive work with Mukwaya prompted action to finalize the transfer of authority. In September 1978, the executive board voted unanimously to recommend Mukwaya to assume the secretary-general position. The bishops at the August 1979 plenary meeting in Zomba, Malawi, formally elected him.[7]

Vincent McCauley's retirement as secretary-general of AMECEA generated abundant praise for his numerous accomplishments. During his fifteen years of formal association with AMECEA, first as chairman and then secretary-general, he was instrumental in launching many projects, including the AMECEA accountancy course at the Nyegezi Social Training Center, the Gaba Pastoral Institute, numerous ecumenical initiatives, the Association of Sisters of Eastern Africa, the social communications and education departments, and the AMECEA documentation Service. AMECEA's honorary president, Cardinal Laurean Rugambwa, had earlier summarized the sentiments of many at this time when he lauded McCauley's assumption of the position of secretary-general in 1973:

> I also wish to take this opportunity to say a special word of thanks to Bishop McCauley. Bishop McCauley was elected Chairman of AMECEA in 1964 and has remained in this function ever since, being re-elected in 1967 and 1970. His influence in shaping our Association into what it is today has been enormous. But over and above the tremendous service he has given to AMECEA as Chairman, Bishop McCauley has [served] for the past year also [in] the role of Secretary General. Fr. Flynn's death could have easily disrupted the smooth running of the AMECEA Office, but due to Bishop McCauley's readiness to fill the gap with his experience and energy, AMECEA has continued to thrive. During the past year a number of important undertakings have been concluded, and the mammoth and complex preparations for this Plenary meeting have been precisely without a hitch. I am sure that all of you join wholeheartedly with me in extending a vote of thanks and appreciation to Bishop McCauley.[8]

Many of McCauley's associates, members of Holy Cross and others, view his work at AMECEA as the high point of his episcopal career. Robert Hesse, C.S.C., stated it clearly and succinctly, "The greatest work he did was at AMECEA."[9] McCauley's AMECEA colleagues praised him for shaping the Church in Africa and beyond with his vision:

> During his 15 years as Chairman and Secretary General of AMECEA, Bishop McCauley's warm personality, vision, and efficiency shaped the Association into what it is today, strengthened its collegiality and won for it many friends both in Africa and abroad.[10]

This author concurs with the above sentiments. McCauley's work in Fort Portal, while significant, did not have the far-reaching effect of his efforts at AMECEA. His foresight, extraordinary dedication, and significant accomplishments energized the entire Eastern African Church and placed it in a receptive position for local clergy to assume responsibilities. Clearly, McCauley's vision needed the broader audience. Fortunately for the African Church, this became a reality.

McCauley's formal retirement from leadership in AMECEA did not mean that his presence and influence ceased to be needed and felt in the Eastern African Church. In its letter of gratitude to McCauley for his long service to AMECEA, the executive board unanimously requested that he "continue assisting the organization and to guide Fr. Mukwaya in his new position."[11] In many ways McCauley and Mukwaya simply changed positions, with the bishop assisting as needed in the AMECEA organization. McCauley wrote his family:

> Little by little the word is getting around that Fr. Mukwaya is the new boss at AMECEA. Putting him in the lime-light is part of my task . . . while working behind the scenes to make it and him look good. I think it is what the Lord wants, so I'm trying to make it work.[12]

While McCauley had no official position, extant correspondence shows at times McCauley was "acting" secretary-general, or chairman. He informed some friends, "My successor, Fr. Mukwaya, took off on Thursday for 3 months study and prayer in the Holy Land, so I am back in the saddle full time."[13] He sent many letters on behalf of the Catholic Higher Institute of Eastern Africa (CHIEA).[14]

McCauley never truly retired from AMECEA. Although not handling all the details of day-to-day operations, he was always held in high esteem as the "consulting elder, . . . acting [in] the grandfather role."[15] He wrote his family:

> If the two months since my return are any indication of the future, I think I'll go back to work. The retirement program is overwhelming me. I seem to be doing the same things as always, but with only one secretary instead of three. Then, too, my Bishop and friends have been calling up to say: "Now that you are retired you won't mind helping us. . . . In no time my calendar is filled for six months.[16]

Formal retirement from AMECEA did, however, provide McCauley with the time and opportunity to once again connect with his beloved Uganda. Fallout from the Amin years was significant and it weighed heavily upon the aging bishop. He wrote,

> Uganda is very much on our minds these days. We thought things would be OK when Idi Amin was overthrown. But now the various factions within the country are squabbling among themselves: Socialists and Communists shout down the moderates and conservatives. The country is in disorder. We are still trying to help the poor, but it is very difficult.[17]

He told his family that he was involved with restoration and rehabilitation programs in six Ugandan dioceses. He traveled to Uganda for meetings, ordinations, and to rally the people.[18]

McCauley's continued assistance with AMECEA was evident as well in the preparations for the 1982 plenary session, originally scheduled for Lusaka, Zambia. As a member of the planning committee, McCauley hosted a brainstorming session in April 1981. After many discussions, the participants from all AMECEA member nations suggested the theme: "The Family: Truly Christian and Truly African." The idea arose from a talk given by Pope John Paul II in Zaire. Particular emphasis on the family "in the context of small Christian communities" was recommended.[19] The bishops hoped that each member nation would nominate a couple to attend the plenary.

The planned plenary, however, experienced some significant problems necessitating major shifts. First, as with some previous plenaries, there was a need to change the venue. Bishop Medardo J. Mazombwe of Chipata, Zambia, reported, "The present state of affairs in the Archdiocese of Lusaka is not conducive to create an atmosphere required of the nature of [an] AMECEA Plenary Conference." Thus, on rather short notice, the plenary was shifted to the Kenya Technical Teachers' College in Nairobi.[20] This last-minute shift created a situation that led to the cancellation of the study session on the family, as the new venue could only host the bishops for sufficient time for the business agenda. In order not to waste the preparation, however, a substitute half-day session was held during the plenary business meeting. The session concluded that validating irregular marriages and assisting those in broken relationships was the main preoccupation with those who ministered to families. The bishops suggested that each episcopal conference should work on the national level and that the bishops should issue pastoral letters on Christian marriage and family life.[21]

McCauley attended some of the sessions, but due to ill health
could not be fully present.

McCauley's "retirement" years in Nairobi also allowed him
to reconnect with a ministry of the Congregation of Holy
Cross. In May 1982, he journeyed to Rome, along with John
Croston, C.S.C., and William Blum, C.S.C. (the district superior), to attend the beatification of Brother Andre Bessette,
C.S.C. While there, McCauley encountered Patrick Peyton,
C.S.C., the priest with whom he had communication about
his rosary films back in the early days in Fort Portal. Peyton
asked the bishop's assistance in the establishment of a Family
Rosary Center in Nairobi. At the 1982 AMECEA plenary session, the project received 100 percent backing of the assembled
bishops, including the offer of personnel.[22]

Catholic Higher Institute of Eastern Africa

In November 1973, Cardinal Angelo Rossi, prefect of
the Sacred Congregation for the Evangelization of Peoples,
requested the apostolic nuncio in Uganda, Archbishop Luigi
Bellotti, to consult all African episcopal conferences about the
possibility of "a center of High Theological Studies for the
Native Clergy of the English-speaking countries of this continent." Rossi also requested the opinion of the Uganda Episcopal Conference on the opportunity, location, and guidelines
for such an institution. Lastly, Rossi wanted to know if the
conference were favorable to the plan and would support it
financially.[23]

The idea was raised at subsequent AMECEA and SECAM
plenary sessions. Writing on behalf of AMECEA, McCauley
reported:

> The recommendation from Rome to set up such a Col-
> lege to suit the needs of African students was accepted in

principle. However, it would not be feasible for AMECEA to undertake and staff such a project at present.[24]

The idea received a more generous response from the SECAM bishops meeting in Rome in September 1975. The decision was made to form an ad hoc committee, composed of representatives from each of the SECAM regions, to review the proposal more fully and report to a scheduled July 1976 meeting in Nairobi.[25] Bishop Patrick Kalilombe, of the ad hoc committee, in turn wrote to McCauley asking that AMECEA again be queried on the proposal at its forthcoming 1976 plenary.[26]

The initial work of the ad hoc committee became more formalized in 1976. Archbishop Francis Arinze, another member of the ad hoc committee, was assigned the task of presenting the committee's findings to the AMECEA plenary and to form a permanent committee to move the project forward. Through Arinze's efforts, each quadrant of the Church in Africa elected a representative for a permanent committee.[27] The permanent committee, with Arinze acting as convener, first met August 31 to September 1, 1977, at Bigard Seminary in Enugu, Nigeria.[28] The meeting proposed two possible locations of the school, Kenya or Nigeria, and suggested the prospective students would be clerics who had finished theology. A major step was taken when Edouard Trudeau, S.J., was chosen as director of planning for the institute.[29] Trudeau took the job on an interim basis until the Jesuits released him. He took charge of the project officially in January 1979.[30]

Trudeau worked closely with McCauley in preparing for the first official meeting of the episcopal executive board on February 19, 1979. At the meeting, an academic commission was established to research programs for the proposed institution and a board of governors was appointed to oversee the project. Cardinal Maurice Otunga of Nairobi chaired the governors; McCauley was a member. The final business item for the initial meeting was to change the name of the school to the Catholic Higher Institute of Eastern Africa (CHIEA).[31]

The formal initiation of an effort in Eastern Africa to inaugurate a Catholic institution of higher education did not answer the question of whether a similar project should be started in Western Africa. In October 1978, Propaganda Fide and the Sacred Congregation for Catholic Education had suggested that one university be built, as funds would only support one such project. However, in March 1980, the chairman of the permanent committee for CHIEA, Archbishop Francis Arinze, stated that the Association Episcopal Conference for Anglophone West Africa (AECAWA) also wanted a school. This had been the recommendation at the 1978 SECAM plenary. After meeting with all the episcopal conferences of all member nations, Trudeau voiced the same sentiments.[32] Rome thus changed its view, responding that there was no objection to two institutions, but that already existing seminary facilities should be utilized if possible. Eventually the CHIEA permanent committee, meeting March 4–5, 1980, acknowledged the need for a college in West Africa.[33]

Once AMECEA decided to go forward with the Catholic university project, the difficult task of financing the effort took center stage. McCauley's vast experience in development made him the natural selection to head the fundraising efforts. Working with the secretary-general, Joseph Mukwaya, McCauley, as a member of the CHIEA Finance Committee, championed the drive, seeking funds, as was his custom, from all possible venues. Besides Misereor and Missio, appeals were sent to the Swiss Catholic Lenten Fund, the Canadian Catholic Conference of Bishops, and the Canadian Religious Conference. Additionally, McCauley was asked by Cardinal Otunga, chairman of the CHIEA executive committee (board of governors), "to inquire about the possibility of obtaining funds in the U.S.A."[34] These initial inquiries led to the inauguration of a formal fundraising campaign in Europe, the United States, and Canada. Despite all these efforts, McCauley realized that AMECEA would still have to raise $1 million on its own.[35]

Simultaneous with fundraising efforts was the physical construction of the institution. Again, McCauley's previous experience with the Gaba National Seminary and the Virika Cathedral was invaluable in the construction of CHIEA. He worked with Edouard Trudeau and the Kenya Episcopal Conference to secure the necessary land for the school. In April 1979, the Kenyan bishops voted unanimously to give CHIEA fifteen acres on the grounds of St. Thomas Aquinas Seminary.[36] McCauley, accompanied by Joseph Kelly, C.S.S.p., visited the property. In his visionary perspective he stated, "This could become a great Catholic University."[37] With McCauley as a member, the CHIEA building committee first met June 17–18, 1980. The initial plan was for a four-phase construction, with an estimated cost of $1.5 million.[38] The initial estimate was soon raised to $2 million, as rising material and labor costs burdened the project from the outset.[39] Construction of the institute was completed in early 1984.

The physical plant and sufficient funds for its proper construction were essential, but as with any institution of higher learning, the academic program lay at the school's central core. Before construction of the school began, the aforementioned academic commission first met in April 1979. As secretary-general, McCauley called this initial meeting, serving as chair until the election of Father John Lemay, W.F., as permanent chairman. The commission's initial idea was for CHIEA to offer a two-year licentiate program. The program was geared toward priests with baccalaureate degrees.[40] Seven different academic specialties were planned: biblical, moral, dogmatic, pastoral, spiritual, Church history, and liturgy. The CHIEA board of governors charged the academic commission with the preparation of a preliminary program of studies, to set up

academic structures and by-laws, as well as make suggestions
for both a dean of students and a rector.[41] The commission
recommended Father Paul Kalanda, who had served as rector
of Katigondo seminary in Uganda as the first CHIEA rector.
Kalanda never served, however, as he was appointed bishop
of Moroto, Uganda. Father Augustin Ndeukaya replaced
Kalanda as rector.[42]

In June 1980, Joseph Mukwaya reported to the AMECEA
bishops that the Sacred Congregation for the Evangelization
of Peoples had approved "the launching of the Institute."[43]
Bishop Medardo Mazombwe, chairman of AMECEA, officially inaugurated CHIEA on September 3, 1984, welcoming twenty-one priest-students. Courses in biblical theology,
dogmatics, moral theology, pastoral studies, liturgy, Church
history, spiritual theology, Church law, management, social
communications, pastoral counseling, and catechesis were
available. CHIEA's aim was

> to be the cradle of a Catholic University for Eastern Africa
> and to cater for specialized and advanced ecclesiastical
> studies through teaching and research in an African cul-
> tural environment.[44]

One year later, on August 18, 1985, Pope John Paul II formally opened the school.[45]

Vincent McCauley's contribution to the foundation of
CHIEA was based on his persistent belief in building the
local church. Father Neil Ryan, C.S.C., has commented, "He
realized that in order for the church in Africa to truly have
influence it needed people with degrees, not certificates. He
was able to get the bishops to understand this."[46] He did not
believe in sending priests abroad for training if adequate
education was present locally. While McCauley did not
live to see the complete fulfillment of his dream, he was
clearly, "the innovator of the Catholic Institute," and its

true guiding light.[47] The university library, named in honor of Bishop McCauley, testifies to this fact.

Journey to Death

As described earlier, Vincent McCauley suffered from facial skin cancer for the majority of his adult life, a situation that necessitated numerous surgeries. Yet, he heroically bore this cross and never complained. Serapio Magambo spoke for many in describing McCauley's valiant battle:

> His pain and suffering and the numerous operations he had on his body did not deter him from return-ing to Africa till the end. Another person, after so many operations—I believe they were in the region of 50—would have recoiled and ended his days disgruntled and complaining. Not so with Vince. All the time I was with him I never heard him complaining about his suffering.[48]

As he grew older, the natural aging process brought McCa-uley more acute health problems. In September 1976, he had a plastic aorta inserted at the Mayo Clinic. In July 1980, a second heart surgery repaired an aneurysm in another section of the aorta. In his 1980 Christmas letter he wrote: "The sur-gery to repair an aneurism [sic] on the aorta was successful, the recovery slower than I hoped for, but with the excellent care provided me, the recovery is complete."[49] Nineteen months later he was again hospitalized with pneumonia. Extant min-utes of various AMECEA committees upon which McCauley served reveal that he was often absent between 1980 and 1982 due to various health issues.[50]

Despite receiving a "clean bill of health" in an October 1981 Mayo Clinic visit, McCauley continued to experience health problems that became increasingly more severe.[51] Beginning in July 1982, he experienced several acute pulmonary hemorrhages. He wrote his family: "On the morning of the 12th [July] I had my lung gusher. Fr. Croston rushed me to the hospital. He anointed me in the car. The doctors stopped the flood and put me to bed."[52] John Croston, C.S.C., explained the situation to the Holy Cross Generalate in Rome:

> The Bishop has been having difficulty with one of his lungs. [He] coughs up a good bit of blood from time to time but the doctor thinks he has it under control. [He] never complains and continues to work like a beaver.[53]

McCauley's ill health was noticed by members of Holy Cross at the new Dandora parish in Nairobi. As one man commented, "He was obviously sick."[54]

McCauley's condition only continued to deteriorate as September arrived. He was deeply appreciative of Croston's faithful presence: "Big John Croston is a busy man. While so many bishops are in town still he finds time to check up on me regularly. Without him I would be lost." The bishop's affection was mutual with Croston, who believed McCauley "knew his days were numbered." He continued, "It was a great privilege to have been with the Bishop in his last days—as well as through the years."[55] Eventually McCauley realized his condition necessitated medical treatment in the United States. In his always lighthearted manner, he wrote to the superior general, Thomas Barrosse, C.S.C.:

> One finger in the dike is OK for a short time. When two fingers are needed the repair job becomes more urgent. The one finger Nairobi treatment doesn't seem to be enough for my leaky lung, so I thought I better not delay the repairs at Mayo Clinic.[56]

In October 1982, McCauley traveled with Croston to the United States for treatment. As was the bishop's custom, they stopped at Lourdes to ask Mary's guidance and intercession. The pair arrived at the Mayo Clinic where initial tests revealed no problem. The positive report allowed McCauley to visit his family in Iowa. A week later the pair met in Omaha and then traveled to Notre Dame. While staying at Holy Cross House, the community infirmary, McCauley again experienced a severe hemorrhage. Thus, he returned to the Mayo Clinic with Croston, who reported,

> His spirits are upbeat but he's aware that he's a high-risk patient and isn't taking it lightly. With his medical history, physical condition and age it would be rash for anyone to even venture a guess about the recovery period.[57]

The doctors recommended exploratory surgery, even with the risks involved. McCauley told the medical team to press forward as it was the only way he would be able to return to Africa.[58]

At 6:30 p.m. on November 1, 1982, while undergoing surgery, Vincent McCauley died. At the bishop's side through the whole ordeal, John Croston lovingly gave McCauley a final tribute: "I still maintain that as the evening sun cast its soft shadow to signal the end of another day in Rochester, a *man* died on the operating table but at the same instant *a saint* [emphasis Croston] was born." He continued, "I can mourn for him but not feel sorry for one who has opened his eyes to the wonders of heaven."[59]

In East Africa, the news of McCauley's death was received when many bishops were gathered in Kampala to celebrate the episcopal ordination of Joseph Mukwaya, held on October 31 at the Rubaga Cathedral. On November 2, the bishops thus assembled celebrated a memorial Mass at the Gaba National Seminary.[60] On November 4, Cardinal Maurice Otunga celebrated a second memorial Mass at the Holy Family Basilica in Nairobi. In his homily William Blum, C.S.C., spoke of McCauley the priest:

All of us who had the privilege to live and work with Bishop McCauley knew very well how much he was a priest. In so many ways he was a priest for priests. His smile in the midst of suffering, his welcome, his comment, "What can I do to help you?" was the way so many of us knew him.[61]

Vincent McCauley was buried on November 4 in the Holy Cross community cemetery at Notre Dame, with his family present. At the funeral Mass, Father Arnold "Gus" Fell, C.S.C., who had accompanied McCauley on the initial 1958 investigative trip to Africa, spoke of the bishop's character, faith, and commitment:

If I were to use one word to identify Bishop Vince I would say: GALLANT. It is a term you rarely hear these days. Gallant: brave and cheerful against all odds; chivalrous defender of the weak; unselfish rescuer of the needy; carrying off his battles with a youthful flair, and always with a touch of class. He was the gallant knight of Our Lady, his great love; his lance always for the right: slaying the dragons of other persons' needs and troubles and injustices; jousting with the Black Knights of personal pain and constant threat of death.[62]

When McCauley was buried, a fitting but unusual event occurred. Father Richard Warner, C.S.C., provincial of the Indiana Province of Holy Cross and presider at the committal ceremony tells the story:

It was a cool, crisp fall afternoon with clear skies and sun, but a relatively cold temperature even for that time of year. Once the [funeral] procession arrived at the cemetery, I took my place at the head of his coffin to lead those present in the final commendation and farewell. As the ceremony ended and people began to sprinkle his casket with holy water, there was one cloud in the otherwise cloudless sky and for just a few moments, and in the midst of the sunshine, a few snow flurries fell. I was shocked at the occurrence because I remember the bishop telling me perhaps almost 10 years earlier, why he named his cathedral Our Lady of the Snows or Virika.[63]

McCauley's rather sudden, although not totally unexpected, death brought forth tributes from all fronts. Speaking on behalf of AMECEA, its chairman, Bishop Medardo Mazombwe, wrote:

> Indeed we have lost a brother Bishop whose caliber, service and dedication is [sic] irreplaceable. . . . During the 18 years of dedicated service, Bishop McCauley not only facilitated the growth of our Association but also created an atmosphere of collegiality and solidarity among us. . . . Such is the genius of the man we are going to miss; a person who we can rightly call "the Father of AMECEA."[64]

In various tributes he was described as "a gentleman bishop" who lived the saga of a "valiant man of God."[65] Appropriately, the superior general of Holy Cross, Thomas Barrosse, C.S.C., lauded his life of simplicity as religious and missionary:

> He was an extraordinary man, and I thank God for having blessed Holy Cross, our missions in Eastern Bengal of forty years ago, and the Church of East Africa today with so simple, generous, dedicated and joyful a religious and prist [sic].[66]

Summary

In 1979, Vincent McCauley retired as secretary-general of AMECEA, the organization that he had guided closely for fifteen years. Yet, his work for the bishops and Church of Eastern Africa did not end. Utilizing his skills of organization and financial development and his remaining physical energy, he answered the call to serve in many venues of AMECEA's varied activities. He became the understudy to his former protégé, Joseph Mukwaya, but that did not deter him from becoming integrally involved with the planning of the 1982 AMECEA plenary session in Nairobi, as well as serving as a trusted advisor for all in the association. The majority of his time was dedicated to a long-held dream, the establishment of a Catholic university in Eastern Africa for the education of the clergy. When the opportunity arose through the Sacred Congregation for the Evangelization of Peoples to initiate the Catholic Higher Institute for Eastern Africa, McCauley jumped in with both feet, getting involved in virtually every preparatory commission, exercising especially his vast experience in fundraising, through various European, United States, and Canadian Church groups. When God called Vincent McCauley home, his pet project was well on the road to its ultimate completion. A valiant servant of God, Vincent McCauley was a missionary at heart. He worked long and hard in the service of God's people through promotion of the local church. Thus, it is certain that on November 1, 1982, the Feast of All Saints, he heard the words of Jesus, "Come, you that are blessed by my Father, inherit the kingdom prepared for you from the foundation of the world" (Mt 25:34b).

Epilogue:
Vincent McCauley, C.S.C.:
The Man and His Legacy

Vincent McCauley, truly a valiant servant of God, died as he had lived, never wanting anything for himself, but always freely giving his life away for the sake of others. Like Jesus, the one whom he followed, McCauley was a quiet leader, who through talent, but more importantly the proper application of his gifts, accomplished significant things for God's people in venues across the world. He was a missionary at heart, believing that it was absolutely necessary to construct a local church structure, both institutionally and in personnel. This book, I believe, has adequately demonstrated McCauley's multiple and praiseworthy efforts, initially in Bengal as teacher and parish priest, in Washington, D.C., as formation director and fundraiser, and in his leadership in the Eastern African Church, starting in Fort Portal but quickly extending outward to the entire region through his work with AMECEA and SECAM. While McCauley's construction of the kingdom of God in our world has been told, there is one final and important piece of his life that must be

337

addressed—the personality and spirituality from which all of his accomplishments flowed. While many of the qualities of Vincent McCauley are apparent in the pages of this biography, it is appropriate as we close this story to synthesize the essence of the man. What drove him? What qualities made him great and drew so many people to his side to share the ministry, which was his life? Lastly, it is necessary to explore the legacy that Bishop Vincent McCauley left to the Church and the world.

Leadership Qualities

Vincent McCauley's success as a missionary priest was supported by many important leadership qualities. Many who worked closely with him described McCauley as "a man of vision who could look far and plan accordingly."[1] His vision was not only manifest in great projects such as the Virika Cathedral, the Gaba Pastoral Institute, and the Catholic Higher Institute of Eastern Africa, but in his ability to adapt to the situation. He described his own reaction to the African scene:

> Africa is changing rapidly. The surge of independence has created new situations in every field. It behooves us as Christ's agents to adapt our thinking and our ministry to the new circumstances. The Church must not lag behind; rather She should lead.[2]

His vision allowed him to be a great animator and motivator of people; he could see people's potential and had the ability to utilize it well and properly. Additionally, he saw his own ability and was confident he could perform to high standards.[3] He had the ability to act differently as the situation warranted. Joseph Mugenyi, auxiliary bishop of Fort Portal, stated, "McCauley could change his tone and approach depending on the need. When it was necessary he could be tough. He could recognize when one tone or another was best."[4] He was a man of great principles and standards; he had the ability to see to the reality of most all situations.[5]

McCauley, in describing the qualities of a good missionary, unwittingly detailed his own personality and leadership ability. He wrote:

It takes exceptional humility and generosity. No sensitive thin-skinned extrovert who demands the lime-light will succeed. The missionary we need must *love* [emphasis McCauley] the people he is working for, take his "personal fulfillment" from the fact that he is cooperating with Our Lord in raising up a People to know Him and serve Him with genuine African love.[6]

He was a transparent man; he was genuine to all people and situations. Brother Tad Las, C.S.C., stated, "He impressed me as a man of what you saw is what you got. He was open, very sincere, and treated you as an individual. . . . Everyone was the same to him."[7] He strongly advocated a spirit of poverty in the mission mentality:

It is true that extravagance is not so predominant in the missions, but the norms of extravagance can apply here too, when we consider the lot of the people around us. Our imported standards and the mentality that is responsible for them can, and often does, create a gap between us and our people.[8]

Another integral element of McCauley's leadership ability was the instinctive and very strong personal work ethic and the almost boundless energy he possessed for ministry. Many members of Holy Cross and other contemporaries speak of his dedication to purpose and task and enthusiasm for what he did. One Holy Cross religious stated, "He never did anything slowly or quietly, but always with great bursts of energy."[9] Thomas Barrosse, C.S.C., well expressed how McCauley's contemporaries perceived his energy:

> He spent himself generously and enthusiastically on
> whatever endeavor fell to his responsibility, but always
> with humility and readiness to let others take the places
> of prominence. His piety was simple and warm, as was his
> life with his fellow religious whenever he had the oppor-
> tunity to be with us.[10]

McCauley always practiced what he preached; he never asked
anyone to do what he was not willing to do. John Croston,
C.S.C., has written, "He would never refuse a request no matter the exertion involved and often did things for others that
others would have been more capable of doing for him. That
was the way he wanted it."[11]

As discussed in various contexts, both when he was bishop
of Fort Portal and in more direct service with AMECEA,
McCauley was a leader in the promotion of an ecumenical
spirit in Eastern Africa. His influence cut across all lines; he
was a universal man. His successor in Fort Portal, Serapio
Magambo, once wrote:

> Vince was loved and appreciated by everybody in Fort
> Portal—young and old, men and women, rich and poor,
> black and white, Catholics and non-Catholics. He cut
> across all cultural, religious, racial and ethnic boundaries.
> It is rare nowadays to find such persons but then Vince
> was that rare person.[12]

He was a friend to all, but especially the poor and marginal-
ized.[13] He asked others to see people as they were, made in
the image and likeness of God, whether Protestant, Muslim,
child, or adult. McCauley's ability to work with all peoples and
groups made him a unifying factor in the fractured society in
which he lived.[14]

McCauley's leadership skills were manifest through his
ability as a great communicator. Although he never mastered
African languages, he had no problem communicating. He

was a great conversationalist, making a point to interact with as many people as possible when he entered a room. He prided himself on knowing names. His engagement of others was real. One Holy Cross religious commented, "He never came off as phony."[15]

Spirituality and Personal Qualities

Vincent McCauley proved that he was a great leader, but the base of his life as a religious and priest was his spirituality, as manifest principally through prayer and holiness of life. Those who knew him best described him as a man of frequent and deep prayer. His prayer was both public and private, but in both cases he always seemed to pray for others, never himself.[16] He was always doing things for others. John Croston, C.S.C., once commented: "Whatever he could do for you he would do it—whether it was financial support, moral support, or support in a religious context. He was a holy man and helped many people in that way."[17] Joseph Kelly, C.S.S.p., describes McCauley's faithfulness to others. Even when hospitalized, he at times would "sneak out" of his hospital room in the early morning, preside at Mass for a convent of sisters, and then return to the hospital with no one knowing he had left.[18] Many people saw McCauley as a saintly person, a man of God. His faith was simple, but very profound.

Possibly the most significant and manifest aspect of his spirituality was his devotion to the Blessed Virgin Mary. McCauley's friend Arnold Fell commented:

> You cannot understand him at all apart from his devotion to Our Blessed Mother Mary. It is a great love story. She was his heroine, his inseparable companion. He spoke and wrote of her as if she was right by his side.[19]

On his regular trips to the United States and Europe, both for medical treatment and fundraising, McCauley invariably

stopped at Lourdes. John Croston relates, "He seemed trans-
fixed, as if she was speaking to him personally. I saw a statue,
but he saw a woman with whom he spoke person to person."[20]
He shared his dedication to Mary with others: "Devotion to
Our Blessed Mother is one of our basic themes in developing
the spiritual life in our African seminarians."[21] His devotion to
Mary was sealed in a very concrete way through the motto on
his episcopal coat-of-arms: *Mariam Sequens Non-Divias* (Following Mary, You do not Go Astray). He wanted any success
in the Diocese of Fort Portal to be attributed to her.[22]

McCauley's spirituality of prayer and holiness grew from
his basic love for others. His love for the people he served was
manifest in great respect for their ability as seen in his support
of indigenization in all aspects of his ministry. This policy
endeared him to others, especially native clergy and bishops.[23]
McCauley always made time for others; he demonstrated a
genuine interest in what others did or said. John Croston,
C.S.C., commented: "He was a man who never thought ill of
another and never hesitated a moment to lend a helping hand
where it was needed. He truly loved people."[24] Another Holy
Cross religious stated, "He treated you as if you were the most
important person in his life at that moment."[25] In special ways
he made a significant impact by simply being present to others. Serapio Magambo once commented, "Socially, no other
bishop I know in East Africa, black or white, has had so much
influence with the Africans, black or white, as Bishop McCauley."[26] He was relaxed in the presence of others and enjoyed a
good time. He told lots of jokes and was an avid bridge player.
McCauley gave every person full respect based on their inher-
ent human dignity.

His love for people was manifest especially for children and
youth. He regularly visited St. Mary's minor seminary and
spoke and played table tennis with the students as a father
would to his son. In the bush villages, he always brought

candy and made time to interact and speak with the children. Additionally, his promotion of education was a paramount endeavor to provide opportunities today and improve the future lot of children more universally.[27]

The love McCauley held for others was completely mutual and was expressed in many ways. People were inspired by the bishop, especially his attitude that encouraged people to be all they could possibly be. He was a "cheerleader"; he stood on the side of others who had ideas to pursue and dreams to achieve.[28] The African bishops themselves expressed the greatest manifestation of love for McCauley. His AMECEA colleague, Joseph Healey, M.M., once commented, "The fact that strikes you most is the warm affection, almost veneration of the African bishops for their Bishop Vince. Many of them have said to me: 'He is our Father.'"[29] His successor, Serapio Magambo, wrote, "I replaced a wonderful man. . . . I must confess I learnt a lot from him and highly value the experience I have gained under him."[30]

Bishop McCauley's love for others was also manifest in his great kindness in word and action. He was well known for his gentleness in all situations and he possessed a good sense of humor that helped him engage others. He was, thus, able to make friends easily as people were attracted to him like a magnet. He took people at face value; he did not expect anything save what was given. In his relationships with others, disagreements naturally arose, especially in his position as local ordinary. But all testify that McCauley never held a grudge against anyone.[31]

A central tenet to McCauley's kind disposition was his openness to others. John Croston, C.S.C., once wrote: "He was accessible and extremely approachable. . . . Everyone was welcomed and made to feel important."[32] McCauley had an open-door policy; appointments were not needed to speak with him. He welcomed other opinions. One fellow Holy

Cross religious put it well: "I never had the sense I would have to hold back an opinion from McCauley."[33] People could dialogue with him on any issue; he always treated others with grace and respect. He was open to learning from others and his surroundings; he was a good listener.[34]

McCauley was a very compassionate and caring man. He never told people what to do, but rather asked, "What and how are you doing?"[35] His work with refugees exemplified his compassionate nature. Bishop Magambo once commented, "He could not see a poor or needy person and remain unmoved. He would always go for help, whether this was a spiritual or material need."[36] McCauley's compassionate side was even clear to seminarians during his Washington, D.C., days. One seminarian of the period commented, "I was struck by his constant concern for others who were having problems; he was always looking after somebody."[37]

The bishop's compassion was often manifest in his great generosity. He gave freely of his time, talent, and resources. Whenever a member of Holy Cross went on vacation, the religious would hear McCauley say, "Do you have enough money? Are you sure?"[38] As evidenced by his almost daily distribution of funds to refugees, McCauley could rightly be called, "generous to a fault." But when he was challenged by others who felt he was being "taken," McCauley would always respond, "I know that at least nine out of ten are thieves, but I don't want to reach heaven and find that I could have helped somebody and didn't."[39] Clearly he could quietly yet forcefully disarm his critics.

McCauley encapsulated his personality and spirituality by conducting his daily affairs in humility. He never complained about anything, as manifest most clearly through the cross of physical pain he bore constantly and bravely. He never spoke of himself, but rather promoted the Church and its needs.

His friend and long-time associate, Arnold Fell, C.S.C., put it well:

> He was truly a humble man, yet an out-going, ever-joyful positive one. . . . He always tried to pass unnoticed. To which, I would add, however, that he never passed without noticing you with a greeting, a word of encouragement or praise or a happy word. You always felt better after meeting him, no matter what your trouble at the time.[40]

The Legacy of Vincent McCauley

The ministerial career of Vincent McCauley, spanning almost half a century and exercised on three continents, was significant for many reasons. His work ethic, expertise, magnetic personality, and overall kindness allowed him to leave his mark in every avenue of ministry he engaged, in Bengal, the United States, and Eastern Africa. As a missionary in Bengal his work was a significant boost to the local church, especially the training of future indigenous clergy. His time in Washington was also marked as a formator of young religious.

Vincent McCauley will be remembered in history, however, for his contributions to the Church in Eastern Africa. As the founding local ordinary in Fort Portal, McCauley set up the ecclesiastical, educational, and financial structures and institutions necessary for the diocese to operate. He readied the diocese and its people for an indigenous bishop, resigning his post as soon as this turnover was feasible. Following the devastating 1966 earthquake, McCauley rebuilt, bigger and better, the cathedral that the tremor destroyed. For the wider Ugandan Church, McCauley was the point man to promote ecumenism through the Uganda Joint Christian Council, and the one who brought the teachings of Vatican II to clergy and laity through his English translation and publication of the documents and a series of talks by fellow Holy Cross religious,

Edward Heston. McCauley's active involvement with the
Uganda Episcopal Conference was capped by his oversight of
the construction of the new Gaba National Seminary.

In a wider context, his work with AMECEA, initially as
chairman (1964 to 1973) and then secretary-general (1973 to
1979), provided him with greater opportunities for influence.
Present on the ground floor of the association, McCauley
assisted in the body's formation. After the third session of Vatican II and AMECEA's formal launching, McCauley's leadership was responsible for the initiation of numerous significant
programs and institutions, including the Gaba Pastoral Institute, construction of AMECEA's Nairobi headquarters, several
ecumenical and pastoral programs, such as the accounting
course at the Nyegezi Social Training Center, the formation of
SECAM, and the foundation of the Catholic Higher Institute
of Eastern Africa (CHIEA). Bishop Paul Kalanda synthesized
McCauley's contribution to the African Church:

> Bishop MacCauley [sic] played a key role. He has left a
> mark everywhere he passed and everywhere he worked:
> First in Fort Portal diocese, in the Uganda Episcopal
> Conference and then AMECEA in Nairobi, Kenya, and
> in Eastern Africa as a whole.[41]

Besides the more visible programs and institutional undertakings, Vincent McCauley's legacy may rest in the common
everyday ways he influenced peoples' lives. The respect granted
him by indigenous clergy demonstrates how his presence
positively affected their lives. In a more general sense, Serapio
Magambo spoke of McCauley's personal generosity of spirit:

> It was by giving himself, his time, his money, his material
> and spiritual goods, nay his life itself, that he made Fort
> Portal, Eastern Africa and Madagascar what they are now
> as far as Catholicism is concerned.[42]

In a more specific way he continued:

> Bishop McCauley was, I believe, your greatest ambassador
> to Uganda and to Eastern Africa. In great simplicity, love,
> and suffering he made us understand how you Americans
> and particularly Holy Cross love us and are interested in
> our total development in body and soul.[43]

In a similar way, Cardinal Maurice Otunga of Nairobi claimed McCauley the region's unifying factor: "Whatever unity we bishops in Eastern Africa have, we owe it to Bishop McCauley."[44] His AMECEA colleague, Joseph Kelly, C.S.S.p., might have put it best: "He had good initiative, great faith, long patience and almost unimagineable charity."[45]

Possibly, Vincent McCauley's contribution can best be seen by comparisons drawn between him and other notables of his day. James Rahilly stated that McCauley's appointment to Africa was "the grace of God working through the Holy Cross administration." He claimed, "McCauley was to Africa what Hesburgh was to Notre Dame." John Keefe went even further: "What John XXIII was to the Church, McCauley was to East[ern] Africa. He opened the doors, he brought in a new life. He had a different vision; he surprised everyone."[46]

Summary

In his famous stage play, *A Man for All Seasons*, English playwright Robert Bolt portrays the courage of St. Thomas More, who sought to cross boundaries between church and state while holding fast to the true faith which he professed. He was never cowed by his inability to win the support of others, but rather was content to be right rather than popular. In a similar but more successful way, Vincent Joseph McCauley crossed many national, cultural, and religious boundaries as a missionary in Bengal and Eastern Africa. Like More, he was never cowed by opponents or naysayers who suggested his dreams were too lofty or impracticable. On the contrary, he believed and practiced the ethic that if he reached his goals they were not set high enough. He courageously defended his staunch belief in the promotion of the lay Church, in transferring both power and authority to local people so they could aid an indigenous clergy. McCauley was highly successful, especially in the latter half of his life in Africa, in building institutions and creating a self-sustaining local church. His secret for success was a simple but fervent spirituality, not worn on his sleeve but evident nonetheless, a strong personal constitution and work ethic, and a winning combination of personal qualities that endeared him to most everyone. He understood his role as a servant in the construction of God's kingdom in our world. His life is an inspiration and serves as a model for people in the twenty-first century.

Notes

Introduction

1. John Croston, C.S.C., interview with the author, July 7, 2005, Archives Holy Cross Priests Indiana Province, Notre Dame, IN (hereafter AHCFI).

2. As is related in chapter one, many seminarians sought spiritual direction and guidance from McCauley. Additionally, his more open approach to religious formation, generated through his personality and previous experience in Bengal, was well appreciated and served as a significant contrast to the stricter, more traditional formation of Holy Cross College.

3. Burton Smith, interview with the author, April 8, 2006, AHCFI.

4. Mbarara is interchangeably spelled Mbarrara. In this book the more contemporary spelling (Mbarara) is used, save direct quotations when the older spelling is used. Also, for clarity and consistency the religious designation W.F. (White Fathers) is used throughout. Today, the Missionaries of Africa use the religious designation M. Afr. The historical time period and documents reviewed in this biography all used the former (W.F.) designation.

5. Vincent McCauley, C.S.C., to Theodore Mehling, C.S.C., 1 September, 1961, 38:48, Mehling Papers, AHCFI.

6. This episcopal body was originally formed in 1961 at Dar es Salaam as the Interterritorial Episcopal Board of Eastern Africa (ITEBEA). At Vatican II, the bishops changed the name and the direction of the body to be more proactive in its operations. McCauley's selection by his fellow prelates clearly demonstrated the respect he had gained, even as a very junior bishop.

7. Vincent McCauley, C.S.C., to Maurice Otunga, 23 October 1970, unmarked box, AMECEA Correspondence, Archives

Diocese of Fort Portal, Uganda, Fort Portal, Uganda (hereafter ADFP).

8. Paulinas Bagambaki, interview with the author, February 1, 2006, AHCFI.

9. The material on Holy Cross is found mainly in James T. Connelly, C.S.C., "Holy Cross in East Africa, 1958–1980," (1981) Archives Indiana Province, Notre Dame, IN (hereafter AIP). McCauley is mentioned in a few articles, most prominently in Joseph G. Healey, M.M., "Two AMECEA Giants," The African Ecclesial Review (AFER) 26, nos. 1–2 (February–April 1986): 22–25, an essay that highlights the contribution of McCauley and Killian Flynn to AMECEA.

1. The Early Years: 1906–1936

1. Stephen Neill, *A History of Christian Missions* (Middlesex, England: Penguin Books, 1979), 22–23.

2. At the Council of Jerusalem the momentous decision was made that it was not necessary for Gentiles to follow Jewish ways in their conversion to Christianity. This highly significant decision allowed Christianity to move forward as a separate religion and not a sect of Judaism. See Acts of the Apostles 15:1–29.

3. Inculturation is the concept that local culture is respected and utilized by conquering and/or missionary groups. Acculturation rejects the local culture and utilizes the conquering or missionary force culture as normative.

4. Angelyn Dries, O.S.F., *The Missionary Movement in American Catholic History* (Maryknoll, NY: Orbis Books, 1998), 43–45.

5. Ibid., 43–62.

6. The Congregation of Holy Cross received final approbation for its Constitutions on May 13, 1857. This was achieved after Moreau agreed to two requests of the Holy See: to make an institutional commitment of the congregation to the Bengal missions (described in chapter 2) and to separate the women religious into

a distinct congregation. Thus, Moreau's original idea of sisters, brothers, and priests ministering side-by-side in the same congregation was short-lived. For more information concerning the need to separate women from men in Holy Cross see: Thomas Barrosse, C.S.C., *Moreau: Portrait of a Founder* (Notre Dame, Indiana: Fides Publishers, Inc., 1969), 229–233; Gary MacEoin, *Father Moreau: Founder of Holy Cross* (Milwaukee: Bruce Publishing Company, 1962), 132–166; Etienne Catta and Tony Catta, trans. Edward Heston, C.S.C., *Basil Anthony Mary Moreau*, Vol. II (Milwaukee: Bruce Publishing Company, 1955), 255–258.

7. Joseph A. Kehoe, C.S.C., "Holy Cross in Oregon, 1902–1980," (1982) AIP, 1–2.

8. There is no exhaustive history of the Congregation of Holy Cross. More information on the origins of the congregation are found in: Catta and Catta, *Moreau*, Vol. I, 338–453; Barrosse, *Moreau*, 76–272. It should be noted that East Africa refers to Uganda, Kenya, and Tanzania. Eastern Africa encompasses those nations plus others in the surrounding region.

9. For more information on the NCWC and Mexico in the 1920s and 1930s see: Douglas Slawson, "The National Catholic Welfare Conference and the Church-State Conflict in Mexico, 1925–1929," *The Americas* 47, no. 1 (July 1990): 55–93 and "The National Catholic Welfare Conference and the Mexican Church-State Conflict of the mid-1930s: A Case of Déjà Vu," *Catholic Historical Review* 80, no. 1 (1994): 58–96.

10. See Christopher Kauffman, *Ministry and Meaning: A Religious History of Catholic Health Care in the United States* (New York: Crossroad Publishing Company, 1995). Pages 170–192 present material on the early years of the Catholic Hospital Association.

11. Dries, *Missionary Movement*, 105; 104.

12. Data sheet on Vincent McCauley, C.S.C., n.d., 811, Doss. 1, Holy Cross Generalate Papers, Archives of the University of Notre Dame, Notre Dame, IN (hereafter AUND).

13. Robert Hoffman, C.S.C., interview with the author, April 24, 2006, AHCFI.

14. Mary Joan Larsen, interview with the author, May 8, 2006, AHCFI; Gene Burke, C.S.C., interview with the author, April 21, 2006, AHCFI.

15. Vincent McCauley, C.S.C., to Larry Tracy, 24 February 1978, Personal Papers of Larry Tracy (hereafter PPLT); Mary Joan Larsen interview.

16. Vincent McCauley to Harverd Tracy, 14 February 1948, Personal Papers of Mary Joan Larsen (hereafter PPMJL). Gertrude Tracy, wife to Harverd, was a first cousin to Vincent McCauley. He regularly corresponded with this couple and later with Mary Joan (Tracy) Larsen and Larry Tracy, children to Harverd and Gertrude.

17. Frank E. Pellegrin, "The Story of Bishop Vince," *Our Lady's Bulletin*, 13, no. 12 (February 1977): 10; James Nichols, C.S.C., "Vincent McCauley," essay, 109 Bishop McCauley Papers, Archives of Holy Cross Fathers East Africa, Kampala, Uganda (hereafter AHCFEA).

18. Vincent McCauley, C.S.C., to George Finnegan, C.S.C., 27 September 1924, Confidential Personal File, AHCFI.

19. McCauley took four years of Latin, math, and English, and two years of Greek. Sonia Palumbo, e-mail message to author, 22 January, 2007.

20. Eleanor McCandless, interview with the author, April 3, 2006, AHCFI.

21. McCauley to Finnegan, 27 September 1924; Vincent McCauley, C.S.C., to George Finnegan, C.S.C., 5 October 1924, Confidential Personnel File, AHCFI.

22. Data sheet on Vincent McCauley, C.S.C.

23. Raymond J. Clancy, C.S.C., *The Congregation of Holy Cross in East Bengal, 1853–1953 with a Brief History of the Church in Bengal* (Washington, D.C: Holy Cross Foreign Mission Seminary, 1953), 77–78; Edmund N. Goedert, C.S.C., "Holy Cross

Priests in the Diocese of Dacca, 1853–1981," (1983) AIP, 16–17; *The Bengalese* 11, no. 8 (September 1930): cover page; George Marr, C.S.C., to James Burns, C.S.C., 9 September 1931, 3:31, Burns Papers, AHCFI.

24. For more information about the call of the hierarchy to centralize theological studies in Washington, D.C., see C. Joseph Nuese, *The Catholic University of America: A Centennial History* (Washington, D.C.: The Catholic University of America Press, 1990), 168. Nuese says that by 1916 there were seven religious houses of study in the general area. During the tenure of the University's first rector, Bishop John J. Keane, an invitation was extended to religious communities to locate their houses of theological studies on or adjacent to the University's campus. Three examples of foundations were: the Marists in 1892, Paulists in 1894, and the Dominicans in 1903. See Patrick Henry Ahern, *The Catholic University of America 1887–1896: The Rectorship of John J. Keane* (Washington, D.C.: The Catholic University of America Press, 1948), 84–89.

25. Vincent McCauley, C.S.C., to James Burns, C.S.C., 15 July 1934, 12:46, Burns Papers, AHCFI; James Burns, C.S.C., to Vincent McCauley, C.S.C., 18 July 1934, 12:46, Burns Papers, AHCFI.

26. Vincent McCauley, C.S.C, "The Churches and Development in Africa," (lecture at Creighton University, Omaha, NE, May 7, 1971), 910.1, McCauley Papers, Archives of the Diocese of Fort Portal, ADFP.

27. John Croston interview, July 7, 2005; John Croston, C.S.C., interview with the author, April 5, 2006, AHCFI; George Lucas, C.S.C., interview with the author, April 17, 2006, AHCFI.

28. Patrick Peyton, C.S.C., known as the "rosary priest," popularized the phrase, "The family that prays together stays together." He was internationally known for his promotion of family prayer through the rosary. By means of dozens of rosary

crusades held between 1948 and 1985, Peyton brought his simple but profound message to the world. McCauley would later cross paths with Peyton shortly after the former became bishop of Fort Portal, Uganda, in 1961. For more information on Peyton please see: Richard Gribble, C.S.C., *American Apostle of the Family Rosary: The Life of Patrick J. Peyton, CSC* (New York: Crossroad, 2005).

29. Vincent McCauley, C.S.C., homily on the Feast of the Immaculate Conception, n.d., 811, Doss. 1, Holy Cross Generalate Papers, AUND.

30. James Burns, C.S.C., to Vincent McCauley, C.S.C., 8 August 1934, 12:46, Burns Papers, AHCFI. It should be noted that McCauley professed the "fourth vow" for missionary service. This vow stated: "I, N., unworthy that I am, but nevertheless relying on the Divine Mercy and moved by the desire to serve the most Holy Trinity, I vow forever to Almighty God, before our Lord Jesus Christ, the Immaculate Virgin Mary, and her worthy husband Joseph and all the heavenly court, poverty, chastity, obedience, (and a willingness to go anywhere the Superior General may wish to send me,) according to the sense of the Constitutions of the Congregation of Holy Cross." Thus, McCauley was ultimately under obedience to the superior general for assignment.

31. In the mid- to late-nineteenth century Holy Cross religious were active in starting schools and orphanages throughout the Midwest and as far east as Baltimore, Camden, New Jersey, and Philadelphia. Many of the schools were short-lived but these foundations demonstrate the zeal of the community to answer the call of the Church.

32. The American provincials, James Burns (1927–1938) and Thomas Steiner (1938–1950) did not actively promote eastern foundations. Fear of expansion due to lack of funds and personnel, and the desire to promote the fortunes of Notre Dame created a narrow view of the community's future possibilities.

33. "Chronicles of Holy Cross," September 18, 1933, December 8, 1933, Archives Stonehill College, North Easton, MA (hereafter ASC).

34. Frederick Lothrup Ames had amassed a fortune from his family shovel business and his prize Guernsey cowherd. The history of the Ames family is colorful and multifaceted. For detailed information see: Winthrop Ames, *The Ames Family*, privately published, 1938, and William L. Chaffin, *History of the Town of Easton, Massachusetts* (Cambridge, MA: John Wilson and Son, 1886), 648–660.

35. Ames Family History Fact Sheet, Ames Family Papers; *Brockton Daily Enterprise*, March 5, 1937, ASC; *Providence Visitor*, July 22, 1948, North Easton File, AHCFI.

36. "Chronicles of Holy Cross," October 17, 1935, ASC. With a minor seminary in North Easton and a novitiate in North Dartmouth, Holy Cross decided to solidify its foundation by expansion of its holdings. Two hundred acres of the Ames estate remained with the owner, Edith Cutler, who was eager to sell. Thus, in late 1936 Holy Cross purchased the remaining land. In September 1948, Stonehill College was founded on the North Easton site.

37. Vincent McCauley, C.S.C., to Harverd and Gertrude Tracy, 3 November 1935, PPMJL.

38. Ibid.

39. Vincent McCauley, C.S.C., to James Burns, C.S.C., June 18, 1934 [*sic*–1936], 14:10, Burns Papers, ACHFI.

2. Missionary to Bengal: 1936–1944

1. Goedert, C.S.C., "Holy Cross in Dacca," 1. For more information on the relationship between the Vatican and Portugal in the period of the *Padroado*, please see: M. N. Pearson, *The New Cambridge History of India*, Vol. I, *The Portuguese in India* (Cambridge: Cambridge University Press, 1987), 118–120; Michael Edwards, *A History of India From the Earliest Times to Present*

Day (London: Thames and Hudson, 1961), 143–153; Vincent A. Smith, *The Oxford History of India*, Part I (Oxford: Clarendon Press, 1958), 329–335.

2. *Catholic Encyclopedia*, Vol. 6 (New York: The Universal Foundation, Inc, 1913): 603.

3. Ibid. See also Stephen Neill, *A History of Christianity in India: The Beginnings to AD 1707* (Cambridge: Cambridge University Press, 1984), 358.

4. In Latin America, through a series of Papal bulls, most especially *Inter caetera* (Alexander VI, May 4, 1493) and *Universalis ecclesiae* (Julius II, July 28, 1508), the Spanish government was given the right of patronage over the Church. This meant that the Spanish crown controlled Church activities and personnel. This rare privilege was given (1) because the Spanish had just resecured their borders with the final defeat of the Moors in 1492, and (2) the Church did not have the economic resources necessary to adequately set up the necessary institutions. The Patronato Real system led to many conflicts between church and state until the dawn of the period of independence in the nineteenth century. For more information on the Patronato Real see: Eugene W. Shiels, *King and Church: The Rise and Fall of the Patronato Real* (Chicago: Loyola University Press, 1961).

5. Goedert, "Holy Cross in Dacca," 4. The full story of the Vicariate Apostolic in Bengal is told in Clancy, *Holy Cross in East Bengal*, xliv–lxi, 26–35.

6. Ibid., 4–5.

7. Quoted in Ibid., 6.

8. Ibid., 7.

9. Ibid., 6.

10. Ibid., 7–8. It should be noted that in 1866, due to many pressures, Moreau was forced to resign as superior general. Pierre Dufal was elected as his successor, but after a very short period it was clear he did not have the constitution for the position. Thus, he returned to Bengal and Edward Sorin was elected the third

superior general, serving in the United States simultaneously as president of Notre Dame.

11. Three men from Indiana, Fathers Michael Fallize, Francis Boeres, and Bonnet Roche, and two from Canada, Father Aime-Marie Fourmond and Mr. Pierre Fichet, were the team sent in 1888. Roche and Fourmond were veterans of the Bengal mission.

12. Goedert, "Holy Cross in Dacca," 10–11.

13. Ibid., 12–14.

14. Clancy, "Holy Cross in East Bengal," 70.

15. Goedert, "Holy Cross in Dacca," 28–29.

16. Ibid., 15.

17. Richard Timm, C.S.C., ed., *150 Years of Holy Cross in East Bengal Mission* (Dhaka, Bangladesh: Congregation of Holy Cross, 2003), 29; Goedert, "Holy Cross in Dacca," 16–19.

18. Goedert, "Holy Cross in Dacca," 19–21; Timm, *Holy Cross in Bengal*, 34; Clancy, *Holy Cross in East Bengal*, 64.

19. Clancy, C.S.C., *Holy Cross in East Bengal*, 73, 120–21. Some statistics demonstrate the gravity of the financial loss to the missions:

Date	Donations	Monies From Holy Cross
1929–1930	No record	$42,273.4
1930–1931	$4,672.22	$32,196.54
1931–1932	$5,257.00	$28,653.45
1932–1933	$1,711.00	$9,618.00

See Timothy Crowley, C.S.C., to "Dear Fathers and Brothers," March 27, 1933, 712, Holy Cross Generalate Papers, AUND.

20. Ibid., 72.

21. James Burns, C.S.C., to Timothy Crowley, C.S.C., 10 April 1933, 4:48, Burns Papers, AHCFI.

22. Timothy Crowley, C.S.C., to James Burns, C.S.C., 9 May 1933, 4:48, Burns Papers, AHCFI.

23. Timothy Crowley, C.S.C., to James Burns, C.S.C., 5 July 1933, 4:48, Burns Papers, AHCFI.

24. Michael Mangan, C.S.C., to James W. Donahue, C.S.C., 21 November 1934, 712, Dacca Holy Cross Chapters, Holy Cross Generalate Papers, AUND.

25. Timothy Crowley, C.S.C., to James W. Donahue, C.S.C., 8 August, 1933, 711, Doss. 3, Holy Cross Generalate Papers, AUND.

26. Timothy Crowley, C.S.C., to James W. Donahue, C.S.C., 4 July 1934, 711, Doss. 3; Andrew Steffes, C.S.C., to Timothy Crowley, C.S.C., 10 July, 1935, 711, Doss. 3, Holy Cross Generalate Papers, AUND. Brother Andrew Steffes, C.S.C., was headmaster at Holy Cross High School in Bandhura. The imminent return of one brother to the United States due to illness prompted Steffes to implore Crowley, "Most humbly and respectfully I wish to point out that three men are the minimum with which the present institution at Bandhura can be run."

27. Timothy Crowley, C.S.C., to James W. Donahue, C.S.C., 14 June 1936, 711, Doss. 3, Holy Cross Generalate Papers, AUND.

28. James W. Donahue, C.S.C., to Timothy Crowley, C.S.C., 8 September 1936, 711, Doss. 3, Holy Cross Generalate Papers, AUND.

29. James Burns, C.S.C., to Vincent McCauley, C.S.C., 22 June 1936, 14:10, Burns Papers, and June 26, 1936, 7:44, Burns Papers, AHCFI.

30. James Burns, C.S.C., to Francis Goodall, C.S.C., 15 August, 1936, 7:45, Burns Papers, AHCFI; Francis Goodall, C.S.C., to James Burns, C.S.C, 12 August 1936 and 26 October 1936, 7:45, Burns Papers, AHCFI. Goodall reported that McCauley raised $500 during his begging tour.

31. Francis Goodall, C.S.C., to James Burns, C.S.C., 22 July 1936, 7:45, Burns Papers, Holy Cross Generalate Papers, AUND; James Burns, C.S.C., to Francis Goodall, C.S.C., 22 July 1936, 7:45, Burns Papers, Holy Cross Generalate Papers, AUND; Francis Goodall, C.S.C., to James Burns, C.S.C., 11 September

1936, 7:45, Burns Papers, Holy Cross Generalate Papers, AUND;
James Burns, C.S.C., to Francis Goodall, C.S.C., 6 September
1936, 7:45, Burns Papers, Holy Cross Generalate Papers, AUND.
Switalski served in the Bengal mission from 1928 to 1954. See
Raymond Switalski, C.S.C., Personnel Card, AHCFI.

32. *The Bengalese* 17, no. 9 (November 1936): 18, AHCFI.

33. Francis Goodall, C.S.C., to James Burns, C.S.C., 26
October 1936, 7:45, Burns Papers, AHCFI.

34. Francis Goodall, C.S.C., to James Burns, C.S.C., 18
August 1936, 7:45, Burns Papers, AHCFI; Vincent McCauley,
C.S.C., to Francis Goodall, C.S.C., 1 November 1936, McCauley
File, Holy Cross Mission Center Papers, AHCFI.

35. James W. Donahue, C.S.C., to Vincent McCauley,
C.S.C., 2 January 1937, 811, Doss. 2, Holy Cross Generalate
Papers, AUND; Vincent McCauley, C.S.C., to James W. Dona-
hue, C.S.C., 5 February 1937, 811, Doss. 2, Holy Cross Gen-
eralate Papers, AUND; James W. Donahue, C.S.C., to Vincent
McCauley, C.S.C., 16 March 1937, 811, Doss. 2, Holy Cross
Generalate Papers, AUND.

36. Clancy, *Holy Cross in East Bengal*, 127; Vincent McCauley,
C.S.C., to Francis Goodall, C.S.C., 23 November 1936, McCauley File, Holy Cross Mission Center Papers, AHCFI.

37. Vincent McCauley, C.S.C., "Fifteen Hours By Boat," *The
Bengalese* 18, no. 5 (May 1937): 8–9; Clancy, *Holy Cross in East
Bengal*, 111; Timothy Crowley, C.S.C., to James Burns, C.S.C.,
30 November 1936, 7:36, Burns Papers, AHCFI.

38. McCauley to Goodall, 23 November 1936.

39. Vincent McCauley, C.S.C., to Harriet Gartland, 7
March 1937, McCauley File, Holy Cross Mission Center Papers,
AHCFI.

40. Francis Goodall, C.S.C., to Vincent McCauley, C.S.C.,
16 February 1937, McCauley File, Holy Cross Mission Center
Papers, AHCFI.

41. Timm, *Holy Cross in Bengal*, 41; Clancy, *Holy Cross in East Bengal*, 103–105; *The Bengalese* 18, no. 2 (February 1937): 13; Vincent McCauley, C.S.C., "Dreams Become Reality," *The Bengalese* 25, no. 4 (1944): 6, 15.

42. McCauley, "Dreams Become Reality," 6–7; Vincent McCauley, C.S.C., to Francis Goodall, C.S.C., 17 January 1937 and 25 July 1938, McCauley File, Holy Cross Mission Center Papers, AHCFI.

43. Vincent McCauley, C.S.C., to Francis Goodall, C.S.C., 23 March 1937, McCauley File, Holy Cross Mission Center Papers, AHCFI.

44. McCauley to Goodall, 25 July 1938.

45. Vincent McCauley, C.S.C., to Harriet Gartland, 30 September 1938, McCauley File, Holy Cross Mission Center Papers, AHCFI.

46. McCauley to Goodall, 23 March 1937; Vincent McCauley, C.S.C., to Francis Goodall, C.S.C., 21 June 1937, McCauley File, Holy Cross Mission Center Papers, AHCFI.

47. Vincent McCauley, C.S.C., to Harverd and Gertrude Tracy, 21 August 1939, PPMJL.

48. *The Bengalese* 27, no. 6 (September 1946): 9, AHCFI.

49. Quotes in Clancy, *Holy Cross in East Bengal*, 66. Crowley was referring to the Apostolic Letter *Maximum Illud* of Pope Benedict XV, November 30, 1919.

50. Vincent McCauley, C.S.C., to Dear Monsignor [Thomas Steiner], 6 May 1944, 27:05, Steiner Papers, AHCFI.

51. Vincent McCauley, C.S.C., to Mr. and Mrs. Charles McCauley, 31 August 1942, PPMJL.

52. Vincent McCauley, C.S.C., to Harverd Tracy, 26 April 1942, PPMJL. McCauley magnified the problem by stating that Italian- and German-born missionaries had been placed in internment camps, thus further reducing the already slim ranks of expatriates.

53. Vincent McCauley, C.S.C., to Harverd and Gertrude Tracy, 10 December 1940, PPMJL.

54. McCauley to Harverd Tracy, 26 April 1942.

55. Vincent McCauley, C.S.C., to Thomas Fitzpatrick, C.S.C., 28 January 1944, McCauley File, Holy Cross Mission Center Papers, AHCFI.

56. Vincent McCauley, C.S.C., to Anonymous, n.d. [1943], McCauley File, Holy Cross Mission Center Papers, AHCFI.

57. Vincent McCauley, C.S.C., to Harverd Tracy et al., 23 March 1943, PPMJL.

58. Vincent McCauley, C.S.C., to Anonymous, n.d. [1943], McCauley File, Holy Cross Mission Center Papers, AHCFI.

59. McCauley to Dear Monsignor [Steiner], 6 May 1944.

60. Goedert, "Holy Cross in Dacca," 22–25.

61. Clancy, *Holy Cross in East Bengal*, 158; Vincent McCauley, C.S.C., to Francis Goodall, C.S.C., 6 June 1937, McCauley File, Holy Cross Mission Center Papers, AHCFI.

62. Clancy, *Holy Cross in East Bengal*, 182; Donald MacGregor, C.S.C., "The Hill Tipperach Kukis," *The Bengalese* 18, no. 3 (March 1937): 14.

63. MacGregor, "The Kukis," 14; Clancy, *Holy Cross in East Bengal*, 184; Joseph Voorde, C.S.C., to Francis Goodall, C.S.C., 15 March 1938, Voorde File, Holy Cross Mission Center Papers, AHCFI. Mariamnagar village was very isolated. It was accessible from Dacca via a combination of train, horse-drawn trolley, and foot. It is now in the Indian state of Tripura.

64. John Kane, C.S.C., to James W. Donahue, C.S.C., 23 September 1936, 713.2, Doss. 1, Holy Cross Generalate Papers, AUND.

65. Joseph Voorde, C.S.C., to Peter (John) [Harrington], 3 August 1939, Voorde File, Holy Cross Mission Center Papers, AHCFI. See also Clancy, *Holy Cross in East Bengal*, 188.

66. Thomas Steiner, C.S.C., to Timothy Crowley, C.S.C., 8 January 1939, 3:27, Steiner Papers; Francis Goodall, C.S.C., to

Vincent McCauley, C.S.C., 17 January 1939, McCauley File, Holy Cross Mission Center Papers, AHCFI.

67. Vincent McCauley, C.S.C., to Francis Goodall, C.S.C., 29 May 1939, McCauley File, Holy Cross Mission Center Papers, AHCFI.

68. Vincent McCauley, C.S.C., to Joseph and Harriet Gartland, 7 July 1939, McCauley Papers, Holy Cross Mission Center Papers, AHCFI.

69. McCauley to Goodall, 29 May 1939.

70. Timothy Crowley, C.S.C., to Albert Cousineau, C.S.C., 23 February 1940, 711, Doss. 2, Holy Cross Generalate Papers, AUND.

71. Vincent McCauley, C.S.C., to Harverd Tracy, 1 August 1943, PPMJL.

72. McCauley to Joseph and Harriet Gartland, 7 July 1939.

73. Vincent McCauley, C.S.C., to Harverd and Gertrude Tracy, 28 January 1940, PPMJL. The remote environment of the mission to the Kukis was described by McCauley: "The new villages are at the other end of our little domain; let's say it is ten miles to the station, sixty miles by train, sixteen miles on foot up and down 400-500 foot hills, to the place of the weekly bazaar. There the catechists were to meet the villagers who would show them the way eight or nine miles farther to the first of the new villages." See McCauley to Joseph and Harriet Gartland, 7 July 1939.

74. McCauley to Harverd and Gertrude Tracy, 28 January 1940.

75. *The Bengalese* 21, no. 1 (January 1940): 12, AHCFI.

76. McCauley to Harverd and Gertrude Tracy, 28 January 1940.

77. Vincent McCauley, C.S.C., to Francis Goodall, C.S.C., 22 January 22 1940, McCauley Papers, Holy Cross Mission Center Papers, AHCFI.

78. Vincent McCauley, C.S.C., to Harverd and Gertrude Tracy, 24 June 1940, PPMJL.

79. Ibid.

80. Quoted in Clancy, *Holy Cross in East Bengal*, 136–137.

81. Ibid.

82. John Kane replaced Michael Mangan as regional superior in Bengal in 1938.

83. John Kane, C.S.C., to Albert Cousineau, C.S.C., 30 December 1941, 3 March 1942, 18 May 1942, 713.2, Doss. 1, Holy Cross Generalate Papers, AUND.

84. Timothy Crowley, C.S.C., to Dear Brethren, 1 August 1940, 711, Doss. 2, Holy Cross Generalate Papers, AUND; Timothy Crowley, C.S.C., to Thomas Steiner, C.S.C., 6 June 1940, 3:27, Steiner Papers, AHCFI.

85. Vincent McCauley, C.S.C., to E. J. Murphy, 16 June 16, 1942, PPMJL; Vincent McCauley, C.S.C., to Murphy Family, 23 July 1944, PPMJL; McCauley to Harverd Tracy, 30 June 1942, PPMJL.

86. Vincent McCauley, C.S.C., to Harverd and Gertrude Tracy, 3 June 1940, PPMJL.

87. McCauley to Harverd Tracy, 26 April 1942.

88. McCauley to Harverd and Gertrude Tracy, 3 June 1940.

89. Vincent McCauley, C.S.C., to Joseph Gartland, 28 January 1941, McCauley Papers, Holy Cross Mission Center Papers, AHCFI.

90. Clancy, *Holy Cross in East Bengal*, 106; "Chronicles Bandhura, 1940–1962," D-9, Bengal Missions, AHCFI.

91. List of Assignments, n.d., 27:05, Steiner Papers, AHCFI; McCauley to Harverd Tracy, 1 August 1943.

92. McCauley to Joseph Gartland, 28 January 1941. In another letter, McCauley wrote, "I am sure you will forgive me for being 'sold' on the idea of training priests for Christ. There is nothing I would rather be 'afflicted with' if we can put it that way." See McCauley to Harverd Tracy, 1 August 1943.

93. Vincent McCauley, C.S.C., to Harverd and Gertrude Tracy, 3 March 1941, PPMJL.

94. McCauley to Thomas Fitzpatrick, 28 January 1944.

95. Thomas More Beere, C.S.C., interview with the author, April 21, 2006, AHCFI.

96. McCauley to Harverd and Gertrude Tracy, 10 December 1940.

97. McCauley to Dear Monsignor [Steiner], 6 May 1944.

98. McCauley to Thomas Fitzpatrick, 28 January 1944.

99. Michael D'Rozario, C.S.C., to the author, 1 August 2005.

100. Vincent McCauley, C.S.C., to Harverd Tracy, 26 February 1942, PPMJL.

101. McCauley to Harverd Tracy, 30 June 1942.

102. McCauley to Thomas Fitzpatrick, 28 January 1944.

103. Ibid.; Vincent McCauley, C.S.C., to Harverd Tracy, 12 December 1940, PPMJL.

104. John Kane, C.S.C., to Albert Cousineau, C.S.C., 8 April 1943, 713.2, Doss. 1, Holy Cross Generalate Papers, AUND; *The Bengalese* 24, no. 8 (October 1943): 12, ACHFI.

105. Vincent McCauley, C.S.C., to unknown, n.d. [1943], McCauley Papers, Holy Cross Mission Center Papers, AHCFI.

106. McCauley to Mr. and Mrs. Charles McCauley, 31 August 1942. See also Clancy, *Holy Cross in East Bengal*, 179–181.

107. Vincent McCauley, C.S.C., to E. J. Murphy, 6 June 1942, PPMJL; McCauley to Harverd Tracy, 30 June 1942.

108. Vincent McCauley, C.S.C., to Murphy Family, 2 August 1944, PPMJL; McCauley to Harverd Tracy, 1 August 1943.

109. Vincent McCauley, C.S.C., to Gertrude Tracy, 10 July 1941, PPMJL.

110. McCauley to Thomas Fitzpatrick, 28 January 1944.

111. John Kane, C.S.C., to Albert Cousineau, C.S.C., 12 November 1941, 713.2, Doss. 1, Holy Cross Generalate Papers, AUND.

112. Vincent McCauley, C.S.C., to Eleanor McCauley, 28 July 1941, Personal Papers of Nonnie Frenzer (hereafter PPNF).

113. Ibid.

114. John Kane, C.S.C., to Albert Cousineau, C.S.C., 11 January 1944, 713.2, Doss. 1, Holy Cross Generalate Papers, AUND.

115. Timothy Crowley, C.S.C., to Thomas Steiner, C.S.C., 8 February 1944, 27:5, Steiner Papers, AHCFI.

116. Thomas Steiner, C.S.C., to Timothy Crowley, C.S.C., 27:5, Steiner Papers, AHCFI.

117. John Kane, C.S.C., to Albert Cousineau, C.S.C., 28 April 1944, 713.2, Doss. 1, Holy Cross Generalate Papers, AUND.

118. Timothy Crowley, C.S.C., to Thomas Steiner, C.S.C., 9 May 1944, 27:5, Steiner Papers, AHCFI; John Kane, C.S.C., to Thomas Steiner, C.S.C., 16 May 1944 and 29 May 1944, 27:5, Steiner Papers, AHCFI.

119. Pellegrin, "Bishop Vince," 10–11; Theodore Hesburgh, C.S.C., eulogy for Bishop McCauley, November 3, 1982, 811, Doss. 1, Holy Cross Generalate Papers, AUND; John Kane, C.S.C., to Albert Cousineau, C.S.C., (telegram), 28 August 1944, 713.2, Holy Cross Generalate Papers, AUND.

120. Vincent McCauley, C.S.C., to Thomas Steiner, C.S.C., 8 September 1944, 22:4, Steiner Papers, AHCFI.

121. Al Neff, C.S.C., to Harriet Gartland, 3 October 1944, McCauley File, Holy Cross Mission Center Papers, AHCFI; Arnold Fell, C.S.C., funeral homily for Vincent McCauley, C.S.C., November 4, 1982, 811, Doss. 1, Holy Cross Generalate Papers, AUND.

3. The Foreign Mission Society: 1944–1958

1. The Bengalese 25, no. 8 (November 1944): 22.

2. John Kane, C.S.C., to Thomas Steiner, C.S.C., 7 October 1944, 27:5, Steiner Papers, AHCFI.

3. Vincent McCauley, C.S.C., to Thomas Steiner, C.S.C., 16 November 1944, 22:4, Steiner Papers, AHCFI.

4. Thomas Steiner, C.S.C., to Vincent McCauley, C.S.C., 9 September 1944, 22:4, Steiner Papers, AHCFI.

5. McCauley visited Cousineau in New York City, the location of the Holy Cross Generalate at the time. Cousineau commented about McCauley, "How thin and tired he was looking." See Albert Cousineau, C.S.C., to John Kane, C.S.C., 2 October 1944, 713.2, Doss. 1, Holy Cross Generalate Papers, AUND. See also Pellegrin, "Bishop Vince," 13.

6. Thomas Steiner, C.S.C., to John Kane, C.S.C., 30 September 1944, 27:5, Steiner Papers, Holy Cross Mission Center Papers, AHCFI; McCauley to Steiner, 8 September 1944; Joseph Voorde, C.S.C., to Thomas Fitzpatrick, C.S.C., 2 November 1944, Voorde File, Holy Cross Mission Center Papers, AHCFI.

7. Vincent McCauley, C.S.C., to Harverd Tracy, 3 November 1944.

8. McCauley to Thomas Steiner, 16 November 1944. McCauley wrote, "I had hoped to see you at N.D. long before this but my legs have not done so well as expected. A few days ago another clot developed in my right leg and forced me back to bed. There is a reaction in both arms also; it is something like rheumatism. It may disappear when the clot dissolves."

9. Christopher O'Toole, C.S.C., to Vincent McCauley, C.S.C., 18 November 1944, 22:4, Steiner Papers, AHCFI.

10. Joseph Voorde, C.S.C., to Thomas Fitzpatrick, C.S.C., 13 December 1944, Voorde File, Holy Cross Mission Center Papers, AHCFI.

11. Arthur C. Brown, M.D., to Thomas Steiner, C.S.C., 12 January 1945, 7:4, Steiner Papers, AHFCI; Christopher O'Toole, C.S.C., to Brown, 17 January 1945, 7:4, Steiner Papers, AHFCI.

12. Vincent McCauley, C.S.C., to The Tracy Family, 18 March 1945, PPMJL; *The Bengalese* 26, no. 2 (March 1945): 22.

13. *The Bengalese* 26, no. 7 (November 1945): 22; *The Bengalese* 27, no. 1 (December 1945–January 1946): 20.

14. *The Bengalese* 27, no. 6 (September 1946): 9.

15. Robert Pelton, C.S.C., interview with the author, April 26, 2006, AHCFI; Robert Hoffman interview; Wil Menard, C.S.C., interview with the author, April 21, 2006, AHCFI; Gene Burke interview.

16. Al Croce, C.S.C., interview with the author, April 19, 2006, AHCFI; Thomas Tallarida, C.S.C., interview with the author, April 5, 2006, AHCFI; Richard Timm, C.S.C., to the author, 1 August 2005, AHCFI.

17. Ibid. Also, Gene Burke interview.

18. Francis Zagorc, C.S.C., interview with the author, April 25, 2006, AHCFI; Thomas Tallarida interview; Wil Menard interview, April 21, 2006.

19. As one example, McCauley requested special permission of the provincial for one seminarian to travel home for "the spiritual welfare" of his family. While the required permission was not secured, nevertheless, the incident demonstrates how McCauley stood shoulder to shoulder with his seminarians. See Vincent McCauley, C.S.C., to Thomas Steiner, C.S.C., 2 May 1949, 21:9, Steiner Papers, AHCFI; Thomas Steiner, C.S.C., to Vincent McCauley, C.S.C., 27:9, Steiner Papers, AHCFI.

20. Thomas Tallarida interview.

21. Robert Pelton interview; Thomas Tallarida interview.

22. Vincent McCauley, C.S.C., to Thomas Steiner, C.S.C., 31 March 1950, 27:9, Steiner Papers, AHCFI.

23. Christopher O'Toole, C.S.C., to Vincent McCauley, C.S.C., 3 April 1950, 27:9, Steiner Papers, AHCFI. Theodore Mehling, C.S.C., who succeeded Steiner as provincial in 1950, also demonstrated his confidence in McCauley: "Personally, I am satisfied to accept your recommendations." See Theodore Mehling, C.S.C., to Vincent McCauley, C.S.C., 18 May 1951, 33:61, Mehling Papers, AHCFI.

24. Thomas Tallarida interview; William Simmons, C.S.C., interview with the author, April 5, 2006, AHCFI.

25. Michael D'Rozario to the author, 1 August 2005; Vincent McCauley, C.S.C., to Theodore Mehling, C.S.C., 4 October 1950, 33:61, Mehling Papers, AHCFI. The order of the day at the FMS, beginning at 5:30 a.m. and ending at 10:30 p.m., was as follows: rising, meditation and Mass, breakfast, obediences, classes at Holy Cross, lunch/rest, work, study, visit to Blessed Sacrament, supper, recreation, study, retire.

26. Ibid.

27. Wil Menard interview, April 21, 2006; Robert Hoffman interview.

28. Vincent McCauley, C.S.C., to Thomas Steiner, C.S.C., 3 December 1947, 7:8, Steiner Papers, AHCFI.

29. William Smith to Thomas Steiner, C.S.C., 8 August 1947; Thomas Steiner, C.S.C., to Smith (telegram), n.d [August 1947], 21:8, Steiner Papers, AHCFI.

30. The five talks and their titles were: October 2, 1949, "Fire on the Earth"; October 9, 1949, "Making Nobody Somebody"; October 16, 1949, "Contact With Missionaries"; October 23, 1949, "Queen of the Missions"; October 30, 1949, "The Missionary Christ."

31. Vincent McCauley, C.S.C., "Contact With Missionaries" (NCCM radio talk), October 16, 1949, PDRP 2/03.05, McCauley Drop File, AUND.

32. John Croston interview, April 5, 2006.

33. Vincent McCauley, C.S.C., to Harverd Tracy, 18 October 1949, PPMJL.

34. Vincent McCauley, C.S.C., "Queen of the Missions" (NCCM radio talk), October 23, 1949, PDRP 2/03.05, McCauley Drop File, AHCFI; Vincent McCauley, C.S.C., to Harverd Tracy, 29 December 1949, PPMJL.

35. Minutes, Faculty Meeting, Holy Cross College, 1937–1959, 17 October 1949, Holy Cross College Papers, AHCFI.

36. Al Croce interview; Wil Menard interview, April 21, 2006.

37. Ibid. Also, Gene Burke interview; Richard Timm to the author, 1 August 2005; Harry Bride, C.S.C., to the author, 14 May 2006, AHCFI.

38. Vincent McCauley, C.S.C., to Christopher O'Toole, C.S.C., 17 September 1948, 414 (FM), Holy Cross Generalate Papers, AUND.

39. Vincent McCauley, C.S.C., to Thomas Steiner, C.S.C., 26 January 1949, 21:9, Steiner Papers, AHCFI; McCauley to Harverd Tracy, 29 December 1949.

40. Michael D'Rozario to the author, 1 August 2005; Wil Menard interview, April 21, 2006.

41. Wil Menard, C.S.C., interview with the author, August 31, 2005, AHCFI; Canonical Visit 1957, 33:64, Mehling Papers, AHCFI.

42. Vincent McCauley, C.S.C., to Christopher O'Toole, C.S.C., 1 October 1952, 811, Doss. 1, Holy Cross Generalate Papers, AUND.

43. Eleanor McCandless interview. McCauley's mother, Mary Wickham McCauley, died on November 18, 1951.

44. All say that McCauley possessed a heavy foot when he drove.

45. Francis Zagorc interview; Robert Hoffman interview.

46. Robert Hoffman interview.

47. Vincent McCauley, C.S.C., "First Thing First," *Holy Cross Missions* I, no. 2 (September 1956): 22, AHCFI.

48. Francis Zagorc, C.S.C., interview with James Connelly, C.S.C., May 12, 1980, AHCFI.

49. "The Bricklayer," August–November 1957, PPMJL.

50. Ibid.; Foreign Mission Seminary Chronicle, March 10, 1957, AHCFI.

51. Each local house is governed by a superior and his council. McCauley was a member of the Foreign Missionary local council for three years.

52. *The Bengalese* 34, no. 10 (December 1953): 11, AHCFI.

53. Wil Menard, C.S.C., interview with the author, April 4, 2006, AHCFI.

54. Michael J. McInerney, M.D., to Christopher O'Toole, C.S.C., 9 September 1950, 811, Doss. 1, Holy Cross Generalate Papers, AUND. McInerney wrote, "Father McCauley has regained his former state of good health and is in good physical condition at this time. It is my opinion that Father McCauley is now able to resume his Foreign Mission Work in India."

55. Vincent McCauley, C.S.C., to Theodore Mehling, C.S.C., 28 December 1951, 33:62, Mehling Papers, AHCFI; Theodore Mehling, C.S.C., to Vincent McCauley, C.S.C., 16 May 1951, 33:61, Mehling Papers, AHCFI; Vincent McCauley, C.S.C., to Theodore Mehling, C.S.C., 16 May 1952, 33:62, Mehling Papers, AHCFI; Canonical Visit, October 1954, 33:63a, Mehling Papers, AHCFI; Theodore Mehling, C.S.C., to Vincent McCauley, C.S.C., 22 February 1954, 33:69, Mehling Papers, AHCFI.

56. Vincent McCauley, C.S.C., to Theodore Mehling, C.S.C., 6 May 1955, 33:69, Mehling Papers, AHCFI.

57. Theodore Hesburgh, eulogy for Vincent McCauley; Foreign Mission Chronicle, February 4, 1958, AHCFI.

4. Superior of the Uganda Mission: 1958–1961

1. The Algiers foundation was initiated in 1840, but missionaries were recalled in 1842. Another attempt was made in 1844 but a recall was made in 1853. Other missionary foundations were Chile in March 1943, Brazil in January 1944, Haiti in 1944, Ghana in September 1957, and Peru in September 1963.

2. Dries, *Missionary Movement*, 149.

3. Ibid., 149–152.

4. Ibid., 155.

5. Quoted in Ibid., 171.

6. Christopher O'Toole, C.S.C., to Thomas Fitzpatrick, C.S.C., 11 March 1958, 810.3, Holy Cross Generalate Papers, AUND; John Keefe, C.S.C., interview with the author, April 7,

2006, ACHFI; Robert Malone, C.S.C., interview with the author, March 20, 2006, AHCFI.

7. Vincent McCauley, C.S.C., interview with James Connelly, C.S.C., April 22, 1978, AHCFI; Connelly, "Holy Cross in East Africa," 1; Arnold Fell, C.S.C., "Uganda Safari," *Holy Cross Missions*, n.d. [1958], 810.1, Holy Cross Generalate Papers, AUND; Christopher O'Toole, C.S.C., to Theodore Mehling, C.S.C., 11 March 1958, 810.3, Holy Cross Generalate Papers, AUND.

8. Vincent McCauley, C.S.C., to Father General [Christopher O'Toole, C.S.C.], 13 April 1958, 811, Doss. 2, Holy Cross Generalate Papers, AUND.

9. Report on the Mbarara Diocese, May 1958, 38:45, Mehling Papers, AHCFI.

10. McCauley to Father General [O'Toole], 13 April 1958.

11. Report on the Mbarara Diocese, May 1958.

12. Ibid. The report stated, "This type of Foreign Mission work could provide what might be considered a welcome change from the present main mission work of the Congregation, specifically that in East Pakistan. The Congregation's thinking and practice for decades has necessarily been geared to the rather 'hopeless' apostolate to the Muslims. . . . The mission apostolate to the Muslims is almost entirely indirect, with no possibility of conversions in the foreseeable future. . . . On the other hand, in Uganda the opportunities for conversion are at this time seemingly Providential. Converts are all but knocking at the Church's door."

13. Ibid.

14. Ibid.

15. McCauley interview with James Connelly.

16. Vincent McCauley, C.S.C., to Theodore Mehling, C.S.C., 15 May 1958, 38:45, Mehling Papers, AHCFI; Vincent McCauley, C.S.C., to Christopher O'Toole, C.S.C., 23 May 1958, 810.3, Holy Cross Generalate Papers, AUND.

17. Christopher O'Toole to Thomas Fitzpatrick, 11 March 1958, 810.3, Holy Cross Generalate Papers, AUND; Christopher

O'Toole, C.S.C., to Vincent McCauley, C.S.C., 23 June 1958 and 28 May 1958, 810.3, Holy Cross Generalate Papers, AUND.

18. Theodore Mehling, C.S.C., to Christopher O'Toole, C.S.C., 24 May 1958, 810.3, Holy Cross Generalate Papers, AUND.

19. Christopher O'Toole to Theodore Mehling, 11 March 1958.

20. Vincent McCauley, C.S.C., "Report of the Visit of Father McCauley to Beirut, April 1958," 2 May 1958, The Uganda Mission File, Holy Cross Mission Center Papers, AHCFI. McCauley, "Note from Trip," 260 History of Holy Cross in East Africa, Archives Holy Cross East Africa, Kampala, Uganda (hereafter AHCEA).

21. Christopher O'Toole, C.S.C., to Vincent McCauley, C.S.C., 28 May 1958, 810.3, Holy Cross Generalate Papers, AUND.

22. Vincent McCauley, C.S.C., to Christopher O'Toole, C.S.C., 9 June 1958, 810.3, Holy Cross Generalate Papers, AUND.

23. Christopher O'Toole, C.S.C., to Theodore Mehling, C.S.C., 16 June 1958 and 28 June 1958, 810.3, Holy Cross Generalate Papers, AUND.

24. Theodore Mehling to Christopher O'Toole, 23 June 1958. A medical examination reported McCauley "in excellent shape," although caution was advised against overexposure to the sun. See E. B. Floersch, M.D., to Theodore Mehling, C.S.C., 21 August 1958, 38:45, Mehling Papers, AHCFI.

25. It was assumed by all that the northern region of Mbarrara, where Holy Cross would minister, would become its own diocese. Thus, the man chosen to head the mission would be the most likely candidate for bishop once the diocese was established.

26. Theodore Mehling, C.S.C., to Christopher O'Toole, C.S.C., 23 September 1959, 811, Doss. 2, Holy Cross Generalate Papers, AUND.

27. Theodore Mehling, C.S.C., to Vincent McCauley, C.S.C., 29 July 1958, 38:45, Mehling Papers, AHCFI.

28. Vincent McCauley, C.S.C., to Theodore Mehling, C.S.C., 30 July 1958, 38:45, Mehling Papers, AHCFI.

29. Vincent McCauley, C.S.C., to Theodore Mehling, C.S.C., 26 June 1958, 810.3, Holy Cross Generalate Papers, AUND.

30. McCauley to Theodore Mehling, 30 July 1958.

31. Christopher O'Toole, C.S.C., to Vincent McCauley, C.S.C., 9 August 1958, 810.3, Holy Cross Generalate Papers, AUND.

32. Robert Hesse, C.S.C., interview with the author, February 22, 2006, AHCFI; Francis Zagorc interview with James Connelly.

33. Adrian Hastings, *The Church in Africa 1450–1950* (Oxford: Clarendon Press, 1994), 298–300.

34. Roland Oliver, *The Missionary Factor in East Africa* (London: Longmans, 1969), 11. The association of Christianity with the anti-slavery campaign was made clear by Sir Bartle Frere, British governor of Bombay: "I regard the spread of Christianity as practically the same thing as the extinction of both [the] slave-trade and slavery." See William B. Anderson, *The Church in East Africa, 1840–1974* (Dodoma: Central Tanganyika Press, 1977), 9.

35. Quoted in Hastings, *Church in Africa*, 251–252.

36. Oliver, *Missionary Factor*, 7. Additionally, Oliver comments on Livingstone's death: "A revolution was set in motion which was to bring a new kind of missionary into Africa and a new and more numerous class of subscribers to the Society's [CMS] lists." See Oliver, *Missionary Factor*, 34. See also Elizabeth Isichei, *A History of Christianity in Africa: From Antiquity to the Present* (Grand Rapids, MI: William B. Eerdman's Publishing Company, 1995), 128.

37. Hastings, *Church in Africa*, 250.

38. Oliver, *Missionary Factor*, 35–42, 51–52, 66–67.

39. Isichei, *Christianity in Africa*, 133.

40. Oliver, *Missionary Factor*, 60–61, 68.

41. Ibid., 290; Hastings, *Church in Africa*, 274. An interesting twist to this discussion is provided by Elizabeth Isichei, who adds that many women became Christians to assist with problems associated with child mortality, general illness, and poverty. See Isichei, *Christianity in Africa*, 240.

42. Hastings, *Church in Africa*, 270, 282–290; Oliver, *Missionary Factor*, 100–103, 163–164; Thomas Spear, "Toward the History of African Christianity," in *East African Expressions of Christianity*, ed. Thomas Spear and Isaria N. Kimambo, (Athens: Ohio University Press, 1999), 4. This situation was greatly exacerbated by the arrival in the 1880s of German missionaries. Before this time, Arab traders generally left the Christian missions alone; Christians did not challenge Arab hegemony in certain regions. Oliver claims, due to the German invasion of the region, "Between 1884 and 1888, however, the attitude of Arabs towards the missionaries changed abruptly all over Central Africa."

43. Ian Leggett, *Uganda* (Oxford: Oxfam Foundation Publishers, 2001), 1; Phares Mutibwa, *Uganda Since Independence: A Story of Unfulfilled Hope* (Trenton, NJ: Africa World Press, Inc., 1992), 3; Charles Miller, *The Lunatic Express* (New York: Macmillan, 1971), 116, 119.

44. Samwiri R. Karugire, "The Arrival of the European Missionaries: The First Fifteen Years or So" in *A Century of Christianity in Uganda, 1877–1977*, ed. Tom Tuma and Phares Mutibwa (Nairobi: Afro Press Limited, 1978), 7.

45. Hastings, *Church in Africa*, 384. Buganda, located adjacent to Lake Victoria, is the name of the most prominent kingdom in what became the nation of Uganda. The country was an amalgamation of several different kingdoms.

46. Anderson, *Church in East Africa*, 18–22; Miller, *Lunatic Express*, 124.

47. Karugire, "The Arrival of the European Missionaries," 4.

48. Anderson, *Church in East Africa*, 23–24.

49. Hastings, *Church in Africa*, 248.

50. Lavigerie was educated at Saint Sulpice in Paris, and was thus influenced by the "moderate Gallicanism" that reigned there. He worked in Lebanon and Syria and was appointed Auditor of the Roman Rota in 1861. His experiences convinced him that the Church needed to be more universal and open to society. He was a friend of Popes Pius IX and Leo XIII. He served as the ordinary for the Diocese of Nancy until he was called to Algiers in 1867. It is interesting to note that as learned as he was, Lavigerie had some misguided preconceived ideas about Africans, especially religion and ignorance. He once stated, "It is doubtful if the blacks of the interior have any ideas at all about the after life or about the immortality of the soul. In any case they do not seem to have any religion, but only gross superstitions, without any form of worship, which resemble witchcraft. Their idea of God is so vague that certain explorers have been able to say they had none. As for morality, since the foundation is absolutely lacking, it can be said that it does not exist. All the vices are found among them, and the scanty notions which they possess concerning right and wrong are nothing more than the dying rays of that light which God gave humanity at its origins." See Frederick Tusingire, *The Evangelization of Uganda: Challenges and Strategies* (Kisubi, Uganda, 2003), 26–32, 40.

51. Hastings, *Church in Africa*, 255.

52. Tusingire, *The Evangelization of Uganda*, 37–40; Yves Tourigny, W.F., *So Abundant a Harvest: The Catholic Church in Uganda 1879–1979* (London: Darton, Longman, & Todd, 1979), 21, 25–28. The other three in the party arrived on June 25, 1879. The group left Marseilles on April 21, 1878.

53. Tourigny, *So Abundant a Harvest*, 30–31; Thomas P. Ofcansky, *Uganda: Tarnished Pearl of Africa* (Boulder, CO: Westview Press, 1996), 18.

54. Possible reasons for Mwanga's hostility toward the Christian missionaries were (1) fear that Europeans were closing in on him, and (2) influence from Muslims in his court. See Karugire, "The Arrival of the European Missionaries," 8–9.

55. The Ugandan martyrs, twenty-two of whom were Catholic, were beatified on June 6, 1920, by Pope Benedict XV and canonized on Mission Sunday, October 18, 1964, by Pope Paul VI. Today the Ugandan martyrs stand as a national symbol of Uganda's strong Catholic faith and tradition.

56. Karugire, "The Arrival of the European Missionaries," 10–12; Hastings, *Church in Africa*, 381–382.

57. James Ndyabahika, "Inter-Faith Relations in Uganda as the Area of Dialogue and Spirituality, 1960–1996," *The Asia Journal of Theology* 12, 12 (October 1998): 396.

58. Tourigny, *So Abundant a Harvest*, 22–23; Tusingire, *The Evangelization of Uganda*, 47–48.

59. Mutibwa, *Uganda Since Independence*, 2. See also Tournigny, *So Abundant a Harvest*, 54–55.

60. Samwiri R. Karugire, *A Political History of Uganda* (London: Heinmann, 1980), 70.

61. Quoted in Tournigny, *So Abundant a Harvest*, 56.

62. Ibid., 56–58. See also Frederick B. Welborn, *Religion and Politcs in Uganda, 1952–62* (Nairobi: East African Publishing House, 1965), 7. The St. Joseph Society for Foreign Missions (Mill Hill Fathers) were founded in Great Britain in 1866 by Herbert Vaughn with the aim of evangelizing "the many peoples of other lands, particularly in the British Empire." See Tusingire, *The Evangelization of Uganda*, 32–34.

63. Tusingire, *The Evangelization of Uganda*, 34–36; Tourigny, *So Abundant a Harvest*, 84–85. In 1867, Daniel Comboni in Verona, Italy, founded the Comboni or Verona Fathers. His idea, "Plan for the Regeneration of Africa," was based on the idea or slogan, "Save Africa with Africa." The last few years of the nineteenth century saw several other groups come to Africa, including

Belgian Jesuits, Redemptorists, Benedictines, Pallottines, Divine Word Missioners, and Irish Holy Ghost Fathers. See Hastings, *Church in Africa*, 417–418.

64. Tusingire, *The Evangelization of Uganda*, 120.

65. Tournigny, *So Abundant a Harvest*, 66; Tusingire, *The Evangelization of Uganda*, 13–31. The growth of Catholicism in Uganda is seen in these statistics: 1896—32,753; 1906—100,025; 1916—218,824; 1927—227,597.

66. Hastings, *Church in Africa*, 565–566.

67. Quoted in Hastings, *Church in Africa*, 296. Francis Libermann was born into a Jewish family in Alsace, France, in 1802. He converted to Christianity while in training to become a rabbi. After ordination as a priest, he established a small religious order, "The Missionaries of the Immaculate Heart," for service in Africa. Later, the Vatican merged this group with the older and more stable Congregation of the Holy Ghost (Spiritans). Thus, Libermann is known as the "Second Founder" of the Spiritans.

68. It should be noted that many Christian groups entered the African continent in the first decades of the twentieth century. Dr. J. H. Oldman, organizing secretary for the famous 1910 Edinburgh [Ecumenical] Council, was also the driving force behind the Conference of Missionary Societies in Great Britain and Northern Ireland. This group worked to assure that Africans received the same care and attention as others served by missionary groups. In Uganda specifically, other Christian groups present were African Inland Mission (1922), Seventh Day Adventists (1927), Salvation Army (1931), and Bible Church Men's Missionary Society (1933). American Pentecostal churches came later. See C. Groves, *The Planting of Christianity in Africa*, 4 Vols. (New Haven, CT: Lutterwort Press, 1990), 187.

69. Oliver, *Missionary Factor*, 289–290.

70. *Rerum Ecclesiae* (February 28, 1926—Pius XI), paragraph 19 emphasized the importance of native clergy: "Before everything else, We call your attention to the importance of building

up a native clergy. If you do not work with all your might to attain this purpose, We assert that not only will your apostolate be crippled, but it will become an obstacle and an impediment to the establishment and organization of the Church in those countries. We gladly recognize and acknowledge the fact that in some places steps have already been taken to provide for these needs by the erection of seminaries in which native youths of promise are well educated and prepared to receive the dignity of the priesthood, and are trained to instruct in the Christian Faith members of their own race. But in spite of all this work, we are still a great distance from the goal, which we have set for ourselves." In *Maximum Ilud* (November 30, 1919—Benedict XV) a similar exhortation to the promotion of native clergy is given: "For since the native priest by birth, temper, sentiment, and interests is in close touch with his own people, it is beyond all controversy how valuable he can be in instilling the Faith in the minds of his people. The native priest understands better than any outsider how to proceed with his own people. Such being the case, he can often gain access to places where foreign priests would not be permitted to enter." In paragraph 20, the document reads, "The true missionary is not an agent of his country, but an ambassador of Christ."

71. Ibid., 233–234, 240; Tusingire, *The Evangelization of Uganda*, 90–91; Tournigny, *So Abundant a Harvest*, 104–107.

72. Oliver, *Missionary Factor*, 229–230.

73. St. Charles is one of the twenty-two martyrs whose feast is celebrated June 3.

74. Hastings, *Church in Africa*, 572–573.

75. Tusingire, *The Evangelization of Uganda*, 141.

76. John Paige, C.S.C., "Preserving Order Amid Chaos: The Survival of Schools in Uganda, 1971–1986," (Ph.D. diss., University of Maryland, 1998), 42.

77. Ibid., 44–45.

78. Quoted in Tusingire, *The Evangelization of Uganda*, 104.

79. Quoted in Isichei, *Christianity in Africa*, 236.

80. Ibid., 229. John Paige, C.S.C., also comments: "The CMS mission, together with the Catholic missions, did indeed have a monopoly on education and as such acted as educational agencies for the state. This educational engagement served Church purposes certainly, but was also of great importance for the colonial state, as it provided trained manpower. The government, therefore, looked with great sympathy upon the CMS mission's educational enterprise." See Paige, "Preserving Order Amid Chaos," 46.

81. Oliver, *Missionary Factor*, 197, 240–241.

82. Quoted in Tournigny, *So Abundant a Harvest*, 120. The Phelps-Stokes Commission of 1924 was a British-based, missionary-inspired, and privately funded group that called for partnership between religious missions and government, not separate development. See: F. Musgrove, "What Sort of Facts?" *African Affairs* 5, no. 205 (October 1952): 313–318 and Edward H. Berman, "American Influence on African Education: The Role of the Phelps-Stokes Fund's Education Commissions," *Comparative Education Review* 15, no. 2 (June 1971): 132–145.

83. Ibid., 134.

84. Hastings, *Church in Africa*, 398.

85. Quoted in ibid., 432.

86. Karugire, "The Arrival of the European Missionaries," 2.

87. Kenneth Ingham, *The Making of Modern Uganda* (London: George Allen and Unwin, 1958), 43; Hastings, *Church in Africa*, 402; E. S. Odhiambo, "The Paradox of Collaboration: The Uganda Case," *East Africa Journal 9* (October 1972): 20.

88. Tusingire, *The Evangelization of Uganda*, 8–12.

89. Jan Jelmert Jorgensen, *Uganda: A Modern History* (New York: St. Martin Press, 1981), 80–81.

90. Isichei, *Christianity in Africa*, 231.

91. Thomas Apuuli Kisembo, "One Hundred Years of Catholic Faith in Fort Portal Diocese," Booklet, n.d. [1995], 8, 13, 16–18, History of Fort Portal Diocese, ADFP.

92. Ibid., 20.

93. Quoted in ibid., 34, 38–39.

94. Ibid., 25–27. One account during the period described the situation with catechists: "Every year we lose the best ones. Those who have received better instruction and who know well how to read and write are the first ones to leave us and to put themselves at the service of a Chief who gives them a higher pay."

95. Tourigny, *So Abundant a Harvest*, 138; Kisembo, "Fort Portal Diocese," 58.

96. Foreign Mission Chronicle, October 16–26, 1958; Robert Hesse interview. McCauley et al. were scheduled for an audience with Pius XII, but he died. The coronation of John XXIII was scheduled one day after the group's planned departure to Africa and they requested from the superior general a short reprieve to be present, but the request was not granted.

97. Robert Hesse interview; *Petit Echo*, no. 488 (February 1959), Archives White Fathers Kampala, Lourdel House, Kampala, Uganda (hereafter AWFK); Vincent McCauley, C.S.C., to Christopher O'Toole, C.S.C., 5 November 1958, 813.2, Holy Cross Generalate Papers, AUND.

98. Robert Chaput, W.F., opened St. Augustine's Teacher Training College on February 23, 1955. Its purpose was to serve the kingdoms of Bunyoro and Toro. It opened with minimal facilities, but still attracted 146 students divided into two levels— pre-professional and professional. See J. Keenan, "Story of a College: The Birth and Growth of St. Augustine's Teacher Training College, Butiti [*sic*] –Uganda," *Overseas Education* 30, no. 1 (April 1958): 12–18.

99. Francis Zagorc interview.

100. Jean Ogez, W.F., to Christopher O'Toole, C.S.C., 19 November 1938, 813.2, Holy Cross Generalate Papers, AUND.

101. McCauley to Christopher O'Toole, 5 November 1958; Christopher O'Toole, C.S.C., to Vincent McCauley, C.S.C., 10 October 1958, 810.3, Holy Cross Generalate Papers, AUND; Vincent McCauley, C.S.C., to Theodore Mehling, C.S.C., 5

December 1958, 38:45, Mehling Papers, AHCFI. Being on site, McCauley was convinced the Butiiti training center was better than Fort Portal. Additionally, with McCauley at the Teacher Training College, the group was in close proximity.

102. Vincent McCauley, C.S.C., to Christopher O'Toole, C.S.C., 24 January 1959, Box 109, Bishop McCauley Papers, AHCEA.

103. Cyril Kadoma, interview with the author, January 28, 2006, AHCFI.

104. John Harrington, C.S.C., interview with James Connelly, C.S.C., September 20, 1980, AHCFI; Vincent McCauley, C.S.C., to Christopher O'Toole, C.S.C., 2 January 1959, 812.2, Holy Cross Generalate Papers, AUND; Christopher O'Toole, C.S.C., to Vincent McCauley, C.S.C., 30 January 1959, Box 109, Bishop McCauley Papers, AHCEA.

105. Connelly, "Holy Cross in East Africa," 13–14.

106. From a canonical point of view McCauley had not yet been appointed superior, as the Holy Cross foundation did not meet canonical requirements for such a structure. The superior general, Christopher O'Toole, C.S.C., had written McCauley, "For the present, in order to simplify administration, the project in Uganda is considered as a house of the Indiana Province with yourself in charge." See Christopher O'Toole, C.S.C., to Vincent McCauley, C.S.C., 2 April 1959, Box 109, Bishop McCauley Papers, AHCEA.

107. Christopher O'Toole, C.S.C., to Vincent McCauley, C.S.C., 8 January 1959, Box 109, Bishop McCauley Papers, AHCEA.

108. Christopher O'Toole, C.S.C., to Vincent McCauley, C.S.C., 1 September 1959, 811, Doss. 2, Holy Cross Generalate Papers, AUND. It should be noted that at the outset some dissatisfaction with the mission was expressed. One of the pioneers felt the Holy Cross community was being asked to "fill holes" where

there were personnel gaps in the diocese. See Francis Zagorc interview with James Connelly.

109. Questionnaire, Bukwali Parish, n.d., Box 920, History of the Diocese of Fort Portal, ADFP; Vincent McCauley, C.S.C., to Christopher O'Toole, C.S.C., 26 February 1959, Box 109, Bishop McCauley Papers, AHCEA; Kisembo, "Fort Portal Diocese," 59. King George Rukeidi III gave Kaijakwamya the land upon his retirement as a Gombolola Chief.

110. Christopher O'Toole, C.S.C., to Vincent McCauley, C.S.C., 1 September 1959, Box 109, Bishop McCauley Papers, AHCEA; Christopher O'Toole, C.S.C., to Vincent McCauley, C.S.C., 9 January 1960, 811, Doss. 2, Holy Cross Generalate Papers, AUND.

111. Vincent McCauley, C.S.C., to Christopher O'Toole, C.S.C., 29 June 1959, 813.2, Holy Cross Generalate Papers, AUND.

112. *Uganda Drum* I, 4 (August–September 1959) Uganda Drum Group 400, Box 450.1, AHCEA. McCauley described his jubilee celebration to his family: "My jubilee was much more of 'an affair' than I thought possible. The young priests (CSCs) decided it should be an occasion. So they invited all the missionaries of the District. We had the first Solemn Mass that anyone can remember. . . . The school choir did credibly and Fr. Heyes, the pastor, gave a sermon on the priesthood. There were 18 priests and Brothers here for the noon meal—a buffet. A perfect day." See Vincent McCauley, C.S.C., to the Larsen Family, 29 June 1959, PPMJL.

113. "Report on Visitation to the Holy Cross Project in the Diocese of Mbarara," August 1959, 38:46, Mehling Papers, AHCFI.

114. Francis Zagorc interview with James Connelly.

115. Quoted in Serapio Magambo, "Twenty-Five Years of [the] Holy Cross Congregation Sharing with the People of East Africa," n.d. [1973], Group 800, Box 801.1, AHCEA.

116. Vincent McCauley, C.S.C., to Theodore Mehling, C.S.C., 18 February 1959, 38:46, Mehling Papers, AHCFI.

117. Vincent McCauley to the Larsen Family, 29 June 1959.

118. Vincent McCauley, C.S.C., to Harverd Tracy, n.d., PPMJL; Quoted in Magambo, "Twenty-Five Years."

119. Vincent McCauley, C.S.C., to Christopher O'Toole, C.S.C., 3 February 1960, 811, Doss. 2, Holy Cross Generalate Papers, AUND.

120. Christopher O'Toole, C.S.C., to Vincent McCauley, C.S.C., 22 December 1958, 813.2, Holy Cross Generalate Papers, AUND.

121. Gene Burke, C.S.C., to Christopher O'Toole, C.S.C., 31 July 1958, 810.3, Holy Cross Generalate Papers, AUND.

122. Charles Byaruhanga to Christopher O'Toole, C.S.C., 2 November 1969, 811, Doss. 2, Holy Cross Generalate Papers, AUND.

123. John Keefe interview, April 7, 2006; Connelly, "Holy Cross in East Africa," 9; Francis Zagorc interview. Keefe suggests that any disagreement was not significant, but arose mainly from different ways of operation and at times ignorance.

124. Robert Malone, C.S.C., interview with James Connelly, C.S.C., February 28, 1980, AHCFI.

125. Burton Smith interview.

126. Vincent McCauley, C.S.C., to Christopher O'Toole, C.S.C., 4 January 1961, 811, Doss. 2, Holy Cross Generalate Papers, AUND.

127. John Keefe interview, April 7, 2006.

128. McCauley to Christopher O'Toole, 3 February 1960. McCauley is referring to Father George DePrizio, C.S.C., provincial of the Eastern Province of Priests and Brothers, and Brother Ephrem O'Dwyer, C.S.C., provincial of the Eastern Province of Brothers. McCauley could not understand DePrizio's stance at all: "This is the Fr. DePrizio who wanted the mission assigned to his Province and was sure he could find men to staff it. Now he 'may'

have one man to spare, and in a couple of years we will see. So in five years the Eastern Province will 'spare' two men for the missions. What a change in attitude!"

129. Ibid.

130. Louis Durrieu, W.F., to F. X. Lacoursiere, W.F., 2 February 1955, 022–37, Correspondence Rwenzori, AWFK; F. X. Lacoursiere, W.F., to J. R. Knox, 11 May 1955, 022–37, Correspondence Rwenzori, AWFK; F. X. Lacoursiere, W.F., to Dear Fathers and Brothers, 11 February 1955, 022–37, Correspondence Rwenzori, AWFK; F. X. Lacoursiere, W.F., to J. R. Knox, 11 May 1955, 022–37, Correspondence Rwenzori, AWFK.

131. "Report on the Diocese of Mbarara," n.d. [1958], 38:45, Mehling Papers, AHCFI.

132. Cornelius Ryan, C.S.C., interview with the author, March 30, 2006, AHCFI.

133. Theodore Mehling, C.S.C., to Vincent McCauley, C.S.C., 20 March 1959 and 1 August 1959, 38:46, Mehling Papers, AHCFI.

134. Agreement between the Reverend Bishop of Mbarara, Uganda, and the provincial superior of the Indiana Province of the Priests of the Congregation of Holy Cross, September 9, 1959, 813.2, Holy Cross Generalate Papers, AUND. Mehling signed the document on September 22, 1959, and Ogez on October 22, 1959.

135. "Report on Visitation to the Holy Cross Project in the Diocese of Mbarara," August 1959, 38:46, Mehling Papers, AHCFI.

136. "Division of the Diocese of Mbarara," n.d. [March 1958], 810.3, Holy Cross Generalate Papers, AUND.

137. J. Garitan, W.F., to Leo Volker, W.F., 6 April 1960, 022–11, Correspondence, AWFK.

138. Vincent McCauley, C.S.C., to Theodore Mehling, C.S.C., 15 December 1959, 38:46, Mehling Papers, AHCFI. McCauley's reticence at the time was known by the White Fathers,

whose local superior wrote their superior general, "Although he [McCauley] expects that one day Toro-Bunyoro will be entrusted to their Society, he is not in a hurry to take over." J. Garitan to Leo Volker, 6 April 1960.

139. McCauley to Theodore Mehling, 15 December 1959. McCauley related his feelings about the situation to the provincial of the Eastern Province of Priests and Brothers, George DePrizio, C.S.C.: "The coming separation of the Diocese is the topic of conversation in mission circles and out of it. Many wonder why there is much delap [sic]. Personally, I am glad for it gives us time to size up a very complex situation, and gives our young missionaries much needed experience. It also provides your superior in the upper echelon an opportunity to consider the advantages and needs of this new venture." See Vincent McCauley, C.S.C., to George DePrizio, C.S.C., 29 September 1960, 310.2.59, DePrizio Papers, AHCFE.

140. Theodore Mehling, C.S.C., to Vincent McCauley, C.S.C., 30 December 1959, 38:46, Mehling Papers, AHCFI. Mehling should not have been surprised by Ogez's desire for rapid separation, as this was what he learned when he made his initial visit to the region in December 1958, only a few weeks after the four initial Holy Cross religious arrived. See Theodore Mehling, "Visit to the Uganda Mission," n.d. [December 1958], 38:45, Mehling Papers, AHCFI. In a very interesting note, McCauley claimed in a 1978 interview that he had no idea Ogez was planning to split the diocese. All extant data contradicts his statement. See McCauley interview with James Connelly.

141. Christopher O'Toole to McCauley, 9 January 1960; Christopher O'Toole, C.S.C, to Theodore Mehling, C.S.C., 9 January 1960, 811, Doss. 2, Holy Cross Generalate Papers, AUND.

142. Theodore Mehling, C.S.C., to Vincent McCauley, C.S.C., 10 March 1960, 38:47 Mehling Papers, AHCFI.

143. Christopher O'Toole, C.S.C., to Cardinal Gregory Peter Agagianian, 3 February 1961, 811, Doss. 2, Holy Cross Generalate Papers, AUND.

144. Christopher O'Toole, C.S.C., to Theodore Mehling, C.S.C., 20 July 1960, 811, Doss. 2, Holy Cross Generalate Papers, AUND; Theodore Mehling, C.S.C., to Christopher O'Toole, C.S.C., 28 July 1960, 811, Doss. 2, Holy Cross Generalate Papers, AUND; Theodore Mehling, C.S.C., to Vincent McCauley, C.S.C., 10 August 1960, 38:47, Mehling Papers, AHCFI; Theodore Mehling, C.S.C., to Vincent McCauley, C.S.C., 13 September 1960, 38:47, Mehling Papers, AHCFI.

145. Vincent McCauley, C.S.C., to Christopher O'Toole, C.S.C., 28 August 1960, 811 Doss. 2, Holy Cross Generalate Papers, AUND.

5. Bishop of Fort Portal—The First Years: 1961–1973

1. Vincent McCauley, C.S.C., to Christopher O'Toole, C.S.C., 17 April 1959, 109 Bishop McCauley Papers, AHCEA. John Keefe, C.S.C., has stated that the first generation of African clergy were well trained by the White Fathers. When Holy Cross arrived, this generation was dying out and few had replaced them. John Keefe, C.S.C., interview with the author, April 11, 2006, AHCFI.

2. Quoted in Magambo, "Twenty-Five Years."

3. Vincent McCauley, C.S.C., to Christopher O'Toole, C.S.C., 14 December 1959 and 19 October 1960, 811, Doss. 2, Holy Cross Generalate Papers, AUND.

4. "Report on Visitation to the Holy Cross Project in the Diocese of Mbarara," August 1959, 38:46, Mehling Papers, ACHFI.

5. Vincent McCauley, C.S.C., to George DePrizio, C.S.C., 3 February 1960 310.2.59, DePrizio Papers, AHCFE.

6. Vincent McCauley, C.S.C., to Christopher O'Toole, C.S.C., 4 January 1961, 811, Doss. 2, Holy Cross Generalate Papers, AUND. Robert Hesse, C.S.C., one of the original

three newly ordained who accompanied McCauley to Uganda in November 1958 stated, "He [McCauley] would never say he would be bishop. I don't know if he wanted it. I hope he did for he was a very talented man, especially in relations with other people." Robert Hesse interview.

7. Vincent McCauley, C.S.C., to Christopher O'Toole, C.S.C., 12 March 1961, 811, Doss. 2, Holy Cross Generalate Papers, AUND. It seems that McCauley was somewhat surprised by the appointment. In a 1978 interview he stated, "We only heard about the division [of the Mbarara diocese] long after it had been agreed by the Superior General. We didn't know they were negotiating because we were looking for the five year agreement." See McCauley interview with James Connelly.

8. Christopher O'Toole, C.S.C., to Gregory Peter Cardinal Agagianian, 18 March 1961, 811, Doss. 2, Holy Cross Generalate Papers, AUND.

9. *South Bend Tribune*, May 17, 1961, 811, Doss. 1, Holy Cross Generalate Papers, AUND.

10. Unfortunately the Zephir did not last long. McCauley was a notoriously fast driver who literally drove the bottom off the vehicle through almost constant contact with the dirt roads. Later he obtained a blue Mercedes Benz that, despite his efforts, lasted some time.

11. *Catholic News Bulletin*. Kampala Uganda, July 2, 1960 [*sic*–1961], 811, Doss. 1, Holy Cross Generalate Papers, AUND.

12. Vincent McCauley, C.S.C., to Christopher O'Toole, 4 September 1961, 811, Doss. 2, Holy Cross Generalate Papers, AUND.

13. McCauley interview with James Connelly; Francis Zagorc interview with James Connelly; Vincent McCauley, C.S.C., to Mr. and Mrs. Roger Slakey, 17 May 1967, 910.1, Bishop McCauley Papers, ADFP.

14. James Tumusiime, ed., *Uganda 30 Years 1962–1992* (Kampala, Uganda: Fountain Publishers, Ltd., 1992), 22–23;

Mutibwa, *Uganda Since Independence*, 11–13; Ofcansky, *Uganda: Tarnished Pearl*, 34–35.

15. Quoted in Richard F. Long, "Journey to Africa," *Syracuse Herald-Journal*, December 12, 1960, Uganda Mission File, Holy Cross Mission Papers, AHFCI.

16. Phares Mutibwa, "The Church of Uganda and the Movements for Political Independence, 1952–1962," in *A Century of Christianity in Uganda, 1877–1977,* ed. Tom Tuma and Phares Mutibwa (Nairobi: Afro Press Limited, 1978): 132–133; Welborn, *Religion and Politics*, 16; Tumusiime, *Uganda 30 Years*, 23; Grace Ibingira, *The Forging of an African Nation* (Kampala, Uganda, Viking Press, 1973), 76–77.

17. David Apter, *The Political Kingdom in Uganda* (Princeton, NJ: Princeton University Press, 1967), 340; Donald Anthony Low, *Buganda in Modern History* (Berkeley: University of California Press, 1971), 182–183; Ibingira, *Forging of an African Nation*, 80. It should be noted that sources differ on the foundation date of the Democratic Party. Some sources suggest it was 1956, not 1954 as stated in the text. See James Tumusiime, *Uganda 30 Years*, 86, and Terence Hopkins, "Politics and Uganda: The Buganda Question," in *Boston University Papers on Africa,* ed. Jeffrey Butler and A. A. Castagno (New York: Praeger, 1967), 256.

18. Ibingira, *Forging an African Nation*, 86.

19. Ibid., 87; Jorgensen, *Uganda*, 221; Mutibwa, *Uganda Since Independence*, 16.

20. Cherry Gertzel, "How Kabaka Yekka Came to be, *Africa Report* (October 1964): 10–11; S. R. Karugire, *A Political History of Uganda* (London: Heinemann, 1980), 186.

21. Quoted in Tumusiime, *Uganda 30 Years*, 24; Victor C. Ferkiss, "Religion and Politics in Independent African States: A Prolegomenon," in *Boston University Papers on Africa,* ed. Jeffrey Butler and A.A. Castagno (New York: Praeger, 1967), 19; Harry Eckstein and David E. Apter, *Comparative Politics: A Reader* (New York: Glencoe, 1963), 651. Apter writes in a more general sense:

"The problem of religious division extends far beyond the competition between major religious groupings—Moslem, Hindu, Christian—and far beyond ordinary variation in values. The classic conflicts in the West, between the spiritual and secular spheres of life, is not what is at stake here, but rather competing spiritualities: the values of government and leadership, moral properties of state action—all these are involved in the religious sphere, no less than we generally thing [sic] of as religious matters. It is no accident that the language of nationalism is often the language of religious usage, and the 'political kingdom' is both a claim to secular authority and an ecclesiastical allusion, the one reinforcing the other."

22. Welborn, *Religion and Politics*, 11–12.

23. William B. Anderson, *The Church in East Africa, 1840–1974* (Dedoma, Tanzania: Central Tanganyika Press, 1977), 135. One should note that Catholics were not the only oppressed minority. Terence Hopkins has commented, "If the Roman Catholics felt somewhat aggrieved about their position in Uganda society, however, the Muslims have felt really discriminated against—which, in the kind of consciously Christian society that was being developed in Uganda during overrule, they undoubtedly were." See Hopkins, "Politics in Uganda: The Buganda Question," 267.

24. Vincent McCauley, C.S.C., to Patrick Peyton, C.S.C., 30 November 1961, 811, Doss. 2, Holy Cross Generalate Papers, AUND. McCauley commented: "Politics continue to obsess the country. The situation is still flamable [sic] but most of the leaders seem to have softened their tone a bit now that they are faced with the practical realities of running an independent country. It is no longer enough to rail against the colonial powers. So we are hopeful that conditions will improve." See Vincent McCauley, C.S.C., to George DePrizio, C.S.C., 23 April 1962, 310.2.59, DePrizio Papers, AHCFE.

25. Ibingira, *Forging of an African Nation*, 188; Tournigny, *So Abundant a Harvest*, 167–168; Karugire, *Political History of Uganda*, 177–179.

26. Ibingira, *Forging of an African Nation*, 200.

27. Low, *Buganda in Modern History*, 216–217; Karugire, *Political History of Uganda*, 182–185. The concessions given were (1) Buganda was given the privilege to have direct or indirect elections of its representatives to the National Assembly, (2) Buganda was also given the privilege to control its local civil service, without supervising interference from the Federal Uganda government, and (3) control of the Protectorate police during the period of internal self-government was vested in local governors, not the prime minister.

28. Vincent McCauley, C.S.C., to Leandre M. Frechet, C.S.C., 18 February 1962, 811, Doss. 2, Holy Cross Generalate Papers, AUND. McCauley expressed similar sentiments to his family: "Politics are still the hot topic, and the anti-groups like to put us on the spot. . . . Fortunately long ago I have taken a position on non-interference in politics, and refused to be drawn into the controversy, or even to express an opinion." See Vincent McCauley, C.S.C., to the Larsen Family, 13 April 1962, PPMJL.

29. Hopkins, "Politics in Uganda," 268.

30. Vincent McCauley, C.S.C., to Bernard Mullahy, C.S.C., 19 April 1962, 41:77, Mullahy Papers, AHCFI.

31. Milton Obote, "The Footsteps of Uganda's Revolution," *East Africa Journal* 5 (October 1968): 7.

32. Connelly, "Holy Cross in East Africa," 11–12.

33. Leggett, *Uganda*, 1.

34. Mutibwa, *Uganda Since Independence*, 24.

35. Adrian Hastings, "Uganda Today: The New Politicians," *The Tablet* (December 5, 1959): 1055. In a similar prophetic tone, journalist Richard Long wrote shortly after independence: "There seems to be an ominous clash on the horizon between these ancient kings and the leaders of both major political parties.

One represents the old, tribal Africa, and the other the new breed yearning for their place in the sun." See Richard Long, "Independent Uganda: Christianity's Role in the Problems and prospects Confronting a Young Nation," *America* 107, 28 (October 13, 1962): 885.

36. Hopkins, "Politics in Uganda," 251.

37. Mutibwa, *Uganda Since Independence*, 24; Low, *Buganda in Modern History*, 206–214. It should be noted that the various tribes spoke different dialects. Divisions were somewhat national and had been present for centuries before Europeans came to the region in the mid-ninteenth century.

38. Mutibwa, *Uganda Since Independence*, 27; Long, "Independent Uganda," 885.

39. Quoted in Long, "Independent Uganda," 891.

40. Vincent McCauley, C.S.C., "The Church's Response to the Nationalist Challenge in Uganda" (position paper), n.d., 652 Missionary Sisters of Africa, ADFP.

41. Vincent McCauley, C.S.C., to the Larsen Family, 26 September 1962, PPMJL.

42. Catholic Diocese of Fort Portal, Uganda, East Africa, Quinquennial Report.

43. McCauley interview with James Connelly.

44. Transcribed interview with Samson B. Katemba, July 16, 1964, 910.1, Bishop McCauley Papers, ADFP. Many Holy Cross religious who lived and worked with McCauley over the years verify that he insisted that his priests and religious refrain from all public political statements, viewing such participation as detrimental to the promotion of the faith.

45. Mutibwa, *Uganda Since Independence*, 30; Tumusiime, *Uganda 30 Years*, 27.

46. Jan Jorgensen, *Uganda*, 213–214.

47. Cherry Gertzel, "Kabaka Yekka," 3.

48. Mutibwa, *Uganda Since Independence*, 29, 41.

49. Richard Long, "Uganda's Independence," 22.

50. Meeting minutes, Board of Consultors, Diocese of Fort Portal, April 2, 1968, 440.1, Board of Consultors Meeting Minutes, ADFP.

51. Tumusiime, *Uganda 30 Years*, 32–33; Ofcansky, *Uganda: Tarnished Pearl*, 40–41; Mutibwa, *Uganda Since Independence*, 34–35; Peter M. Gukiina, *Uganda: A Case Study in African Political Development* (Notre Dame, IN: University of Notre Dame Press, 1972), 122–127.

52. Vincent McCauley, C.S.C., to Joanie and Dick Larsen, 9 January 1864 [*sic*–1964], PPMJL.

53. Gukiina, *Uganda: A Case Study*, 128–129. The facts are unclear as to whether the Kabaka had any plans to overthrow Obote. It is true, however, that between 1962 and 1966, Mutesa II did petition the United Nations, the British government, and the Organization of African Unity to intervene and restore the precepts of the 1962 constitution which, in the mind of Mutesa, had been repeatedly violated by Obote. None of these government organizations responded to Mutesa.

54. Tumusiime, *Uganda 30 Years*, 34; see Mutibwa, *Uganda Since Independence*, 39. In addition to his position as secretary-general of the UPC, Ibingira was the Uganda Minister of State. The dragnet, which Obote ordered, also claimed Dr. E. B. S. Lumu (Minister of Health), Balaki Kirga (Minister of Mineral and Water Resources), Mathias Ngobi (Minister of Agriculture), and George Magezi (Minister of Housing and Labor). Further, Obote elevated Idi Amin to the post of Army Commander and abolished the posts of president, held by Edward Mutesa II, and vice president. The removal of the Kabaka led to open rebellion in Buganda, which sought to secede from the country. In the Battle of Mengo, Obote's forces, led by Amin, defeated those of the Kabaka. Eventually Mutesa was forced into exile and died in London in 1969.

55. Obote, "The Footsteps of Uganda's Revolution," 13.

56. Mutibwa, *Uganda Since Independence*, 63–64.

57. Jorgensen, *Uganda*, 230.

58. Mutibwa, *Uganda Since Independence*, 36, 59, 64.

59. Statement of the Bishops of Uganda, June 27, 1967, 229, UEC Commissions, Joint Christian Council, ADFP.

60. Bishop Serapio Magambo, "An Appreciation of Bishop Vincent McCauley, C.S.C.," December 14, 1982, 811, Doss. 1, Holy Cross Generalate Papers, AUND.

61. Ibid.; Joseph Mukwaya, interview with the author, February 4, 2006, AHCFI.

62. Hastings, "The Pattern of African Mission Work," n.d. [1960s], found in 635.2, Priests Meetings, ADFP.

63. Joseph Blomjous, "Whither the Missions?" (talk), n.d. [1965], 480.2 Presbyterial Council Correspondence, ADFP. Blomjous presented five specific tensions that needed to be addressed: (1) tension between traditional missionary concepts and the present mission situation; (2) tension between the universal mission of the Church and the necessary respect for human freedom; (3) tension between mission and religious pluralism; (4) tension between the mission of the Church and its unity; the Church is not only Western, which requires the need for pluriformity—different ways to live the gospel message; and (5) tension between the mission of the Church and the temporal order, seen especially in the role of traditional Church institutions.

64. James Ferguson, C.S.C., interview with the author, April 4, 2006, AHCFI.

65. Vincent McCauley, C.S.C., to John Donoghue, 25 June 1965, 823, Holy Cross Generalate Papers, AUND.

66. Vincent McCauley, C.S.C., to Leo Volker, W.F., 21 November 1966, 641, Missionaries of Africa, ADFP.

67. Ibid.

68. Ibid.; Vincent McCauley, C.S.C., to H. Goetz, 28 January 1972, 720.5, Misereor, ADFP; Vincent McCauley, "Priests Conference 1968, Introduction," 811, Doss. 3, Holy Cross Generalate Papers, AUND.

69. Vincent McCauley, C.S.C., to Germain Lalande, C.S.C., 22 July 1965, 811, Doss. 3, Holy Cross Generalate Papers, AUND.

70. McCauley to Leo Volker, 21 November 1966.

71. Vincent McCauley, C.S.C., "Holy Cross in Africa," 1976 Provincial Chapter, PCSC 5/13, AUND.

72. Joseph Mukwaya interview.

73. As one example of how McCauley suggested the need for greater inculturation on the part of religious communities, he wrote the local superior of the White Sisters: "The missionary spirit of our White Sisters has always been exemplary. It still is. Their effectiveness, however, has sometimes been hampered by a few out-dated rules and traditions." He suggested that the sisters too often do not seem to understand what is happening in the local community. He continued, "In other words, the Sisters are not a part of the community; they are foreigners with a life of their own to live away from and untouched by local society." See Vincent McCauley, C.S.C., to Mother Maria Mechtildis, W.F., 12 December 1964, 652, Missionary Sisters of Our Lady of Africa, ADFP.

74. McCauley, "Holy Cross in Africa."

75. Vincent McCauley, C.S.C., "For the Good of the Church, "memorandum to the Uganda Episcopal Conference, March 1968, 811, Doss. 3, Holy Cross Generalate Papers, AUND.

76. Vincent McCauley, C.S.C., to Fathers, Brothers and Sisters, 16 March 1968, 910.1, Bishop McCauley Papers, ADFP. In a similar vein, McCauley wrote his family: "I feel the Church will be stronger and the people here better Catholics as a result of the personal participation and sacrifice we are trying [to] make the basis of operation for the Church. Otherwise I see nothing but a dependant attitude prevailing. . . . What we want is to build up the Church so that the native clergy can take over, and the native Catholics can not only support their Church but make it grow

from an inner viability." See Vincent McCauley, C.S.C., to Harverd Tracy, 13 March 1962, PPMJL.

77. Quoted in *Transmission* VI, no. 2 (November 1983): 6, AHCFI. Archbishop Charles Schleck, C.S.C., expressed similar ideas about McCauley's promotion of local clergy: "He remained there [Fort Portal] until such time as he had prepared one of the local priests to take over as local Bishop, which clearly indicated to all that he was not attached to the role there but considered himself as placed there to prepare a strong and good local clergy as Bishop as quickly as possible." See Charles Schleck, C.S.C., to the author, 6 August 2005.

78. Joseph Mukwaya interview.

79. Vincent McCauley, C.S.C., to Antonio Mazzi, 22 June 1967, 220.4 UEC Seminaries Gaba, ADFP.

80. McCauley, "For the Good of the Church."

81. Ibid.

82. Ibid.

83. "A Memorandum to the Secretary for the Religious Affairs Presented by Indigenous Priests of the Fort Portal Diocese," n.d. [1969], 470.2, Chancery Correspondence, ADFR.

84. Catholic Diocese of Fort Portal, Uganda, East Africa, Quinquennial Report, 1961–1965, 114, *Ad Limina* Visits, ADFP.

85. Vincent McCauley, C.S.C., to Germain Lalande, C.S.C., February 2, 1973, 811, Doss. 3, Holy Cross Generalate Papers, AUND. In this letter, McCauley describes a memorandum from the Uganda Priests Association that advocates married deacons and priests. He says, despite the nature of the memorandum, the concept of Africanization needed to be promoted.

86. Vincent McCauley, C.S.C., to Leo Volker, W.F., 7 April 1965, 022.045, Correspondence AWFK.

87. Vincent McCauley, C.S.C., to Harry Heyes, W.F., 1 April 1965, 641, Missionaries of Africa, ADFP.

88. See William Blum, C.S.C., interview with the author, March 22, 2006, AHCFI; Robert Hesse interview; John Keefe interview, April 11, 2006.

89. McCauley to Bernard Mullahy, 19 April 1962.

90. Francis Zagorc interview; George Lucas interview; Cornelius Ryan interview.

91. George Lucas interview.

92. Robert Hesse interview; John Croston, C.S.C., interview with the author, April 7, 2006, AHCFI; Burton Smith interview.

93. Vincent McCauley, C.S.C., to Harriet Gartland, 21 October 1971, McCauley File, Holy Cross Mission Center Papers, AHCFI.

94. Bonaventura Kasaija, interview with the author, January 30, 2006, AHCFI; George Lucas interview; William Blum interview.

95. Religious have stated that when McCauley went to bush villages he often promised the local people things without full realization of what he was saying. This was particularly true when requests came in Rutoro, the local tribal language that McCauley never knew that well. See John Keefe interview, April 7, 2006.

96. Richard Potthast, C.S.C., interview with the author, February 6, 2006, AHCFI.

97. Vincent McCauley, C.S.C., to Your Highness, n.d. [March 1966], 952, Kingdom of Toro, ADFP.

98. Constitution of the Toro Joint Advisory Welfare Committee, n.d. [July 1962]; meeting minutes, Toro Joint Advisory Welfare Committee, July 17, 1962, 952, Kingdom of Toro, ADFP. The Constitution gave additional areas the committee sought to engage: (1) foster unity among members, (2) elicit resources of member organizations, (3) procure and provide information, (4) arrange and provide facilities for local community meetings, lectures, and conferences, and (5) collect and distribute charitable monies for various projects in the local community.

99. Meeting minutes, Toro Joint Advisory Welfare Committee, March 29, 1966, 952, Kingdom of Toro, ADFP.

100. Vincent McCauley, C.S.C., to Y. B. Bigirwa, 11 December 1964, 272, Hoima Diocese, ADFP.

101. Long, "Independent Uganda," 891; Vincent McCauley, C.S.C., to Permanent Secretary, Ministry of Housing and Labour, 28 May 1965, 952, Kingdom of Toro, ADFP.

102. Vincent McCauley, C.S.C., to Charles Walker, Sr., 1 June 1968, 910.1 Bishop McCauley Papers, ADFP.

103. McCauley, "The Churches and Development in Africa."

104. John Croston interview, April 5, 2006.

105. Meeting minutes, Board of Consultors, Fort Portal Diocese, March 10, 1970, 440.1, Board of Consultors, ADFP.

106. Cornelius Ryan interview; Richard Potthast interview; Paulinus Bagambaki interview.

107. Vincent McCauley, C.S.C., to All the Priests, 30 October 1969, 480.1, Presbyterial Council Meeting Minutes, ADFP.

108. Henri Valette, W.F., interview with the author, February 23, 2006, AHCFI; Paulinus Bagambaki interview; Joseph Mugenyi, interview with the author, February 6, 2006, AHCFI.

109. The four geographic zones were parish groupings: (1) Virika, Yerya, Bubombwa, and Bukwali, (2) Nsenyi, Kasanga, and Kasese, (3) Butiiti and Wekomire, and (4) Kahunge and Kitagwenga.

110. Catholic Diocese of Fort Portal, Uganda, East Africa, Quinquennial Report.

111. Cardinal Gregory Peter Agagianian to Vincent McCauley, C.S.C., 18 July 1968, unmarked box, AMECEA Correspondence, ADFP.

112. Vincent McCauley, C.S.C., to Your Eminence [Cardinal Gregory Peter Agagianian], 3 February 1965, 811, Doss. 3, Holy Cross Generalate Papers, AUND; Vincent McCauley, C.S.C., to Guido del Mestri, 27 July 1965, 811, Doss. 3, Holy Cross Generalate Papers, AUND; McCauley interview with James Connelly.

113. McCauley to Leo Volker, 7 April 1965; Germain Lalande to McCauley, 6 June 1965.

114. Tourigny, *So Abundant a Harvest*, 158; Connelly, "Holy Cross in East Africa," 19; Guido del Mestri to Your Excellencies, 12 September 1965, 272, Hoima Diocese, ADFP.

115. Vincent McCauley, C.S.C., to H. H. Wagner, 19 January 1966, 910.1, Bishop McCauley Papers, ADFP.

116. History of the Cathedral of Our Lady of the Snows, Diocese of Fort Portal, n.d., 920, History of the Fort Portal Diocese, ADFP; "Earthquake Cripples Catholic Church in Toro," n.d. [March 1966], 952, Kingdom of Toro, ADFP.

117. *Uganda Drum*, March 20, 1966, 450.1, AHCEA; "Appendix List," March 26, 1966, 952, Kingdom of Toro, ADFP. McCauley described the effects of the earthquake: "Here at Virika the damage is staggering. The cathedral is too badly damaged to bother about. The architect and engineer from Kampala condemned it. Their report is known to the government. We can do nothing but tear it down." See Vincent McCauley, C.S.C., to Richard Sullivan, C.S.C., 26 March 1966, 526.05.1, Overseas Apostolates, AHCFE.

118. Vincent McCauley, C.S.C., to Germain Lalande, C.S.C., 26 March 1966, 811, Doss. 3, Holy Cross Generalate Papers, AUND.

119. Vincent McCauley, C.S.C., to Arnold Fell, C.S.C., 28 March 1966, 910.1, Bishop McCauley Papers, ADFP.

120. Vincent McCauley, C.S.C., to Antonio Mazza, 28 July 1967, 220.4, UEC Commissions, Seminaries, Gaba; Vincent McCauley, C.S.C., to Dear Monsignor [H. Goetz], 26 October 1966, 720.5, Misereor, ADFP.

121. James Rahilly, interview with the author, March 26, 2006, AHCFI; meeting minutes, Board of Consultors, September 30, 1966, 440.1, Board of Consultors Papers, ADFP.

122. Meeting minutes, Board of Consultors, October 4, 1967, 440.1, Board of Consultors Papers, ADFP.

123. John Croston, C.S.C., to Howard Kenna, C.S.C., 24 April 1968, 35:6, Kenna Papers, AHCFI.

124. Vincent McCauley, C.S.C., to Howard Kenna, C.S.C., 21 May 1968, 35:6, Kenna Papers, AHCFI.

6. The Pastoral Missionary: 1961–1973

1. Thomas Smith, C.S.C., interview with the author, April 4, 2006, ACHFI.

2. John Keefe interview, April 7, 2006; Cornelius Ryan interview; Robert Hesse interview.

3. Vincent McCauley, C.S.C., to Guido del Mestri, 2 October 1965, 920, History of the Diocese of Fort Portal, ADFP.

4. Robert Malone interview, March 20, 2006. Safaris were a routine of travel for several days to Catholic communities in remote rural areas. The conferring of sacraments and catechesis were central ministries during these trips.

5. Louis Rink, C.S.C., interview with the author, April 24, 2006, AHCFI. A typical safari day can be described. The priest (or bishop) would arrive via automobile and go to the village chapel. Generally he would be greeted by the local catechist(s) who would "beat the drum" announcing the arrival of "Tata." Confessions would be heard and then Mass celebrated. If necessary, other sacraments would be celebrated. A meal would end the visit. See *Uganda Drum* I, no. 4 (August–September 1959), 450.1, AHCEA.

6. McCauley to Guido del Mestri, 2 October 1965.

7. Stephen Gibson, C.S.C., interview with the author, April 27, 2006, AHCFI.

8. Interestingly, one missionary, speaking of McCauley's language difficulty, stated that the bishop shied away from situations where Rutoro was required. He stated, "Had he been able to converse better, he would have been closer to the people and the people to him." See Robert Malone interview, March 20, 2006.

9. James Rahilly interview.

10. The complete story of the ministry of Patrick Peyton, C.S.C., well known to many as the "rosary priest," is presented in Richard Gribble, C.S.C., *American Apostle of the Family Rosary: The Life of Patrick J. Peyton, CSC* (New York: Crossroads, 2005). For information on the African crusades of 1955 see pages 126–127.

11. McCauley to Mehling, 1 September, 1961. He wrote to the provincial: "I hope you will understand that, loathe [*sic*] as I am to take on anything outside of Fort Portal, and above all to lose a man of Fr. Zagorc's caliber, I feel constrained by the conviction that the Church will benefit and Holy Cross influence will spread throughout Africa."

12. Christopher O'Toole, C.S.C., to Vincent McCauley, C.S.C., 13 September 1961, 811, Doss. 2, Holy Cross Generalate Papers, AUND.

13. The crusade Peyton had designed and implemented in dioceses around the world was an extensive program of meetings, media coverage, and public rosary rallies that necessitated extensive commitments of personnel, economic resources, and time.

14. Bernard Mullahy, C.S.C., to Vincent McCauley, C.S.C., December 13, 1961, 41:77, Mullahy Papers, AHCFI. It should be noted that all the world's bishops were invited by Peyton to view the rosary films during the ongoing Second Vatican Council in the fall of 1965.

15. Vincent McCauley, C.S.C., to Charles Walker, 27 November 1967, 910.1, Bishop McCauley Papers, ADFP.

16. Vincent McCauley, C.S.C., to Arnold Fell, C.S.C., 24 October 1967, 910.1, Bishop McCauley Papers, ADFP. There is no extant data that the program was repeated.

17. The Batutsi were the ruling tribe in Rwanda. In 1961, their king was exiled, allowing the rival tribe, the Bahutu, to attain power. The Bahutu immediately began to harass the Batutsi, who spilled over the border into Uganda. This same conflict, only much more magnified, was central to the genocide in Rwanda in 1994.

18. Report "Refugees 1966," 728.28, Catholic Relief Services, ADFP; Vincent McCauley, C.S.C., to Cardinal Peter Gregory Agagianian, 22 June 1964, 728.28, Catholic Relief Services, ADFP.

19. Vincent McCauley, C.S.C., to Larry and Mary Tracy, Christmas 1964, PPMJL.

20. Report "Refugees 1966."

21. Ibid.

22. Vincent McCauley, C.S.C., to Johnny and Adele, 25 May 25, 1967, McCauley Folder, Holy Cross Mission Center Papers, AHCFI.

23. Vincent McCauley, C.S.C., to Monsignor Kaiser, 11 April 1962, 200.4 Uganda Episcopal Conference, Archives Archdiocese of Kampala, Kampala, Uganda (hereafter AAK).

24. Vincent McCauley, C.S.C., to Dear Monsignor, 14 April 1964, 229, UEC Commissions, Joint Christian Council, ADFP.

25. Vincent McCauley, C.S.C., "Long Term Problems Facing Refugees in Central Africa," 72.28, Catholic Relief Services, ADFP.

26. Vincent McCauley, C.S.C., to Dr. T. Stark, 25 July 1967, 720.28, Catholic Relief Services, ADFP.

27. Robert Hesse interview. Brother Orlando's kindness and holiness were noted by many both in Holy Cross and outside of the congregation.

28. Vincent McCauley, C.S.C., to Pietro Sigismandi, 16 September 1965, 720.28, Catholic Relief Services, ADFP; Vincent McCauley, C.S.C., to Richard Walsh, W.F., 25 May 1964, 641, Missionaries of Africa, ADFP.

29. Joseph Mugenyi interview.

30. *Uganda Drum* IX, no. 3 (April 1967), 450.1, AHCEA; Vincent McCauley, C.S.C., to Jean J. Chenaud, 4 January 1965, 720.28, Catholic Relief Services, ADFP; George MacInnes, C.S.C., to Vincent McCauley, C.S.C., 23 November 1965, 330.7, Kahunge Parish, ADFP.

31. Meeting minutes, Board of Consultors, October 8, 1968, 440.1, Board of Consultors, Kitagwenda Parish, ADFP; Robert Hesse, C.S.C., to Vincent McCauley, C.S.C., 19 September 1968, 330.8, Kitagwenda Parish, ADFP; Serapio Magambo to Felix Rwambareli, 15 April 1969, 330.8, Kitagwenda Parish, ADFP; Robert Hesse, C.S.C., "Safari to Kitagwenda," n.d. [March 1966], 330.8, Kitagwenda Parish, ADFP.

32. Vincent McCauley, C.S.C., to Dear Father, 14 November 1961, 720.28, Catholic Relief Services, ADFP.

33. McCauley to Monsignor Kaiser, 11 April 1962, 200.4. The Uganda government also sought the assistance of Catholic Relief Services for the Batutsi refugees.

34. Report "Refugees 1966."

35. John Keefe interview, April 11, 2006.

36. Vincent McCauley, C.S.C., to Salvatore Milone, 23 January 1967, 910.1, Bishop McCauley Papers, ADFP. It should be noted that McCauley was equally appreciative of the efforts of the White Fathers. He wrote, "No word of commendation from me can do justice to their zeal and generosity." See Vincent McCauley, C.S.C., to James Smith, W.F., 13 March 1968, 022–45, Correspondence, AWFK.

37. Vincent McCauley, C.S.C., to Germain Lalande, C.S.C., 11 April 1964, 811, Doss. 3, Holy Cross Generalate Papers, AUND.

38. Vincent McCauley, C.S.C., to Louis Meyer, C.S.C., 7 January 1965, 35:5, Kenna Papers, AHCFI.

39. Bonaventura Kasaija interview; Meeting minutes, Priests' Senate, June 15, [1971], 480.1 Presbyterial Council Meeting Minutes, ADFP.

40. Banyatereza Sisters, group interview with the author, January 28, 2006, AHCFI.

41. Vincent McCauley, C.S.C., "Priests' Conference," 1968, 635.2, Priests Meetings, ADFP.

42. Report of Priests' Annual Conference, June 1–3, 1964, 635.2 Priests' Meeting Minutes, ADFP; Clerical Conference, February 13–15, 1967, 635.2 Priests' Meeting Minutes, ADFP; Priests' Conference 1970, 635.2 Priests' Meeting Minutes, ADFP; Vincent McCauley, C.S.C., to Priests of the Diocese of Fort Portal, 13 January 1971, ADFP.

43. Katwe Catholic Council to Vincent McCauley, C.S.C., 14 April 1962, 910.1, Bishop McCauley Papers, ADFP. From extant data, this group continued to press McCauley for a few years on this issue. It is clear, however, that the group's agenda was more generically nationalistic. For example, in February 1965, McCauley received a letter that demanded that all parish priests be Africans, the appointment of an African as vicar general, and that Africans be appointed as seminary professors. See Katwe Catholic Council to Vincent McCauley, C.S.C., February 19, 1965, 910.1, Bishop McCauley Papers, ADFP. Others have verified the situation noted by the Katwe group at the outset. See Paulinus Bagambaki interview.

44. Robert Malone, C.S.C., interview with the author, March 6, 2006, AHCFI; William Blum interview. Blum suggests individual religious in the two communities did have social interaction.

45. Robert Hesse interview; Cornelius Ryan interview; James Rahilly interview; Francis Zagorc interview with James Connelly.

46. Regular Visitation in the Diocese of Fort Portal, n.d., 023, Visitations, AWFK.

47. George Lucas interview; William Blum interview; Francis Zagorc interview.

48. James Ferguson interview.

49. McCauley to Leo Volker, 21 November 1966.

50. Fort Portal General Report, March 11, 1964, 023, Visitations, AWFK. This report also demonstrates that the White Fathers felt the need to reduce their influence so Holy Cross and the African diocesan priests could take the lead positions. The report states, "I felt that some Holy Cross Fathers were resenting

that key posts were still in White Fathers' hands. Without mentioning that to Bishop McCauley, I suggested to him that it might be good to give all the key posts to Holy Cross Fathers and African priests, in order to prevent any ill feeling that White Fathers wanted to remain in command. His Lordship told me as he had done before that it [*sic*–he] would do so when possible, but that there was no Holy Cross Father who could fill thoses [*sic*] posts for the time being."

51. Regular Visitation in the Diocese of Fort Portal. Another report also demonstrates McCaulcy's impartial usc of pcrsonncl.

52. McCauley to Germain Lalande, 11 April 1964.

53. Kisembo, "Fort Portal Diocese," 67. Kisembo's number of fifty-two Holy Cross religious is probably an inversion of the real number of approximately twenty-five.

54. Vincent McCauley, C.S.C., to Richard Walsh, W.F., 13 July 1962, 641, Missionaries of Africa, ADFP.

55. Vincent McCauley, C.S.C., to Oscar Braun, W.F., 17 July 1963, 641, Missionaries of Africa, ADFP.

56. Vincent McCauley to James Smith, 13 March 1968, 641, Missionaries of Africa, ADFP.

57. Vincent McCauley, C.S.C., to Kathleen Cuzzi, 8 May 1970, 910.1, McCauley Papers, ADFP.

58. McCauley to Guido del Mestri, 2 October 1965; Cardinal Peter Gregory Agagianian to McCauley, 18 July 1968.

59. Vincent McCauley, C.S.C., to Richard Sullivan, C.S.C., 24 October 1967, 526.05.1, Overseas Apostolates, AHCFE.

60. Germain Lalande, C.S.C., to Vincent McCauley, C.S.C., 6 June 1965, 811, Doss. 3, Holy Cross Generalate Papers, AUND.

61. Francis Zagorc interview with James Connelly; John Croston interview, July 7, 2005.

62. The Lake Saka House was opened in 1962. After the earthquake of 1966 destroyed the building, a new structure was built in 1967. The house served for many years as a place of rest and relaxation for Holy Cross religious, especially on Sunday

evenings when the community gathered to recreate together. Today the Saka house is the novitiate for Holy Cross in Eastern Africa.

63. Quoted in *Transmission* VI, no. 2 (November 1983): 6, AHCFI. In a similar vein, McCauley's successor in Fort Portal, Serapio Magambo, once wrote of his friend and mentor: "Alone, without the Holy Cross Congregation advising and supporting him, he might have done little or nothing. He was a Congregation man and relied heavily on Holy Cross for support." See Serapio Magambo, sermon, September 3, 1983, 801.1 Fort Portal Letters from Diocesan Office, AHCK.

64. Robert Malone interview, March 20, 2006; Robert Hesse interview; Richard Potthast interview; Thomas Smith interview; John Croston interview, April 5, 2006; Thomas McDermott, C.S.C., interview with the author, April 21, 2006, AHCFI. McDermott relates a comical but illustrative story of McCauley at a Holy Cross social function. In January 1982, McCauley was present at a Holy Cross function in Nairobi. He was playing bridge. He called out "McDermott, get me a drink!" Dutifully the young priest got the bishop a drink. Some time later, the bishop again called out, "McDermott, get me a drink!" Again the young priest got the bishop a drink. Some time later the bishop again called for a drink, but the local superior, observing these events told McDermott, "The bishop is drunk; don't get him a drink." But McDermott replied, "I am only a junior priest who knows little, but that man over there started and guided the Diocese of Fort Portal for several years and besides he just bid and won three no trump with lousy cards. I think I am going to get the bishop another drink."

65. John Keefe interview, April 7, 2006; Francis Zagorc interview; Louis Rink interview, April 24, 2006; Francis Zagorc interview with James Connelly.

66. Francis Zagorc interview.

67. Ibid.

68. Meeting minutes, Holy Cross Meeting, November 4, 1968, 642.1, Holy Cross, ADFP.

69. Francis Zagorc interview with James Connelly; Francis Zagorc interview; John Keefe interview, April 7, 2006. John Keefe, C.S.C., provides additional insight into these events. In 1974, he drove McCauley from Uganda to Nairobi. During the long trip McCauley told Keefe how hurt he was by the efforts of some Holy Cross religious to secure his ouster as bishop in Fort Portal. For McCauley it was not the sentiment but the method that was most troubling. For Keefe this was a very dry period for community life and fraternal brotherhood within Holy Cross in East Africa. See John Keefe interview, April 11, 2006.

70. Catholic Diocese of Fort Portal, Uganda, East Africa, Quinquennial Report.

71. Vincent McCauley, C.S.C., to Mother Theodosia, 23 December 1969, 651, Banyatereza Sisters, ADFP; Banyatereza Sisters interview, January 28, 2006.

72. Magambo, sermon; Banyatereza Sisters interview, January 28, 2006.

73. From Diocesan Office, AHCEA.

74. Vincent McCauley, C.S.C., "The Challenge Before Us" (panel discussion, audio tape), C4420, audio, AUND.

75. *Petit Echo* no. 636 (1973), AWFK.

76. Ibid. The magazine reported that solutions similar to McCauley's "experiment" had been utilized in at least three other places. In Austria, Brazil, and Zaire (Democratic Republic of Congo), women religious had assumed roles traditionally more clerical due to lack of clergy. In all cases, those who were served reported satisfaction.

77. Banyatereza Sisters interview, January 28, 2006; Harry Heyes, W.F., to Edward Heston, C.S.C., 28 May 1964, 267.76, FP10, Holy Cross Generalate Papers, AUND; Edward Heston, C.S.C., to Harry Heyes, W.F., 2 June 1964, 267.76, FP10, Holy Cross Generalate Papers, AUND; Vincent McCauley, C.S.C., to

Edward Heston, C.S.C., 20 March 1968, 267.76, FP10, Holy Cross Generalate Papers, AUND; James Rahilly, C.S.C., to Edward Heston, C.S.C., 31 May 1968, 267.76, FP10, Holy Cross Generalate Papers, AUND.

78. Profile of Monsignor Vincent J. McCauley, Bishop of Fort Portal, March 18, 1968, 920, History of the Diocese of Fort Portal, ADFP. The Ladies of Mary, later called the Daughters of Mary and Joseph, arrived in Toro in 1959. They had been invited by the White Sisters to assist due to their lack of personnel. They came at a time of the reorganization of teacher education. Thus, when the opportunity to assist at Kinyamasaka Teachers College arose, they took the ministry. Within a short amount of time, Kinyamasika became the center of teacher education in Fort Portal. See Kisembo, "Fort Portal Diocese," 69.

79. McCauley was deeply appreciative of the "magnificent work that the White Sisters have done for the Church here in Fort Portal." But he also hoped that the Sisters' retrenchment was not permanent: "All of us . . . wish to re-iterate our insistence that Fort Portal be included in your future plans for the White Sisters Apostolate." See Vincent McCauley, C.S.C., to Mother Mary Seward, W.S., 28 February 1969, 652, Missionary Sisters of Our Lady of Africa, ADFP.

80. Vincent McCauley, C.S.C., to Mother Benedict, S.C.M.M., 23 September 1958, McCauley File, Holy Cross Mission Center Papers, AHCFI; fact sheet, Medical Mission Sisters, n.d., 652, Missionary Sisters of Our Lady of Africa, ADFP.

81. Vincent McCauley, C.S.C., to Larry and Mary Tracy, 27 March 1962, PPMJL; Kisembo, "Fort Portal Diocese," 71.

82. Vincent McCauley, C.S.C., "The Church's Response to the Nationalist Challenge in Uganda" (position paper) n.d., 652, Missionary Sisters of Our Lady of Africa, ADFP.

83. Extant data shows that McCauley had actually first contacted Misereor in September 1963 about plans for a nurses' training center in Fort Portal. See W. Rowenkamp to Vincent

McCauley, C.S.C., 7 October 1963, 526.1, Virika Hospital, ADFP.

84. Vincent McCauley, C.S.C., to Monsignor Dossing, 2 October 1964, 526.1, Virika Hospital, ADFP.

85. Vincent McCauley, C.S.C., to Father Benedict, 20 November 1965, 526.1, Virika Hospital, ADFP; Nurses Home and Training Center—information sheet, n.d.,; Vincent McCauley, C.S.C., to Dick and Joan Larsen, 9 November 1966, PPMJL.

86. Vincent McCauley, C.S.C., "Priests Conference," 1968, 635.2, Priests Meetings, ADFP.

87. Banyatereza Sisters interview, January 28, 2006; Richard Potthast interview; McCauley, "The Challenge Before Us."

88. Joseph Mugenyi interview; Vincent McCauley, C.S.C., to Guido del Mestri, 3 July 1965, 267.76, FP 11, Holy Cross Generalate Papers, AUND. The *Pro Ecclesia et Pontifice* was established by Pope Leo XIII on July 17, 1888, to commemorate the golden jubilee of his ordination. It is given to clergy and lay people for distinguished service to the Church.

89. Robert Hesse interview; Robert Malone interview, March 6, 2006.

90. Lay Apostolate in Fort Portal Diocese, Annual Report, 1966, 556.1, Lay Apostolate Fort Portal, ADFP. The ten committees were (1) education, (2) social, (3) family, (4) economic, (5) press and political, (6) land, (7) Church officials, (8) study, (9) finance, and (10) liturgical.

91. Ibid.

92. Meeting minutes, Diocesan Pastoral Council, March 11, 1972, 801.6, Fort Portal Diocesan Meetings, AHCEA.

93. Catholic Action, as defined by Pope Pius XI in *Ubi Arcano* (1922) as the work of the laity in support of the bishops, was very popular in the 1930s through the 1950s, beginning in Europe and moving to the United States. Groups such as Grail, Young Christian Workers, and the Christian Family Movement received strong institutional support. Other programs, such as Friendship

House and the Catholic Worker Movement, were very popular, but, having no close ties to the work of local bishops, were considered more secondary works of Catholic Action. An excellent summary of the various Catholic Action groups, especially as manifest in the United States is Debra Campbell's "The Heyday of Catholic Action and the Lay Apostolate, 1929–1959," in *Transforming Parish Ministry: The Changing Roles of Catholic Clergy, Laity, and Women Religious*, ed. Jay P. Dolan, R. Scott Appleby, Patricia Byrne, and Debra Campbell (New York: Crossroad, 1989), 222–252.

94. Henri Valette interview.

95. Lay Apostolate in Fort Portal Diocese, Annual Report, 1966; McCauley to Guido del Mestri, 2 October 1965.

96. McCauley to Guido del Mestri, 2 October 1965.

97. Banyatereza Sisters interview, January 28, 2006; Salomi Mujasi, interview with the author, January 21, 2006, AHCFI.

98. Adrian Hastings, "Ecumenism In Africa" (essay) n.d. [1960s], 635.2, Priests Meetings, ADFP.

99. Thomas Smith interview.

100. John Poulton, "Uganda Sets the Pace" (unpublished essay), n.d., 229, UEC Commissions, Joint Christian Council, ADFP.

101. Hastings, "Ecumenism In Africa."

102. Ibid.

103. Vincent McCauley, C.S.C., to Beloved in Christ, 7 June 1965, 910.1, Bishop McCauley Papers, ADFP.

104. Vincent McCauley, C.S.C., Pastoral Letter 1967, 401, Official Acts, Pastoral Letters, ADFP.

105. Vincent McCauley, C.S.C., memorandum for the Uganda Joint Christian Council (UJCC), 30 August 1967, 229, UEC Commissions, Joint Christian Council, ADFP.

106. Vincent McCauley, C.S.C., to Germain Lalande, C.S.C., 14 April 1964, 811 Doss. 3, Holy Cross Generalate Papers, AUND.

107. McCauley, memorandum for the UJCC, 30 August 1967; Vincent McCauley, C.S.C., Pastoral Letter, Lent 1967, 401, Official Acts Pastoral Letters, ADFP. In his Pastoral Letter, McCauley wrote: "Every effort must be made to heal the break that separates Christians. Our motivation must be that of Jesus Himself. The night before He suffered and died for us, He prayed to His Father: 'That they may be one as Thou Father in me and I in Thee.' The charity of Christ should inspire all of our dealing with our Protestant neighbors. There must be no place in our hearts for animosity. There should be no harsh words from our mouths; no unkind actions that will be offensive to our fellow Christians. On the contrary we should pray for them and do and say in charity only what will bring us all together in Christ."

108. Thomas Smith interview. Henri Valette, W.F., stated, "It was really a big achievement." See Henri Valette interview.

109. Vincent McCauley, C.S.C., to Archbishop Erica Sabiiti, 12 December 1970, 229, UEC Commissions, Joint Christian Council, ADFP; News clipping, December 1971, 276, Kasese Diocese, ADFP; Beatrice Nyakaanu, interview with the author, February 6, 2006, AHCFI.

110. Vincent McCauley, C.S.C., to Professor H. P. Dinwiddy, 20 March 1967, 229, UEC Commissions, Joint Christian Council, ADFP.

111. Robert Hesse interview; James Rahilly interview; Joseph Mugenyi interview.

112. Henri Valette interview.

113. McCauley was a member of the Commission for Inter-Faith Cooperation in Uganda, but his contribution was more in ecumenical realms with Protestants. See James Rahilly, C.S.C., to Yves Tournigny, W.F., 30 January 1967, 641 Missionaries of Africa, ADFP. The UJCC was the first joint Christian council in which the Catholic Church participated.

114. Report of the Chairman of the Uganda Joint Christian Council, n.d. [1967], 229, UEC Commissions, Joint Christian Council, ADFP.

115. McCauley, "The Churches and Development in Africa"; Draft Constitution of the Uganda Joint Christian Council, n.d. [1963], 229, UEC Commissions, Joint Christian Council, ADFP. The UJCC committees were Education (May 1964), Communications (June 1964), Social Services (July 1964), Medical Services (August 1964), Ecumenical (July 1968).

116. Draft Constitution of the Uganda Joint Christian Council.

117. Uganda Christian Council information sheet, n.d., 229, UEC Commissions, Joint Christian Council, ADFP.

118. Report of the Chairman of the Joint Christian Council, n.d. [1967].

119. Uganda Christian Council information sheet; meeting minutes, Uganda Episcopal Conference, April 17, 1964, 211.1, UEC Plenary Meetings, ADFP.

120. McCauley to Germain Lalande, 11 April 1964.

121. Meeting minutes, Uganda Joint Christian Council, March 7, 1967, 229, UEC Commissions, Joint Christian Council, ADFP.

122. McCauley, "The Churches and Development in Africa."

123. Vincent McCauley, C.S.C., to Archbishops and Bishops of Uganda, 21 January 1968, 212.2, Uganda Episcopal Conference, AAK.

124. Meeting minutes, Uganda Joint Christian Council, October 12, 1966 and April 13, 1972, 229 UEC Commissions, Joint Christian Council, ADFP.

125. Vincent McCauley, C.S.C., chairman's remarks, Uganda Joint Christian Council, 229, UEC Commisisons, Joint Christian Council, ADFP.

126. Theodore Hesburgh, eulogy for Vincent McCauley. In a similar vein, Serapio Magambo stated, "Bishop McCauley suffered

a lot in his body yet there was a cheerfulness about him that radi-
ated contentment, concern for others and for the Church." See
Magambo, sermon.

7. An Educator in the Faith: 1961–1973

1. Quoted in Richard Long, "Journey to Africa," *Syracuse-
Herald Journal*, December 13, 1960, McCauley File, Holy Cross
Mission Center Papers, AHCFI.

2. See John Croston interview, April 5, 2006.

3. Joesph Mukwaya interview.

4. Vincent McCauley, C.S.C., to Fabius Dunn, C.S.C., 16
January 1971, 910.1, Bishop McCauley Papers, ADFP.

5. Richard Potthast interview.

6. Vincent McCauley, C.S.C., to E. E. Blommaert, 5 April
1971, 910.1, Bishop McCauley Papers, ADFP.

7. Vincent McCauley, C.S.C., to All Christians of Fort Portal Diocese, 16 April 1971, 480.1, Presbyteral Council Meeting
Minutes, ADFP.

8. Vincent McCauley, C.S.C., to Arnold Fell, C.S.C., 10
August 1967, McCauley File, Holy Cross Mission Center Papers,
AHCFI.

9. Vincent McCauley, C.S.C., to Cardinal Peter Gregory Agagianian, 1 June 1967, 586, Catechists, ADFP; Richard Potthast
interview; *The Rwenzori Echo* (January 1973): 16, 810.51, *Rwenzori Echo*, AHCEA. It should be noted that the White Fathers had
been integral to the start of the catechist training program before
the formation of the Fort Portal diocese. Ibanda is almost directly
south of Fort Portal; Mugalike is northeast of Fort Portal.

10. Vincent McCauley, C.S.C., to Raymond Ettledorf, 2 April
1968, 586, Catechists, ADFP.

11. Ephrem O'Dwyer, C.S.C., to Christopher O'Toole,
C.S.C., 29 September 1961, 813.2, Holy Cross Generalate Papers,
AUND; John Harrington interview with James Connolly.

12. John Donoghue, C.S.C., to Bonaventure Foley, C.S.C., 6 February 1964, 813.2, Holy Cross Generalate Papers, AUND.

13. The educational system in Uganda, public and parochial, is set up on three levels: (1) Elementary level, P1–P7, (2) Ordinary, S1–S4, and (3) Advanced level, S5–S6.

14. Report of the Common Inquiry into the Recent Strike at Leo's College, Virika, July 1965, 575, St. Leo's Senior Secondary School (SSS), ADFP; Chronicles of St. Leo's College, 1961–1962, Chronicles of East Africa Communities, Archives Holy Cross Brothers, Eastern Province, Valatie, New York (hereafter AHCBE). St. Leo's became a senior secondary school in 1960.

15. Vincent McCauley, C.S.C., to Germain Lalande, C.S.C., 17 June 1963, 811, Doss. 3, Holy Cross Generalate Papers, AUND.

16. Ibid.

17. Vincent McCauley, C.S.C., to Howard Kenna, C.S.C., 17 June 1963, 35:4, Kenna Papers, AHCFI.

18. "Chronicles of St. Leo's College," 1965–1966, Chronicles of East Africa Communities, AHCBV; Vincent McCauley, C.S.C., to John Donoghue, C.S.C., 21 July 1965, 823, Holy Cross Generalate Papers, AUND.

19. Vincent McCauley, C.S.C., to Edward Heston, C.S.C., 22 July 1965, FP 1, Holy Cross Generalate Papers, AUND.

20. James Rio, C.S.C., interview with the author, June 15, 2006, AHCFI.

21. John Donoghue, C.S.C., to Germain Lalande, C.S.C., n.d. [July 1965], 823, Holy Cross Generalate Papers, AUND. James Rio, C.S.C., who was working at St. Leo's during the strike, believes that the genesis of the disturbance was a solidarity move with similar demonstrations then ongoing in the Congo. See James Rio interview, June 15, 2006.

22. John Donoghue, C.S.C., to Vincent McCauley, C.S.C., 6 July 1965, 823, Holy Cross Generalate Papers, AUND.

23. Vincent McCauley, C.S.C., to Germain Lalande, C.S.C., 20 July 1965, 811, Doss 3, Holy Cross Generalate Papers, AUND.

24. Germain Lalande, C.S.C., to John Donoghue, C.S.C., 25 July 1965, 823, Holy Cross Generalate Papers, AUND.

25. John Donoghue to McCauley, 6 July 1965. Donoghue was referring to the fact that many brothers had left the Uganda mission after a relatively short stay. He commented, "Those who return are beaten men and I fear that within four years that most of them will have left the community—a fear not based on a hunch." It should also be noted that several Holy Cross priests present in Fort Portal at the time echoed the need for greater preparation, especially cultural sensitivity, on the part of the brothers. Another element to be considered is that the brothers had little if any contact with African clergy and thus no significant path to enter into some relationship with the local church.

26. Vincent McCauley, C.S.C., to John Donoghue, C.S.C., 25 June [sic–July] 25, 1965 and 21 July 1965, 823, Holy Cross Generalate Papers, AUND. McCauley wrote on July 25: "Brother, we are here as missionaries. We are 'wanted' by God; we are 'needed' by the Church. Of course we are not wanted by those who do not want Religion, who oppose the Church, who reject Catholic education. We would be naïve, indeed, to think that the government and many of the people . . . even some Catholics . . . 'want' us for the reasons that motivate our coming here. The only reason many of them want us is for what they can get out of us in material and cultural advantages."

27. Germain Lalande, C.S.C., to John Donoghue, C.S.C., 4 September 1965, 823, Holy Cross Generalate Papers, AUND. It should be noted that other strikes arose, such as in February 1970, but nothing was as significant as the 1963 and 1965 disturbances.

28. The bishop made use of St. Ann's Junior Secondary School, near the Virika Cathedral, renaming it St. Maria Goretti

and advancing its academic status to senior secondary level. It served almost exclusively Banyatereza Sisters and aspirants to their community.

29. General Council minutes, Sisters of the Holy Cross, C1.5, July 26, 1961 to April 1, 1967, Archives Sisters of the Holy Cross, Notre Dame, IN (hereafter AHCS).

30. Report on African Visit, April 3–10, 1965, K 8.3, St. Maria Goretti School, AHCS.

31. General Council minutes, Sisters of the Holy Cross.

32. Sister Catherine di Ricci, C.S.C., had previous missionary experience in Brazil; Sister Madeline Patrice, C.S.C., had experience in East Pakistan (Bengal).

33. Chronicles, Holy Cross Convent, St. Maria Goretti School, July 1967, K 8.3, St. Maria Goretti School, AHCS; Catherine de Ricci, C.S.C., to Mother Kathryn Marie Gibbons, C.S.C., 10 April 1967, K 8.3, St. Maria Goretti School, AHCS.

34. Vincent McCauley, C.S.C., to Mother Olivette, C.S.C., 15 September 1967, K 8.3, St. Maria Goretti School, AHCS. Sister Olivette, C.S.C., was elected superior general necessitating her return to the United States and her title change of "Mother."

35. Vincent McCauley, C.S.C., to Sr. Marie Esperie, C.S.C., 26 August 1971, 910.1 Bishop McCauley Papers, ADFP.

36. Vincent McCauley, C.S.C., to Mother Kathryn Marie Gibbons, C.S.C., 25 October 1966, K 8.3, St. Maria Goretti School, AHCS. This was a projected number by the St. Maria Goretti staff.

37. Chronicles, Holy Cross Convent, St. Maria Goretti School. From the Civil War forward, Sisters of the Holy Cross were very active in hospital and general health care ministries. For full details see: Kauffman, *Ministry & Meaning*, 86–87, 93–93, 111–115, 162–164.

38. Vincent McCauley, C.S.C., to Sr. M. Espirit, C.S.C., 6 June 1969, 910.1 Bishop McCauley Papers, ADFP. It should be noted that Catherine de Ricci, C.S.C., was headmistress of St.

Maria Goretti for the remainder of McCauley's tenure as bishop. In January 1972, the year McCauley left the diocese, there were 193 students at the school. By this time most of the students were actually lay students. See Chronicles, Holy Cross Convent, St. Maria Goretti School.

39. Vincent McCauley to Christopher O'Toole, 26 February 1959. White Fathers staffed the school at the time.

40. Vincent McCauley, C.S.C., to Christopher O'Toole, C.S.C., 24 March 1959, 813.2, Holy Cross Generalate Papers, AUND.

41. Parish Visitation, St. Mary's Seminary, Fort Portal, November 14–16, 1966, 023, Visitations, AWFK; Catholic Diocese of Fort Portal, Uganda, East Africa, Quinquennial Report.

42. James Holland, C.S.C., to John Donoghue, C.S.C., 20 October 1966, Donoghue Papers, AHCBV.

43. Bonaventura Kasaija interview.

44. Vincent McCauley, C.S.C., to Antonio Mazza, 29 July 1967, and 10 April 1972, 611, St. Mary's Seminary, ADFP. McCauley was constantly begging funds from Mazza, and was often successful, receiving over $30,000 in 1965 alone.

45. Vincent McCauley, C.S.C., to Edward Jennings, 910.1, Bishop McCauley Papers, ADFP.

46. Inspection report on St. Mary's Seminary, Fort Portal, September 12, 1968, 611, St. Mary's Seminary, ADFP.

47. "Chronicles of St. Mary's Seminary," 1966–1967, Chronicles of East Africa, AHCBV.

48. John Croston, C.S.C., to Howard Kenna, C.S.C., 29 November 1966, 35:4, Kenna papers, AHCFI.

49. Parish Visitation, St. Mary's Seminary, Fort Portal, November 14–16, 1966, 023, Visitations, AWFK; J. A. Smith, W.F., to Vincent McCauley, C.S.C., 023, Visitations, AWFK.

50. Vincent McCauley, C.S.C., to Arnold Fell, C.S.C., 11 July 1967, Bishop McCauley File, Holy Cross Mission Center Papers, AHCFI.

51. "Chronicles of St. Mary's Seminary"; Contract—Diocese of Fort Portal and Holy Cross Brothers, n.d. [January 1968], 823, Holy Cross Generalate Papers, AUND. Three of the major stipulations in the contract were (1) salary, (2) at least four college graduate brothers to be assigned, and (3) brothers' provincial, after consultation with the bishop, would appoint the headmaster.

52. Vincent McCauley, C.S.C., to Germain Lalande, C.S.C., 823, Generalate Papers, AUND.

53. Confidential report of Brother Francis Ellis, C.S.C., on his trip to Uganda, n.d. [August 1969], Uganda File, Bransby Papers, AHCBV. The report clearly stated that the brothers wanted to stay at the seminary and were very anxious to work out the problems as soon as possible. The rector of the institution was in overall control of religious formation; the headmaster was responsible for the academic side of the program.

54. Ibid.

55. James Rio, C.S.C., to Elmos Bransby, C.S.C., 27 May 1970, Uganda File, Bransby Papers, AHCBV.

56. Elmo Bransby, C.S.C., to James Rio, C.S.C., 8 June 1970, Uganda File, Bransby Papers, AHCBV.

57. Observations and Recommendations Concerning St. Mary's Seminary, March 6, 1971, 611, St. Mary's Seminary, ADFP.

58. Tad Las, C.S.C., and James Gulnac, C.S.C., joint interview with the author, May 17, 2006.

59. Ibid. Las stated that McCauley justified his edict based on his role as bishop in a missionary territory. Under the rules of Propaganda Fide, which governed missionary territories, the local bishop had ultimate control over all who ministered in the region. Thus, he used his authority to set up the seminary along lines that he wanted.

60. The published line was that Fotusky went on home leave in March 1972. However, he never resumed his position at the seminary. James Rio, C.S.C., suggests that McCauley came to see

Fotusky as a principal source of the brother/priest conflict. See James Rio interview, June 15, 2006.

61. Meeting minutes, Priest Senate, April 12, 1972, 642.1, Holy Cross, ADFP. The Senate strongly recommended an African to lead the seminary. The minutes read, "If the Africans are the only people who have to live here for the rest of their lives, why shouldn't they be in charge of the future?" The meeting concluded by stating: "Practically with the present situation, we recommend strongly that there should be one head, be it priest or brother. This is the first thing to be done in the process of solving the problems of the seminary." Thus, it seems, McCauley followed the advice of his priests. It should also be noted that some questioned Kasaija's appointment because there was no consultation in the process. See Thomas Keefe, C.S.C., to Hugh McCabe, C.S.C., 25 November 1971, 811, Doss. 3, Holy Cross Generalate Papers, AUND.

62. Vincent McCauley, C.S.C., to Bonaventura Kasaija, 13 March 1972, 611, St. Mary's Seminary, ADFP. When Serapio Magambo succeeded McCauley as bishop of Fort Portal in January 1973, Fotusky was removed from the seminary.

63. Thomas Keefe, C.S.C., to Hugh McCabe, C.S.C., 27 September 1971, St. Mary's Seminary File, McCabe Papers, AHCBV.

64. James Rio, C.S.C., to Thomas Keefe, C.S.C., 2 December 1971, St. Mary's Seminary File, McCabe Papers, AHCBV. Extant data does not indicate who the "two one-sided men" were. Rio said later, "I don't think he [McCauley] had a grasp on what was going on." See James Rio interview, June 15, 2006.

65. Vincent McCauley, C.S.C., to Hugh McCabe, C.S.C., 25 November 1971, 811, Doss. 3, Holy Cross Generalate, AUND.

66. Vincent McCauley, C.S.C., to Germain Lalande, C.S.C., 25 November 1971, 811, Doss. 3, Holy Cross Generalate Papers, AUND.

67. John Keefe interview, April 11, 2006, AHCFI.

68. James Nichols, C.S.C., to Hugh McCabe, C.S.C., 25 November 1971, 811, Doss. 3, Holy Cross Generalate Papers, AUND.

69. Hugh McCabe, C.S.C., to Germain Lalande, C.S.C., 30 November 1971, 811, Doss. 3, Holy Cross Generalate Papers, AUND. Interestingly, James Rio said he had "no problem" with the arrangement that made him "director of studies" and Bonaventura Kasaija the rector. See James Rio, C.S.C., interview with the author, June 16, 2006, AHCFI.

70. Robert Malone interview, March 20, 2006; Vincent McCauley, C.S.C., to Germain Lalande, C.S.C., 4 January 1972, 811, Doss. 3, Holy Cross Generalate Papers, AUND. Malone stated, "I think McCauley was terrified that he would lose the Holy Cross Brothers from St. Mary's and at times it looked like this would happen."

71. McCauley to Bonaventura Kasaija, 13 March 1972.

72. John Donoghue, C.S.C., to Germain Lalande, C.S.C., 29 September 1965, 823, Holy Cross Generalate Papers, AUND.

73. John Croston interview, April 5, 2006; Robert Malone interview, March 20, 2006.

74. Meeting minutes, Uganda Episcopal Conference, April 17, 1964, 211.1, UEC Plenary Meetings, ADFP. Monsignor Bonaventura Kasaija claims that McCauley was the driving force behind the national seminary idea. Kasaija says that he spoke with McCauley about introducing the idea of combining Gulu, Gaba, and Katigondo. McCauley, in turn, took the idea to the bishops. See Bonaventura Kasaija interview.

75. George Lucas interview.

76. McCauley to Antonio Mazza, 22 June 1967.

77. Vincent McCauley, C.S.C., to Antonio Mazza, 18 May 1967, 220.4, UEC Seminaries, Gaba, ADFP; "meeting of Special Committee of Senior Seminary Staff," February 15, 1967, 220.4, UEC Seminaries, Gaba, ADFP.

78. Draft "Uganda National Seminary" n.d., 220.4, UEC Commissions, Seminaries, Gaba, ADFP; Antonio Mazza to Vincent McCauley, C.S.C., 4 July 1966, 220.4, UEC Commissions, Seminaries, Gaba, ADFP.

79. Guido del Mestri to Vincent McCauley, C.S.C., 5 December 1966, 220.4, UEC Commissions, Seminaries, ADFP.

80. Vincent McCauley, C.S.C., to Cardinal Peter Gregory Agagianian, 19 October 1966, 220.4, UEC Commissions, Gaba, ADFP.

81. Vincent McCauley, C.S.C., to Dear Bishop [Adrian Ddungu and James Odongo], 19 December 1966, 220.4, UEC Commissions, Gaba, ADFP.

82. McCauley to Antonio Mazza, 22 June 1967.

83. Vincent McCauley, C.S.C., to Guido del Mestri, 1 July 1967, 229, UEC Commissions, Joint Christian Council, ADFP.

84. Vincent McCauley, C.S.C., to Antonio Mazza, 15 July 1967, 220.4, UEC Commissions, Gaba, ADFP.

85. Vincent McCauley, C.S.C., to Adrian Ddungu and James Odongo, 16 September 1967, 220.4, UEC Commissions, Gaba, ADFP; Vincent McCauley, C.S.C., to Antonio Mazza, 5 June 1970, 220.4, UEC Commissions, Gaba, ADFP.

86. Vincent McCauley, C.S.C., to Antonio Mazza, 28 November 1968, 220.4, UEC Commissions, Gaba, ADFP.

87. Vincent McCauley, C.S.C., to Antonio Mazza, 21 January 1969, 220.4, UEC Commissions, Gaba, ADFP.

88. Antonio Mazza to Vincent McCauley, C.S.C., 18 February 1969, 220.4, UEC Commissions, Gaba, ADFP.

89. Vincent McCauley, C.S.C., to Nicolaus Mund, 15 July 1969, 220.4, UEC Commissions, Gaba, ADFP. He acknowledged a gift of $220,000.

90. Vincent McCauley, C.S.C., to Albert Schlitzer, C.S.C., 11 February 1970, 220.4, UEC Commissions, Gaba, ADFP.

91. Vincent McCauley, C.S.C., to Director Adveniat [Aachen, Germany], 6 February 1970, 220.4, UEC Commissions, Gaba, ADFP.

92. Meeting minutes, Uganda Episcopal Conference, August 1, 1970, 202.2, AMECEA Plenary Meetings (misfiled), ADFP.

93. Emmanuel Nsubaga to Vincent McCauley, C.S.C., 18 July 1970, 204.1, AMECEA Secretariat Correspondence (misfiled), ADFP.

94. Vincent McCauley, C.S.C., Gaba National Seminary Dedication (speech, October 21, 1970), 220.4, UEC Commissions, Gaba, ADFP.

95. Vincent McCauley, C.S.C., to Antonio Mazza, 1 March 1971 and 8 August 1971, 220.4, UEC Commissions, Gaba, ADFP.

96. Vincent McCauley, C.S.C., to Msgr. Wilhelm Wissing, 2 December 1971, 720.3, Missio, ADFP.

8. An Influential Bishop: 1961–1973

1. Many fine historical sources on Vatican II have been published. A representative sample follows: Robert McAfee Brown, *Observer in Rome: A Protestant Report on the Vatican Council* (Garden City, NY: Doubleday, 1964); Anthony J. Cernera, ed., *Vatican II: The Continuing Agenda* (Fairfield, CT: Sacred Heart University Press, 1997); Henri De Lubac, S.J., "The Church in Crisis," *Theology Digest* 17 (1969): 312–25; Dennis M. Doyle, *The Church Emerging from Vatican II: A Popular Approach to Contemporary Catholicism* (Mystic, CT: Twenty-third Publications, 1992); Adrian Hastings, ed., *Modern Catholicism: Vatican II and After* (New York: Oxford University Press, 1991); Christopher Hollis, *The Achievements of Vatican II* (New York: Hawthorn Books, 1967); Rene Latourelle, ed., *Vatican II Assessment and Perspectives Twenty-Five Years After* (1962–1987), 5 vols., (New York: Paulist Press, 1988); Timothy G. McCarthy, *The Catholic Tradition: Before and After Vatican II 1878–1993* (Chicago: Loyola

University Press, 1994); Timothy E. O'Connell, ed., *Vatican II: An American Appraisal* (Wilmington, DE: Michael Glazier, 1986); John W. O'Malley, S.J., "Developments, Reforms, and Two Great Reformations: Towards a Historical Assessment of Vatican II," *Theological Studies* 44 (1983): 373–406. Joseph Ratzinger, *Theological Highlights of Vatican II* (New York: Paulist Press, 1966); Xavier Rynne, *Vatican Council II* (Maryknoll, NY: Orbis Books, 1999); Edward Schillebeeckx, O.P., *The Real Achievement of Vatican II* (New York: Herder and Herder, 1967); Alberic Stacpoole, ed., *Vatican II Revisited by Those Who Were There* (Minneapolis: Winston Press, 1986); Herbert Vorgrimler, ed., *Commentary on the Documents of Vatican II*, 5 vols., (New York: Herder and Herder, 1969); Alberto Melloni and Christoph Theobald, eds., *Vatican II: A Forgotten Future?* (London: SCM Press, 2005); Giuseppe Alberigo, *History of Vatican II*, 5 vols., ed. Joseph Komonchak (Maryknoll, NY: Orbis Press, 1995); Giuseppe Alberigo, *A Brief History of Vatican II*, trans. Matthew Sherry (Maryknoll, NY: Orbis Press, 2006).

2. Karl Rahner, S.J., *Theological Investigations,* Vol, XX, *Concern for the Church* (London: Darton, Longman, and Todd, 1981), 77–89, especially 82–84.

3. William Blum interview. Blum stated, "Bishop McCauley played a significant role at Vatican II for the bishops and countries in Eastern Africa." McCauley saw his task as one of duty to the African Church. He explained to the superior general, "I have been asked to live with the African Bishops again during the next session of the Council. It is much more pleasant at the Generalate, but duty must be done." See Vincent McCauley, C.S.C., to Germain Lalande, C.S.C., 11 April 1964, 310.2.59, DePrizio Papers, AHCFE.

4. Vincent McCauley, C.S.C., to Harry Heyes, W.F., 28 September 1964, 641, Missionaries of Africa, ADFP. The reference to ITEBEA was to Inter-Territorial Episcopal Board Eastern Africa. In "Chairman of AMECEA" and "Secretary-General

of AMECEA," McCauley's long-standing association with this group, known after 1964 as the Association of Member Episcopal Conferences in Eastern Africa (AMECEA) is detailed.

5. Vincent McCauley, C.S.C., to Edward Heston, C.S.C., 4 April 1964, 267.76 FP1, Holy Cross Generalate Papers, AUND.

6. John Croston interview, April 5, 2006.

7. Fell, funeral homily for Vincent McCauley. Many other Holy Cross religious have expressed similar comments about McCauley's role at Vatican II. All agree he had a very positive influence and was the driving force that allowed the Eastern African hierarchy to believe it had something to contribute to the Council proceedings.

8. At the Council, McCauley wrote to his family stating that ecumenism was "The Big Topic of the Council." See Vincent McCauley, C.S.C., to Harverd Tracy, 16 November 1963, PPMJL.

9. Edward Heston, C.S.C., to Vincent McCauley, C.S.C., 19 August 1963, 267.76, FP1, Holy Cross Generalate Papers, AUND; Vincent McCauley, C.S.C., to Edward Heston, C.S.C., 27 August, 1963 and 30 May 1965, 267.76, FP1, Holy Cross Generalate Papers, AUND.

10. Vincent McCauley, C.S.C., to Edward Heston, C.S.C., 3 May 1965 and 30 May 1965, 267.76, FP1, Holy Cross Generalate Papers, AUND. On November 30, 1919, Pope Benedict XV issued *Maximum Illud*, an apostolic letter on evangelization and missions. In the letter, the pope spoke of norms for local bishops, vicars, and apostolic prefects, pastoral care for missionaries, collaboration between religious and diocesan clergy, formation of native clergy, and the need to avoid nationalism and to study indigenous languages. McCauley did not want to detract from the schema on mission, but felt it was necessary as well to review the 1919 Instruction as it was the basis upon which religious communities and local ordinaries would build their working relationships. The

establishment of the local church set up possible conflict between missionary orders and the local bishop.

11. Vincent McCauley, C.S.C., to Edward Heston, C.S.C., 5 May 1965, 267.76, Holy Cross Generalate Papers, AUND.

12. On October 1, 1963, however, the second day of the second session, Cardinal Laurean Rugambwa of Tanzania made an intervention reminding the Council Fathers of the critical missionary function of the Church. See Yves Tourigny, W.F., "Birth of the Decree," *AFER* IX, no. 1 (January 1967): 5.

13. Tourigny, "Birth of the Decree," 5–14. The leading African voice was Cardinal Rugambwa. The only Ugandan bishop to speak on the Council floor at this time was Cyprian Kihangire, Auxiliary in Gulu and soon-to-be ordinary in Hoima. McCauley did not address the issue from the floor. For a fine summary of this initial debate on the mission schema see: Xavier Rynne, *Vatican Council II* (Maryknoll, NY: Orbis Books, 1968), 383–387.

14. Vincent McCauley, C.S.C., to Bishop Dennis Durning, 15 June 1965, 206.2, CHIEA, Archives Association of Member Episcopal Conferences in Eastern Africa, Nairobi (hereafter AAMECEA). McCauley wondered if some sort of lobby or active discussion with bishops would be advisable to save the traditional view in the final document.

15. Blomjous, "Whither the Missions?"

16. Ibid.

17. Report on the General Background of the Propagation of the Schema *De Activitate Missionale Ecclesiae*, March 6, 1965, 202.2, AMECEA Plenary Meetings, ADFP.

18. McCauley to Edward Heston, 30 May 1965.

19. McCauley to Edward Heston, 3 May 1965.

20. Vincent McCauley, C.S.C., "Findings of the Special Study Conference on the Schema, July 9, 1965, 202.2, AMECEA Plenary Meetings, ADFP.

21. Tourigny, "Birth of the Decree," 14–15; McCauley to Bishop Dennis Durning, 15 June 1965. McCauley's comment

about confirmation bore fruit in the final document. In *Ad Gentes* paragraphs 4 and 42 there are references to the Blessed Virgin Mary. Paragraph 11 reads: "The Church must be present in these groups through her children, who dwell among them or who are sent to them. For all Christians, wherever they live, are bound to show forth, by the example of their lives and by the witness of the word, that new man put on at Baptism and that power of the Holy Spirit by which they have been strengthened at Confirmation. Thus other men, observing their good works, can glorify the Father (cf. Mt 5:16) and can perceive more fully the real meaning of human life and the universal bond of the community of mankind."

22. Henri Valette interview.

23. John Keefe interview, April 7, 2006.

24. Vincent McCauley, C.S.C., Pastoral Letter to the Clergy, n.d. [1965], 401, Official Acts, Pastoral Letters, ADFP.

25. Vincent McCauley, C.S.C., priests' conference, 1968, 635.2, Priests' Meetings, ADFP.

26. Vincent McCauley, C.S.C., foreword to *Vatican II Documents*, March 1, 1966, AAK.

27. William Blum interview; John Croston interview, April 5, 2006. Heston was eminently qualified to give informed talks on Vatican II. During the first session of Vatican II, he served as the moderator of the American bishops' press panel. In sessions II, III, and IV he was director of the English language section of the Ecumenical Press Office. An expert in Latin, he attended all the Council sessions, made summaries of the discussions, and communicated this information to the press.

28. John Croston, C.S.C., to Howard Kenna, C.S.C., 26 July 1966, 35:4, Kenna Papers, AHCFI.

29. Robert Chaput, W.F., to Edward Heston, C.S.C., 17 September 1966, 267.76, FP 11, Holy Cross Generalate Papers, AUND.

30. Meeting minutes, Pastoral Commission, Diocese of Fort Portal, January 27, 1968, 480.2, Presbyteral Council Correspondence, ADFP.

31. Vincent McCauley, C.S.C., to Priests and Religious, 24 July 1965, 910.1 Bishop McCauley Papers, ADFP.

32. Vincent McCauley, C.S.C., to Dear Fathers, 12 May 1965, 910.1, Bishop McCauley Papers, ADFP. Later that same year, McCauley reasserted his authority by promulgating rubrics for the new Mass. He wrote, "These are the prescribed rubrics, hereby officially promulgated. The old rubrics are no longer to be used and no options to be introduced at Masses offered publicly in the Diocese of Fort Portal." See McCauley to Priests and Religious, 24 July 1965.

33. Meeting minutes, Senate of Priests, April 12, 1972, 480.2, Presbyteral Council Correspondence, 480.1, Presbyteral Council Correspondence, ADFP; McCauley to All the Priests, 30 October 1969.

34. Vincent McCauley, C.S.C., to Fathers and Religious, 24 May 1967, 910.1, Bishop McCauley Papers, ADFP.

35. Vincent McCauley, C.S.C., memorandum to the priests of the diocese, 3 May 1972, 641, Missionaries of Africa, ADFP.

36. George MacInnes, C.S.C., "The African Parish: Is There a Problem?" *AFER* XI, no. 3 (1969): 224.

37. Ibid., 220, 226–227, 233.

38. Yves Tourigny, W.F., "The Uganda Catholic Secretariat" (essay), November 24, 1982, 905.7, Tourigny Papers, AAK. The administrative structure of the UEC evolved and was made more complex with time. The secretariat served as the overseeing body for day-to-day operations for the various departments. The general secretary was responsible to the chairman of the UEC for daily operations. During McCauley's tenure as bishop of Fort Portal, the UEC comprised seven departments: Pastoral, Education, Medical, Social Services, Youth, Social Communication, and Lay

Apostolate. See Regulations of the Uganda Episcopal Conference, March 11, 1967, 210, UEC Regulations and Statutes, ADFP.

39. Vincent McCauley, C.S.C., to Archbishop A. Paullidrinni, 3 March 1967, 202.5. AMECEA Correspondence. ADFP.

40. Joseph Willigers, M.H.M., to the author, 12 March 2006.

41. Paul Kalanda to the author, 14 March 2006.

42. Robert Hesse interview; Banyatereza Sisters interview, January 28, 2006.

43. John Croston interview, July 7, 2005.

44. Vincent McCauley, C.S.C., to Joseph Kiwanuka, 24 August 1961, 200.4., Uganda Episcopal Conference, AAK.

45. Barnabas R. Halem 'Imana to Killian Flynn, O.F.M., Cap., 12 June 1967, 202.5, AMECEA Correspondence, ADFP; Regulations of the UEC Secretariat, September 15, 1969, 210, UEC Regulations and Statutes, ADFP; meeting minutes, Uganda Episcopal Conference, October 21, 1970, 202.2, AMECEA Plenary (misfiled), ADFP; S. C. Lea to Bishops' Executive Episcopal Conference, 25 June 1963, 200.5, Uganda Episcopal Conference, AAK.

46. Vincent McCauley, C.S.C., to Cardinal Jean Villot, 3 May 1972, 141 *Cor Unum*, ADFP. Villot was President of *Cor Unum*. Pope Paul VI established the Pontifical Council *Cor Unum* for Human and Christian Development in his letter *Amoris Officio* of July 15, 1971. The office's aims were (1) to assist the pope and be his instrument for carrying out special initiatives in the field of humanitarian actions when disasters occur, or in the field of integral human promotion; (2) to foster the catechesis of charity and encourage the faithful to give a concrete witness to evangelical charity; and (3) to encourage and coordinate the initiative of Catholic organizations through the exchange of information and by promoting fraternal cooperation in favor of integral human development.

47. Report of Brother Bartholomew, March 26, 1970, 203, Uganda Episcopal Conference, AAK; meeting minutes, Ecumenical Commission of the UEC, 203, Uganda Episcopal Conference, AAK.

48. Vincent McCauley, C.S.C., to Edward Heston, C.S.C., 13 May 1972, 224, UEC Social Communications Commission, ADFP.

49. Feasibility study for a central publishing house in Uganda, October 2, 1972, 224, UEC Social Communication Commission, ADFP; Sister Mary Connell, F.S.P., to Vincent McCauley, C.S.C., 17 February 1972, 224, UEC Social Communication Commission, ADFP.

50. Meeting minutes, Uganda Episcopal Conference, Social Communication Commission, May 11, 1970, 224, UEC Commissions, Social Communications, ADFP.

51. Meeting minutes, Uganda Hierarchy, October 10, 1961, 200.4, 208, Uganda Episcopal Conference, AAK; meeting minutes, Uganda Catholic Medical Bureau, December 15, 1966, 208, Uganda Episcopal Conference, AAK.

52. Meeting minutes, Uganda Catholic Medical Bureau, November 26, 1963, 208, Uganda Episcopal Conference, AAK.

53. Meeting minutes, Ecumenical Medical Conference, January 22–23, 1971, 208, Uganda Episcopal Conference, AAK.

54. Quoted in Tourigny, *So Abundant a Harvest*, 188–189.

55. Unsigned to Paul Marcinkas, n.d. [March 1969], 107, Pastoral Visits, ADFP.

56. Hastings, "The Church in Uganda," 239.

57. Meeting minutes, Catholic Secretariat of Uganda, March 21, 1969, 107, Pastoral Visits, ADFP; notes from meeting held on March 6, 1969, 107, Pastoral Visits, ADFP. The original members of the Episcopal Committee were Archbishop Nsubuga, chair, and Bishops Adrian Ddungu, James Odongo, and Cyprian Kihangire.

58. *Monitor* (San Francisco), August 7, 1969, 107, Pastoral Visits, ADFP.

59. Speech of the Anglican Archbishop of Uganda, Rwanda, and Burundi, August 2, 1969, The Secretariat for Promoting Christian Unity, Information Service No. 8, September 1969, 201.4, SECAM Newsletters, ADFP.

60. Tourigny, *So Abundant a Harvest*, 187; Paul Zoungrana, speech to SECAM, July 28, 1969, 201.3, SECAM Documentation; Vincent McCauley, C.S.C., chairman's report, August 3–10, 1970, AMECEA Plenary Session, 1970, 202.2, AMECEA Plenary, ADFP.

61. Symposium Bulletin I, no.1, n.d. [1976], 201.4, SECAM Newsletters, ADFP.

62. Ibid.

63. Tourigny, *So Abundant a Harvest*, 188.

64. Vincent McCauley, C.S.C., to Sergio Pignedoli, n.d. [1969], 201.1, SECAM Correspondence, ADFP; Vincent McCauley, C.S.C., to Amleto Poggi, 20 November 1968, 201.1, SECAM Correspondence, ADFP.

65. Record of the Symposium of the All Africa and Madagascar Bishops, Gaba Institute, Kampala, July 28–31, 1969, 201.2, SECAM Minutes, ADFP.

66. Ibid.; "The Clergy in Africa" (position paper), June 1, 1970, 201.2, SECAM Minutes, ADFP.

67. *Petit Echo* no. 601 (September–October 1969), AWFK.

68. Pope Paul VI, speech at Namugongo, August 2, 1969, Secretariat for Promoting Christian Unity, Information Service, No. 8, September 1969, 201.4, SECAM Newsletters, ADFP.

69. Vincent McCauley, C.S.C., to Adrian Ddungu, 31 August 1971; McCauley to Joseph Osei, 12 July 1971, 201.1, SECAM Correspondence, ADFP.

70. Joseph Osei to Vincent McCauley, C.S.C., 11 July 1971, 201.1, SECAM Correspondence, ADFP.

71. Paul Zoungrana to Vincent McCauley, C.S.C., 22 August 1969, 201.1, SECAM Correspondence, ADFP.

72. Acts of Second Plenary Assembly of SECAM, n.d. [1970], 201.3, SECAM Documentation, ADFP.

73. Ibid.; notes of meeting between Bishop McCauley and Father Flynn, September 29, 1969, 202.5, AMECEA Correspondence, ADFP.

74. Vincent McCauley, C.S.C., memorandum, 22 October 1969 [sic–1970], 201.1, SECAM Correspondence, ADFP.

75. Vincent McCauley, C.S.C., to Killian Flynn, O.F.M. Cap., 4 June 1970, unmarked box, AMECEA Correspondence, ADFP.

76. Meeting minutes, SECAM, August 18–28, 201.1, SECAM Correspondence, ADFP.

77. McCauley to Joseph Osei, 12 July 1971, 201.1, SECAM Correspondence, ADFP.

78. SECAM Third Plenary Central Committee Meeting, June 13, 1972, SG 174, SECAM Assemblies, Secretary General, AAMECEA.

79. SECAM Plenary Session, n.d. [1972], 201.2, SECAM Minutes, ADFP; Committee for African Internal Affairs: SECAM Interim Report (1972-1975), 201.2, SECAM Minutes, ADFP.

80. Meeting minutes, SECAM Standing Committee, December 4–7, 1972, SG 175, SECAM Standing Committee Minutes, Secretary General, AAMECEA. Joseph Healey, M.M., believes that McCauley's departure from SECAM was based on his consistent belief in Africanization. Thus, after serving to get the organization going, he desired to bow out in favor of an African. See Joseph Healey, M.M., interview with the author, October 2, 2006, AHCFI.

81. Vincent McCauley, C.S.C., to Joseph Osei, 5 August 1976, SG 174, SECAM Correspondence, Secretary General, AAMECEA.

82. Vincent McCauley, C.S.C., to Henri Valette, W.F., 21 May 1977 and 29 May 1978, SG 174, SECAM Correspondence, Secretary General, AAMECEA.

83. Vincent McCauley, C.S.C., to Joseph Osei, 5 May 1978, SG 174, SECAM Correspondence, Secretary General, AAMECEA.

84. Joseph Osei to Vincent McCauley, C.S.C., 5 March 1973 and 13 October 1977, SG 174, SECAM Correspondence, Secretary General, AAMECEA.

9. Transition and Resignation: 1969–1973

1. Some have suggested that McCauley's original choice to succeed him was Boniface Masiko, but when this priest was crippled from a motorcycle accident, he was forced to change, thus choosing Magambo.

2. Vincent McCauley, C.S.C., to Francis Sullivan, C.S.C., 13 January 1971, 910.1, Bishop McCauley Papers, ADFP.

3. Vincent McCauley, C.S.C., to Serapio Magambo, 25 October 1966, 470.2, Chancery Correspondence, ADFP.

4. Quoted in *The Rwenzori Echo* (July–August 1969), 745, Fort Portal Publications, AWFK.

5. Tourigny, *So Abundant a Harvest*, 192.

6. John Croston, C.S.C., to Father Frechet, 16 August 1969, 811, Doss. 3, Holy Cross Generalate Papers, AUND.

7. John Croston, C.S.C., to Howard Kenna, C.S.C., 8 January 1970, 35:6, Kenna Papers, AHCFI.

8. Vincent McCauley, C.S.C., to Harold Duffus, 1 October 1970, 910.1, Bishop McCauley Papers, ADFP.

9. Vincent McCauley, C.S.C., to Charles Walker, 26 February 1972, 910.1, Bishop McCauley Papers, ADFP.

10. Magambo, sermon.

11. Vincent McCauley, C.S.C., to Sergio Pignedoli, 20 February 1971, unmarked box, AMECEA Correspondence, ADFP.

12. Program, the Alpha Sigma Nu lecture, May 2, 1971, 910.1, Bishop McCauley Papers, ADFP.

13. Hastings, "The Church in Uganda," 243. More generically, the church-state situation in Africa was described in a position paper given at the 1970 SECAM Plenary Meeting in Abijan, Ivory Coast: "The relationship between Church and State varies from simple toleration in officially Muslim countries to full religious freedom and even strong Christian influence where Christians are the best organized single group. In general the State permits less and less religious privilege; the clergy cannot form power structures but must participate in the common national effort and assume the role of spiritual service to the society in which the Church lives." See Theo van Asten, "The Clergy in Africa" (position paper), June 19, 1970, 201.2, SECAM Minutes, ADFP.

14. Some of the issues that began to push Amin and Obote apart were (1) Obote failed to provide the army with new accommodations, vehicles, and equipment, (2) the government's failure to consult with the army on policy matters and promotions, (3) the alleged downgrading of the army in favor of the general service unit, and (4) discrimination against West Nile and Acholi officers in favor of officers from Obote's home region of Langi. See Jorgensen, *Uganda*, 268–269.

15. Mutibwa, *Uganda Since Independence*, 71–74, 78; Jorgensen, *Uganda*, 268–269.

16. Mutibwa, *Uganda Since Independence*, 78; "2 WF's Die in Uganda Military Coup," *White Fathers Magazine* (March 1, 1971): 6–7, Uganda Mission, Holy Cross Mission Center Papers, AHFCI.

17. Idi Amin to Archbishop Emmanuel Nsubuga, 22 June 1971, 641, Missionaries of Africa, ADFP.

18. Quoted in Amii Omara-Otunnu, *Politics and the Military in Uganda, 1890–1985* (London: Macmillan Press, 1987), 99.

19. Ibid., 92–93, 96–97.

20. Ibid., 93.

21. Quoted in Mutibwa, *Uganda Since Independence*, 81–83.

22. Tumusiime, *Uganda 30 Years*, 40–42.

23. Mutibwa, *Uganda Since Independence*, 85–87.

24. Joint Religious Council to Idi Amin Dada, 20 February 1971, 229, UEC Commissions, Joint Christian Council, ADFP.

25. *Uganda Drum* 14, no. 2 (June 1971), 450.1, *Uganda Drum*, AHCEA.

26. Francis Zagorc interview with James Connelly.

27. Vincent McCauley, C.S.C., to Sr. Mary Felicitas, B.V.M., 9 April 1971, 910.1, Bishop McCauley Papers, ADFP.

28. Vincent McCauley, C.S.C., to Mrs. Richard F. Mitchell, 25 January 1972, 910.1, Bishop McCauley Papers, ADFP.

29. Vincent McCauley, C.S.C., to Charles Walker, 13 May 1972, 910.1, Bishop McCauley Papers, ADFP.

30. F. J. Ravenhill, "Military Rule in Uganda: The Politics of Survival," *African Studies Review* 7, no 1 (April 1974): 250.

31. Mutibwa, *Uganda Since Independence*, 84–85.

32. Ibid., 100–101.

33. Tumusiime, *Uganda 30 Years*, 43; Mutibwa, *Uganda Since Independence*, 87–89.

34. Bert Adams and Mike Bristow, "The Politico-Economic Position of Ugandan Asians in the Colonial and Independent Eras." *Journal of Asian and African Studies* XIII, nos. 3–4 (1978): 157.

35. Ibid., 157, 158.

36. Idi Amin Dada, speech, December 8, 1971, *East Africa Journal* (1972): 2. Amin claimed that Allah had told him in a dream to expel all Asians from Uganda.

37. Eventually Amin even forced Asians who were Ugandan citizens to leave the country.

38. Ravenhill, "Military Rule in Uganda," 245. A few illustrative statistics about the economic downturn were: between 1971 and 1978 production of products plummeted significantly—cement–85 percent, sheets–87 percent, steel ingredients–55

percent, corrugated iron and roofing–94 percent, blankets–88 percent. See Jorgensen, *Uganda*, 294–298.

39. Cardinal Emmanuel Nusbuga to The President of Uganda [Idi Amin], 12 August 1972, 201.2, SECAM Minutes, ADFP.

40. Omara-Otunnu, *Politics and the Military in Uganda*, 111; Jorgensen, *Uganda*, 306; Donald Anthony Low, "Uganda Unhinged," *International Affairs* (London) 49, no. 2 (April 1973): 226.

41. Still, the Seventh Day Adventists operated many excellent free medical clinics. Other Protestant denominations provided important services, despite Amin's edict. See Robert Malone interview, March 20, 2006.

42. Kevin Ward "Catholic–Protestant Relations in Uganda: An Historical Perspective," *African Theological* Journal 13, no. 3: 182.

43. Vincent McCauley, C.S.C., to Marianne Bold, 7 July 1975, SG 88, Misso, Secretary General, AAMECEA.

44. Mutibwa, *Uganda Since Independence*, 112. Luwum was killed in a staged accident. The ostensible reason for the murder was a letter from the Church of Uganda to Amin asking that he loosen his grip on the Christian churches.

45. James Ferguson interview; James Ferguson, C.S.C., interview with James Connelly, C.S.C., May 19, 1980, AHCFI.

46. Arnold Fell, C.S.C., to Relatives of Holy Cross Priests and Brothers in Uganda, 10 November 1973, Uganda Mission, Holy Cross Mission Center Papers, AHCFI. Much of Amin's anti-American rhetoric was due to the United States's support for Israel, a nation Amin had rejected. At the time, however, Fell stated that John Keefe, C.S.C., superior of the mission, had informed the former that he did not see any direct danger to Holy Cross religious in the country.

47. Under the statutes of the congregation, all provinces and districts meet in chapter every three years to discuss issues and elect (as necessary) those for leadership positions.

48. East Africa District Chapter Decrees and Recommendations, January 1973, 401.1, District Chapter Legislation, AHCEA.

49. The Congregation of Holy Cross is divided into geographic provinces and districts. Provinces are autonomous; districts are responsible to their parent province. In 1973 (and today as well), the District of East Africa is under the jurisdiction of the Indiana Province. Thus, all its chapter legislation must be reviewed and approved by the provincial chapter.

50. Proceedings of Provincial Chapter, 1973, Recommendation #5, Provincial Chapter Papers, AHCFI. This incident is an illustration of the somewhat disconnected relationship between the Indiana Province and the District of East Africa. John Keefe, C.S.C., claims that the provincial administration generally had little contact with the dictrict. All administrative matters were handled directly from the Foreign Mission Society, headed by Father Arnold Fell, C.S.C., headquartered in Washington, D.C. See John Keefe interview, April 11, 2006.

51. Connelly, "Holy Cross in East Africa," 26–27. All three goals set by the 1976 District Chapter were met. In September 1977, Thomas McDermott, C.S.C., a seminarian, came for a regency year program. In July 1978, Fathers William Blum, C.S.C., and James Rahilly, C.S.C., arrived in Nairobi to live and work in Dandora Parish. In 1979, the Congregation of Holy Cross welcomed its first native African candidate.

52. McCauley, "Holy Cross in Africa."

53. John Croston to Howard Kenna, 24 April 1968.

54. Vincent McCauley, C.S.C., to Edward Heston, C.S.C., 13 August 1968, 267.76, FPS, Holy Cross Generalate Papers, AUND.

55. Vincent McCauley, C.S.C., to Germain Lalande, C.S.C., 11 March 1970, 811, Doss. 3, Holy Cross Generalate Papers, AUND.

56. Cardinal Emmanuel Nsubuga to Cardinal Angelo Rossi, 18 April 1972, 209.2, Uganda Episcopal Conference, AAK.

57. Vincent McCauley, C.S.C., to Nora McCarthy, 1 December 1972, 910.1, Bishop McCauley Papers, ADFP; Vincent McCauley, C.S.C., to Mrs. Vallie Kumalac, 14 December 1972, 910.1, Bishop McCauley Papers, ADFP.

58. Vincent McCauley, C.S.C., to Sergio Pignedoli, n.d. [1972], unmarked box, AMECEA Correspondence, ADFP.

59. Quoted in *The Rwenzori Echo* (January 1973): 8, 801.51, *Rwenzori Echo*, ΛΗСΕΛ.

60. Quoted in Tourigny, *So Abundant a Harvest*, 200.

61. Thomas Kisembo to Vincent McCauley, C.S.C., 28 December 1972, 480.2, Presbyterial Council Correspondence, ADFP.

62. John Croston interview, July 7, 2005.

63. Thomas Smith interview.

64. Joseph Willigers, M.H.M., to the author, 12 March 2006.

65. George Lucas, C.S.C., sees McCauley's resignation as consistent with the independence drive, Africanization, and the attempt by the Ugandan government to remove expatriates who were simply holding on and give the positions to Africans. Louis Rink, C.S.C., suggests that McCauley's popularity forced the government to pressure his resignation as the only means to snuff out his influence. Speaking of possible reasons for McCauley's resignation, Thomas Smith, C.S.C., has suggested, "I think the pressures of 1972—Amin's increasing rhetoric against Westerners and his advance of Arab culture—would have an effect." Henri Valette, W.F., has stated that Amin's targeting of Americans must be at least partially responsible for McCauley's decision to resign when he did. See George Lucas interview; Louis Rink interview, April 24, 2006; Thomas Smith interview.

66. "The Living Dead Bishop," *The Rwenzori Echo* 2, no. 1 (January–February 1983): 11–12.

67. John Croston interview, July 7, 2005. James Ferguson agrees with Croston that neither nationalism nor government pressure were factors in McCauley's resignation. See James Ferguson interview. It is interesting to note that Croston did indicate McCauley was somewhat pressured, but from a nationalism/Africanization perspective. When Magambo was made auxiliary in Fort Portal he wrote, "We are happy with the choice and it will pose no problem to work with Bishop Magambo when Bishop McCauley steps down. In that we are the smallest Diocese and have two Bishops, this may force Bishop McCauley to step up his time-table to field some pretty hot questions." See John Croston, C.S.C., to Howard Kenna, C.S.C., 17 July 1969, 35:6, Kenna Papers, AHCFI.

68. John Keefe, C.S.C., interview with the author, April 9, 2006, AHCFI; Francis Zagorc interview.

69. Stephen Gibson interview.

70. For reasons that are not extant, Amin attended the installation. Most likely he was invited to demonstrate the practice of Africanization. He gave McCauley $100 as a gift.

71. Quoted in *The Rwenzori Echo* (January 1973): 16, 810.51, *Rwenzori Echo*, AHCEA.

10. Chairman of AMECEA: 1964–1973

1. Tourigny, *So Abundant a Harvest*, 186.

2. "Short History of AMECEA—1961–1973," n.d., AMECEA History, AAMECEA.

3. Ibid.; Joseph Kelly, C.S.S.p., "AMECEA's Forward-Looking Chairman," AFER 26 nos. 1–2 (February–April 1986): 13. The subtitle for the study conference was: "Looking Toward an Indigenous Church in Independent African States with a Pluralistic Society, and Considering Fields for Cooperation Between Hierarchies, as well as the Church's Special Interest in Education." Besides Blomjous, the other members of the steering committee

were Archbishop Del Mestri and representatives of the five national episcopal conferences.

4. Ibid.; John Mutiso-Mbinda, "AMECEA Bishops' Consultations," AFER 26, nos. 1–2 (February–April 1986): 17.

5. AMECEA Review of First Seven Years, n.d. [1968], 202.3,
AMECEA Plenary Meetings, ADFP.

6. Vincent McCauley, C.S.C., to Bishop William G. Connare,
16 July 1967, 202.5, AMECEA Correspondence, ADFP.

7. The nine paper topics were (1) "The African Diocesan
Priest," (2) "The Pastoral Work of the Indigenous Church," (3)
"The Church and Other Religious Groups," (4) "Church and
State," (5) "The Church and the School," (6) "The Church and the
Teacher," (7) "The Church and Social Justice," (8) "The Church
and the Mass Media of Communications," and (9) "Fields for
Cooperation Between the Hierarchies." See "Short History of
AMECEA—1961–1973," n.d., AMECEA History, AAMECEA
and Kelly, "AMECEA's Forward-Looking Chairman," 13.

8. "Short History of AMECEA—1961–1973." The original
representatives to ITEBEA were Bishops Billington (Uganda),
Blomjous (Tanganyika), Cavallera (Kenya), Hardmann (Malawi),
and Archbishop Kozlowiecki (Zambia).

9. Guido Del Mestri to Your Excellencies, 3 October 1961,
200.4 Uganda Episcopal Conference, AAK; meeting minutes,
ITEBEA, September 12–14, 1961, ITEBEA Board and Plenary
Meetings, 1961–1964, Secretary General, AAMECEA.

10. Meeting minutes, ITEBEA, November 20, 1962,
ITEBEA Board and Plenary Meetings, 1961–1964, Secretary
General, AAMECEA.

11. Report of the AMECEA Representatives to Misereor, February 7, 1979, SG 89, Misereor, Secretary General, AAMECEA.

12. H. Goetz to Vincent McCauley, C.S.C., 3 September
1969, 720.5 Misereor, ADFP.

13. Vincent McCauley, C.S.C., to H. Goetz, 13 September
1969, 720.5, Misereor, ADFP. McCauley continually expressed

gratitude for the efforts of the German bishops to financially assist the Africa mission. One typical comment is illustrative: "Your decision to set up a common fund for pastoral projects is, I believe, unique in the world. I am sure that the missionaries in developing countries will be greatly heartened to hear that you are making special efforts to assist them in their vital need." See Vincent McCauley, C.S.C., to Msgr. Wilhelm Wissing, 11 November 1971, unmarked box, AMECEA Correspondence, ADFP.

14. Meeting minutes, ITEBEA, November 17, 1963 and November 23, 1963, ITEBEA Board and Plenary Meetings, 1961–1964, Secretary General, AAMECEA.

15. "AMECEA Milestones," *AFER* 26, nos. 1–2 (February–April 1986): 8; chairman's report, AMECEA Plenary Session, September 4–11, 1967, AMECEA Plenary Session, 1967, Secretary General, AAMECEA.

16. While the executive board had met in 1962 and 1963, no plenary session of ITEBEA had been held since the inaugural 1961 meeting at Dar es Salaam.

17. Report on the Plenary Meeting of the Bishops of Eastern Africa, November 4, 1964, 202.2, AMECEA Plenary Session, ADFP.

18. At the 1967 plenary, the name was shortened to Association of the Episcopal Conferences in Eastern Africa, but the acronym AMECEA was kept because it was well known. Later the original title was restored. See notes AMECEA Third Plenary, September 1967, 202, AMECEA Regulations, ADFP. It is important to note that AMECEA was restricted in its jurisdiction. The 1964 constitution read: "The Association is not an Episcopal Conference or legislative organ as contemplated by ecclesiastical law. The resolutions adopted at meetings of the Association do not have in themselves the force of law." See AMECEA Constitution, November 4, 1964, 202, AMECEA Regulations, ADFP.

19. "Short History of AMECEA—1961–1973." The new executive board was Vincent McCauley (Uganda), Gervais

Nkalanga (West Tanganyika), Eberhart Spiess (East Tanganyika), William Dunne (Kenya), Nicholas Agnozzi, O.F.M. Cap. (Zambia), and Jean Louis Jobidan, W.F. (Malawi).

20. Vincent McCauley, C.S.C., chairman's report, AMECEA 1967, 202.5, AMECEA Correspondence, ADFP.

21. Laurean Rugambwa to Maurice Otunga, 17 June 1970, 204.1, AMECEA Secretariat Correspondence, ADFP.

22. Vincent McCauley, C.S.C., to Mother Benedict, 6 October 1964, 526.1, Virika Hospital, ADFP; McCauley to H. Goetz, 13 September 1969.

23. Report on the Plenary Meeting of the Bishops of Eastern Africa, November 4, 1964, 202.2, AMECEA Plenary Sessions, ADFP; meeting minutes, AMECEA Plenary Meetings, November 12, 1964, 202.2, AMECEA Plenary Sessions, ADFP.

24. AMECEA Plenary Meetings, November 12, 1964, 202.2, AMECEA Plenary Sessions, ADFP.

25. Statutes of AMECEA, n.d., 202, AMECEA Regulations, ADFP.

26. Kelly, "AMECEA's Forward-Looking Chairman," 12.

27. Chairman's report, AMECEA Plenary, September 4–11, 1967, AMECEA Plenary Sessions, Secretary General, AAMECEA.

28. "Short History of AMECEA—1961–1973." The 1929 Instruction was still in effect in 1964. It entrusted mission dioceses to the care of missionary institutes. The time was right to make dioceses independent of mission congregations; thus the instruction needed to change. The re-draft was submitted to the Propaganda Fide.

29. Chairman's report, AMECEA Plenary, September 4–11, 1967. Joseph Healey interview.

30. Chairman's report AMECEA Plenary, September 4–11, 1967.

31. Ibid.

32. Joseph Kelly, C.S.S.p., AMECEA Documentation Service, "Proposal for Establishing," April 17, 1972, 202.4, AMECEA Documentation, ADFP.

33. Vincent McCauley to Bishop William G. Connare, 16 July 1967. Nothing happened initially with McCauley's efforts with the American bishops. Eventually in 2001, the United States Catholic Conference of Bishops (USCC) published *A Call to Solidarity with Africa*. The document stated: "Responding to the call of the church in Africa, as pastors in the United States we recognize the mutual bonds of solidarity that unite us—bonds that have been forged through the life, death and resurrection of Jesus Christ. We stand in solidarity with the Church and the peoples of Africa, to recognize and support their courageous commitment to peace, justice and reconciliation." In November 2004, an ad hoc committee for the Church in Africa was founded.

34. Minutes of Extraordinary Meeting of AMECEA Executive Board, January 25–26, 1967, 202.3, AMECEA Executive Board, ADFP; John Mutiso-Mbinda, "AMECEA Bishops' Consultations," 18.

35. "Short History of AMECEA—1961–1973." The seven papers were (1) "Episcopal Authority and Modern Pastoral Problems," (2) "The Pastoral Council and Other Aspects of Diocesan Organizations," (3) "Re-evaluation of Pastoral Agencies and Methods of Evangelization and Consolidation," (4) "Discussion Points from the Priestly Formation Seminar at Katigondo," (5) "Ecumenism in Africa," (6) "Marriage and Customs," and (7) "The Government of the Young Churches."

36. The General Secretariat, composed of the secretary-general and the heads of AMECEA Departments, was given the following mandates: (1) serve as an organ for the exchange of information and experience, (2) serve as an organ for contact and collaboration between member conferences, (3) execute mandates of plenary sessions and executive board decisions, (4) establish and maintain relations with similar associations, and (5) carry out studies and

research on problems common to member conferences. See Statutes of AMECEA, n.d., 202, AMECEA Regulations, ADFP.

37. Joseph Healey interview. Joseph Glynn, M.M., the
regional superior for Maryknoll in East Africa, was asked at the
1967 AMECEA plenary if Maryknoll had a trained priest for
social communications. Joseph Healey, M.M., ordained in 1966,
had received training at the University of Missouri in international
communication for future assignment to East Africa. He was the
natural selection for the AMECEA post.

38. "Short History of AMECEA—1961–1973"; Fortunatus
Lukanima, "AMECEA's Social Communication Department,"
AFER 26, nos. 1–2 (February–April 1986): 55.

39. Joseph Kelly, C.S.S.p., "A Gentleman Bishop Sharing
Christ's Daily Cross," (unpublished essay).

40. Joseph Kelly, C.S.S.p., AMECEA Documentation Service,
"Proposal for Establishing."

41. Vincent McCauley, C.S.C., memorandum, 5 June 1973,
unmarked box, AMECEA Correspondence, ADFP.

42. Joseph Gremillon to Vincent McCauley, C.S.C., 10
August 1967, 202.5, AMECEA Correspondence, ADFP.

43. Proposal to Set Up a Justice and Peace Commission in East
Africa, n.d. [1967], 202.5, AMECEA Correspondence, ADFP.

44. Chairman's report AMECEA Plenary Session, August
9–10, 1970, AMECEA 1970, Secretary General, AAMECEA.
The justice and peace desk, a branch of the pastoral department,
was established in 2002. It has several goals: (1) the establishment of a network of the justice and peace commissions in the
AMECEA region and the formation of a global African justice
and peace network, (2) capacity for building and supporting the
formation of new justice and peace commissions where they do
not exist yet, (3) formation programs on justice and peace and
social teaching in order to create awareness about these issues
and foster a commitment to them, (4) building a culture of peace
and working toward the resolution of conflicts in the region, (5)

developing and fostering a spirituality of justice and peace, (6) fostering the commitment of the Church and Christians to live the preferential option for the poor, (7) lobbying regional and international organizations to make the voice of the Church heard on issues influencing the life of the people in the AMECEA region, (8) networking and supporting the justice and peace commissions and dioceses working with refugees, (9) the formation of pastoral agents working with refugees, and (10) giving information on and analyzing issues related to justice and peace affecting the region.

45. Vincent McCauley, C.S.C., "Some Thoughts in Advance of Our Meeting in Fort Portal," n.d. [1970], unmarked box, AMECEA Correspondence, ADFP. McCauley wrote, "If [Cardinal] Zoungrana persists with the Second All-Africa [Conference] in 1970 none of the epis[copal] conf[erence] chairmen or appointees to that meeting in West Africa will come to the AMECEA Plenary."

46. "Short History of AMECEA—1961–1973." The position papers were (1) "The Theology and Sociology of the Priesthood," (2) "Solutions in the Shortage of Priests," (3) "Priestly Ministry, Rural and Urban," (4) "Vocations and Junior Seminaries," and (5) "Major Seminary Adaptation."

47. Vincent McCauley, C.S.C., to Cardinal Agostino Bea, S.J., 4 August 1967, 202.5, AMECEA Correspondence, ADFP. McCauley also corresponded with J. G. M. Willebrands, secretary for the Secretariat for promoting Christian Unity, pushing the idea of a Joint Ecumenical Council for Eastern Africa. See J. G. M. Willebrands to Vincent McCauley, C.S.C., 22 August 1967, 202.5, AMECEA Correspondence, ADFP.

48. The position papers were (1) "Principles of Ecumenism," (2) "Social Position," (3) "Education in Ecumenism," (4) "Joint Prayers, Mixed Marriages, Baptism (Recognition of Protestants)," and (5) "AMECEA Commitment to the WCC and Other Protestant Bodies." See notes of meeting between Bishop McCauley

and Father Flynn, September 29, 1969, 202.5 AMECEA Correspondence, ADFP.

49. Killian Flynn, O.F.M., Cap., to Chairman of Episcopal Conferences of Kenya, Malawi, Tanzania, Uganda, and Zambia, 27 October 1969, unmarked box, AMECEA Correspondence, ADFP.

50. In early December 1969, McCauley reported that some of the position papers had not been received. Additionally Tom Stransky was elected superior general of the Paulists, creating a vacuum in the secretariat, resulting in insufficient attention and preparation for the proposed January meeting at Langata. Thus, McCauley was forced to write, "Most regretfully, I have no alternative but to give notice today to all concerned that the seminar cannot take place on the dates specified." See Vincent McCauley, C.S.C., to Tom Stransky, C.S.P., 2 December 1969, unmarked box, AMECEA Correspondence, ADFP.

51. *Petit Echo* no. 609 (1970): 250, AWFK. The Protestant observers were Samuel Amissah of the All Africa Conference of Churches, John Gatu, secretary-general of the Presbyterian Church of East Africa, and John Thompson, council for religious education of the Association for the Teaching of Christian Churches.

52. Ibid.

53. Short report on the Seminar on Ecumenism Held in Nairobi from March 31 to April 4, 1970, n.d. [1970], 204.1, AMECEA Secretariat Correspondence, ADFP.

54. *Petit Echo* no. 609: 250–251.

55. Vincent McCauley, C.S.C., chairman's report, AMECEA Plenary Session, August 3–10, 202.2, AMECEA Plenary Sessions, ADFP.

56. Cardinal John Willebrands to Vincent McCauley, C.S.C., 1 June 1970, 204.1, AMECEA Secretariat, ADFP.

57. "The Church and Development" (seminar, December 1–4, 1970, Limuru, Kenya), 202.5, AMECEA Documentation, ADFP.

The topics discussed included: (1) theology of development, (2) nature of the partnership between governments and church in the matter of development, (3) roles of government, hierarchy, and the laity in socio-economic development, (4) how the Church should organize its development planning, (5) Church-sponsored private institutions in development, and (6) relationship of episcopal commissions and other Church private agencies in development planning and implementation.

58. AMECEA Documentation Service, January 30, 1974, 202.4, AMECEA Documentation Service, ADFP.

59. Vincent McCauley, C.S.C., to Members of the AMECEA Executive Board, 1 November 1969, 202.5, AMECEA Correspondence, ADFP.

60. Sergio Pignedoli to Vincent McCauley, C.S.C., 9 December 1969, 202.5, AMECEA Correspondence, ADFP.

61. Vincent McCauley, C.S.C., to Sergio Pignedoli, 16 December 1969, 202.5, AMECEA Correspondence, ADFP.

62. Vincent McCauley, C.S.C., to My Lords [Bishops of AMECEA Executive Board], 202.5, AMECEA Correspondence, ADFP.

63. Vincent McCauley, C.S.C., to Pierluigi Sartorelli, 25 June 1970, unmarked box, AMECEA Correspondence, ADFP.

64. Vincent McCauley, C.S.C., chairman's report, AMECEA Plenary Session, August 3–10, 1970, 202.2 AMECEA Plenary Session, ADFP.

65. Dominic Conway to Vincent McCauley, C.S.C., 10 June 1970, unmarked box, AMECEA Correspondence, ADFP.

66. McCauley, chairman's report, August 3–10.

67. Minutes of Emergency Meeting of AMECEA Executive Board, September 29, 1970, 202.3, AMECEA Executive Board, ADFP. The reference to the All Africa Bishops' Symposium demonstrates how much SECAM depended upon AMECEA in its initial days.

68. Joseph Mukwaya interview.

69. Vincent McCauley, C.S.C., to Sergio Pignedoli, 20 September 1971, unmarked box, AMECEA Correspondence, ADFP.

70. See "An Influential Bishop: 1961–1973," note 46.

71. Vincent McCauley, C.S.C., to Killian Flynn, O.F.M. Cap., 4 April 1972, 141 *Cor Unum*, ADFP.

72. Minutes of AMECEA Executive Board, July 17–18, 1974, 202.3, AMECEA Executive Board, ADFP.

73. Vincent McCauley, C.S.C., to Missio, 21 March 1972, 720.3 Missio, ADFP.

74. Vincent McCauley, C.S.C., chairman's report, December 12–13, 1973, AMECEA Plenary 1973; Vincent McCauley, C.S.C., to James Odongo, 10 February 1976, SG 10, Executive Board, Secretary General, AAMECEA.

75. Memorandum "Establishment of a Catechetical College," 23 February 1966, SG 102, AMECEA Pastoral Institute, Secretary General, AAMECEA.

76. Ton Simons, W.F., memorandum, "Establishment of a Catechetical Pastoral Institute for East and Central Africa," June 1966, SG 21, AMECEA Pastoral Institute, Secretary General, AAMECEA.

77. Meeting minutes, AMECEA Executive Board, September 8, 1966, AMECEA Executive Board, ADFP.

78. Statutes of Establishment, Pastoral Institute of Eastern Africa, September 4, 1967, 206.1, AMECEA, CHIEA, ADFP.

79. Ibid.

80. Joseph Healey interview. Healey stated that McCauley had a vision for the catechetical training of personnel and Gaba was to be his flagship project.

81. Emmanuel Nsubuga to Vincent McCauley, C.S.C., 15 November 1966, SG 21, AMECEA Pastoral Institute, Secretary General, AAMECEA. The two stipulations made by Nsubuga were (1) the rector of the Katigondo seminary must assure there is room for Gaba seminarians, and (2) ownership of the buildings

and land remains with the archdiocese. If the institute leaves, all reverts back to the archdiocese.

82. "Short History of AMECEA—1961–1973."

83. Vincent McCauley, C.S.C., to James Smith, W.F., 12 July 1967, 205, AMECEA Pastoral Institute, Secretary General, AAMECEA.

84. Guido del Mestri to Vincent McCauley, C.S.C., 20 August 1967, 205, AMECEA pastoral institute, ADFP; Vincent McCauley, C.S.C., to Dominic Conway (Propaganda Fide), 12 June 1968, 205, AMECEA pastoral institute, ADFP. According to records, $20,000 was secured in August 1967 and $10,000 in June 1968.

85. Pamphlet, AMECEA, McCauley File, Holy Cross Mission Center Papers, AHCFI. Part I of the ten-month course was a basic overview of African pastoral anthropology, scripture, pastoral theology, liturgy, and religious education. Part II concentrated on select themes and problems studied in a more pragmatic and less theoretical approach.

86. James Ferguson interview. Ferguson was the first member of Holy Cross to attend Gaba.

87. The faculty members were Ton Simons, W.F., principal; Aylward Shorter, W.F., African Anthropology; Sr. Gertrude Maley, M.M., Methodology; G. Heuthorst, M.H.M., Scripture. Miss Frances Scott was the institute's librarian. The Board of Governors consisted of elected members of AMECEA's executive board, the local ordinary, secretary-general of AMECEA, and the director of Gaba. Statutes of AMECEA Pastoral Institute, September 4, 1967, as amended in 1972 and 1976, 202, AMECEA Regulations, ADFP and Adrian B. Smith, "Africa's New Pastoral Institute," *AFER* IX no. 4 (October 1967): 319.

88. Vincent McCauley, C.S.C., to To Whom it May Concern, 22 February 1972, 206.1, AMECEA, CHIEA, ADFP.

89. This recognition was never received. Today Gaba, located in Eldoret, Kenya, is affiliated with the Catholic University of Eastern Africa (CUEA).

90. Meeting minutes, Uganda Episcopal Conference, April 20–24, 1971, 206.2, AMECEA, CHIEA, ADFP; Vincent McCauley, C.S.C., to Ferdinand Luthiger, 22 March 1972, 206.2, AMECEA, CHIEA, ADFP; "Short History of AMECEA—1961–1973." *The African Ecclesial Review* (*AFER*) was started in 1959 by Father J. Geerdes and published in Kisubi, Uganda. In 1964, the bishops of AMECEA agreed that *AFER* should come under the responsibility of AMECEA and appointed a board responsible for the journal's overall policy. In 1967, at the AMECEA plenary session, the bishops approved the statutes of *AFER* and agreed that responsibility and control for the journal should be transferred to an *AFER* board of directors appointed by AMECEA. Finally in August 1971, control over *AFER* was given to the Gaba Institute.

91. Joseph Healey interview.

92. Pastoral Institute of Eastern Africa (PIEA) report of the director, n.d. [1971], 206.1, AMECEA, CHIEA, ADFP.

93. Ton Simons, W.F., to Vincent McCauley, 10 January 1971, 205, AMECEA Pastoral Institute, ADFP.

94. PIEA report of the director.

95. Ton Simons, W.F., to AMECEA Executive Board, 19 June 1971, 204.1, AMECEA Secretariat Correspondence, ADFP.

96. Ton Simons, W.F., to Vincent McCauley, C.S.C., 16 August 1971, 206.1 AMECEA, CHIEA, ADFP.

97. McCauley to To Whom it May Concern, 22 February 1972; McCauley to Gerard Laliberte, W.F., 24 June 1970, 204.1, AMECEA Secretariat Correspondence, ADFP. McCauley constructed the story that Simons was ill to cover a difficult situation. He wrote to Robert Chaput, W.F., about Simon's "strange and erratic behavior." McCauley was concerned that scandal might arise. He continued, "Ton is a disturbed man. We must help him

and try to save him as a priest." Joseph Healey, M.M., claims that Simons was planning to leave the priesthood. See Vincent McCauley, C.S.C., to Robert Chaput, W.F., 11 January 1972, 206.1, AMECEA, CHIEA, ADFP and Joseph Healey interview.

98. Vincent McCauley, C.S.C., to the Larsen Family, 6 July 1975, PPMJL.

99. Meeting minutes, AMECEA Executive Board, August 11, 1972, 206.1, AMECEA, CHIEA, ADFP. It should be noted that the problem of finding qualified Africans to serve in Gaba positions persisted for some time. A triennial report (1977–1979) showed that for the first eleven years of the institute (1968–1979) only six of thirty-seven priests and religious who were Gaba staff members were Africans. The report stated, "These figures reveal a situation which leaves some doubt with regard to the seriousness with which the AMECEA Bishops and religious Superiors accept the importance of Africanization of their Pastoral Institute's staff. Certainly a better balance between African and non-African personnel could be reached." See Gaba Triennial Report 1977–1979, 206.1, AMECEA, CHIEA, ADFP.

100. John Lemay, W.F., to Serapio Magambo, June 12, 1973, 206.1, AMECEA, CHIEA, ADFP. Lemay wrote, "I wanted . . . to give you a solid assurance that there is no risk at all in sending students to Gaba. The conditions in Uganda are increasingly stable."

101. Vincent McCauley, C.S.C., to All AMECEA Bishops, 2 July 1975, 206.1, AMECEA, CHIEA, ADFP.

102. Report of the meeting to discuss transfer of ownership of Loreto Convent, Eldoret, Kenya, July 2, 1975, 206.1, AMECEA, CHIEA, ADFP.

103. Gaba Triennial Report 1977–1979, 206.1, AMECEA, CHIEA, ADFP. Since the Gaba facility was no longer used, the institute took the name AMECEA Pastoral Institute.

104. Vincent McCauley, C.S.C., to Bishops of the Uganda Episcopal Conference, 16 October 1969, 901.1, Bishop McCauley Papers, ADFP.

105. McCauley, chairman's report, August 3–10, 1970. McCauley continued to heap praise on Gaba, stating, "that the reputation of the AMECEA Pastoral Institute has spread throughout the world." See Secretary General to the AMECEA Plenary, n.d. [1977], 202.2, AMECEA Plenary Meetings, ADFP.

106. Vincent McCauley resigned his official duties with AMECEA in 1979, but a very exciting and interesting evolution of the institute's programming occurred the next year. In 1980, the institute's residential course was suspended in lieu of the Gaba staff offering specialized programs on location in each of the AMECEA countries. The programs were integrative of scripture, anthropology, theology, religious education, and communication, as was the residential course. This idea had been initially proposed by the institute's board of governors in 1978 and endorsed by the AMECEA plenary session in 1979. Seven courses, of varied durations, were offered. The program was highly successful. A report read, "The year has been a very positive experience from the viewpoint of both the Gaba staff and of the participants in the five countries. This would seem to imply that short courses should become a regular feature of the Gaba format." See John Lemay, W.F., to All AMECEA Bishops, 30 October 1979, 206.1 AMECEA, CHIEA, ADFP; PIEA report on the 1980 Programs, n.d. [1981], 206.1 AMECEA, CHIEA, ADFP.

107. AMECEA Documentation Service, January 10, 1975 and June 22, 1977, AAMECEA; "AMECEA Milestones," July 1979, 202.3, AMECEA Plenary Sessions, ADFP.

108. John Mutiso-Mbinda to Vincent McCauley, C.S.C., 30 January 1979, SG 21, AMECEA Research Department, Secretary General, AAMECEA; progress report, n.d. [1983], SG 21, AMECEA Research Department, Secretary General, AAMECEA.

11. Secretary General of AMECEA: 1973–1979

1. Matt Campbell to Vincent McCauley, 18 July 1968, 202.5, AMECEA Correspondence, ADFP; Vincent McCauley, C.S.C., to Stanley Lea, W.F., 27 March 1967, 641, Missionaries of Africa, ADFP.

2. Minutes of Emergency Meeting of AMECEA Executive Board, January 29, 1970, 202.3, AMECEA Executive Board, ADFP. Since McCauley represented Uganda, Flynn represented Zambia, and the AMECEA headquarters was in Kenya, it was hoped that a qualified candidate could be found from Tanzania or Malawi.

3. Vincent McCauley, C.S.C., to Members of the Executive Board of AMECEA, 8 May 1968, 202.5, AMECEA Correspondence, ADFP. The original vote of the bishops was fifty-one to two in favor of placing Flynn forward to be named a bishop. However, when the Kenyan bishops unanimously voted no, McCauley drew back. Interestingly, only three years later, in 1971, Archbishop Maurice Otunga of Nairobi wrote McCauley that the annual Episcopal Conference Meeting in Nairobi had voted unanimously that Flynn should be granted "Episcopal Dignity." See Archbishop Maurice Otunga to Vincent McCauley, C.S.C., 17 November 1971, unmarked box, AMECEA Correspondence, ADFP.

4. Laurean Rugambwa to Killian Flynn, 4 July 1970, 202.5, AMECEA Correspondence, ADFP.

5. Vincent McCauley, C.S.C., to Your Grace, 2 March 1970, unmarked box, AMECEA Correspondence, ADFP.

6. Vincent McCauley, C.S.C., to Laurean Rugumbwa, 4 March 1972, unmarked box, AMECEA Correspondence, ADFP.

7. Ibid.; minutes of AMECEA Executive Board Annual Meeting, August 11, 1972, 202.3, AMECEA Executive Board, ADFP. Healey served in this temporary capacity "in name only"; it was short-lived. His task was "to hold down the fort." Joseph Healey interview.

8. Healey, "Two AMECEA Giants," 23.

9. Vincent McCauley, C.S.C., chairman's report, AMECEA Plenary Session, December 14–21, 1973, 202.3, AMECEA Plenary Meetings, ADFP.

10. Vincent McCauley, C.S.C., to P. Bosa, 23 December 1972, 910.1, Bishop McCauley Papers, ADFP. Many were elated that McCauley would stay in Eastern Africa. His friend from SECAM, Joseph Osei, wrote, "I am very happy that you are still with us and very much in the thick of the battle, just where action is needed; and that's where you belong." See Joseph Osei to Vincent McCauley, C.S.C., 5 March 1973, SG 174, SECAM Correspondence, Secretary General AAMECEA.

11. Meeting minutes, AMECEA Executive Board, January 15–16, 1973, 202.3, AMECEA Executive Board, ADFP.

12. Vincent McCauley, C.S.C., to Mr. and Mrs. Joseph Dellere, 30 December 1972, 910.1, Bishop McCauley Papers, ADFP. McCauley took the secretary general position contingent, "on the condition that they give me a qualified African to train." See Vincent McCauley, C.S.C., to Dick and Joanie Larsen, 4 February 1973, PPMJL

13. Joseph Healey interview.

14. Joseph Willigers, M.H.M., to the author, 12 March 2006.

15. Charles Schleck to the author, 6 August 2005.

16. Joseph Healey interview.

17. While McCauley was secretary-general, he was also wearing, at least for this period, the hat of chairman of AMECEA. When McCauley resigned his position in Fort Portal he was forced to move out of the country. Due to government problems between Uganda and Kenya, he was forced to go first to Rome and then to Nairobi. McCauley's possession of a Vatican passport made things somewhat easier for his travel, but restrictions were still present. He explained the situation in a letter to his family: "As Chairman and Secretary General of AMECEA I practically had to move to Nairobi . . . although I originally wanted to operate from Gaba

National Seminary in Uganda. President Idi Amin's tough policy in Uganda makes that impossible. Since Amin 'sold out' to the Muslims, the Catholic Church has become . . . in his mind . . . 'the opposition.' He got rid of Asians, then most of the British, so now he is focusing on the Catholics. We expect to lose a minimum of 30% and possibly as much as 70% of our mission personnel unless there is a drastic change in the Government's policy. So, as the former Bishop of Fort Portal, I could not stay and work in Uganda." See McCauley to Dick and Joanie Larsen, 4 February 1973; Joseph Healey interview.

18. Statutes of AMECEA, n.d., 202, AMECEA Regulations, ADFP.

19. Vincent McCauley, C.S.C., to Germain Lalande, C.S.C., 17 April 1973, 811, Doss. 1, Holy Cross Generalate Papers, AUND.

20. Joseph Healey interview.

21. Meeting minutes, AMECEA Plenary Meeting, December 14–21, 1973, 202.2, AMECEA Plenary Meetings, ADFP; meeting minutes, AMECEA Plenary Meeting, August 18, 1979, 202.2, AMECEA Plenary Meetings, ADFP; meeting minutes, AMECEA Executive Board, September 22–23, 1977, 202.3, AMECEA Executive Board, ADFP. In 1993, Eritrea was also granted membership to AMECEA as part pf the Catholic Bishops' Conference of Ethiopia and Eritrea.

22. McCauley to Dick and Joanie Larsen, 4 February 1973.

23. The AMECEA office doubled as a residence. Killian Flynn's office and bedroom adjoined each other. Joseph Healey's office was in the parlor of the home. The Kenyan bishops were contemplating the construction of a large Catholic Center in Nairobi. McCauley hoped that AMECEA could get some space in the proposed building. When this plan did not materialize, however, it was decided to tear down the original colonial home on Gitanga Road and replace it with a new building for offices and residences. During this transition period, January 1973 to September 1975,

all AMECEA clerical personnel resided in local parishes. See Joseph Healey interview.

24. The breakdown in costs for the new headquarters building was (in Kenyan shillings): Missio–451,533 KES; Misereor–239,928 KES; AMECEA Documentation Service–52,500 KES; McCauley–408,951 KES. See Statement of Account, August 1974–June 1976, AMECEA Building Project, 202.2, AMECEA Plenary Meetings, ADFP.

25. Meeting minutes, AMECEA Executive Board, March 12–13, 1975, 202.3, AMECEA Executive Board, ADFP; Secretary General report to the Plenary, n.d. [1976], 202.2, AMECEA Plenary Meetings, ADFP.

26. Secretary General report to the Plenary, July 13–23, 1976, AMECEA Plenary, Secretary General, AAMECEA.

27. Minutes of AMECEA Executive Board, August 11, 1972 and January 15–16, 1973, 202.3, AMECEA Executive Board, ADFP. The working papers presented were (1) "Personnel: Training, Selection and Distribution," (2) "Marriage and the Family," (3) "Religious Education," (4) "Social Service and Distribution," and (5) "Specialized Apostolates." See "Planning for the Church in Africa in the 1980s," overview document summary, n.d. [1973], AMECEA Plenary, Secretary General, AAMECEA.

28. Vincent McCauley, C.S.C., to Mr. and Mrs. David Frenzer, 11 February 1982, PPNF.

29. AMECEA Documentation Service, May 11, 1976, 202.4, AMECEA Documentation Service, ADFP. The 1973 AMECEA Study Conference concluded concerning SCC: "We have to insist upon building Church life and work on Basic Christian Communities in both rural and urban areas. Church life must be based on the communities in which everyday life and work takes place: those basic and manageable social groups whose members can experience real inter-personal relationships and feel a sense of communal belonging, both in living and working." Quoted in Joseph Healey, M.M. and Donald Sybertz, M.M., *Towards an*

African Narrative Theology (Maryknoll, NY: Orbis Books, 2004), 138.

30. Meeting minutes, AMECEA Plenary, December 14–21, 1973, 202.2, AMECEA Plenary, ADFP.

31. Meeting minutes, AMECEA Executive Board, March 12–13, 1975, 202.3, AMECEA Executive Board, ADFP.

32. Monsignor F. Mkhori to Vincent McCauley, C.S.C., 31 July 1975, AMECEA Plenary Session, 1976, Secretary General, AAMECEA; Vincent McCauley, C.S.C., to Bishop James Sangu, 14 August 1975, AMECEA Plenary Session, 1976, Secretary General, AAMECEA; Bishop James Sangu to Vincent McCauley, C.S.C., September 9, 1975, AMECEA Plenary Session, 1976, Secretary General, AAMECEA.

33. Meeting minutes, AMECEA Plenary, July 13–23, 1976, AMECEA Plenary, 1976, Secretary General, AAMECEA.

34. Mutiso-Mbinda, "AMECEA Bishops' Consultations," 20. The 1976 AMECEA Study Conference stated emphatically: "Systematic formation of Small Christian Communities should be the key pastoral priority in the years to come in Eastern Africa." See Healey and Sybertz, *Towards an African Theology*, 138.

35. Vincent McCauley, C.S.C., to Dick, Joanie, Susie, and Anne Larsen, 30 July 1976, PPMJL.

36. Synods of Bishops, a post–Vatican II phenomenon, were held in 1968, 1969 (extraordinary), 1971, 1974, 1977, and 1980, during McCauley's life.

37. Vincent McCauley, C.S.C., to Dick and Joanie Larsen, 29 September 1977 and 28 October 1977, PPMJL; report of the Secretary General to the AMECEA Executive Board, February 22, 1978, SG-10, Secretary General, AAMECEA.

38. The Fourth Ordinary Synod of Bishops was held September 30 to October 29, 1977. The bishops' discussions raised thirty-four propositions and nine hundred suggestions. Six general areas were treated in these recommendations: (1) the importance of catechetical renewal, (2) the nature of true catechesis, (3) the

persons involved in catechesis, (4) the ongoing need for catechesis for all Christians, (5) the means and channels of catechesis, and (6) the special aspects affecting catechesis.

39. Meeting minutes, AMECEA Executive Board, September 22–23, 1977, 202.3, AMECEA Executive Board, ADFP.

40. James J. Odongo to All AMECEA Bishops, 7 November 1978, AMECEA Plenary 1979, Secretary General, AAMECEA.

41. In December 1978, McCauley acknowledged that an invitation had been received from Bishop Matthias Chimote to host the 1979 AMECEA plenary in Zomba, Malawi. The proposed dates were August 5–19, 1979. See Vincent McCauley, C.S.C., to Matthias Chimote, 15 December 1978, AMECEA Plenary 1979, Secretary General, AAMECEA.

42. Meeting minutes, AMECEA Executive Board, February 22–23, 1978, 202.3 AMECEA Executive Board, ADFP; Vincent McCauley, C.S.C., to Eminences and Excellencies, 15 January 1979, AMECEA Plenary 1979, Secretary General, AAMECEA.

43. Meeting minutes, AMECEA Plenary, August 18, 1979, 202.2, AMECEA Plenary, ADFP.

44. Mutiso-Mbinda, "AMECEA Bishops' Consultations," 20.

45. Additionally, the conference described the missionary role of Eastern African SCC: "SCC can be an effective way of developing the mission dimension of the Church at the most local level and of making people feel that they are really part of the Church's evangelizing work." Quoted in Healey and Sybertz, *Towards an African Narrative Theology*, 150, 348.

46. Vincent McCauley, C.S.C., to Father Benedict, 6 June 1978, SG 89, Misereor, Secretary General, AAMECEA.

47. Meeting minutes, AMECEA Plenary Session, July 13–23, 1976, 202.2, AMECEA Plenary Sessions, ADFP; meeting minutes, AMECEA Executive Board, October 29–30, 1975, 202.3, AMECEA Executive Board, ADFP; AMECEA Documentation Service, September 2, 1975, AAMECEA.

48. Report of General Secretary to AMECEA Executive Board, February 17, 1977 and February 22, 1978, 202.3, AMECEA Executive Board, ADFP; meeting minutes, AMECEA Plenary Session, 202.2, AMECEA Plenary Sessions, ADFP; Meeting minutes, AMECEA Executive Board, March 1–3, 1980, 202.3, AMECEA Executive Board, ADFP. The accounting program at the Social Training Center continues to operate today.

49. Killian Flynn, O.F.M. Cap., memorandum, 29 April 1971, 204.1, AMECEA Secretariat Correspondence, ADFP.

50. Meeting minutes, AMECEA Executive Board, August 20, 1971, 202.3, AMECEA Executive Board, ADFP.

51. Meeting minutes, AMECEA Executive Board, August 11, 1972 and October 2–3, 1973, 202.3, AMECEA Executive Board, ADFP. The proposal was to be funded as follows: AMECEA, $25,000; Missio, $18,000; Sacred Congregation for Non-Believers, $1,000; Private Sources, $1,000.

52. Evaluation report of the 1974 Interdisciplinary Seminar on Urban and Industrial Concerns, n.d. [1975] SG 54, Ecumenism, Secretary General, AAMECEA.

53. Secretary General's Report to the AMECEA Executive Board, July 1974–March 1975, March 1, 1975, 202.3, AMECEA Executive Board, ADFP; minutes of AMECEA Executive Board, July 17–18, 1974, 202.3, AMECEA Executive Board, ADFP; evaluation report of the 1974 Interdisciplinary Seminar on Urban and Industrial Concerns, n.d. [1975], SG 54, Ecumenism, Secretary General, AAMECEA. Among the participants were seven different religious denominations, thirteen nations, twenty-two total people (fourteen clergy and eight lay men and women).

54. Vincent McCauley, C.S.C., to Cardinal Maurice Otunga, 21 November 1974, SG 54, Ecumenism, Secretary General, AAMECEA.

55. Burgess Carr to Vincent McCauley, C.S.C., 1 October 1974, SG 43, AACC, Secretary General, AAMECEA; Vincent

McCauley, C.S.C., to Burgess Carr, 2 October 1974, SG 43, AACC, Secretary General, AAMECEA.

56. Vincent McCauley, C.S.C., to Sarwart G. Shebata, 29 June 1979, SG 43, AACC, Secretary General, AAMECEA.

57. AMECEA Documentation Service, October 12, 1976, 202.4, AMECEA Documentation Service, ADFP.

58. Vincent McCauley, C.S.C., to Cardinal John Willebrands, 17 September 1974, SG 38, Secretary for Christian Unity, Secretary General, AAMECEA; Charles Moeller to Vincent McCauley, C.S.C., 12 December 1975, SG 38, Secretary for Christian Unity, Secretary General, AAMECEA.

59. CORAT Africa consisted of an executive board of eleven professional laymen and an advisory board of several heads of churches in Africa: Lutheran, Anglican, Roman Catholic, Presbyterian, Methodist, Baptist, and African International Church. The organization offered training courses, consulting, professional advice on organization and administration, training and research, personnel selection, and vocational guidance. See First Report on the Work of CORAT (Africa), December 1975, SG 167, CORAT Africa, Secretary General, AAMECEA.

60. G. S. Snell to Vincent McCauley, C.S.C., 18 July 1974, SG 167, CORAT Africa, Secretary General, AAMECEA.

61. Vincent McCauley, C.S.C., to Archbishop Simon Lourdusamy, 24 July 1974, SG 167, CORAT Africa, Secretary General, AAMECEA.

62. Progress report, March 27–June 30, 1975, SG 167, CORAT Africa, AAMECEA; Vincent McCauley, C.S.C., to Paul Mukasa, 12 June 1975, SG 167, CORAT Africa, AAMECEA.

63. Vincent McCauley, C.S.C., to All AMECEA Bishops, 22 August 1975, SG 167, CORAT Africa, Secretary General, AAMECEA.

64. D. H. Trollop to Vincent McCauley, C.S.C., 18 June 1981, SG 167, CORAT Africa, AAMECEA. As an example, one of McCauley's lay associates in Nairobi wrote to the bishop, "It is

through your intimate connection with the Executive Officers of CORAT that I was considered above all others and selected for the job." See Damien Tamale to Vincent McCauley, C.S.C., 5 May 1977, SG 167, CORAT Africa, Secretary General, AAMECEA.

65. Meeting minutes, AMECEA Executive Board, January 15–16, 1973, 202.3, AMECEA Executive Board, ADFP; Mary Victoria Chirwa, "Regional Cooperation Among the AMECEA Religious Women," *AFER* 26 nos. 1–2 (February–April 1986): 67.

66. AMECEA Documentation Service, October 10, 1974, AAMECEA.

67. Sister M. T. Gacambi to Conference of Religious Women in Five AMECEA Countries, 1 March 1974, M55, AMECEA Sisters, Secretary General, AAMECEA.

68. Summary sheet, September 1974, M35, AMECEA Sisters, Secretary General, AAMECEA.

69. Vincent McCauley, C.S.C., to Werenfried Van Straaten, O. Praem, 3 December 1975, M55 AMECEA Sisters, Secretary General, AAMECEA; *Tanzamakenuga (Sisters Speak)* 1, no. 1 (July 1, 1975), M55 AMECEA Sisters, Secretary General, AAMECEA.

70. Vincent McCauley, C.S.C., to Archbishop Simon Lourdusamy, 11 April 1976, M55 AMECEA Sisters, Secretary General, AAMECEA.

71. Vincent McCauley, C.S.C., to Msgr. Wilhelm Wissing, 18 August 1975, M55, AMECEA Sisters, Secretary General, AMECEA.

72. Meeting minutes, AMECEA Executive Board, August 20, 1971, 202.3, AMECEA Executive Board, ADFP.

73. Richard Kiley, F.S.C., to Dear Fellow Religion Teachers, 21 December 1969, 206.2, AMECEA, CHIEA, ADFP; Alden Pierce to Colin Davies, 1 November 1970, 206.2, AMECEA, CHIEA, ADFP.

74. Memorandum—Re: Active Non-Catholic Participation in producing the GABA R. E. Syllabus, 13 June 1971, 206.2, AMECEA, CHIEA, ADFP.

75. Emmanuel Nsubuga to Idi Amin Dada, 2 August 1972, 210.1, SECAM Correspondence, ADFP.

76. Vincent McCauley, C.S.C., to Mother M. Agnes Walsh, 23 April 1972, 206.2, AMECEA, CHIEA, ADFP.

77. AMECEA Evolution Meeting, May 15, 1979, AMECEA History, AAMECEA.

78. Meeting minutes, AMECEA Plenary, December 14–21, 1973, 202.3, AMECEA Plenaries, ADFP.

79. Richard Kiley, F.S.C., to Vincent McCauley, C.S.C., 28 February 1976, SG 10, Executive Board, Secretary General, AAMECEA.

80. Jimmy K. Tindigarukayo, "Uganda, 1979–85: Leadership in Transition," in *The Journal of Modern African Studies* 26, no. 4 (December 1988): 6-8.

81. Ibid., 608.

82. Tumusiime, *Uganda 30 Years*, 51. The immediate time after Amin's ouster was a period of great confusion and political instability. Yusuf Lule, the head of the UNLF, was installed as president, but he remained in office only sixty-eight days. Historian Thomas Ofcansky attributes his short tenure to his inability to establish a working relationship between the UNLF and the political wing of the Uganda National Liberation Army (UNLA). On June 19, Lule was replaced by Godfrey Binaisa, who had served as attorney general in Obote's government. Although a political neophyte, he sought to accomplish an ambitious program. By April 1980, however, his regime began to unravel. On May 13, 1980, Binaisa was placed under house arrest. Binaisa's departure brought a military council to power until December. National elections held at this time brought the Uganda People's Congress and its leader, Milton Obote, back into prominence and power. See Ofcansky, *Uganda: Tarnished Pearl*, 48–51;

Tindigarukayo, "Uganda, 1979–85," 609–617; Mutibwa, *Uganda Since Independence*, 125, 130–138.

83. Vincent McCauley, C.S.C., to Harriet Gartland, 4 July 1977, McCauley File, Holy Cross Mission Center Papers, AHCFI.

84. Vincent McCauley, C.S.C., to Anthony Connix, W.F., 4 January 1978, SG 39, Refugees, Secretary General, AAMECEA.

85. Vincent McCauley, C.S.C., to Joseph M. Glynn, M.M., 9 May 1978, SG 39, Refugees, Secretary General, AAMECEA.

86. Vincent McCauley, C.S.C., to Dick and Joanie Larsen, 31 January 1978, PPMJL. McCauley explained further: "As you can well imagine, the parishes, the religious houses, including the cardinal and the Nuncio, have refugees at their doors everyday. I had 75 yesterday and 20 today. We try to help the most desparate cases that do not qualify at the J[oint] R[efugee] S[ervice] of K[enya] agency. As you well know, not all of them are deserving cases, but we do not have a staff of social workers to follow up all the cases. We just do what we can with the little we have." See McCauley to Joseph M. Glynn, 9 May 1978.

87. Paraphrase of "Christ is at the Door," in Joseph Healey, M.M., *African Stories for Preachers and Teachers* (Nairobi: Pauline Publications Africa, 2005): 83.

88. Vincent McCauley, C.S.C., to William Madden, M.M., 28 August 1979, SG 39, Refugees, Secretary General, AAMECEA.

89. Vincent McCauley, C.S.C., to Msgr. Leo Schwarz, 30 January 1978, SG 89, Misereor, Secretary General, AAMECEA.

90. Jospeh Mukwaya interview; John Croston interviews, July 7, 2005 and April 7, 2006.

91. AMECEA Documentation Service, December 7, 1977, AAMECEA.

92. Ibid.

93. Vincent McCauley, C.S.C., to Elizabeth Winkler, 6 April 1978, SG 39, Refugees, Secretary General, AAMECEA. Winkler, secretary-general of the International Migration Committee in Geneva, Switzerland, was encouraging AMECEA to set up a formal department or commission to handle ministry to nomads. McCauley responded, "We are grateful for the concern you have expressed and the offer to assist us. However, we feel that it would be premature for us to set up a special office for the nomadic apostolate. Our own personnel are fully engaged. Perhaps at some time in the future the situation may develop sufficiently to justify the kind of organization that you envisage."

94. Bishop Colin Davies to Vincent McCauley, C.S.C., 8 February 1979, SG 20, Apostolate to the Nomads, Secretary General, AAMECEA.

95. McCauley to Germain Lalande, 17 April 1973.

96. Copy of radio news announcement, February 26, 1977, 260, History of Holy Cross in East Africa, AHCEA.

97. Connelly, "Holy Cross in East Africa," 26. Some members of Holy Cross did not find out about the cancellation until after their arrival in Kampala.

98. Vincent McCauley, C.S.C., to Thomas Barrosse, C.S.C., 18 May 1977, 811, Doss. 1, Holy Cross Generalate Papers, AUND; Vincent McCauley, C.S.C., to Louis LeDuc, C.S.C., n.d. [1977], 811, Doss. 1, Holy Cross Generalate Papers, AUND.

99. Vincent McCauley, C.S.C., to Larry and Mary Tracy, 9 June 1979, PPMJL.

100. Isichei, *Christianity in Africa*, 247.

101. Report on the Visitation to the Holy Cross Project in the Diocese of Mbarara, August 1959, 38:46, Mehling Papers, AHCFI.

102. John Croston interview, April 7, 2006; Robert Hesse interview. Hesse commented, "We were afraid we would start a seminary program, then we would be 'kicked out' and the seminarians would be left without support."

103. John Harrington interview with James Connelly. Sacred Heart and Christian Brothers had taken many local vocations, but many had left and few completed the program, with the result of a huge financial loss to the parent religious congregations.

104. Francis Zagorc interview; John Croston interview, April 5, 2006, Thomas Smith interview.

105. Howard Kenna, C.S.C., to William Blum, C.S.C., 12 September 1973, 35:9, Kenna Papers, AHCFI. In 1974, McCauley told Father Richard Warner, C.S.C., that he was happy that Holy Cross was now seeking African vocations. See Richard Warner, C.S.C., to the author, 3 November 2006.

106. Discussion of Apostolic Plan, August 28, 1972, 420.1, District Meetings Prior to 1988, AHCEA.

107. Meeting minutes, Holy Cross Religious, June 3–5, 1977, 420.1 District Meetings Prior to 1988, AHCEA.

108. Meeting minutes, Holy Cross Religious, September 9, 1979, 420.1, District Meetings Prior to 1988, AHCEA. Bashabora first showed interest in Holy Cross in the late 1960s, but the aforementioned fears and roadblocks delayed any action on his request. After candidacy, he was admitted to the novitiate. Eventually, however, he returned to his diocese.

109. Holy Cross Community Meeting, September 24, 1977, 420.1 District Meetings Prior to 1988, AHCEA; James Ferguson, interview with James Connelly, C.S.C., May 9, 1980, AHCFI.

110. Meeting minutes, Holy Cross Religious, April 11, 1977, and September 24, 1977, 420.1, District Meetings Prior to 1988, AHCEA. Some of the reasons given for choosing Nairobi as the expansion site were (1) Swahili, the vernacular language, was more universal and easier to learn, (2) the urban setting was considered advantageous, and (3) Nairobi was close enough to Uganda to keep close watch on people and operations there. See William Blum, C.S.C., interview with James Connelly, C.S.C., June 24, 1978, AHCFI.

111. Today Holy Cross Parish Dandora is a flourishing Catholic community with an excellent elementary school, low-cost medical dispensary, and many other outreach programs to people in the general area.

12. Retirement and Death: 1979–1982

1. Secretary General's report to the Executive Board, July 1974–March 1975, March 1, 1975, 202.3, AMECEA Executive Board, ADFP. This reticent attitude is consistent with Joseph Healey's claim that Africans liked expatriates for their organizational skills. Thus, as long as McCauley or other capable people were present, there was no absolute need to propose Africans for top jobs in the Church.

2. Record of Evaluation Meeting of AMECEA Department, November 28, 1977, AMECEA History, AAMECEA; meeting minutes, AMECEA Executive Board, February 22–23, 1978, 202.3, AMECEA Executive Board, ADFP.

3. McCauley presented a systematized list of ideas central to the post of secretary-general: (1) the secretary-general needs time to think and to consult knowledgeable people, (2) he should come to opinions and decisions with the AMECEA team and then propose them to the executive board, (3) he should find a better way of involving the executive board and making it aware of what the general secretariat (those who work at AMECEA headquarters) and departments are doing, (4) he ought to foster sharing among departments to develop shared visions and priorities, and (5) he should encourage departments to be open to discussing the needs of the Church in East Africa. See AMECEA Interdepartmental Evaluation Meeting, June 19, 1981, AMECEA History, AAMECEA.

4. Charles Schleck to the author, 6 August 2005.

5. Report of the Secretary General to AMECEA Staffing Commission, February 1977, SG 10, Executive Board, Secretary General, AAMECEA.

6. Secretary General's report to AMECEA Executive Board, February 21–23, 1979, 202.3, AMECEA Executive Board, ADFP.

7. Meeting minutes, AMECEA Plenary Session, August 5–19, 1979, 1979 AMECEA Plenary Session, Secretary General, AAMECEA.

8. Laurean Cardinal Rugambwa, opening address to AMECEA Plenary Session, December 14, 1973, 202.3, AMECEA Plenary Meetings, ADFP.

9. Robert Hesse interview.

10. Healey, "Two AMECEA Giants," 25.

11. Meeting minutes, AMECEA Executive Board, February 21–23, 1979, 202.3, AMECEA Executive Board, ADFP; meeting minutes, AMECEA Plenary, August 18, 1979, 202.3, AMECEA Plenary Meeting, ADFP.

12. Vincent McCauley, C.S.C., to the Larsen Family, 16 January 1980, PPMJL.

13. Vincent McCauley, C.S.C., to Kathy and John, 1 March 1981, Personal Papers of Paul McCandless (hereafter PPPM).

14. The Catholic Higher Institute of Eastern Africa is described in full in "Retirement and Death: 1979–1982."

15. Vincent McCauley, C.S.C., to Paul McCandless and Family, 5 September 1982, PPPM.

16. Vincent McCauley to the Larsen Family, 16 January 1980. As one example McCauley relates an incident where he was asked to fill in at the last minute at a local parish confirmation when Cardinal Maurice Otunga of Nairobi was involved in an automobile accident and unable to attend. He said he administered confirmation to five hundred and it took one full hour for he and two priests to distribute communion to some three thousand people. He wrote, "I enjoyed the day very much, but I'll admit that it was a real work out for a 76-year old bishop." See Vincent McCauley, C.S.C., to Frenzer Family, 22 April 1982, PPNF.

17. Vincent McCauley, C.S.C., to Nonnie Frenzer, 29 June 1979, PPNF.

18. Vincent McCauley to the Larsen Family, 16 January 1980.

19. Report to AMECEA Executive Board, July 27–28, 1981, AMECEA 1982 Plenary, Secretary General, AAMECEA.

20. M. J. Mazombwe to Joseph Mukwaya, 14 July 1982, 1982 AMECEA Plenary, Secretary General, AAMECA; John Croston, C.S.C., to Louis LeDuc, C.S.C., 31 August 1982, 1982 Plenary Sessions, Secretary General, AAMECEA.

21. Meeting minutes, AMECEA Plenary, August 23–27, 1982, 1982 AMECEA Minutes and Documents, Secretary General, AAMECEA.

22. Vincent McCauley, C.S.C., to Paul McCandless and Family, 26 July 1982, PPPM. Today, the center of the Holy Cross Family Ministries in East Africa is in Kampala, Uganda, with representatives in Kenya and Tanzania.

23. Apostolic Pro-Nunio to Archbishop Emmanuel Nsubuga, 5 November 1973, SG 155 (D), CHIEA Correspondence, Secretary General, AAMECEA.

24. Vincent McCauley, C.S.C., to Eminence and Excellencies, 9 September 1975, SG 155 (D), CHIEA Correspondence, Secretary General, AAMECEA.

25. P. A. Kalilombe to Ad-Hoc Committee for Setting Up a Higher Institute of Ecclesiastical Studies in English Africa, 23 March 1976, SG 155 (D), CHIEA Correspondence, Secretary General, AAMECEA. The ad hoc committee members were Archbishop George F. Daniel (Pretoria, South Africa), Archbishop Francis Arinze (Onitsha, Nigeria), Bishop Joseph Gasi (Tambola, Sudan), and Bishop Patrick Kalilombe (Lilongwe, Malawi).

26. P. A. Kalilombe to Vincent McCauley, C.S.C., 3 April 1976, SG 155 (D), CHIEA Correspondence, Secretary General, AAMECEA. It is very interesting to note that McCauley had been calling for such a Catholic university in East Africa since the early

1960s. Robert Pelton, C.S.C., recalls conversations with McCauley when the former was chairman of the University of Notre Dame Theology Department from 1959 to 1963. The bishop wanted Pelton's advice in an initial exploration of establishing such an institution. See Robert Pelton, C.S.C., interview with the author, April 26, 2006, AHCFI.

27. Meeting minutes, AMECEA Plenary, July 13–23, 1976, 202.2, AMECEA Plenary Meetings, ADFP; "The Permanent Planning Committee for Higher Ecclesiastical Institute for English-Speaking Africa," July 12, 1976, SH0155 (D), CHIEA Correspondence, Secretary General, AAMECEA.

28. The permanent committee members were Archbishops Francis Arinze and George Daniel, and Bishops Joseph Gasi and Medardo Mazombwe.

29. Francis Arinze et al., memorandum to All English-Speaking Episcopal Conferences in Africa, 1 September 1977, SG 155 (D), CHIEA Correspondence, Secretary General, AAMECEA. McCauley had done some research prior to the meeting and discovered Trudeau's availability for the position and his desire to serve. See Vincent McCauley, C.S.C., to Francis Arinze, 8 June 1977, SG 155 (D), CHIEA Correspondence, Secretary General, AAMECEA.

30. Vincent McCauley, C.S.C., to Polycarp Toppo, S.J., 30 November 1978, SG 155 (D), CHIEA Correspondence, Secretary General, AAMECEA.

31. Progress report, CHIEA, August 1979, SG 155 (D), CHIEA Correspondence, Secretary General, AAMECEA; Edouard Trudeau, S.J., to Dear Fathers, 21 February 1979, SG 155 (D), CHIEA Correspondence, Secretary General, AAMECEA; Catholic Higher Institute of Eastern Africa Progress Report, August 1979, 206.1, AMECEA CHIEA, ADFP.

32. Archbishop Simon Lourdusamy to Francis Arinze, 12 October 1978; Meeting Minutes, Executive Committee, CHIEA, August 5, 1979, SG 155 (D), CHIEA Correspondence, Secretary

General, AAMECEA; Francis Arinze et al., memorandum, Higher
Institute of Ecclesiastical Studies for English-Speaking Africa,
March 1980, SG 155 (D), CHIEA Correspondence, Secretary
General, AAMECEA; meeting minutes, AMECEA Plenary, 1979,
202.3, AMECEA Plenary, ADFP.

33. Francis Arinze to Cardinal Angelo Rossi, 6 March 1980,
204.1, AMECEA Secretariat Correspondence, ADFP. A French-
speaking university was started in 1967 in Abidjan, Ivory Coast. In
1975, it became the Catholic Institute of West Africa and today
the Catholic University of West Africa. An English-speaking
Catholic Institute of West Africa in Port Harcourt, Nigeria, was
approved in May 1994.

34. Joseph Mukwaya to Msgr. Wilhelm Wissing, 3 Decem-
ber 1980, SG 155 (A), CHIEA—Finances, Secretary General,
AAMECEA; Vincent McCauley, C.S.C., to James Ferguson,
C.S.C., 2 July 1980, SG 155 (A), CHIEA—Finances, Secretary
General, AAMECEA; Vincent McCauley, C.S.C., to William
McCormick, 27 February 1982, SG 155 (A), CHIEA—Finances,
Secretary General, AAMECEA.

35. McCauley to James Ferguson, 2 July 1980.

36. Meeting minutes, AMECEA Executive Board, February
21–23, 1979, 202.3 AMECEA Executive Board; progress report,
CHIEA, August 1979, 206.1, AMECEA, CHIEA, ADFP.

37. Quoted in Joseph Healey interview.

38. CHIEA Building Project, August 25, 1979, Appendix, SG 155 (D), CHIEA Correspondence, Secretary General,
AAMECEA. Phase I, 1980, construction of the library and the
foundations for all other buildings for $300,000. Phase II, 1981,
construction of twenty-four student residences for $400,000.
Phase III, 1982, construction of twelve teacher residences, administrative offices, classrooms, and dining hall for $400,000. Phase
IV, construction of twelve additional student residences, staff
housing, and completion of general work for $400,000. Thus, a
total of $1.5 million was needed for the project.

39. Edouard Trudeau, S.J., to Msgr. Wilhelm Wissing, 1 June 1980, SG 155 (D) CHIEA Correspondence, Secretary General, AAMECEA; CHIEA Building Project (1980-1984), SG 155 (D) CHIEA Correspondence, Secretary General, AAMECEA.

40. Meeting minutes, CHIEA Academic Commission, April 18–20, 1979, SG 155 (C), CHIEA Academic Matters, Secretary General, AAMECEA; CHIEA Program of Studies—Draft, n.d. [1980], SG 155 (C), CHIEA Academic Matters, Secretary General, AAMECEA.

41. Progress report, CHIEA, August 1979, 206.1, AMECEA CHIEA, ADFP.

42. Adrian Ddungu to Bishop Medardo Mazombwe, 17 June 1980, SG 155 (D), CHIEA Correspondence, AAMECEA; meeting minutes, CHIEA Executive Committee, February 17, 1981, SG 155 (D), CHIEA Correspondence, AAMECEA; Paul Kalanda to Eminences, Excellencies and Reverend Fathers, 30 November 1980, 206.1, AMECEA, CHIEA, ADFP.

43. Joseph Mukwaya to All AMECEA Ordinaries, 25 June 1980, 202.5, AMECEA Correspondence, ADFP; Joseph Mukwaya to Paul Kalanda, 29 May 1980, SG 155 (D), CHIEA Correspondence, Secretary General, AAMECEA.

44. AMECEA communication sheet, 1982, AMECEA History, AAMECEA.

45. Catalog CHIEA Bulletin No. 1, 1984–1984, SG 155 (C), CHIEA Academic Matters, Secretary General, AAMECEA; Catholic University of Eastern Africa (CUEA) Program of Studies, 2001–2004, 1. In 1986, the Graduate School of Theology at CHIEA started negotiations with the Commission of Higher Education in Kenya toward the establishment of the Catholic University of Eastern Africa. In 1989, the school obtained the "Letter of Interim Authority." After three more years of intensive negotiations between the authority of the Graduate School of Theology (CHIEA) and the Commission for Higher Education, the faculty of arts and sciences was established. Finally on November

3, 1992, a civil charter was received and the Catholic University of Eastern Africa (CUEA) officially began. Today CUEA serves a wide range of students from across the continent in numerous major disciplines.

46. Cornelius Ryan interview; James Ferguson interview.

47. Joseph Mukwaya interview; John Croston interview, April 7, 2006.

48. Magambo, "An Appreciation."

49. Vincent McCauley, C.S.C., "Christmas Letter 1980," PPPM.

50. Nichols, "Vincent McCauley," 109, Bishop McCauley Papers, AHCEA; Vincent McCauley, C.S.C., "Christmas Letter 1980"; Vincent McCauley, C.S.C., to Dick and Joanie Larsen, 9 February 1982, PPMJL.

51. John Croston, C.S.C., to Holy Cross Fathers, 27 October 1981, 109, Bishop McCauley Papers, AHCEA.

52. Vincent McCauley to Paul McCandless and Family, 26 July 1982.

53. John Croston to Louis LeDuc, 31 August 1982.

54. Thomas McDermott interview.

55. Vincent McCauley, C.S.C., to Louis LeDuc, C.S.C., 24 August 1982, 811, Doss. 1, Holy Cross Generalate Papers, AUND; John Croston, C.S.C., to Louis LeDuc, 3 January 1983, 811, Doss. 1, Holy Cross Generalate Papers, AUND.

56. Vincent McCauley, C.S.C., to Thomas Barrosse, C.S.C., 18 September 1982, 811, Doss. 1, Holy Cross Generalate Papers, AUND.

57. John Croston, C.S.C., to Dear All, 27 October 1982, 109, Bishop McCauley Papers, AHCEA. It was revealed later that McCauley had a few hemorrhage episodes while visiting his family.

58. John Croston interview, April 7, 2006. Not only did McCauley want to get back to Africa and his ministry with AMECEA, but also an extra incentive, the forthcoming episcopal

ordination of his friend and colleague Joseph Mukwaya, scheduled for October 31, drove him to take the risk of surgery.

59. John Croston, C.S.C., to Larry and Mary Tracy, 8 December 1982, PPMJL.

60. Joseph Healey interview.

61. William Blum, C.S.C., homily for Vincent McCauley,
November 4, 1982, 109, Bishop McCauley Papers, AHCEA.

62. Fell, funeral homily for Vincent McCauley.

63. Richard Warner, C.S.C., to the author, 3 November
2006.

64. "A Word from Bishop Medrardo Mazombwe on the
Death of Bishop V. J. McCauley," *Rwenzori Echo* II, no. 2 (April–
June, 1983): 13.

65. AMECEA Documentation Service no. 253, November
8, 1982, 109, Bishop McCauley Papers, AHCEA; "The Story of
Bishop McCauley, CSC," n.d., History of the Diocese of Fort
Portal, ADFP; Healey, "Two AMECEA Giants," 25.

66. Thomas Barrosse, C.S.C., to Richard Warner, C.S.C., 10
November 1982, 811, Doss. 1, Holy Cross Generalate Papers,
AUND.

Epilogue: Vincent McCauley, C.S.C.: The Man and His Legacy

1. Bishop Joseph Mugengi, interview with the author, February 6, 2006, AHCFI.

2. Vincent McCauley, C.S.C., Pastoral Letter, 27 December
1963, 401, Official Acts Pastoral Letters, ADFP.

3. Solom Mujasi interview; Henri Valette interview.

4. Joseph Mugengi interview.

5. Bonaventura Kasaija interview.

6. Vincent McCauley, C.S.C., "Notes," April 19, 1967,
McCauley File, Holy Cross Mission Center Papers, AHCFI.

7. Tad Las interview.

8. Vincent McCauley, C.S.C., to Germain Lalande, C.S.C., 17
March 1972, 403.5, Richard Wunsch Superior Papers, AHCEA.

9. Al Croce interview; Cyril Kadoma interview; Beatrice Nya-kaanu interview; Richard Potthast interview.

10. Thomas Barrosse, C.S.C., to Archbishop D. S. Lour-dusamy, 10 November 1982, 811, Doss. 1, Holy Cross Generalate Papers, AUND.

11. John Croston to Larry and Mary Tracy, 8 December 1982.

12. Magambo, "An Appreciation."

13. Louis Rink, C.S.C., interview with the author, April 4, 2006, AHCFI. Rink relates that when McCauley went on safari to an outstation village, he always asked the local pastor to take him to the poorest section of the parish first. Only after this ini-tial visit did villagers gather in a central location for the bishop's official visit.

14. Richard Potthast interview; Banyatereza Sisters, group interview with the author, February 6, 2006, AHCFI; Beatrice Nyakaanu interview.

15. John Croston interview, April 7, 2006; Thomas Smith interview.

16. Joseph Mukwaya interview; Paulinas Bagambaki interview.

17. John Croston interview, July 7, 2005, AHCFI.

18. Kelly, "A Gentleman Bishop."

19. Fell, funeral homily for Vincent McCauley.

20. John Croston interview, April 7, 2006, AHCFI.

21. Vincent McCauley, C.S.C., to Paul McCandless, 7 March 1981, PPPM.

22. Magambo, "An Appreciation."

23. Healey, "Two AMECEA Giants," 25.

24. John Croston, C.S.C., to Tracy Family, 8 December [1982], PPMJL.

25. George Lucas interview.

26. Magambo, "Twenty-Five Years."

27. Paulinus Bagambaki interview; Beatrice Nyakoanu, interview with the author, February 6, 2006, AHCFI; Aquirinus Kibira, interview with the author, January 31, 2006, AHCFI.

28. Joseph Healey, M.M., to Arnold Fell, C.S.C., 9 January 1981, McCauley File, Holy Cross Mission Center Papers, AHCFI; Henri Valette interview; Bonaventura Kasaija interview.

29. Healey, "Two AMECEA Giants," 25.

30. Serapio Magambo to Poor Clare Sisters, 28 April 1973, 910.1, Bishop McCauley Papers, ADFP.

31. Richard Timm to the author, 1 August 2005; Francis Zagorc interview; James Ferguson interview.

32. *Transmission* VI, no. 2 (November 1983): 6, AHCFI.

33. Beatrice Nyakoanu interview; Thomas Smith interview.

34. Bonaventura Kasaija interview.

35. Louis Rink interview, April 4, 2006.

36. Magambo, "An Appreciation."

37. Gene Burke interview.

38. Tad Las interview.

39. Richard Potthast interview.

40. Arnold Fell, C.S.C., to Louis LeDuc, C.S.C., 2 March 1983, 811, Doss. 1, Holy Cross Generalate Papers, AUND.

41. Paul Kalanda to the author, 14 March 2006.

42. Magambo, "An Appreciation."

43. Ibid.

44. Quoted in William Blum interview.

45. Kelly, "A Gentleman Bishop."

46. James Rahilly interview; John Keefe interview, April 9, 2006.

Bibliography

Primary Sources

Archival Repositories

Archives Diocese of Fort Portal (ADFP), Fort Portal, Uganda
Archives Archdiocese of Kampala (AAK), Kampala, Uganda
Archives Holy Cross East Africa (AHCEA), Kampala, Uganda
Archives White Fathers Kampala (AWFK), Kampala, Uganda
Archives Association of Member Episcopal Conferences in Eastern Africa (AAMECEA), Nairobi, Kenya
Archives Holy Cross Fathers, Indiana Province (AHCFI), Notre Dame, Indiana
Archives Indiana Province (AIP), Notre Dame, Indiana
Archives University of Notre Dame (AUND), Notre Dame, Indiana
Archives Holy Cross Brothers Eastern Province (AHCBE), Valatie, New York
Archives Holy Cross Fathers Eastern Province (AHCFE), North Easton, Massachusetts
Archives Stonehill College (ASC), North Easton, Massachusetts

Personal Paper Collections

Personal Papers of Mary Joan Larsen (PPMJL)
Personal Papers of Nonnie Frenzer (PPNF)
Personal Papers of Paul McCandless (PPPM)
Personal Papers of Larry and Mary Tracy (PPLT)

Books and Articles by Vincent J. McCauley, C.S.C.

"And Not a Drop to Drink." *The Bengalese* 26, no. 3 (April 1945): 16–17.

"The Boro Din." *The Bengalese* 35, no. 10 (December 1954): 4–9.

"Dreams Become Reality." *The Bengalese* 25, no. 4 (1944): 6–7, 15.

"Elephant in Rampage." *The Bengalese* 20, no. 10 (December 1940): 8–9, 21.

"Fifteen Hours by Boat." *The Bengalese* 18, no. 5 (May 1937): 8–10.

"Fire of the Earth." *The Bengalese* 33, no. 4 (April 1952): 10–12.

"First Things First." *Holy Cross Missions* I, no. 2 (September 1956): 22.

"Forging Chains of Freedom." *Sunday Visitor Press*, 1948, 32.

"A Full Life." *The Bengalese* 26, no. 7 (1945): 3–5, 21.

"Making Nobody Somebody." *The Bengalese* 33, no. 3 (March 1952): 8–10.

"The Powerhouse." *Holy Cross Missions* I, no. 3 (October 1956): 18–19.

"Queen at the Window." *The Bengalese* 33, no. 5 (May 1952): 8–10.

"Rubbernecking in the Bazaar." *The Bengalese* 18, no. 7 (September 1937): 10–11.

"Salam for Christmas." *Holy Cross Missions* I, no. 5 (December 1956): 14–15.

"The Seeker of Souls." *The Bengalese* 33, no. 6 (June 1952): 22–23.

"They Call us Father." *Holy Cross Missions* 2, no. 10 (June 1958): 20–22.

The Unseen Army. Washington, D.C.: National Conference of Catholic Men (NCCM), 1949.

Secondary Sources

Adams, Bert, and Mike Bristow. "The Politico-Economic Position of Ugandan Asians in the Colonial and Independent Eras." *Journal of Asian and African Studies* XIII, nos. 3–4 (1978): 151–166.

Ahern, Patrick Henry. *The Catholic University of America 1887–1896: The Rectorship of John J. Keane.* Washington, D.C.: The Catholic University of America Press, 1949.

Alpers, Edward A. *Ivory and Slaves in East Central Africa.* London: Heineman, 1975.

"AMECEA Priorities and Privileges." *The African Ecclesial Review* 26, nos. 1–2 (February–April 1986): 43–45.

Amin, Idi. "Speech to the Asian Conference." Speech delivered on December 8, 1971. *East African Journal* (February 1972): 2–5.

Anderson, William B. *The Church in East Africa, 1940–1974.* Dodoma: Central Tanganyika Press, 1977.

Apter, David. *The Political Kingdom in Uganda.* Princeton, NJ: Princeton University Press, 1967.

Barrett, David. *Schism and Renewal in Africa.* Oxford: Oxford University Press, 1968.

Barrosse, Thomas, C.S.C. *Moreau: Portrait of a Founder.* Notre Dame, IN: Fides Publishers, Inc., 1969.

Barry, Colman J., O.S.B. *The Catholic University of America 1903–1909: The Rectorship of Denis J. O'Connell.* Washington, D.C.: The Catholic University of America Press, 1950.

Bataringaga, Basil K. "Religion and the State: Catholic Teaching on the Citizen and the State." *Africa Star* (November 1959): 9–13.

Baur, John. *2000 Years of Christianity in Africa: An African Church History.* Nairobi: Pauline Publications Africa, 1994.

Beetham, T. A. *Christianity and the New Africa.* London: Pall Mall Press, 1967.

Berman, Edward H., "American Influence on African Education: The Role of the Phelps-Stokes Fund's Education Commission." *Comparative Education Review* 15, no. 2 (June 1971): 132–145.

Berman, Edward H., ed. *African Reactions to Missionary Education.* New York: Teachers College Press, 1975.

Bienen, Henry. *Armies and Parties in Africa.* New York: Africana, 1978.

Burke, Fred G. *Local Government and Politics in Uganda.* Syracuse, NY: Syracuse University Press, 1964.

Butler, Jeffrey and A. A. Castagno. *Boston University Papers on Africa.* New York: Praeger, 1967.

Calvert, Alexander. *The Missionary Dimension: Vatican II and the Apostolate.* Milwaukee: Bruce Publishing Company, 1967.

Catta, Etienne, and Tony Catta. *Basil Anthony Mary Moreau.* Translated by Edward Heston, C.S.C. Milwaukee: Bruce Publishing Company, 1955.

Chirwa, Mary Victoria. "Regional Cooperation Among the AMECEA Religious Women." *The African Ecclesial Review* 26, nos. 1-2 (February–April 1986): 67–68.

"The Church and Political Parties," *Leadership* no. 46 (March 1961): 3–10.

Clancy, Raymond J., C.S.C. *The Congregation of Holy Cross in East Bengal, 1853–1953 with a Brief History of the Church in Bengal.* Washington, D.C.: Holy Cross Foreign Mission Seminary, 1953.

Connelly, James T., C.S.C. "Holy Cross in East Africa, 1958–1980." (1981) Archives Indiana Province, Notre Dame, IN.

Crowder, Michael, ed. *The Cambridge History of Africa*, Vol. 8, *1940–1975.* Cambridge: Cambridge University Press, 1984.

Decalo, Samuel. *Coups and Army Rule in Africa: Studies in Military Struggle.* New Haven, CT: Yale University Press, 1976.

Dries, Angelyn, O.S.F. *The Missionary Movement in American Catholic History.* Maryknoll, NY: Orbis Books, 1998.

Dumont, Rene. *False Start in Africa.* London: Andre Deutsch, 1966.

Eckstein, Harvey, and David E. Apter. *Comparative Politics: A Reader.* New York: Free Press of Glencoe, 1963.

Edwardes, Michael. *A History of India From the Earliest Times to the Present Day.* London: Thames and Hudson, 1961.

Gale. H. P. *Uganda and the Mill Hill Fathers.* London: Macmillan, 1959.

Gara, Br. Matthew, C.S.C. "River Stay Away," *The Bengalese* 19, no. 8 (October 1938): 11, 15.

Gershenberg, Irving. "Slouching Towards Socialism: Obote's Uganda." *African Studies Review* 15, no. 1 (April 1972): 79–95.

Gertzel, Cherry. "How Kabaka Yekka Came to Be." *African Report* (October 1964): 9–13.

———. *Party and Locality in Northern Uganda 1945–1962.* London: University of London Athlone Press, 1974.

———. "Report from Kampala." *Africa Report* 9, no. 9: 3–8.

Gingyera-Pinycwa, A. G. G. *Apolo Milton Obote and His Times.* New York: NOK Publishers, 1978.

Grahame, I. *Amin and Uganda: A Personal Memoir.* London: Granada, 1980.

Goedert, Edmund N., C.S.C. "Holy Cross Priests in the Diocese of Dacca, 1853–1981." (1983) Archives Indiana Province, Notre Dame, IN.

Gogan, Cothrai. *History of the Holy Ghost Mission in Kenya.* Nairobi, Kenya: Pauline Publications Africa, 2005.

Groves, C. *The Planting of Christianity in Africa.* 4 Vols. New Haven, CT: Lutterwort Press, 1990.

Gukiina, Peter M. *Uganda: A Case Study in African Political Development.* Notre Dame, IN: University of Notre Dame Press, 1972.

Gwyn, David. *Idi Amin.* Boston: Little, Brown and Company, 1977.

Hansen, Holger B., and Michael Twaddle, eds. *Changing Uganda.* Athens: Ohio University Press, 1991.

Hastings, Adrian. *African Catholicism: Essays in Discovery.* Philadelphia: Trinity Press International, 1989.

———. "The Catholic Church in Uganda." *African Ecclesial Review* XI, no. 3 (1969): 239–244.

———. *The Church in Africa, 1450–1950.* Oxford: Clarendon Press, 1994.

———. *Church and Mission in Modern Africa.* London: Burns & Oates, 1967.

———. "The Ministry of the Catholic Church in Africa, 1960–1975." *Christianity in Independent Africa,* edited by Edward Fashole-Luke. Bloomington: Indiana University Press, 1978, 26–44.

Healey, M.M., Joseph G. "Two AMECEA Giants." *The African Ecclesial Review* 26, nos. 1–2 (February–April 1986): 22–25.

———, and Jeanne Hinton, eds. *Small Christian Communities Today: Capturing the New Movement.* Maryknoll, NY: Orbis Books, 2005.

———, and Donald Sybertz, M.M. *Towards an African Narrative Theology.* Maryknoll, NY: Orbis Books, 2004.

Hearne, Brian. "Vatican II's Vision and AMECEA's Reality." *The African Ecclesial Review* 26, nos. 1–2 (February–April 1986): 26–33.

Hogan, Peter E., S.S.J. *The Catholic University of America 1896–1903: The Rectorship of Thomas J. Conaty.* Washington, D.C.: The Catholic University of America Press, 1949.

Ibingira, Grace. *African Upheavals Since Independence.* Boulder, CO: Westview Press, 1980.

———. *The Forging of an African Nation.* Kampala, Uganda: Viking Press, 1973.

Ingham, Kenneth. *A History of East Africa.* London: Longmans, 1962.

———. *The Making of Modern Uganda*. London: George Allen and Unwin, 1958.

Ingrams, Harold. *Uganda: A Crisis of Nationhood*. London: Her Majesty's Stationery Office, 1960.

Isichei, Elizabeth. *A History of Christianity in Africa: From Antiquity to the Present*. Grand Rapids, MI: William B. Eerdmans Publishing Company, 1995.

de Jong, Albert. *The Challenge of Vatican II in East Africa*. Nairobi: Paulines Publications Africa, 2004.

Jorgensen, Jan Jelmert. *Uganda: A Modern History*. New York: St. Martin's Press, 1981.

Kabwegyere, Tarsis. "The Asian Question in Uganda." *East Africa Journal* 9, no. 6 (June 1972): 10–13.

Kamasu, Joseph, and Andrew Cameron. *Lust to Kill: The Rise and Fall of Idi Amin*. London: Corgi, 1979.

Karugire, S. R. *A Political History of Uganda*. London: Heineman, 1980.

Kelly, Joseph, C.S.S.p. "AMECEA's Forward-Looking Chairman." *The African Ecclesial Review* 26, nos. 1-2 (February–April 1986): 12–16.

———. "Gentleman Bishop Sharing Christ's Daily Cross," Unpublished essay.

Keenan, J. "Story of a College: The Birth and Growth of St. Augustine's Teacher Training College Butiti [*sic*–Butiiti]—Uganda." *Overseas Education* 30, no. 1 (April 1958): 12–18.

Kisembo, Thomas. "One Hundred Years of Catholic Faith in Fort Portal Diocese." Booklist, n.p., 1995.

Kittler, Glenn. *The White Fathers*. New York: Doubleday, Image Books, 1957.

Kollman, Paul V., C.S.C. *The Evangelization of Slaves and Catholic Origins in Eastern Africa*. Maryknoll, NY: Orbis Books, 2005.

Kung, Hans. *Council Speeches of Vatican II*. Mahwah, NJ: Paulist Press, 1964.

Kyemba, Henry. *A State of Blood: The Inside Story of Idi Amin.* New York: Grossett & Dunlap, ACE Books, 1977.

Langley, M., and T. Kiggins. *A Serving People.* Nairobi: Oxford University Press, 1974.

Leggett, Ian. *Uganda.* Oxford: Oxfam Fountain Publishers, 2001.

Legum, Colin, ed. *African Contemporary Record, 1976–1977.* New York: Africana, 1977.

Long, Richard F. "Independent Uganda: Christianity's Role in the Problems and Prospects Confronting a Young Nation." *America* 107, no. 28 (October 13, 1962): 885–86, 891.

———. "Uganda's Independence." *Ave Maria* 97, no. 5 (February 2, 1963): 20–27.

Low, Donald Anthony. *Buganda in Modern History.* Berkeley: University of California Press, 1971.

———. "Uganda Unhinged." *International Affairs* (London) 49, no. 2 (April 1973): 219–228.

Lukanima, Fortunatus. "AMECEA Social Communications Department." *The African Ecclesial Review* 26, nos. 1–2 (February–April 1986): 55–56.

MacEoin, Gary. *Father Moreau: Founder of Holy Cross.* Milwaukee: Bruce Publishing Company, 1962.

MacGregor, Donald, C.S.C. "The Hill Tipperah Kukis." *The Bengalese* 18, no. 3 (March 1937): 14–15.

MacInnes, George, C.S.C. "The African Parish—Is There a Problem?" *The African Ecclesial Review* XI, no. 3 (1969): 219–38.

Mamdani, Mahmood. *Politics and Class Formation in Uganda.* New York: Monthly Review Press, 1976.

———. "Uganda in Transition." *Third World Quarterly* 10, no. 3 (July 1988): 1155–1181.

Marsh, Zoe, and G. W. Kingsworth. *An Introduction to the History of East Africa.* Cambridge: Cambridge University Press, 1965.

Martin, David. *General Amin.* London: Faber and Faber, 1974.

Maxon, Robert. *East Africa: An Introductory History*. Morgantown: West Virgina University Press, 1986.

Magina, Magina. "Uganda at the Crossroads." *Africa* 109 (September 1980): 12–19.

Mazrui, Ali A. *Soldiers and Kinsmen in Uganda: The Making of a Military Ethnocracy*. London: Sage Publications, 1975.

————. "Political Science and Social Commitment in the First Republic of Uganda: A Personal Interpretation." *Kenya Historical Review* 6, nos. 1–2 (1978): 63–83.

————. "Soldiers as Traditionalizers: Military Rule in the Re-Africanisation of Africa." *Journal of Asian and African Studies* XII, nos. 1–4 (1977): 256.

Miller, Charles. *The Lunatic Express*. New York: Macmillan, 1971.

Mittleman, James H. "The State of Research on African Politics: Contribution on Uganda." *Journal of Asian and African Studies* XI (1976): 3–4.

Mujaju, Akiiki. "The Political Crisis of Church Institutions in Uganda." *African Affairs* (London) 75 (1976): 67–85.

Mullin, Joseph. *Catholic Church in Modern Uganda*. London: Geoffrey Chapman, 1965.

Muscat, Richard, ed. *A Short History of the Democratic Party, 1954–1984*. Kampala, Uganda: Foundation for African Development, 1984.

Musgrove, Frederick. "What Sort of Facts?" *African Affairs* 205 (October 1952): 313–318.

Mutesa, Edward (Kabaka of Buganda). *The Descrecration of My Kingdom*. London: Constable, 1967.

Mutibwa, Phares. *Uganda Since Independence: A Story of Unfulfilled Hopes*. Trenton, NJ: Africa World Press, Inc., 1992.

Mutiso-Mbinda, John. "AMECEA Bishops' Consultations." *The African Ecclesial Review* 26, nos. 1–2 (February–April 1986): 17–21.

Nasimya-Wasilu, A., and D. W. Warutu, eds. *Mission in Africa, Christianity: Critical Essays in Missiology.* Nairobi: Acton Publishers, 2000.

Ndyabahika, James. "The Inter-Faith Relations in Uganda in the Area of Dialogue and Spirituality, 1960–1996." *The Asia Journal of Theology* 12, no. 2 (October 1998): 391–408.

Neill, Stephen. *A History of Christianity in India: The Beginnings to AD 1707.* Cambridge: Cambridge University Press, 1984.

————. *A History of Christian Missions.* Middlesex, England: Penguin Books, 1979.

Nthamburi, Zablon. "Toward Indigenization of Christianity in Africa: A Missiological Task." *International Bulletin of Missionary Research* 13, no. 3 (July 1989): 112–118.

Oborji, Francis A. *Trends in African Theology Since Vatican II: A Missiological Interpretation.* Rome: Vicariatus Urbis, 1998.

Obote, A. Milton. "The Footsteps of Uganda's Revolution." *East African Journal* 5 (October 1968): 7–13.

Odhiambo, E. S. "The Paradox of Collaboration: The Uganda Case." *East African Journal* 9 (October 1972): 19–25.

Ofcansky, Thomas P. *Uganda: Tarnished Pearl of Africa.* Boulder, CO: Westview Press, 1996.

Okoth, P. Godfrey, Manual Muranga, and Ernesto Okello Ogwang, eds. *Uganda: A Century of Existence.* Kampala, Uganda: Fountain Publishers, 1995.

Oliver, Roland. *The Missionary Factor in East Africa.* London: Longmans, 1969.

Omara-Otunnu, Amii. *Politics and the Military in Uganda, 1980–1985.* London: Macmillan Press, 1987.

O'Neill, Robert. *Mission to the Upper Nile.* London: Mission Book Service, 1979.

Paige, John Rhodes, C.S.C. "Preserving Order Amid Chaos: The Survival of Schools in Uganda, 1971–1986." Ph.D. diss., University of Maryland, 1998.

Parson, Jack. "Africanizing Trade in Uganda: The Final Solution." *Africa Today* 20, no. 1 (Winter 1973): 590–592.

Pearson, M. N. *The New Cambridge History of India*. Vol. 1, *The Portuguese in India*. Cambridge: Cambridge University Press, 1987.

Pellegrin, Frank E. "The Story of Bishop Vince." *Our Lady's Bulletin* 13, no. 12 (February 1977): 10–18.

Pirouet, M. L. "Religion in Uganda Under Amin." *Journal of Religion in Africa* XI (1980): 13–29.

Ravenhill, F. J. "Military Role in Uganda: The Politics of Survival." *African Studies Review* 17, no. 1 (April 1974): 229–260.

Rupesingle, Kumar, ed. *Conflict Resolution in Uganda*. Athens: Ohio University Press, 1989.

Sarpong, Peter. "A View of Africa: The Continent and its Church." *Origins*, 13 (June 23, 1983): 108–112.

Saul, John. "The Unsteady State: Uganda, Obote and General Amin." *Review of African Political Economy* 5 (January–April 1976): 12–38.

Sebala, L. K. M. "Uganda's Constitution: Unitary or Federal?" *African Star* (November 1959): 7–8.

Short, Philip. "Uganda: Putting It in Perspective." *African Report* 18 (March–April 1983): 34–38.

Smith, Adrian B. "Africa's New Pastoral Institute." *The African Ecclesial Review* IX, no. 4 (October 1967): 417–421.

Smith, Vincent. *The Oxford History of India*. Oxford: Clarendon Press, 1958.

Spear, Thomas, and Isaria N. Kimambo, eds. *East African Expressions of Christianity*. Athens: Ohio University Press, 1999.

Tanner, Ralph E. S. *Transitions in African Beliefs*. New York: Maryknoll Publications, 1967.

Taylor, John V. *The Growth of the Church in Buganda*. London: The SCM Press, 1958.

Tilbe, Douglas. *The Uganda Asian Crisis*. London: Community and Race Relations Unit of the British Council of Churches, 1972.

Timm, Richard W., C.S.C. ed. *150 Years of Holy Cross in East Bengal Mission*. Dhaka, Bangladesh: Congregation of Holy Cross, 2003.

Tindigarukayo, Jummy K. "Uganda, 1979–85: Leadership in Transition." *The Journal of Modern African Studies* 26, no. 4 (December 1988): 607–622.

Tourigny, Yves, W.F. "Birth of the Decree." *The African Ecclesial Review* IX, no. 1 (January 1967): 5–19.

———. *So Abundant a Harvest: The Catholic Church in Uganda, 1879–1979*. London: Longman and Todd, 1979.

Tuma, Tom, and Phares Mutibwa, eds. *A Century of Christianity in Uganda, 1877–1977*. Nairobi: Afro Press Limited, 1978.

Tumusiime, James, ed. *Uganda 30 Years, 1962-1992*. Kampala, Uganda: Fountain Publishers, 1992.

Tusingire, Frederick. *The Evangelization of Uganda: Challenges and Strategies*. Kisubi, Uganda: Marianum Publication Company, 2003.

Twaddle, Michael. "The Amin Coup." *Journal of Commonwealth Political Studies* X (1972): 99–112.

Vonck, Paul, W.F. "The AMECEA Pastoral Institute (Gaba)." *The African Ecclesial Review* 26, nos. 1–2 (February–April 1986): 45–46.

Voorde, Joseph F., C.S.C. "Kukis and Kukiland." *The Bengalese* 21, no. 8 (October 1940): 10–11.

Wanyana, Simeon. "Christian Leadership in Africa." *Leadership* 191 (October 1976): 13–17.

Ward, Kevin. "Catholic—Protestant Relations in Uganda: An Historical Perspective." *Africa Theological Journal* 13, no. 3 (1984): 176–185.

————. "The Church of Uganda and the Exile of Kabaka Mutesa II, 1953–1955." *Journal of Religion in Africa* 28, no. 4 (November 1988): 411–449.

Welborn, Frederick B. *East African Christianity.* London: Oxford University Press, 1965.

————. *Religion and Politics in Uganda, 1952–62.* Nairobi: East Africa Publishing House, 1965.

Willetts, Peter. "The Politics of Uganda as a One-Party State, 1969–1970." *African Affairs* 296 (1975): 278–299.

Woodward, Peter. "Ambiguous Amin." *African Affairs* 307 (1978): 153–164.

Young, M. Crawford. "The Obote Revolution." *Africa Report* II (June 1966): 8–14.

Index

338, 340, 342, 345, 346
Fotusky, C.S.C., Thomas, 108,
205–207
Francais, C.S.C., Adolphe, 43
Franciscans, 11
French, C.S.C., James, 30,

Gaba National Seminary, 5, 214,
215, 234, 315, 329, 346
Gaba Pastoral Institute
Africa Ecclesial Review, 283
Africanization, 284, 285
"Churches Research
on Marriage in Africa"
(CROMIA), 287
founding, 212–215, 280–282
Idi Amin regime, 285, 286
Mutiso-Mbinda, John, 287
Sisters of Loreto, 286
Gandhi, Mahatma, 41, 54
Gara, C.S.C., Matthew, 35
Gerstle, C.S.C., Joseph, 108
Gibson, C.S.C., Stephen, 158
Goedert, C.S.C, Edmund, 18, 28,
117
Goodall, C.S.C., Francis, 34, 36,
37, 39
Gozdowski, C.S.C, Orlando, 162,
168
Grail, The, 78
Graner, C.S.C., Lawrence, 34, 82,
83
Gregory XVI, Pope, 11, 89
Gulnac, C.S.C., James, 108, 195
Gulu Seminary, 210

Hamer, O.P., Jerome, 275
Harrington, C.S.C., John, 35, 37,
50, 104, 117, 171, 195
Hastings, Adrian, 86–90, 93, 95,
98, 126, 133, 180, 181, 247,
271
Healey, M.M., Joseph, 272, 283,

291–294, 303, 306, 311, 321,
343
Hesburgh, C.S.C., Theodore, 188,
192, 347
Hesse, C.S.C., Robert, 4, 83, 84,
102, 106, 142, 163, 166, 323
Heston, C.S.C., Edward, 175,
222, 227, 228, 232, 346
Heyes, W.F., Harry, 119, 142
Hirth, C.S.C., Jean-Joseph, 100
Hoffman, C.S.C., Robert, 70, 83
Hoima, Diocese of, 150, 151, 194,
261
Holy Cross College, 3, 19, 64–66,
68, 74
Holy Ghost Fathers, 11
Hurth, C.S.C., Peter, 29, 30, 43
Hyde, Douglas, 76

Ibingira, Grace, 121–123, 131, 132
In Supremo Apostolatus, 89
International Development,
Association of, 76
International Red Cross, 163
Interterritorial Episcopal Board of
Eastern Africa (ITEBEA), 221,
264, 265–268, 287, 295
Irish Province of Capuchins, 291

James, C.S.C., Lewis, 196
Jesuits, 10-12, 16, 26, 37, 77, 327
Jogues, Saint Isaac, 11
John XXIII, Pope, 76, 102, 155,
218, 347
John Paul II, Pope, 321, 325, 330
Johnson, Sir Harry, 100

Kabaka Yekka (KY), 122, 124,
127, 129–131
Kalanda, Bishop Paul, 231, 330.
346

Richard Gribble, C.S.C., is an associate professor in the Department of Religious Studies at Stonehill College in Easton, Massachusetts. He has a doctorate from the Catholic University of America. He is the author of several books and numerous articles on American Catholicism and spirituality, including *American Apostle of the Family Rosary: The Life of Patrick J. Peyton, C.S.C.; Guardian of America: The Life of James Martin Gillis, C.S.P.*; and *Catholicism and the San Francisco Labor Movement, 1896–1921*.

Celebrate the Tradition of Holy Cross